GLOBAL FINANCE
AND URBAN LIVING

D0023907

INTERNATIONAL LIBRARY OF SOCIOLOGY
Founded by Karl Mannheim

Editor: John Urry
University of Lancaster

GLOBAL FINANCE AND URBAN LIVING

A Study of Metropolitan Change

Edited by
Leslie Budd and Sam Whimster

London and New York

First published in 1992
by Routledge
11 New Fetter Lane, London EC4P 4EE

Simultaneously published in the USA and Canada
by Routledge
a division of Routledge, Chapman and Hall Inc.
29 West 35th Street, New York, NY 10001

© 1992 Leslie Budd and Sam Whimster

Typeset by LaserScript, Mitcham, Surrey
Printed in Great Britain by
Biddles Ltd, Guildford and King's Lynn

All rights reserved. No part of this book may be reprinted or
reproduced or utilized in any form or by any electronic,
mechanical, or other means, now known or hereafter
invented, including photocopying and recording, or in any
information storage or retrieval system, without permission in
writing from the publishers.

British Library Cataloguing in Publication Data

Global finance and urban living: a study of metropolitan
change. – (International Library of sociology).
1. Banking
I. Budd, Leslie *1949-* II. Whimster, Sam *1947-* III.
Series
332.1

Library of Congress Cataloging in Publication Data

Global finance and urban living: a study of metropolitan change
edited by Leslie Budd and Sam Whimster.
p. cm. – (The International library of sociology)
Includes bibliographical references and index.
1. International finance. 2. International finance–Social
aspects. 3. City and town life. 4. Urban economics. 5. Central
business districts. I. Budd, Leslie, 1949- . II. Whimster, Sam
1947- . III. Series.
HG3881.G573 1991
332′.042–dc20   91-14751
                                                                                            CIP

ISBN 0–415–07097–X
ISBN 0–415–03198–2 (pbk)

CONTENTS

CONTENTS

ILLUSTRATIONS

TABLES

IUPUI
UNIVERSITY LIBRARIES
755 W. MICHIGAN ST.
INDIANAPOLIS, IN 46202-5195

CONTRIBUTORS

Leslie Budd is senior lecturer in Economics at City of London Polytechnic. He is currently co-authoring a book on new forms of economic partnership in Europe.

Jerry Coakley is senior lecturer in Economics at City of London Polytechnic. He is co-editor of *The City of Capital: London's Role as a Financial Centre* (Blackwell) and *New Perspectives on the Financial System* (Croom Helm).

Keith Cowlard is Head of Geography at City of London Polytechnic. He is the author of *Decision-making in Geography* (Hodder and Stoughton).

Bob Jessop is professor of Sociology at the University of Lancaster. His previous publications include *Thatcherism* (Polity).

Mike Lenhoff is Portfolio Strategist at Capel-Cure Myers. He has held previous posts in academia and consultancy.

Mike Levi is reader in Criminology at University College of Wales, Cardiff. His publications include *Regulating Fraud. White-collar Crime and the Criminal Process* (Tavistock), *Fraud '89: the Extent of Fraud Against Large Companies and Executive Views on What Should Be Done About It*, with D. Sherwin (Ernst and Young).

Andrew Leyshon is a lecturer in Geography at the University of Hull. He is co-author of *The Rise of the British Provincial Financial Centre* (Pergamon), and *Making Money* (Routledge).

CONTRIBUTORS

Nurun Nabi is an associate professor in the Department of Management at the University of Chittagong. He is currently pursuing doctoral research at the City of London Polytechnic, where he is also a consultant in Asian small businesses to the polytechnic's Access and Community Liaison Programme.

Chris Rhodes is a lecturer in Sociology at City of London Polytechnic. He is currently working on a publication on the state and labour relations.

Nicholas Robinson is Hang Seng Professor of Financial Services at City of London Polytechnic.

Leonard Stafford is an economic consultant and was formerly Head of Economics at City of London Polytechnic. He has authored a number of books on economics and business including *The Modern Economy* (Longman).

Christopher Stanley is a barrister at law and a lecturer in law at the University of Kent. He is currently researching the nature of legal personality.

Rob Stones is a lecturer in the Department of Government at the University of Essex. His field of research is the City of London.

Nigel Thrift is professor of Geography at the University of Bristol. He is co-editor of *Class and Space. The Making of Urban Society* (Routledge), *Political Economy in Perspective* (Unwin Hyman), and co-author of *Making Money* (Routledge).

Sam Whimster is reader in Sociology at City of London Polytechnic. He is co-editor of *Max Weber, Rationality and Modernity* (Allen & Unwin).

Stephanie Williams is an architectural journalist. She has also produced a number of TV programmes on architecture.

Sharon Zukin is professor of Sociology at the City University of New York. Her publications include *Loft Living: Culture and Capital in Urban Change* (Radius) and *Landscapes of Power: From Detroit to Disneyland* (University of California Press).

FOREWORD

There are no 'uns like the old 'uns and during the 1980s there was
an old-fashioned financial boom that, like all booms before it,
drew its sustenance on the belief that the world was different. Of
course it discovered that it was not, and that finance ungrounded
in the reality of production and economic value is a house of cards.

But one of the concepts used by the now embarrassed generation of boomsters to describe why their boom would be different
– financial globalisation – has survived the financial excesses and
lives on; and its very durability suggests it gave vent to a more
serious underlying trend that may affect all our lives. This book
attempts to tease out how.

It has more questions than answers, and the authors who self-
deprecatingly dub themselves *flâneurs* are all too aware of the
tentativeness of their conclusions. What they describe and analyse
may, after all, just be a one-decade wonder; and London's place at
the centre of things could all too easily fade in the decade to come.
But all that said, the globalisation of finance remains. Not internationalisation, whose building blocks are firmly national, but
globalisation, a universe of its own rules and which has genuinely
burst out of national boundaries.

The ferocity of the trend will ebb and flow, but there is little
doubt that global finance represents a new business form. Notably
it allows an apparent detachment of finance from industry in a
centre like London because economic activity which underwrites
all finance is taking place elsewhere in the globe. And the British,
with the openness of their financial system, are affected by the
contagion more than most; our financial institutions have more
readily transmuted themselves into the global finance houses who

are not merely their London peer group but fashionable metropolitan pace-setters.

And because British finance in turn is uniquely powerful, what has been happening is no longer for the City ghetto; it has spread out to define British corporate culture and the way business lives now. So if finance is rootless, individualistic and morally founded on the notion of caveat emptor, so is British business. And to the extent that the career choices of the middle classes have been increasingly dominated directly or indirectly by finance, so has the associated culture impacted on what they consider neighbourly, how they save and where they are prepared to educate their children – and beyond that to the very architecture of the buildings in which they chose to work, live and play. Here is a book that attempts to understand the most important phenomenon of our age – and to bring insights and information into the public domain that have laid dormant or undisclosed. Whether fraud or the yuppie, groundscrapers or the securitisation of the mortgage market it makes connections I for one have not seen anywhere else. Congratulations to all concerned!

Will Hutton,
Economics Editor,
The Guardian.
Oxford, March 1991

ACKNOWLEDGEMENTS

Any journey starts with the first step and any conversation with the first word. But purpose and meaning do depend on context. This work stemmed from our immediate experience as teachers and researchers within the environs of the City of London. Journeys into and across this global financial centre generated manifold conversations. As academic *flâneurs* we try hard to integrate these impressions with a knowledgeable analysis of the abstract forces of global finance. Yet repeatedly the scale and unpredictability of events in the 1980s have defied any one authoritative explanation. The seemingly irresistible rise of the financial services sector and an associated inflation in financial assets have turned widely based city economies into service mono-economies and their central business districts into massive construction sites, and in the process disrupted city residents' sense of their place in the urban environment.

To make some sense of this we have called up the expertise of academics and practitioners to construct a telling account. Our purpose has been to bring together viewpoints from a variety of disciplines. As editors we would like to thank our expert witnesses for the discourse this has generated among ourselves, and we hope the book does as much to stimulate a wider assessment of global finance and its effects.

Professional and personal acknowledgements are always hard to list. We are indebted to a number of colleagues at City of London Polytechnic for their interest and support. We also had innumerable conversations with individuals from a variety of institutions that were both valuable and encouraging. Mike Cowen, Vanessa Davidson, Mike Featherstone, Brian Hall, Stuart Innes at the London Docklands Corporation Development, Liz and the late John Kingston, Lord Limerick, Keith Palmer, Di Perrons, Peter Rees and John Watson at the City Corporation, Cynthia White, Caroline Woodhead and John Urry as series editor deserve our particular thanks. Photographs have been supplied courtesy of Olympia & York (Plates 1 and 5); John Moss (Plates 2, 4, 6 and 7; and Dennis Gilbert (Plate 8). Don Shewan deserves thanks for providing mapwork and artwork, as does Michael Chick for his artwork. Kath Edwards came to the rescue with typing at a crucial point, as did Anthony Sharman and Graham Clarke with help converting computer text. Thanks also to Sue Whimster who had to tolerate the inadequacy of our explanation as to why editing a book should take so much time. Finally, Chris Rojek served as a patient and disciplining editor at Routledge.

London
March 1991

INTRODUCTION

Sam Whimster and Leslie Budd

It was the best of times, it was the worst of times, it was the age of wisdom, it was the age of foolishness, it was the epoch of belief, it was the epoch of incredulity, it was the season of Light, it was the season of Darkness, it was the spring of hope, it was the winter of despair, we had everything before us, and we had nothing before us, we were all going to Heaven, we were all going direct the other way – in short, the period was so far like the present period, that some its noisiest authorities insisted on its being received, for good or evil, in the superlative degree of comparison only.

(Charles Dickens, *A Tale of Two Cities*)

The City of London is a tale of two cities. The one was traditional and stuffy, with codes of conduct reflecting a closely bound world of long-established firms and personal relationships built on trust, and whose banking halls and Portland stone exteriors displayed solidity, permanence and discreet luxury. The financial revolution of the eighties marked the emergence of the new city. The bowler hat, the furled umbrella and the four-button cuff sleeve gave way to the double-breasted Prince of Wales check suit, the filofax and the two-button cuff. Undergraduates from the prestigious universities forsook the attractions of civil service, academia and industry to be snapped up by the new would-be integrated finance houses. Previously one had gone into the City because one was rich, whereas now the attraction for new entrants was to become rich. Down came a third of the City's old buildings. Giant cranes dotted the landscape of the centre, bringing to mind the Martian machines in *The War of the Worlds* that destroyed and reformed in their own image. Out of rubble-filled holes steel skeletons emerged, waiting for their designer façades to be bolted on. The new steel and glass buildings signalled airiness, smartness and a wondrous polyglottism.

Inside the new finance houses the young professionals went to work with puritan zeal, fingers, eyes and brains concentrating on the massive flows of global finance. Just to dip a fingernail into the stream generated super-profitable commissions. Equally, to mis-judge the stream or, worse, for the stream to dry up meant a highly abbreviated career. The City professional was both villain and hero, someone who became rich by fair means or foul, a figure of attraction and of hatred, and as such was both glamorised and vilified by television, film, drama and papers. The yuppie was the cultural hero of the eighties, the embodiment of the 'go for it' enterprise culture. The new individualistic ethos of City professionals represented enterprise as a state of nature, in which benefits and penalties accrued to the will and the wits of the individual. No matter that this state of nature was based upon some of the most sophisticated markets and technology that capitalism has ever devised; here was the illusion that the dealer was somehow free of the constraints of organisation and civil society. As cultural hero the young professional turned everything in his or her life into a 'trade' – whether personal relationships, flats, objects of art or sports cars, the geographically favoured public of property owners in the south and the south-east were invited to join in. The financial revolution meant limitless personal credit with property an ever-inflating collateral, and the individual consumer was invited to make an entrepreneur of him or herself. Assets, pensions, savings, insurance policies, personal equity plans and – above all – consumption were to come under personal control as the avuncular man from the Pru and the friendly bank manager were replaced by the financial services executive. At the same time the media and advertising communi-cated finance as fashion, cash dispensers as pose, play and dance. When the new aesthetic of money crossed with the vector of entrepreneurialism, were we 'all going direct to Heaven' – or were we 'all going direct the other way'?

Disentangling impressions from analysis is not an easy task. Indeed it is part of sociological and economic analysis to reveal how elements of lifestyle and culture as well as conceptions of personality became implicated with the worlds of work and finance. In this introduction we suggest that what has occurred is the interpenetration of areas of life previously separated by hierarchies and boundaries. In Part I we point out that the financial apex of material and economic life is now not only a global phenomenon but that its influence has penetrated to the level of individuals and households. In Part II the essays reveal a repatterning of personality, lifestyle, neighbourhoods and the metropolis. This process can be thought of as a break-up of old hierarchies, disciplines and boundaries in the face of the dissolving properties of global finance, which has allowed a new series of repatterning. These arguments are part of a wider debate concerning the issue of globalisation. This holds that we have to reconstitute our way of thinking in terms of hierarchies: not a simple ascension from the level of the individual to that of household, neighbourhood, city, nation, and the international, but instead the international becomes global and, as such, intrudes into all levels of life. The metropolis is contained to a diminishing degree within a national setting; its economic flows are less exclusively city-wide or national and its neighbourhoods can no longer claim an homogeneity of class or race. In Roland Robertson's formulation we are witnessing the interpenetration of the local by the global and the global by the local (Robertson 1991). Part I takes up this theme in its economic aspect, Part II in its cultural and sociological aspects.

PART I THE LEVELS OF MATERIAL LIFE

Before the issue of interpenetration can be examined, it is necessary to take a conceptual step backwards and to consider the levels of material life as a hierarchy. Take the Bengali community around the locality of Brick Lane. This is a block away from the new Bishopsgate development where rents could command £40 a square foot. The economic basis of Brick Lane looks unlikely to withstand the encroachments of the property developers and their financial backers. If this scenario unfolds – and it assumes the continued attractiveness of City fringe development and it discounts, which it ought not to do, the territorial resistance of a community to piecemeal relocation – it will confirm the power of internationally backed development over an ethnic enclave adjoining the City of London.

While this one-sided contest displays the superiority of global finance over a community whose economic, political and cultural resources are disadvantaged in such a struggle, it is probably a mistake to view this as a simple and immediate causal process. To do so would be to underestimate the extent and scope of global finance to reshape and restructure regions, cities, work and the way people live their lives. To arrive at an understanding of this more pervasive influence, one has to pull out the full chain or hierarchy of how finance relates to capitalism, capitalism to markets, and markets to the basic routines of people's material lives. The formulation of this hierarchy is taken from Braudel (1977: 47–63). There is nothing essentially modern about the place of finance at the apex of this hierarchy, which has existed wherever merchants have been able to pursue long-distance trade. The international merchant has been able to act as a financier, lending and borrowing on the basis of the bills of exchange created to conduct long-distance trade. This, as Braudel has shown, has been a feature of European economic life since the thirteenth century, at the time of the revival of the towns and fairs. Similarly, if the economic structure of Brick Lane is examined, the same hierarchy will be found. At the top are the financiers and international merchants. These are the rich Gujarati and Pakistani families who act as intermediaries in an international flow of goods, predominantly clothing. On the basis of merchant capital accumulated from this trade the most successful families have moved on to property development on the City fringes, thus joining a peculiarly English road to financier status. Beneath the level of international trade in clothing, which is organised by the merchants, lies production for the market. In the Braudelian schema these markets need not be capitalist. So in villages on the Indian subcontinent, or in the back streets of Spitalfields, a predominantly domestically based economy can produce for village or street markets. At the bottom of the hierarchy are the enduring routines of material life as it encompasses domestic life and the rhythms of family existence.

So while City financiers and developers might be about to effect an effortless displacement of the Brick Lane community, this mighty feat should not be misunderstood simply as the ascendancy of sophisticated finance over the village economy. Rather it is the ascendancy of a vastly more powerful and complex hierarchy over a no less differentiated, but unfortunately weaker, hierarchy. Understanding the role and power of financial capitalism, which has revealed its true colours in the 1980s, involves holding the levels of this hierarchy in mind. The sheer and gross visibility of the financial services industry, which forms the apex of the hierarchy, has to be related to the merchant and industrial capitalists and their capitalistic influence on markets, and beneath markets the rhythms of material life at the base of the economy.

The rise of the financial services industry and its linkage to global finance has effected a number of changes in the way in which this hierarchy operates. The role of property led finance and Brick Lane has been mentioned, and more will be said on this. Another illustration is the destabilising effect of financial capitalism on industrial capitalism. As the vast global pot of financial assets restlessly surges through the world's financial centres, looking for the best rates of return and profit, entrepreneurial risk has been reinvented. Formerly industrialists attempted to provide stability by means of size, scale and control over markets. The largest companies in the US and the UK have been shown to be vulnerable to the inroads of finance-led take-overs. The availability of funds, new financial innovations such as securitisation, syndicates and consortia, leveraged bids, management buy-outs, and aggressive mergers and acquisition teams in the leading finance houses have rendered vulnerable even the largest and seemingly most secure companies, such as Nabisco, capitalised at $20 billions.

Theorists might wish to consider this as a triumph of Schumpeter over Hilferding. Both economists saw that the profits of industrial capitalists were translated into financial capital, and that, therefore, the banking and financial systems were theoretically the ultimate arbiters of industrial capitalism. Working from the evidence of continental Europe early in the century, Hilferding argued that bankers would aim to implement an organised, stable existence for industrial capitalism which was the originator of profit in the first instance. Firms would be taken over, oligopolies and cartels created, and market share secured. Until the 1980s that is. Schumpeter's insight was to point out that financiers, unencumbered with the satisficing rationality of the industrialist, have a risk and return view of financial assets (Schumpeter 1939: 223). Where an asset provides a suboptimal return, the banker, according to prescriptive theory, should dispose of the asset and seek a better return.

Given the way national economies were managed, the place of finance within the system of national economic regulation, and the absence of requisite financial instruments and means,

Schumpeter's entrepreneurial logic never obtained. Many of the changes, which have brought about a new level of risk to the business environment, are described in Part 1 of this book. While the very large question of how financial and industrial capitalism have come to redefine their relationship requires further investigation than can be offered here, we are able to note the altered role of the financial apex to the level of industrial and merchant capital. This indicates an enhanced and generalised ability of financial capital to penetrate downwards throughout the hierarchy of material existence.

The role of mortgage finance is illustrative of this new-found ability to affect lives at the level of the supposedly enduring rhythms of material life at the base of the hierarchy. Building societies, like their counterparts in the insurance business, started as mutual friendly societies formed to intermediate between groups of borrowers and lenders within a defined locality. The rise in property values in the 1970s stimulated a search for greater amounts of funds for lending which was met by the wholesale money and capital markets following the liberalisation of credit in the early 1980s. The originally local-based building society, which had built up a national client base, now borrowed from the wholesale money markets. Following this development the wholesalers, national and international banks and consortia, entered the mortgage business. Reacting as competitive companies, building societies, which had by now outgrown their localist and friendly society roots, moved to become fully fledged financial companies. The final twist to this story concerns the securitisation of mortgages. From the borrower's perspective, he or she holds a 25-year debt with the local building society. Unbeknown to the mortgagee, the capital for this loan has been drawn down from the international money markets. Further, the building society will have bundled individual mortgages against the wholesale loan. The wholesale lender may then choose to swap the future flow of income represented by the mortgages for a capital sum of money (this is securitisation), or else swap the mortgages for an entirely different source of income-producing financial asset. The mortgage entered into in Bingley may well end up as part of the portfolio of, say, a Japanese investment trust.

From the institutional viewpoint in the United States these developments have been disastrous. What once was a self-contained local business became one of the largest markets in bonds. In place of borrowing and lending on a fixed differential, American thrifts sold on their liabilities and used the money to invest in speculative junk bonds, the market for which has now collapsed (Lewis 1989: 72–92). The Savings and Loans industry's attempts to recover from its staggering losses will severely reduce the availability of cheap mortgage finance in the future, and pose severe problems for regulators. It was precisely the ease and availability of mortgage finance that allowed individuals to purchase their major capital asset and thereby a degree of insulation from the exigencies of material life. These examples, taken from urban communities, industry and housing finance, illustrate a new ubiquity of finance and its ability to affect people's working and living environments.

From international capital to global finance

Part I of the book charts the emergence of the new global financial system. A number of parallel and related themes are discussed. They include London's status as a financial centre, the international competitive pressure acting on the City of London, the rise of new financial instruments and markets, the role of efficient financial markets, and departures – some notably transgressive – from efficient market behaviour, and lastly, the effects of a global financial system on national economic regulation.

We have preferred the term 'global' to that of 'international' finance and the themes in the chapters of Part I require a brief résumé in order to bring out the decisive differences between the two concepts. While the City of London functioned as a successful international financial centre in the 1970s and 80s, Messrs Stafford and Coakley (Chapters 1 & 2) do not offer an assurance that this will continue in the 90s. They regard London's role in the uncertain environment of global finance as precarious. Another of Braudel's theses is helpful in exploring this issue. Each wave of European market and capitalist development had a geographical centre. Venice held this place when the centre of gravity of the European economy revolved around the Mediterranean. Venice was the great crossroads of both a regional economy and an international trade in oriental luxuries with northern European minerals and furs. Finance was an ancillary to this trade producing international banking, negotiable bills of exchange and, as researched by Max Weber, forms of partnership (*commenda*) in

7

financing high-risk shipping ventures. With the rise of the Atlantic seaboard Amsterdam became the new centre and then in the late eighteenth century, consequent upon England's political ascendancy over the lands with which it traded, London became the hub of the new world system (Braudel 1977: 85–6). London maintained this position, reaching its zenith in the Empire of the late Victorian and Edwardian period. London played the premier role as the switchpoint of trade and finance and London as a city benefited vastly from its political and cultural hegemony over Empire (King 1990: 71–81).

The historical argument shows that the financial centre moves to wherever the hub of the world economic system is located. By the 1930s it was New York and, *pari passu*, one would expect New York to lose its ascendancy to Tokyo in the 1990s. In the Braudel thesis London should experience a decline as a financial centre in proportion to its decline as the beneficiary of its world economic system. The new centres flourish at the expense of the old. So Tokyo and New York exist in two massive economies whose domestic savings provide a very large capital base for financial markets and whose international trade provides opportunities for international financial services. Accordingly, London should have become a minor financial centre. In part, the explanation of this anomaly to the Braudel thesis is that London maintained a formidable position as the centre of a sterling area to which its ex-imperial territories subscribed. Moreover, it held on to this role despite its involvement in two, economically disastrous, world wars. While Britain's economic decline in the international pecking order, as measured by gross domestic product, continued (and continues) unchecked, the City demonstrated an absolute and progressive rate of growth from the 1960s. Had Britain's rate of economic growth matched that of the City, the country would have relegated the Federal Republic of Germany to fourth place as a world economic power.

In part, this is explained by the City of London's ability to hold on to its accepted strengths: as international banker to the sterling area, the maintenance of a surprisingly high profile of British-based multinational companies (despite the decline at home) which required financing, a continued major presence in shipping and insurance – valuable legacies despite the absence of both colonies and merchant navy. The City maintained a core role as financial intermediary between savings and government borrowing. In addition London was always able to capitalise on its reputation of trust, its concentration of expertise, its political stability, and its role as an entrepôt in relation to changing global exigencies..

The other half of the explanation, and as will be seen it is a separable half, is the extraordinary growth in eurocurrency and eurobond business, a trend which started in the 1960s. Jerry Coakley notes in Chapter 2 that London's historic international dominance was based on its role in capital markets, issuing bonds and shares and exporting capital, whereas the rise of the eurocurrency markets in the 1960s transformed the City into a banking-oriented financial centre. London became the leading centre of foreign exchange dealing, daily turnover in 1989 averaging $187 billion with New York on $129 billions and Tokyo on $115 billion; also by the 1970s London was the leading centre for international bank lending (a supremacy, though, that Tokyo had whittled away by 1989). The legal regulatory regime of United States banking laws meant it was more profitable for corporations to locate dollar deposits in London which acted as an offshore banking centre. Structural imbalances between national currencies, a trend dating back to the breaking down of the Bretton Woods agreement, were exacerbated by the arrival of petrodollars from the OPEC countries. London's international banking expanded massively in the mid-1970s. This was the phase of so-called turntable banking, when incoming petrodollars were loaned out by syndicates of banks to Third World and Eastern European countries. By the standards of the 1980s this was a simple and profitable business as banks intermediated between creditor and debtor nations. The Euromarket banking business was an essential prelude, in retrospect for bankers an idyllic one, for the much harder world of global finance.

As the City went into the 1980s with neo-conservative governments in both London and Washington it looked like more of the same, but even better. In an obvious sense these governments were welcome to the City, and opportunities were seized to the full – a phenomenon to which we will return below. But while the consequences of the non-interventionist stance of government looked to benefit the City, it is the structural changes of the move to globalisation of finance that have to be grasped, and these point to discontinuity and new uncertainties.

In the 1970s to speak of the City was to speak of two cities. The first was the domestic city which provided the channel for the nation's savings to become invested in British commerce and industry and also acted as banker to the government. The second city was the international offshore banking centre based on Euromarkets. The domestic city was owned by British finance capital and was under the fairly tight control of the Bank of England. The offshore banking was predominantly foreign-owned and not subject to domestic banking regulation. Coakley notes that in 1988 UK banks 'were responsible for a mere 14 per cent of total international lending on their home territory' (Chapter 2, p.60). The arrival of a Conservative government with an adherence to the practice of free international trade dissolved the separation. In 1979 exchange controls were lifted, freeing the funds of major companies, pension funds, investment trusts and other saving vehicles to seek the best possible return throughout the world's markets. 1983 saw the Parkinson–Goodison accord and deregulation. This abolished the demarcations between banking and finance and the separation of the activities of jobbers (who acted as principals) and brokers (who acted as agents). Leonard Stafford discusses these changes in Chapter 1 and sees them as a forced imperative of the international banks over the traditional and domestic City. Deregulation allowed the much more massively capitalised international banks to own both broking and market-making functions. On the new dealing floors trading became much more competitive and price information more transparent with all prices for stocks and bonds being electronically displayed. The domestic City resisted the reforms, fearing quite correctly the beginning of the end, and for a while the Stock Exchange did not immediately capitulate to complete foreign ownership. But, as Stafford observes, 'every attempt to evade the invasive consequences of the forces in play would have confirmed London's status as an inward-looking, restrictive and declining financial backwater' (Chapter 1, p.36).

Hence one feature of globalisation was the invasion of the domestic by the offshore. In 1985 over four hundred foreign banks were operating in London and these, especially the large American and Japanese banks, were showing the range of activities encompassed in a multifunctional financial house. It was the integration of these functions, enabled by technology, that made globalisation a qualitative advance over being international. Foreign exchange dealing had already established that worldwide trading could be accomplished by computer-backed telephone deals. The integrated finance houses sought to extend this type of operation to any number of other financial markets – futures, options, warrants, equities, bonds and so on. '[D]elays in time and defects in information across the globe had diminished to the extent that trading was not significantly fragmented' (Chapter 1, p.37). Theoretically, global finance could be conducted from just one centre anywhere in the world. But in practice, as will be seen, market share is determined by a number of contingent factors. The other feature of global trading by the large houses was their ability to provide a number of services under one roof. So for instance foreign exchange, bonds and securities markets could be interlinked in a major deal.

Globalisation has been enabled by the continuous development of financial innovations. Securitisation is one such innovation, arguably the one that has most significantly sharpened the impact of global finance. Securitisation is a way of raising a capital sum that employs neither the traditional way of a bank loan, nor a share or rights issue on the stock exchange. Instead the borrower seeks access to wholesale money markets and offers in return a future flow of income against the value of an asset – property, land, companies. This has two important consequences. It has reduced the integuments of physical assets to merely tradeable pieces of paper. Second, borrowers and lenders were able to operate outside the channels – both their confines and constraints – of traditional banking procedures; this latter process is termed dis-intermediation.

Financial building blocks and efficient markets

In Chapter 3 Nicholas Robinson explains the basic mechanics of how paper assets are traded and discusses the measures that have been created to impose some sort of order and assurance within the financial markets. The centrepiece here is the equation between risk and return that investors and borrowers calculate in relation to their particular situation. Hedging a risk is offsetting some of the return of the asset against a reduction in the level of risk of holding the asset, and as such is not too dissimilar from the idea of buying insurance. A company, for instance, can reduce its exposure to risk 'by adding something to its portfolio with the opposite "exposure" or "payoff" to the entity's own exposure'

(Chapter 3, p.78). The financial instrument that allows the holder control of features of the risk and return environment is called a swap – 'the process of integrating the world's financial markets towards a single homogeneous entity owes a great deal to the simple financial instrument or "building block", known as a swap' (Chapter 3, p.77).

This raises the thorny issue, in an era which has seen the demise of national and international forms of regulation (a different system of offsetting devices), of whether the swap does take the volatility out of the system of financial transactions. Commenting on the October 1987 crash, which was presaged by the collapse of the futures index on the Chicago Mercantile Exchange, Stafford comments, 'An irony is that markets and instruments designed to limit risk for investors have sometimes led to a greater fragility in the market as a whole' (Chapter 1, p.43). Holders of financial assets may be able to offset their immediate risks, but the consequences of activating those offsetting devices introduce second and third orders of risk which are difficult to calculate, to say the least. And as the experience of 1987 shows, a collapse in a specific market cannot be easily restricted to one place alone. A global financial system by definition means the interrelatedness of all parts in the system.

Behind the matter of risk is the more fundamental question as to whether asset price reflects the true situation in the economic world. The popular suspicion of stock exchanges is of course that paper profits and killings are made irrespective of, and to the detriment of, the real world. Countering the popular prejudice that exchanges inhabit a world of their own, devoid of reality, is the central theory of the efficient market hypothesis.

This hypothesis holds that the prices at which securities trade broadly reflect all the price information that is available to the market. Michael Lenhoff, who gives an account of the private client stockbroking firm, is well placed to review the theory and practice of the efficient market hypothesis. In its pure form the hypothesis argues that all market information is reflected in the price of a security, and that price adjusts to any change, or anticipation of change, in the environment. While fund managers may outperform the market index for a while, this is because they are taking risks that in the longer term would inevitably have a downside. Lenhoff notes 'professionally managed portfolios cannot outperform randomly selected portfolios of equities with equivalent risk characteristics' (Chapter 4, p.103). This raises the question of whether all asset management is then merely passive. Lenhoff points to the existence of market anomalies, where information is not absorbed into price, and this provides a limited scope for the active assets manager.

Efficient markets would seem to be a characteristic of global finance. The implication of a technologically enabled free flow and exchange of information and trading should be to iron out anomalies between markets. In the perfect model all these differences are arbitraged away (Chapter 1, pp.42–3). There are, however, three classes of departures from the model. First, a number of the contributors to Part I speak of these financial flows as a turbulent sea – massive, unpredictable and sometimes uncontrollable. In a simple sense orderliness is swamped by this sea rather than being rationally processed by markets. Second, there is the well-established phenomenon that misinformation and misreading of market signals leads to a less than perfect market. Third, there are opportunities to manipulate the market. These can range from the legitimate, as in government inspired and disseminated confidence in the Tokyo stock market after the 1987 crash, to the illegitimate, as in the case of the New York arbitrageur, Ivan Boesky.

With the rapid evolution of global finance in the eighties opportunities for fraud and departure from market discipline were unhappily only too readily available. Michael Levi (Chapter 5) estimates the losses to fraud as £4 billion at risk in 1989 in Britain. The case of the somewhat less than transparent market intermediary, Boesky, was estimated to have involved fraudulent dealing of over $1 billion. The regulatory authorities' responses, the public's perceptions and government's attitudes on both sides of the Atlantic have been various. In a technical and legal sense it is now quite clear that the British authorities never really addressed the problem until it was too late, that is, after the bull market in securities was over. In the move to deregulation it was recognised that an effective system of checks needed to be put in place. Indeed, the Office of Fair Trading under Gordon Borrie, prior to deregulation, was concerned to promote an open, free and fair competition in financial services. The OFT initiative was sidelined by the accord reached in 1983 by the Chairman of the Stock Exchange, Goodison, and the Minister at the Department of Trade and Industry, Parkinson. Arguably this accord can be seen as a fairly disastrous and expensive compromise. The Americans had a solution to the problems of deregulation of financial markets in the Securities and Exchange Commission. The SEC was already in place as a large, government-funded agency that combined the roles of regulating, policing and prosecuting infringements of statutory law. The Parkinson–Goodison accord disallowed such a unitary solution and a curious hybrid of the statutory and the voluntary, both in respect to rule making and rule enforcement as well as its institutional status (part governmental, part trade association), was brought into being.

The design weakness of this organisation was (and still is) that responsibility is undefined. The County NatWest and Blue Arrow affair, discussed by Christopher Stanley (Chapter 6), demonstrates the weaknesses of overlapping jurisdictions; in particular, the statutory obligations of the Fraud Squad came to take precedence over immediate proscriptive measures which could have been taken by the self-regulating trade association, The Securities Association. Subsequent moves to reform the Securities and Investment Board toward more conventional banking regulation still leaves legal regulation without the statutory powers or legitimacy of the American Securities and Exchange Commission. One can sympathise with the role of the police authorities who have to cope with the excesses of the market. Michael Levi shows that the detection of fraud is just one of the many concerns of Commissioners of the Metropolitan Police. In a scale of priorities policing fraud did not come high in the Commissioners' list in policing London. Moreover the composition and operation of the Fraud Squad works on a rotation basis; officers assigned to fraud do so as a stint in careers that will see moves, say, to criminal investigation, or traffic. As Levi notes, the success achieved by the Fraud Squad says much for police officers' motivation of 'feeling collars', but any objective assessment points to the lack of resources and management structure weaknesses in combating the criminal professional. Levi notes that recent developments have strengthened the powers of the investigating authorities (Chapter 5, pp. 137–8). These developments include the setting up of a Serious Fraud Office with a director directly responsible to the Attorney-General and with authority to investigate any serious fraud; the draconian powers given to the DTI under the Financial Services Act of 1987 to obtain information; and a preparedness to share information with regulatory authorities in other countries. The outcome of the first Guinness trial is a significant indicator of these new priorities. But whether the new powers will be exercised to the full and with what consequences, especially in the field of international fraud, remains to be seen.

The lax, cavalier and procrastinating attitudes of government towards regulating the City, in opposition, say, to their regulation of social security fraud, tend to justify the suspicion that there is an identity of interest between City and Conservative governments. But the chapters by Coakley and by Jessop and Stones return to the theme of the two cities: the traditional and domestic city and the international city. The former, as we have seen, has been upstaged and incorporated by the latter. The political intent behind these changes would suggest that the Conservatives favoured such a process as part of their free market internationalism. Just as the British economy was to be first ravaged and then invigorated by international competition (in the form of a $2.40 to pound exchange rate), so the City was to receive the same treatment. Indeed, opening up the internal, domestically oriented City to global financial competition was at the same time a way of opening the whole economy to the purview of the new financial regime. The results of this were highly uneven both in the City and, more importantly, in the country. While the radicals controlled the Conservative Party there could only be the dissidence of the old school Tory 'wets' against the destruction of the balanced economy, and the occasional protest as in the parliamentary vignette disclosed by Jessop and Stones: the Tory MP Beaumont-Dark warning that though finance was now international, it didn't follow that international control of domestic finance was good for the country. Jessop and Stones are clear that a Conservative strategy (which they choose to term neo-liberalism) included the suborning of the domestic City, the de-professionalisation of the stock exchange, and for the country a political strategy of 'popular capitalism'. 'Defended by Mrs Thatcher as a "one nation" policy which will transform every man (sic) into a homeowner, share-owner, portable pension owner and stakeholder in local services, this is intended to provide the social basis and legitimation for the Thatcherite regime in its efforts to roll back the social democratic welfare state' (Chapter 7, p.176).

Few tears at the time were shed for the passing of the old City. 'Popular capitalism' proved to be a bonanza for the financial services industry, as it had become known. The relaxation of credit, the encouragement of home ownership, the privatisation issues, the encouragement of tax-subsidised saving and investment schemes – servicing the popular capitalist was a lucrative business. The 1980s saw a massive increase in employment in the financial, banking and business services sector concentrated initially in London but spreading to the south-east, epicentres like Bristol and latterly to northern cities such as Leeds (Chapter 12, pp.284–5). The consequences for the new financial services professional was, what Stanley terms, an anomie of affluence – an insatiable egoism of greed. Or as one observer quoted by Stanley put it, 'Never had so many unskilled 24 year olds made so much money in so little time' (Chapter 6, p.142).

Stanley contends that the Conservative ideology of the enterprise culture was in effect an inducement to individuals to go out and make money by whatever means, and that the language of the market was used to legitimate sociological change. The imperative to become rich led to insider dealing, multiple applications for give-away privatisation issues, illegal share support operations in take-overs, concert parties, share ramping and property speculation; all activities not unknown to the old City but kept in check in their scale by the Bank of England. In the chaos of Big Bang when firms doubled and tripled in size in the space of a year, and the new norms were international hardball, there was neither effective oversight nor the discipline of efficient markets. As Stanley notes, just what efficacy was put in a Secretary of State's legislation on insider dealing when at the same time his own City broker was indulging in share ramping and concert parties. Stanley discriminates between a prescriptive enter- prise culture and the pre-existing normative City culture; the latter having a notion of social regulation built into it. The post-crash City may have seen the back of a transgressing enterprise culture. Meanwhile the City is left with the complexities and cost of an overly legalistic regulation (Chapter 4, pp.101–2).

Global finance and the national economy

The debate on the advantages and disadvantages of the City to the rest of the economy is well rehearsed: the City through its invisible exports is a net contributor to the UK economy, the UK economy grows faster (in terms of Gross National Product) from its return on overseas investment than it would from the return on investment in the domestic economy, and lastly it provides efficient investment and savings facilities. The arguments against the City are that it has failed to provide long-term finance for the restructuring of manufacturing industry, preferring instead the allure of short-term returns; that it has acted as a magnet for scarce and highly qualified graduates who would otherwise have been spread more evenly through the economy; that it has an internationalist not a national economic outlook.

The problem with this presentation is that globalisation of finance and the move to insert the UK economy in a system of international free trade have altered the terms of the argument. At the start of the 1980s neo-conservative governments in Washington and London were set to restore profitability of companies, reduce corporate and personal taxation, and give corporations a far freer hand in their economic decision making by the reduction in the influence of planning and a no less important reduction of the power of organised labour. The role of governments in attempting to attenuate the disparities between geographical regions, between industrial sectors, and through welfare and taxation the disparities of income and wealth, in short the function of governments to provide some sort of framework for economic and societal regulation, was ditched (Chapter 7, p.177). This is not an argument against the importance of national contexts, as the differential experience of Britain and its European partners shows.

The 1980s have been good to the City as long as one is not averse to uncertainty. The future in the 90s, to reiterate Stafford and Coakley's predictions, is going to be more precarious. The new finance houses have invested heavily in offices, technology and manpower, and acquisition. Estimates put their investment at over £6 billion in the 1980s, making the City one of the few areas in the UK equipped for international competition. What then are the reasons for this precariousness? First, the indigenous banking and finance institutions are far less significant. There are no British-owned multifunctional finance houses. Though, against this, as Stafford comments in Chapter 1, the role of the niche player may in aggregate prove to be a more important development. The clearers are weakened by their bad Third World debts and are overly reliant on their preserve of the cheque clearing scheme. The Lloyds-based insurance business is an object lesson in the difficulties of capitalising on international market share, merging the functions of principal and agent, operating self-regulation, and the assessment of risks (Chapter 7, p.175).

The future long-term trends that could operate against London are: the return of funds to domestic markets, in particular the United States and Japan; industrial power and banking may become more closely integrated as in the German model (Chapter 2, p.53); the loss of regulatory asymmetry whereby London was privileged by its absence of controls; the possibility that the UK economy could continue its relative decline further depressing the domestic savings and investment markets. A global financial system means that any centre may compete in any market: new futures markets and a sharpened international market for equities in Paris and Frankfurt will pose a stiff challenge; Tokyo is already overtaking the City on foreign exchange dealing; and London can expect further competition in wholesale capital markets (Chapter 1, pp.46–51; Chapter 2, p.70). Should the flow of funds divert from London due, for instance, to the peripheralisation of London from the process of European monetary union and the move toward continental-based and differentiated capital markets, then a worst case scenario becomes discernible. Finance and banking as the growth sector of the 80s falls back, while the manufacturing sector remains weakened, and competitive redemption is spavined by the increasing deficiencies of Britain's training and education systems (Jessop and Stones, Chapter 7). Whether the City does respond to the investment challenges of the 90s – Eastern European recon- struction, Western European restructuring in the light of agri- cultural and regional imbalances, and new ecological demands – as well as responding to the new market disciplines these will impose, remains to be seen.

PART II LANDSCAPES OF POWER

The dissolving effects of global finance on national economic regulation have their counterparts in the field of cultural patterns and urban sociology. Making sense of the metropolis has always been a challenge. As Sharon Zukin points out (Chapter 8, p.197) New Yorkers and Londoners have always prided themselves on their capacity to adjust to the patchwork quilt of their cities. However, while not presupposing that the metropolis was ever a unified and coherent entity, the changes to the landscape of the city in the 80s have been hard to read and explain. In many ways the debates and analyses of urban structures, social movements and spatial patterns have been overtaken by these events on the ground (Pahl 1989). Just as the project of national economic policy as something preserving an essential balance over regions, sectors, and income and wealth distribution has given way to free market internationalism and neo-conservative politics, so too the idea of the city as an assemblage of communities, different economic sectors, public representation and civic and urban culture, underpinned by a degree of planning and investment in infrastructure, has failed.

The reasons for this take one to the heart of current debates. The difficulties associated with applying the concept of *habitus* is illustrative of some of the perplexities involved in coming to grips with the ways in which our notions of time and space have been reconstituted. The theory of habitus was developed by Pierre Bourdieu and Parisian-based urban sociologists. A district or *quartier* is said to have a particular set of material and cultural characteristics. An identifiable social class lives in the district, the housing is of a certain type, and the collective services such as transport, education and culture are all of a particular type and standard. In short a social class, or part of one, could secure a section of the city, benefit from its collective services, and impose its aspirations upon it. In the hands of Bourdieu (1986: 101) this social fixing of an area becomes part of the process whereby social classes reproduce their position in the class hierarchy over time. A habitus gave the bourgeoisie a place in the city and an identifiable standard which acted as cultural capital that could be passed on to their children. Transferred to London in the 1960s, it was reasonably easy to read the habitus of an area, whether it was St John's Wood, Surbiton or Bethnal Green.

Habitus, as a theory, can accommodate change. Sections of the city become fashionable and attract investment, while others languish and decline. But the changes which have occurred in the 1980s overextend the theory. Habitus assumes a degree of empirically discernible regularity of material and cultural practices, whereas in the 1980s whole areas of London have become hard to recognise and to define. The city, writes Harvey, 'is no longer treated as an entity malleable for broad social ends, but as a collage of spaces and people, of ephemeral events and fragmentary contacts' (Harvey 1988: 33).

Social theory has been hard put to keep abreast. For Frederic Jameson the putative chain of determination became, on the one side, global capitalism as the latest stage in the evolution of capitalism, and, on the other, the culture of postmodernism. Culture had replaced social and class action, and postmodernist culture, for Jameson, entailed the disjuncture between the body, its perception and the built environment. In the architectural extravaganzas of global capitalism – Jameson's example is the Bonaventura hotel in Los Angeles – the individual undergoes the vicarious experience of hyperspace. Politics becomes 'an aesthetic of cognitive mapping' (Jameson 1984: 53–92). Mike Davis injects this same notion with a sharper critical edge. Global capitalism represents the circuits of international rentier capitalism in a hypertrophic financial state, and postmodernism is reviled as the 'Warholesque transformation' of city architecture where the 'postmodern tower is merely "a package of standardized space to be gift-wrapped to the clients' taste"' (Davis 1985: 108–9).

Production as a classic sociological uniformity gave way to a concern with consumption. The nexus of culture and consumption is now receiving intense interest (Warde 1990: 1–5) and looks set to re-establish the Simmelian theme of the city as the place where the individual enjoys a multiplicity of stimuli and sensations. The collapse of broad material determinations into smaller micro-effects, and the fragmentation of culture into the individualising forms of lifestyle and personality are now central features of social theory. Stanley (Chapter 6) suggests that the material hierarchy where markets are a result of production, capitalism a consequence of markets, and finance the enabling mechanism for capitalistic intermediation no longer holds. In a postmodernist analysis, such as Baudrillard's, this material hierarchy is dissolved. Accordingly, money does not represent value created through material processes but becomes a part of an internally generated set of symbols. Money is no longer 'filthy lucre, only that of the sanitized electronic display of the computer monitor' (Chapter 6, p.150). Rothman has noted that 'the conven- tional vector of cause and necessity which points from trade to finance, from things to money, has been reversed' (Chapter 6, p.149). Postmodernist analysis has appropriated Marx's dictum 'everything solid melts into air, everything sacred is profaned'. This literary allusion – to Mephistophelean sorcery – becomes literal in the hands of the postmodernists. Global finance has the literal power to conjure profits from its own transactions devoid of the messiness of a real economy; likewise it has the ability to construct its own temples to mammon and refashion the land- scape in its own image.

A possible rejoinder to this analysis is to accuse it of mistaking the 'as if' for the 'what is'. Yet as Stanley argues, part of the behaviour of the 1980s was people acting 'as if' they did have Faustian powers and could transgress with impunity. However, while generating paper profits from paper transactions might be instantaneous, transforming urban landscapes takes a little longer and is somewhat less ephemeral. The chapters by Zukin, Budd and Cowlard document and search out the operant causal mechanisms for such transformations, and the ways in which global capitalism is reinserted in the urban and social structure at higher levels of complexity.

Before briefly outlining their positions it is worth recalling Robertson's formulation of globalisation. The local appears in the global and the global in the local. Universalist reference points such as the national economy, the capital city and its government, or modernist architecture succumb to new overarching forces: national economic regulation to international monetary movements, city government to global property developers, modernism to fast-track building technology. But the global has a localist presence and appearance. The architecture of the 1980s was full of particularistic references – monster buildings with folksy roofs – the international property developers became the philanthropists of parish-sized communities, and the symbols of civic culture were bypassed in favour of an individualising yuppie culture. The contributions of Part II point up the complex interplays between the material, the cultural and the individual.

Zukin portrays the urban landscape as one of the dominance of the vertical – the polished architecture of the centre – over the horizontal segmentation of vernacular city life that lies around the centre. Modern office blocks rise above the vernacular topography of the city to impose a powerful visual imprint. The vernacular landscape belongs to the old working class, the immigrant ghettos and the artists' colonies. These are areas of 'resistance, autonomy and the originality of the powerless' (Chapter 8, p.198). The centre deploys three sorts of power over the vernacular. Economic and financial power confers the ability to buy up property and devise plans for wholesale reconstruction such as those developments being constructed at Canary Wharf in Docklands and already achieved at Battery Park City in New York. Political power and influence introduces coordination. Zukin cites the example of Nelson Rockefeller who as governor of New York state operated the levers of public and private power to open up central and western Manhattan to redevelopment (Chapter 8, p.206). The final instrument of power is control over symbolic representation: a new visual syntax of consumption styles attuned to the tastes of the business and financial services class takes precedence over the old vernacular. The elimination of immigrant enclaves, gentrification, the replacement of local retail outlets by high-volume chain stores, the redevelopment of wholesale markets and manufacturing sectors into prestige housing, historical artifacts, bistros and 'craft' workshops are the victories of the centre over the vernacular (Chapter 8, p.201).

Just as national economic management falls prey to the international demands of global finance, so city governments seek to attract 'world class players', sacrificing the wider and more balanced concerns of cities to the needs of the centre. In London this process has gone unchecked, especially since the removal by national government of local government (the Greater London Council). In London the case of Docklands is central to the analysis of global finance and the metropolis. Keith Cowlard (Chapter 9) shows that the links between trade, finance and transport came to an end in the late nineteenth century as the port of London lost its pivotal position as an entrepôt. In the 1960s the docks were closing and the city was undergoing an office boom. 'What to do with Docklands?' came on to the political agenda. Despite numerous proposals from both Labour and Conservative governments as well as local authorities, little happened until the mid-1980s when London's business and financial services sector experienced rapid expansion. Local authority control had been sidelined with the transfer of Docklands to the London Docklands Development Corporation (LDDC) in 1980. The Isle of Dogs was made an Enterprise Zone in 1982, conferring on incoming investment capital allowances for ten years as well as a rates holiday.

The project that changed everything was the Canary Wharf scheme, sited on the recently closed West India Docks. As the pile-drivers went to work within the coffer dams, the hopes and plans of a mixture of industrial sectors as well as residential and infrastructural investment, which had been the basis of the Greater London Council's schemes, were finally buried. This was to be the new 'Wall Street on water', a recipe that had worked well for the new developers, Olympia & York, at Battery Park City. Because of the scale of the project – it will cover 71 acres, cost £4 billion, provide employment for a medium sized town (40,000 jobs) and have three massive towers – any future assessment of the success of the free market inspired strategy of urban development corporations will be made on the basis of Canary Wharf. A number of interim observations can be made. When completed it will render the initial commercial and residential developments in Docklands as unplanned, inchoate and tawdry. If the scheme meets its own objectives it will mark a permanent shift of gravity of the central business district of London eastwards. But, at the same time, these objectives look increasingly compromised by the downturn in office demand and the financial services sector and, secondly, by the failure of a strategic planning process to plumb such a massive development into the urban and regional infra-structure of the south-east. Cowlard notes that the completion of the project opens up 'a potentially damaging mismatch between commercial development and infrastructure' (Chapter 9, p. 234).

The one effect it has already had was to administer a galvanic shock to the Corporation of the City of London. Canary Wharf's potential 40,000 workers amount to approximately 13 per cent of the current City work-force. In 1975 only 6 per cent of the City's office stock had been built after 1965 and 50 per cent was still pre-war accommodation. As the expansion in City jobs was gathering pace in the early 1980s the City Corporation still operated a planning regime that gave conservation protection to 70 per cent of the buildings. The Corporation's policy turned about to fall in line with other deregulatory measures on office development which the government had passed (Chapter 9, p.232). As Stephanie Williams reports (Chapter 10), the Chairman of the Corporation's Planning Committee, Michael Cassidy, echoed Hayekian philosophy that the market could not be second guessed; the market knew best on developments, moreover it was also impossible to second guess aesthetic considerations. The Corporation introduced a more permissive planning regime and ripped up previous Corporation plans to allow, for instance, the purchase of air rights over London Wall. The long-running saga of planning inquiries into the Bank and Paternoster Square develop-ments should not obscure the fact that the floorspace completed in the period 1979–89 amounted to 30 per cent of the existing stock as it stood in 1979.

Stephanie Williams considers the pressures of an overheated property market on the new permissive planning regime. Any spare land – a major source is land above railway termini, and belonging to the newly privatised public utilities companies – has been exploited. Also large new sites have been consolidated from existing buildings, some of them as recent as the 1960s. The characteristic shape of the new building is what Williams terms the groundscraper. The public's strong disapproval of the skyscraper (not allowed to frustrate Canary Wharf) has not stopped developers offering square footages of 100,000 and above. Broadgate with its 14 phases and 29 acres provided the first built exemplars of the breed. Broadgate was a first in a number of other respects: it represents the biggest and most imaginative development on railway land yet to be seen in Britain and the pioneering of fast-track building methods. Here each phase was completed within 18 months, buildings have been equipped to meet the high-tech specifications required by finance and banking, and American architects – specifically Chicago's Skidmore Owings & Merrill – have, for the first time, been able to put their stamp on a substantial chunk of London. Groundscrapers have emerged, and continue to emerge, at Beaufort House, Minster Court, Little Britain, London Wall, above the main railway stations at Charing Cross and Cannon Street, and along the realigned Holborn Viaduct, with further monster developments planned for Spitalfields wholesale market, London Bridge City and – the biggest proposed so far – at King's Cross.

In Chapter 11 Leslie Budd discusses the impact of property development on London's urban narrative. The flows of finance capital, just as in any other period of boom, have been channelled into property development and, as we have seen, have extended to sites like Canary Wharf and Kings Cross, previously the least attractive. Also the permeability of finance into and out of property has been enhanced in the 1980s by innovations like securitisation and diversified international property portfolio, where risks can be offset by the differential prospects of widely spread geographical locations. Despite these innovations Budd argues that developers adhere to, and are committed by, the territoriality of land which imposes frictions upon the supposed freedom to conquer time and space hypothesized by certain theorists (Soja 1988; Harvey 1988). Budd uses the concept of an urban narrative to discuss the changes from London's post-war economic and spatial patterns in response to the material imperatives of globalised finance which manifested themselves at the end of the 1980s.

Nigel Thrift and Andrew Leyshon take up the theme of the City's newly moneyed. A recent survey of professionals' salaries in the City came up with a rule of the thumb: multiply age by £1000 to obtain the expected salary. This is probably more meaningful to a public sector professional, not least as an index of relative deprivation. For the City professional, salary is merely a base-line figure. Thrift and Leyshon show that salary is supplemented by performance-related bonuses, share option schemes, subsidised mortgages, company car, free medical assurance and so on (Chapter 12, p.290). The 1980s saw a large expansion in City jobs which, with Big Bang, became a scramble to put together the best teams. Thrift and Leyshon track the route of high income to its conversions into personal wealth, noting the fillip given to wealth accumulation by a series of tax-cutting budgets and the related asset price inflation which has such a marked effect on property prices in London and the south-east. Their chapter shows how the 'newly wealthied' convert money into forms of cultural and symbolic capital, which in the English context means the purchase of a country property and the web of personal associations that can be generated by possession of such unique 'positional' goods. The newly wealthied represent a City Disestablishment who, to quote John Lloyd, are 'meritocratic rather than egalitarian, efficient rather than generous, individualistic rather than corporate' (Chapter 12, p.283). For the Disestablishment, write Thrift and Leyshon, the 'abstract community of money had to be transformed into a concrete community of the moneyed'. Hence the country house and the accoutrements of domestic servants and leisure facilities. Using data drawn from estate agents the authors furnish a glimpse of how the moneyed as a family unit seek to maximise the chances of their offspring – part of Bourdieu's thesis on the reproduction of class advantage.

A query remains over the process of reproduction of familial advantage: are the newly wealthied of the international City salariat old middle class (but paid at a rate beyond the wildest dreams of their fathers) or upwardly mobile from lower down the class hierarchy? This query relates to whether the Disestablishment will become a new City élite. Once again, as in the case of the complexities of habitus, a process of differentiation in the formation and transmission of cultural and material capital may be occurring. Research monographs on the changing economic and political structure of the City and the social background of city positions need to be conducted before adequate answers can be given. (On this see Pahl 1990: 12–17.)

Sam Whimster (Chapter 13) writes on yuppies. As a sociological term it is hopelessly imprecise. But because of the prevalence of its use, both in North America and Britain, and the sorts of emotions the word triggers, its usage became a social and linguistic phenomenon in its own right. Following Raymond Williams, Whimster treats it as a *keyword*. These words have no definitional consistency and they express a welter of arguments and feelings that drag the word in different directions. The validity of the term is justified in part by the move toward a post-industrial society in which the service sector and the control function of information predominate. Whimster explores the paradox of the first generation of babyboomers (the 1960s generation), who were countercultural in orientation, becoming transmogrified into yuppies as second generation babyboomers (the generation of the 1980s). The discontinuities have been much remarked. Whimster argues that certain continuities rooted in the expansion of the resources open to personality marked the character formation of the second generation. The opening up of these resources lay in the historically unique twentieth century phenomenon of counterculture that was adopted on a mass scale in the 1960s. Yuppie egoism is a feature of a differentiated personality that embraces both a much harder and more competitive world of work and career as well as a well-developed sense of the needs of self and personality. The demands of capitalist development and ecology in the nineties promises to give a further twist to the dynamics of personality and socioeconomic structure.

The final chapter by Chris Rhodes and Nurun Nabi discusses the economic and political prospects facing the Asian communities in the area of Brick Lane in the eastern wards of Tower Hamlets. Two urban narratives are set to collide. The one is determined by the investment trusts and property developers who wish to realise the value – both material and cultural – of inner city locations so close to the central business district. The other belongs to the crowded settlement of shops, businesses and homes of the Asian community. Rhodes and Nabi show the close interdependence of familial, work and cultural relationships within this growing community. The former narrative is driven by the goal of redeveloping the wholesale fruit and vegetable market of Spitalfields, which would then take the financial services sector within a block of Brick Lane. Such schemes offer linkages in the forms of shops, workshops and cultural amenities in exchange for planning permission for office development. The question raised by Rhodes and Nabi is whether the economic and cultural structure of Asian businesses is assimilable to the modernising mission contained in the linkage schemes. As Zukin notes with reference to linkages, 'temporarily' displaced businesses and trades rarely come back. Rhodes and Nabi record that this is a scepticism shared by Asian businesses in the area. Decisions on the Brick Lane development will be taken by the local politicians. Here the viability and profitability of Asian businesses will be a key perception. If the self-fulfilling prophecy of the decline of manufacturing is widely held, a modernising strategy through redevelopment gains credence. Against this Rhodes and Nabi report a high level of business optimism in the community. Should the power of the centre prevail over the vernacular, then the taste of the Asian city would become 'thoroughly unwelcome, depressing and dangerous' (Chapter 14, p.352).

To date the 1990s has indicated an emerging recession, has seen the demise of the neo-conservative warriors, Reagan and Thatcher, and has revealed a change of sentiment away from the individualist ethos of the 80s. Keynes observed that bankers are the most romantic and least realistic of men. This appears apposite as bankers contemplate their ever worsening bad debts, though some might choose to express the sentiment more forcibly. This raises the question whether bankers and financiers will return to more prudential calculations, and whether an individualising market logic will give way to structures where stricter parameters are placed upon the risk environment. Just as the bad debts are opportunities foregone, so in the real world the era of global finance will have left a permanent impress on the landscape of the metropolis. Whether the more stable processes of habitus will return in place of the agitations of culture, lifestyle and personality, or whether these hitherto separable reference points are to be permanently interlinked remains to be seen. The following chapters will have performed a service if they clarify the nature and direction of certain causal agencies, and show how those forces affect lives as they are lived in the metropolis.

REFERENCES

Bourdieu, P. (1986) *Distinction: A Social Critique of the Judgement of Taste*, London: Routledge.

Braudel, F. (1977) *Afterthoughts on Material Civilization and Capitalism*, Baltimore: The Johns Hopkins University Press.

Davis, M. (1985) 'Urban renaissance and the spirit of postmodernism', *New Left Review*, 151, pp. 106–15.

Harvey, D. (1988) 'Voodoo cities', *New Statesman & Society*, 1, 17, pp. 33–5.

Hilferding, R. (1910) *Das Finanzkapital*, English translation by Bottomor, T. (1981) *Finance Capital*, London: Routledge & Kegan Paul.

Jameson, F. (1984) 'Postmodernism or the cultural logic of late capitalism', *New Left Review*, 146, pp. 53–92.

King, A.D. (1990) *Global Cities. Post-Imperialism and the Internationalization of London*, London: Routledge.

Lewis, M. (1989) *Liar's Poker. Two Cities, True Greed*, London: Hodder & Stoughton.

Pahl, R.E. (1989) 'Is the emperor naked? Some questions on the adequacy of sociological theory in urban and regional research', *International Journal of Urban and Regional Research*, 13, pp. 709–20.

——(1990) 'New rich, old rich, stinking rich? Review essay', *Social History*, 15, 2, pp. 229–39.

Robertson, R. (1991) 'Social theory, cultural relativity and the problem of globality', in A. King (ed.) *Culture, Globalisation and the World System*, New York: Macmillan.

Schumpeter, J.A. (1939) *Business Cycles. A Theoretical, Historical and Statistical Analysis of the Capitalist Process*, vol. 1, New York and London: McGraw-Hill.

Soja, E. (1988) *Postmodern Geographies: The Reassertion of Space in Social Thought*, London: Verso.

Warde, A. (1990) 'Introduction to the sociology of consumption', *Sociology*, 24, pp. 1–4.

Part I

GROWTH AND DYNAMICS OF FINANCIAL MARKETS

1

LONDON'S FINANCIAL MARKETS

Perspectives and prospects

Leonard Stafford

In the summer of 1986 the City of London was an exciting place, where there was a very special feeling of newness, of adventure, of setting out into unknown territories. Opportunities were there to be seized and risks to be taken. The world seemed to be divided into those who possessed the knowledge, courage or sheer cheek to take the opportunities and to accept the risks and the others who were merely competent, diligent and dull. Energy and daring often seemed quite as important as financial expertise although that quality was present, too. A senior manager in a most respected British merchant bank told the writer that it was traders, barrow boys, that were needed, but he hired graduates. At another firm, where broker-dealers had been absorbed into a financial conglomerate, a distinguised senior partner from the former broking house expressed concern at the problem of dealer burn-out. The City had become powerful, cruel and aware of the need to adapt and compete. Often, though, it did not fully understand the processes which were at work; it is learning to do so.

Financial markets absorb and respond to information but the most vital information concerns conjectures about the essentially unknowable future. Technically, financial markets are about responses to uncertainty. They are also about economic and political power. It is only by taking a view of the processes of change and the way in which they have evolved that the likelihood of future directions can be assessed.

THE PROCESS OF CHANGE

The deregulation of the London Stock Exchange, now known as the International Stock Exchange,[1] was a late response to a process

31

of internationalisation in financial markets which had been growing in power and force for a quarter of a century. In those years, City firms experienced a growing involvement with foreign banking houses, with international lending and with overseas securities markets. The traditional City had an unrivalled ability in the techniques of international banking and the finance of foreign trade. It also had a sound commercial infrastructure: competent and experienced accountancy firms, corporate and financial lawyers, excellent business communications and a reputation for probity. The City was, and is, well-positioned in relation to the international time-zones. In spite of these advantages, the City of the 1960s and 70s tended to be slow to react to change. Its institutions and markets were constrained by convention, by restrictive practices and, to an extent, by legislation. The calm and stability of this highly intelligent but essentially complacent world was upset by the arrival of an increasing number of enterprising and aggressively competitive overseas banks. These overseas, and particularly American, banks were attracted to London partly by the freedom from regulation enjoyed by foreign financial firms in the United Kingdom and partly by London's advantages as a centre for the growing and profitable eurodollar markets. Neither the presence of foreign banks nor operations based on eurodeposits could, of themselves, have changed the ethos, institutions and practices of the City of London but both factors were greatly reinforced during the 1970s in ways that positioned London financial firms precisely to take advantage of the next decade's even more significant developments.

The growth of dollar deposits not located in the United States and of wholesale lending based on these funds was given impetus by the current account imbalances which emerged between major groups of countries in the world economy. Current account imbalances have, in the nature of things, capital claims and the transfer of financial assets as their counterparts. These give rise to international financial pressures which, because they have their origins in fundamental economic conditions, develop great power. The oil price rise of 1973 generated massive surpluses for the oil producers and threw importing countries into deficit. London was well-prepared to accept this OPEC business which, politically, could not go to the United States. With oil contracts denominated in dollars, however, the effect was to give a further, massive boost to the London eurodollar markets. The flow of dollar funds into London was lent-on to developing countries notably in Latin

America but also to borrowers in Africa and to Poland. Dollar lending outside the USA was not constrained by reserve requirements and consequently the international flows were amplified by the eurodollar multiplier effect.[2]

The net size of the eurocurrency markets, which to some extent involved other currencies than dollars, grew from US$11 billion in 1965 to US$661 billion by 1981. Eurodollar lending looked very profitable to the international banking community; the rates charged to borrowers were linked to LIBOR (the London Interbank Offer Rate) and the risks seemed small since the borrowers were usually the governments of sovereign states. Moreover, with interest rate risk reduced by linking the rates charged to borrowers to LIBOR and country risk compensated for by the size of the spread (with less credit-worthy borrowers paying higher rates) and reduced by diversification, eurocurrency lending seemed to make very good sense. Syndicating the loans over a large number of banks enabled the international banking system to handle the enormous sums which were coming onto the market and to achieve the aim of distributing risks widely. The ability to manipulate funds on such a scale, to assess the risks, to assemble the syndicates, some of which involved the cooperation and commitment of scores of banking houses, and to devise appropriate financial mechanisms required great ingenuity in terms of procedures, communications and funds transmission.

London's experience as the centre of eurodollar lending enhanced its banking skills, widened its network of international relationships and gave a new boost to the already impressive rate of technological change in the electronic transmission of funds. At the end of the 1970s the financial kaleidoscope was given a further shake by the second oil price quantum-rise of 1979. This brought the oil exporting countries, who had been drifting into deficit, back into surplus. But in the succeeding years the supply side of the market for crude oil responded to higher prices and the surplus had disappeared by 1982. In the meantime, though, another equally significant factor had become apparent. This was the growth of Japanese trading and manufacturing strength which with its counterpart, the United States deficit, set the scene for much of the decade which followed and provided the thrust for the changes which swept through the financial world.

The pattern of current account balances which developed is shown in Table 1.1.

Table 1.1 Current account balances, 1978 to 1985

US$ billion

	1978	1979	1980	1981	1982	1983	1984	1985
United States	−15.4	−1.0	1.9	6.3	−8.1	−46.0	−107.4	−117.7
Japan	16.5	−8.8	−10.7	4.8	6.9	20.8	35.0	49.7
Other industrial countries	13.4	−15.7	−53.0	−30.0	−21.0	2.2	9.3	14.2
Fuel-exporting developing countries	−6.1	51.4	95.1	31.0	−25.6	−14.8	−8.6	−6.5
Other developing countries	−28.4	−44.3	−67.2	−80.2	−65.3	−44.1	−26.5	−27.6

Source: IMF World Economic Outlook and own calculations

Behind the trends exhibited by the figures lay not only Japanese economic efficiency and vigour, but also the United States' combination of tight monetary policy with a loose fiscal stance. This was a product of the pressures on the US government and the independent attempts by the Federal Reserve Bank to counter the inflationary consequences of government policy. The results were the dual deficits – budgetary and payments – and a tendency towards higher interest rates that inevitably spilled over to other Western economies.

Japan's economy was characterised not only by a determined efficiency in the exporting industries but by a very high savings ratio, that is the ratio of saving to income. Japan, therefore, produced a flow of funds seeking opportunities for investment while America had an urgent need to finance her deficit. With Japanese funds playing a more important and sometimes a dominant role in financial markets, the outlines of the modern system began to emerge. The United States was not alone in pursuing more stringent monetary policies; monetarism was the fashion in many western economies and in consequence inflationary pressures diminished. With interest rates tending to rise but inflation diminishing, real interest rates rose. One estimate (Cline 1983) is that average real interest rates, that is nominal rates less the rate of inflation, stood at a negative figure of -0.8 per cent during the 1970s but that the real rate had risen to 7.5 per cent by

1981 and to 11 per cent by 1982. The negative rates had made borrowing attractive for the developing countries in the earlier period but the strongly positive rates of the early 1980s made their position untenable, with large debtors seeking rescheduling or threatening default. London banks moved away from syndicated eurodollar loans which now seemed decidedly fragile. In their place they were able to apply their knowledge, experience and financial resources to the issuing of medium term notes and bonds. By 1984, the value of eurobond issues, that is of bonds denominated in currencies other than those of the countries in which they were sold, equalled that of eurodeposit loans with new business in both markets running at £100 billion a year. Soon, syndicated loan business was confined to renewals and reschedulings.

The shift in the balance of activity altered the relative influence of investment and commercial banks in the euromarkets and prompted fresh innovations in the design of the financial instruments employed. It also brought large corporate borrowers into the euromarkets and so opened up new and very large sources of finance to industrial and commercial companies in the major economies.

With the emergence of the eurobond markets, the pace of financial change accelerated. The influx of American banks into London increased as United States banks, and particularly New York banks, prohibited from combining investment and deposit banking in the States and facing further problems as a result of legislation in 1980 and 1982, established investment banking subsidiaries in the City.[5] It would have been surprising if the flow of Japanese capital coming into London and New York had not induced Japanese investment banks to follow. The trigger for full Japanese participation in the financial markets was probably the Yen–Dollar agreement of the summer of 1984. With the liberalisation of currency flows coinciding with the substantial Japanese trade surpluses, banking flows between the three major centres – New York, London and Tokyo – were bound to increase still further. The high savings ratio was a domestic feature of long standing in Japan and Japanese banking groups, rigidly defined by their functions in their home markets, were able to deploy capital resources which were much greater than those available to British clearing banks. In the almost unregulated freedom of the international capital markets, they were able to apply their financial muscle with flexibility, determination and an impressive clarity of intention.

By 1985 there were over four hundred foreign banks with major presences in London. These included not only American and Japanese, but also European, banks as continental Europe grew in prosperity. Competition from aggressive and innovative American and Japanese investment banks introduced a briskness of style and pace which induced British financial firms not merely to accept but to embrace with enthusiasm the changes which were taking place around them. The changes were structural, technological and institutional. They were responses to the forces generated by the disequilibria discussed above and together they amounted to the globalisation of financial markets.

The term 'globalisation' implies more than that financial markets were international; the suggestion is that delays in time and defects in information across the globe had diminished to the extent that trading was not significantly fragmented. For most markets, trading could produce a common price and for most financial products arbitrage was possible across the markets. Behind the global financial markets was the *technology* of globalisation: the technology of financial innovation and the technology of information and communication. When there were defects of information or delays in transacting, opportunities for profit tended to induce new practices and innovations. Technological developments made increased financial innovation possible but they also made it more necessary, so that a strong element of positive feedback was introduced into the process with the number of financial innovations increasing year by year. One respected observer recorded thirty-seven major innovations in 1985 alone (Kaufman 1986).

The use of computers and advanced information technology for transmitting, categorising and analysing market information was most developed in foreign exchange (FOREX) trading but it was closely paralleled in the bond and securities markets. The products devised and traded, as Nicholas Robinson describes in Chapter 3, crossed the conventional boundaries of these markets. With the increased volatility which followed more rapid trading and faster response to information as well as with the greater sums in play, there was an acute need to control exchange rate and interest rate risks. This applied not only to banks and financial firms but also to major trading and manufacturing companies, who were becoming increasingly aware of the necessity of managing their treasuries skilfully and profitably. Markets were technically more complex than they had ever been. They absorbed and transmitted vast funds and they were becoming interrelated with major transactions involving foreign exchange markets, bond markets and securities markets in a single deal.

In this situation the complementarities between the traditional City and the more forceful newcomers were apparent in terms of functions, since investment bankers needed access to the Stock Exchange, but the changes required were considerable and were at first resisted. Stock Exchange firms were undercapitalised and single capacity, the separation of agency broking from jobbing (market making) was the rule, and minimum commissions were fixed. The US commercial banks, Japanese banks and major British financial houses needed organisations of greater financial size to operate effectively in the new financial markets; they needed to trade in bonds, securities and currencies as well as offering financial services. There was a need for new, large multi-functional financial institutions. One way or another the financial tides released by the events and trends described would have transformed the institutions and practices of the City of London. Had the Stock Exchange not admitted outside financial firms after the Parkinson–Goodison accord of 1983, first to a limited extent and after March 1986 with full ownership, then other ways would have been found to conduct a London trade in UK and foreign equities and gilts, perhaps through NASDAQ[4] or some alternative and specially devised electronic market. No doubt there would have been defensive legal manoeuvres to delay this, but every attempt to evade the invasive consequences of the forces in play would have confirmed London's status as an inward-looking, restrictive and declining financial backwater. There is no doubt that, before the injection of new money by the emerging financial conglomerates and the deregulation of October 1986, the London securities market was an expensive and uncompetitive place in which to deal. Fortunately, a vigorous insistence on the promotion of competition by the Director General of Fair Trading, even if tempered by legislative compromise, ensured that reconstruction was effectively completed in the three years between the spring of 1983 and March 1986.

All members of the new International Stock Exchange had dual capacity and so had the ability to trade on their own account as well as to offer agency broking services. The markets became strongly competitive and commissions, no longer protected, fell often to as little as 0.2 per cent. Securities firms undertaking to buy and sell a range of stocks at displayed prices with a spread between bid and offer prices became market makers. Alongside the equities markets, of course, was the gilt-edged market. Securities firms with a degree of independence from their parent banks and with an approved level of capitalisation undertook similar obligations in respect of government stocks as *primary dealers* through which the authorities were able to use the market. Immediately after the deregulation of 27 October 1986, there were 35 equities market makers and 29 gilt-edged market makers (or GEMMs).

The rise of the new financial conglomerates in the early and middle years of the 1980s has been described many times but it is seldom realised that they took a diversity of forms. These ranged from the typical investment bank, backed by a major commercial bank, and with a market-making arm formed from a Stock Exchange broking firm and a jobbing firm, to energetic New York financial traders with an important London operation, examples of which are Salomon Brothers, or powerful Japanese investment banks like Nomura International. The origins, organisational structure and capital committed by the parent banks determined the internal cohesion and profitability of the new financial firms. In some respects, financial firms which elected to adopt less flamboyant stances exploited familiar markets in which they possessed exceptional competencies, and the niche players fared better than the larger financial groups.

The major commercial banks were burdened by the increasingly doubtful Third World debt on their balance sheets. They had spent hundreds of millions on the acquisition of Stock Exchange firms, and the influx of foreign banks and foreign capital had heightened competition in both wholesale and retail markets. The total dependence of the financial markets on electronic systems for dealing and for the transmission of information called for heavy investment by the banks and by their Stock Exchange subsidiaries. A major commercial bank could spend £200 million on re-equipment of this kind. In spite of these problems, the commercial banks were returning good results in the spring of 1987, but there were indications of trouble to come in the securities markets with which, of course, the banks were now closely involved. UK banks have not yet experienced the crisis affecting Japanese and American banks at the end of 1990, but domestic bad debt provisions have weakened their balance sheets.

London market makers, unlike their specialist New York counterparts, were locked into a competitive situation and there were too many of them. The financial conglomerates, though, could not afford to abandon their independent access to the Stock Exchange and the advantages which this gave in the provision of complex services to clients. Not the least of these services were those provided by the corporate finance departments of the large financial firms. These very expert departments were among the most profitable components of the big financial groupings and their Mergers and Acquisitions teams, in particular, were ingenious and aggressive in detecting possibilities for mergers, advising the companies involved, and setting up financial backing for the operation. Industrial and commercial companies in the UK and overseas were involved in an upsurge of merger activity often embracing international and strongly contested deals. In 1987, mergers and acquisitions of United Kingdom companies totalled some £15 billion. The merger boom, the inflow of banking funds, the competitive trading of market makers, much of which involved inter-broker dealing, the extravagant promotion of privatisation and other major issues produced an extremely strong bull market. The strongest factor of all, however, was the optimistic tone of the global financial climate which kept the funds flowing from centre to centre as the pressures unwound.

The centres of London, Tokyo and New York and, increasingly, the emerging financial markets in the Far East were electronically bound together just as their internal structures depended on the technology of computers and information. With faster trades, not least in the foreign exchange markets where London's financial firms still handled more business each day than any other centre, and with multi-billion dollar funds in play, it was quite inevitable that securities prices, exchange rates and interest rates should become increasingly volatile.

A year after the deregulation of London's financial markets, the extent of the interpenetration of markets – equities and options, eurobonds with equities, domestic securities markets with foreign markets – had grown. The complexity and sophistication of the instruments devised and traded had increased but so had the skill and knowledge of those who used the financial markets: the fund managers, corporate treasurers and professional investors.

The period of growing complexity and intensity of trading in financial markets coincided with the realisation in both governmental and banking circles that the international debt problem had to be treated as a permanent feature of the financial terrain. While a number of innovative measures were taken to ameliorate the problem it was the largely unanticipated action by the creditor banks most involved, beginning with Chase Manhattan in the spring of 1987 but followed by other commercial banks, to increase their provisions against the debt outstanding on their books, which assuaged fears about any dangers to the system arising from this source. Share values did not suffer; the system was stable and powerful.

The main British stock market index, the Financial Times–Stock Exchange 100 (FT–SE – Footsie–100) stood at 2301.9 at the close of business on 15 October 1987. On the next day, the New York market lost 108.36 points on the Dow Jones index; the London market was unchanged. By Monday the stock market collapse was spreading from market to market around the world from east to west as each centre commenced trading. London closed at 2052.3. The decline was sharp and continued throughout the month and, with less severity, into mid-November.

On 10 November, the lowest value of the FT–SE Index recorded was 1515.0; after that the market recovered a little but values of less than 1600 were common until the first week in December. During 1988, the securities market resumed an upward trend, but it was a modest and very gradual one. The confidence and the *élan* had been shaken; the euphoria induced by the five-year bull market evaporated.

RATIONALITY, EFFICIENCY AND MARKET ADJUSTMENT

A reasonable view of these events, which are reflected in the month-by-month changes in the FT–SE 100 Index shown in Figure 1.1, is that the London market had been swept into a rising trend and had over-valued the securities traded. The October 1987 collapse, on this view, represented an adjustment towards a more realistic equilibrium. It was this revaluation which produced an Index oscillating around 1800 throughout most of 1988. The recovery to a stable level around the 2500 mark, constrained by recession in the UK and US, was a sober one.

40

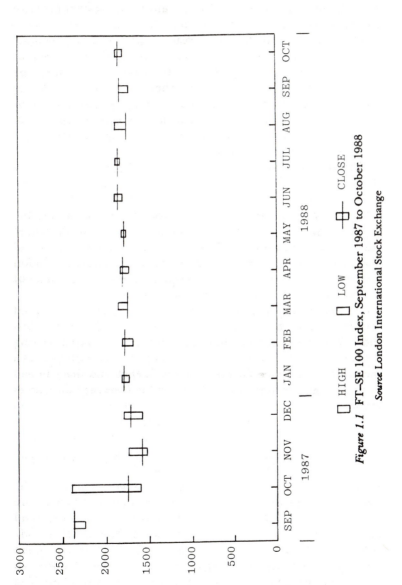

Figure 1.1 FT–SE 100 Index, September 1987 to October 1988

Source London International Stock Exchange

Financial markets adjust quickly as new financial, economic or political information alters trading intentions but it is doubtful, even taking into account disagreements between the US and West German authorities at the time of the 1987 crash about economic and financial policy, that a scrutiny of the record would reveal events that could alter real economic prospects so radically in so short a time. An alternative view is that the financial markets have little to do with the real economy or the prospects of the industrial and commercial companies whose worth they purport to value. In this view, the market is a casino which has become excessively fascinated by its own technology and pretentious about its ability to contribute to the economy. The reality is more complicated than either of these simple views, but it is this reality which will determine the course of future market trends and their eventual economic impact.

An underlying model of the financial sector which offers guidance in analysis is one in which markets are driven by the participants' pursuit of profit that may be impeded by lack of knowledge, by transactions costs, by law or by market regulation but which tends towards a general equilibrium – itself continually moving as conditions and expectations change. In a simple market model, prices adjust towards their market-clearing equilibrium according to the presence of excess demand or supply, with the speed of change of price depending on the magnitude of the discrepancy. In financial markets, adjustment is very fast and information technology has made it more so. Financial assets have a value in the market because they are expected to yield an income stream and, in addition, will have a value when they are sold to another holder or when, as with most bonds, they mature. Market values depend on estimates of these streams. In the case of bonds, for example, such estimates will depend on the coupon, on estimates of the returns on other securities, on the certainty with which the stream may be anticipated – and hence on the credit-worthiness of the issuer – on any conditions attaching to the bond, on the existence of any collateral rights such as warrants, and on many other circumstances. United Kingdom government securities, gilts, will incur no uncertainty about the income stream but their market value will, in general, vary inversely with interest rates. The income streams associated with company equities will depend on expected future corporate earnings, but there will be many factors such as the probability of takeover bids, whether they

42

are likely to be contested, the perceived quality of a company's products and the skills of its management as the market assesses them.

All these things will influence share prices. If financial markets react to information swiftly and accurately all the relevant factors should be absorbed into the prices of the instruments traded. The market is then said to be *efficient* (Fama 1970). There are tests for the efficiency of markets: broadly speaking, divergencies, upward and downward, from a developing trend should be equi-probable. In its strongest form, the efficient markets hypothesis (EMH) suggests that since all the relevant information has already been embodied into the price, it will only be possible to beat the market by the possession of information which is not generally available. To profit from such information necessitates some degree of insider trading.

Rejecting the view that financial markets, and particularly securities markets, are unrelated to the economy or to the prospects for industry, it would be reasonable to conjecture that financial markets would be efficient but imperfectly so. Imperfections arise because financial markets are responsive to so many types of information, are interconnected in complex ways, are subjected to the rapid movement of massive funds from centre to centre and are also influenced by self-referencing changes in market sentiment. This common-sense view is confirmed by more sophisticated analysis: the markets are efficient in absorbing information but they exhibit excess volatility.

The four markets for which the London International Stock Exchange is responsible – UK equities, foreign equities, gilts and traded options – have to be considered alongside the capital markets of various kinds: the newer sorts of market such as those for sterling- and euro-commercial paper, and the growing range of futures markets centred on the London International Financial Futures Exchange (LIFFE). While the efficiency concept is more applicable to the orthodox securities markets than to some of the others mentioned, and while the effectiveness of information transmission and the seriousness of volatility differs between them, they are all interrelated and the general arguments apply. Moreover, where international dealing is involved, exchange rate volatility and its associated risks come into play. An irony is that markets and instruments designed to limit risk for investors have sometimes led to greater fragility in the market as a whole. The use of index futures on the Chicago Mercantile Exchange in association with the protection of large-scale portfolios in anticipation of a falling market is widely believed to have contributed to the severity and suddenness of the October 1987 collapse. The scale of bids and deals in this network of interacting markets had become, even before deregulation, so big that the consequences of failure were beyond contemplation. With both capital markets and stock markets capable of detecting information impressively and instantly, the temptations to prepare markets for a bid or to intervene in order to ensure the success of an issue were irresistible. The need for regulation was clear but, at the time of the design of the regulatory measures which were to be applied, the nature of the system of financial markets and the consequences of changes that were still in train had not become clear.

The system of regulatory bodies set up by the Financial Services Act of 1986 was designed for a less volatile and more precisely defined system of markets. To the regulators, the Securities and Investment Board (SIB) and the Self Regulatory Organisations, codification seemed the key to orderly trading with access to the markets, defined in terms of Registered Investment Exchanges (RIEs), restricted to fit and proper persons. The City considered, and still considers, itself overregulated and with oversight by the DTI, the setting up of the Serious Fraud Office, the establishment, internationally, of more sophisticated rules governing capital adequacy in banking and the inevitability of closer supervision by the agencies of the European Community, its unease may be justified. Trading within and across such com- plex and turbulent markets would certainly be more hazardous without regulation and its uncertainties would be increased. The costs of regulation and of establishing compliance systems are high, however, and, added to the sums committed to computing and information technology, the fixed costs of operating securities houses are increasingly affecting the structure of the financial services industry.

At the end of 1988 it was estimated that the losses of Stock Exchange firms were running at about £600 million a year in the four markets for which the exchange was responsible. Turnover had fallen to half of the 1987 level and offices were overstaffed for the volumes which were being experienced. The synergy which should have existed between banking and securities houses had not developed to an extent that could survive the stock market decline. Possibly a continuation of the bull market would have provided conditions under which the complementaries could have been nurtured into profitability, but the restructuring had come late in an over-volatile and over-hyped market. Had the equities market continued its rise, however, a collapse of the settlements system would have been likely. The gilts market, too, had its troubles. By 1990 the original 29 GEMMs had been reduced to 19. Budget deficits for OECD countries had decreased from an average of 4.3 per cent of GDP in 1983 to 1.2 per cent in 1989 and were accompanied by a decline in yields (*Economist*, 21 July 1990). Perhaps the system which seemed to be evolving strongly and confidently in the mid-eighties could never have attained full maturity in its original form. Globalisation of markets, too, was incomplete and on most technical tests, such as the correlation between saving and investment in national economies, or the persistence of real interest rate differentials, the evidence indicated that international capital flows were not dominant in the financing of real investment.

DECLINE AND RETRENCHMENT

The general atmosphere in the City during the winter of 1988/89 was one of defensiveness and disappointment. By 1990 equities had lost six market makers in addition to the GEMMs already mentioned. Unlike the recession of 1980–81 the recession of 1990 is affecting the service sector more strongly. The prognosis for the City will depend upon its ability to adapt to these straitened circumstances as competition from other European financial markets grows.

The retail markets had become as tough, competitive and over-crowded as the wholesale ones; even domestic lending and branch banking were no longer a comfortable source of profit for a gentlemanly oligopoly. The Trustee Savings Bank had shed its humble image and was buying staff in order to compete directly with the established high street banks. The Building Societies Act of 1986 had opened the door for the Societies to extend the range of their financial services and they, too, were offering fierce and effective competition. The Abbey National prepared to go public and did so in the summer of 1989; the banks bought into local estate agents or formed their own property subsidiaries as did insurers like the Prudential. With over £2 billion invested by building societies, banks and insurance companies in setting up estate agency chains, the collapse of the housing market in 1989 was yet another disaster for the banking and financial sector.

The problems of other sectors of the financial services industry put pressure on the commercial banks to concentrate more on domestic banking where they had competitive strength. The sector was becoming overcrowded, there was room for financial innovation and the forceful marketing of services, but product differentiation was hard to maintain and branch costs were high. The banks' customers had become well-informed and were no longer bound by the traditional loyalties which had served the high street banks so well. The urgent need was to simplify branch banking, to give it a clear purpose in terms of providing finance, advice and other services to corporate and individual clients. To do this with profit in the competitive environment which had evolved, with non-bank financial firms as well as new banking entrants providing similar products and services, it was necessary to reduce costs. One very effective way of doing this was to apply information technology to save staff in the more routine areas of domestic banking and, as well, to standardise procedures and to provide flexibility in the services offered. The provision of financial services to knowledgeable and demanding clients also required computer-linking to the major financial markets though the banks' City offices.

The new realism was the recognition that financial markets were everywhere interconnected, that competition was fierce in every sector, that this involved either defensive or pre-emptive innovation in the design and marketing of financial products, that both access to the markets and the control of costs, including staff costs, depended on a mastery of the most advanced computer technology, that ingenuity and entrepreneurship were not enough; no one was secure.

PROSPECTS FOR THE 1990s

Even as late as 1987, it was tempting to think of the City of London as an island of special competence surrounded by a turbulent and competitive financial ocean. This would have been a misperception; London is a part of the turbulent sea. To use a different metaphor, the City is one of several financial singularities. These are defined by the effects they have on the financial and information flows which pass through them or are generated by them.

It is not the largest such financial singularity; as often as not it is responding to occurrences in the larger centres of New York and Tokyo. In the middle 1980s, the forces which changed the City were consequences of the disequilibria in payments balances, regulatory regimes and technologies. Those that will change the financial markets and their institutions in the 1990s will be rather different.

While the Japanese surpluses and the United States deficit still persist, both are tending to diminish; moreover the US government's fiscal deficit, although still large enough to be of significance in the global financial system, is running at only 3 per cent of GNP and is set to decline. Factors which had determined the course of events in the middle 1980s seem likely to be rather muted in the next decade.

The West German current account surplus had been running at a level of more than US$55 billion in the third quarter of 1989, but by mid 1991 the difficulties of reunification had brought about a sharp reduction in this positive balance. The costs of modernising the eastern provinces also increased the German budget deficit to 5 per cent of the country's GNP. Taken together with the increasingly apparent weaknesses of the Tokyo stock market, any continuance of the massive financial flows of earlier years seems unlikely, although monetary growth in the mid 1990s may have a stimulating effect. The relationships here, however, are complex. The underlying strength of the German economy as well as the growing cohesion of the European Community indicate an even more visible European presence in the international financial markets and in London, which is likely to continue to offer the most convenient and effective European access to global capital markets. An instance of this tendency was the uncontested bid by the West Germany Deutsche Bank for Morgan Grenfell, the London merchant bankers. A probable pattern for the 1990s seems to be of a less active New York-Tokyo axis balanced by increasingly effective and coordinated European centres.

Moves towards a unified securities market, discussed in Chapter 2 by Coakley, would alter the relative importance of the City in other financial sectors as well as in international securities markets. To achieve a unified European market centred on London would greatly augment the United Kingdom's economic and financial status in the Community. To fail to meet this challenge would cause Britain to be relegated to the margins of the

European economy. This, as in other ways, would be a step towards making London an annexe of the New York markets on the one hand and the major occidental centre for Japanese banking and capital markets activity on the other. This is an aspect of the EMU discussion which has not been adequately explored.

In the situation of the 1980s financial flows tended to be intra-OECD, that is from West Germany and Japan towards Britain, the USA and certain European economies. The sophistication of the United States' capital markets as well as the sheer size of the American economy ensured that there was a strong flow back towards Europe and the United Kingdom. Mergers and acquisitions set up and carried through within the European Community grew by a factor of five between 1983 and 1989 and the UK itself was spending more than £20 billion on the acquisition of American companies. The methods applied in the finance of mergers and acquisitions were tending to require very specialised competencies. The parent bank of a major group provided immediate finance on a very large scale and the investment banking arm of the group covered the deal by means of an issue of bonds with terms adjusted towards an optimum by means of swaps or other arrangements. There were three consequences of this type of development. The first was that merger and acquisition commissions, which could be up to 1 per cent of the value of the deal, were seen to be available to merchant banks which had not yet developed a UK client base, provided that finance could be raised quickly and not too expensively. The second was that a regulatory imbalance was again at work, in that there was very little protection for British companies threatened by foreign takeovers. The third was that American, Japanese and European banks increased their involvement in UK merger business and in devising methods of providing finance on terms acceptable to the bidders and sustainable by the businesses acquired. It has, however, to be noted that mergers and acquisitions activity had by the end of 1990 come to a standstill.

Changes in merchant banking strategy tended to divide the industry into the very large investment banks with powerful backing and the more traditional merchant banking operations which depended on close contact with client companies: relationship banking. The bond markets, neither very active nor particularly profitable in 1988, began to pick up, as did the stock market itself, reaching pre-crash levels by the autumn of 1989. It was not only takeover activity that provided buoyancy for the securities markets; the institutions held a great deal of cash, partly as the outcome of considered financial asset preferences and partly in anticipation of future privatisation issues. The availability of cash for the institutions was also a byproduct of the distributional effects of government monetary policy. The track of the ISE equities market is shown in Figure 1.2.

Although the bond markets were becoming more active, bond dealers, unlike market makers in the securities markets, have no obligation to trade and so levels of activity can change quickly. The bonds offered, though, were tending to be less complex, the principal reason being that exotic financial instruments are difficult to dispose of in secondary markets. In 1988, 82 per cent of new bond issues were straights. In 1989 this percentage had fallen but this was due to the increased interest in bonds with equity warrants, which offer an attractive combination of risk, return and commitment to the investment. Japanese issues with equity warrant are currently running at an estimated capitalised value of US$60 billion. The trend towards simplification in new bond issues can also be seen in the reduced percentages of Note Issuance Facilities (NIFs) and other facilities.

While there has been a tendency to retreat from over-elaboration in the design of financial products, the impetus towards innovation is not spent. The use of medium term euronotes (euro MTNs) has grown although only a small number of firms are active in the secondary market. On the technical side, some fund managers have been developing computer models which are directed towards outperforming specifically selected indices or which restructure portfolios according to asset yield comparisons. A development which may appear in the London markets is the offer of futures funds. The issue of ECU bonds has become commonplace as has a variety of other ECU-denominated transactions.

The trend which seems most pronounced in the financial services industry is that towards bigness and consequently towards oligopolistic market structures, at least so far as any one centre is concerned. Because all the major markets are global, if imperfectly so, the situation is one of competitive oligopoly. While the volume of global financing is maintained at an adequate level, industry structures will be sustainable although there may be quite sweeping changes in particular financial centres. The changes in

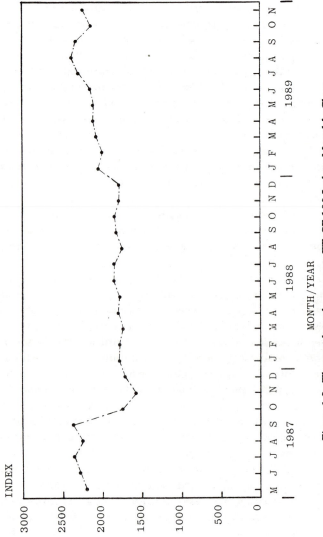

Figure 1.2 The crash and recovery: FT–SE 100 Index: Monthly Close

Source LSE, London

the direction of financial flows are already having such effects in London and in Europe.

The speed and extent of changes in the structure of the London markets depends in some degree on the fate of the United Kingdom economy. A collapse in the level of economic activity, a failure to contain inflation, a slower growth of industrial production or a fall in corporate profitability might lead to a temporary retreat from UK equities by investors. They would come back, but the market to which they returned would be one in which overseas firms were totally dominant, in which the number of market makers was much reduced, perhaps by a half, and in which the major participants' trading tactics were closely coordinated with their parent banks' financial strategies. The reactions of institutional investors to such a situation would be interesting to observe, but the implications for UK companies and for the economy itself would be of more serious concern.

NOTES

1 As from May 1991 it has reverted to its old name, the London Stock Exchange.
2 The eurodollar multiplier is the ratio of the increase in eurodeposits to the primary deposits made. The existence and magnitude of the effect is a matter of contention.
3 Legislation: the *Depository Institutions Monetary Control Act*, 1980, and the *Garn–St.Germain Depository Institutions Act*, 1982.
4 NASDAQ: National Association of Securities Dealers Automated Quotations; a computerised over-the-counter system designed for the US market but which is expanding internationally.

REFERENCES

Cline, W.R. (1983) *International Debt and the Stability of the World Economy*, Washington: Institute of International Economics.
Fama, E.F. (1970) 'Efficient capital markets: a review of theory and empirical work', *The Journal of Finance*, XXV, 2 May 1970.
Kaufman, H. (1986) *Interest Rates, the Markets and the New Financial World*, London: Taurus.
Pecchioli, R.M. (1983) *The Internationalisation of Banking: The Policy Issues*, Paris: OECD.

2

LONDON AS AN INTERNATIONAL FINANCIAL CENTRE[1]

Jerry Coakley

In the 1980s while much of British manufacturing industry languished and declined the City of London was paraded as the international success story of a Thatcherite decade. It had succeeded in carving itself an important niche in the postmodern international division of labour where services and not industry allegedly reigned supreme. Radical deregulatory reforms such as the abolition of exchange controls and the Big Bang liberalisation of the Stock Exchange had served to enhance further the City's international role.[2]

However, at the beginning of a new decade, the City's leading role is not looking as secure as it had been *vis-à-vis* both competing international centres like Tokyo and New York and competing regional European centres. Continuing deregulatory reforms in both the US and Japan are beginning to erode the City's apparently impregnable hegemonic financial role.[3] In addition the move toward a single European market by 1992 and ongoing deregulation is likely to afford new opportunities to some of London's European competitors. All of this is not to deny the City's current leading role in many markets. Rather it is intended as an antidote to the prevailing complacency about the City's current and future role.

In this chapter I examine the dimensions and parameters of London's international role in some of the major financial markets. In the first section I discuss competing notions of international financial centres. Next the importance of London's share of various international banking and other markets is examined. In a final section I evaluate London's future position in the light of the 1992 proposals and moves toward European monetary union.

INTERNATIONAL FINANCIAL CENTRES

Financial markets play a central role in modern capitalism. Indeed, their precise role has formed the basis of a number of famous theories such as Hilferding's (1910) theory of finance capital to which I return below. The influence of financial markets also filters into reports in the more serious financial press. For example, according to a recent *Economist* newspaper capital market survey Europe has two competing capitalist models: the bank-dominated German model and the stock market-dominated Anglo-Saxon model. The competing models are described in the following terms:

> The Anglo-Saxon tradition relies on equity capital, strong shareholders, relatively open capital markets, a range of different sorts of institutions active in them, and arm's-length relations between banks and industry. Banks have only recently been admitted to stock-exchange membership. Investors' interests are served by a wide range of competing products and by disclosure.
>
> West Germans, at the opposite end of the pole, lean on loan finance, as well as on strong links between banks and industry. German banks are members of the underdeveloped equity markets; savers prefer fixed-income assets; and what securities they do own they probably bought through their bank branch. Financial products are more restricted, and so are the methods by which they are sold.[4]

The West German model in the above quotation resembles Hilferding's (1910) concept of finance capital. Hilferding, drawing on the German experience, argued that a bank–industry nexus would emerge in which the banks were the dominant partner. In his model of advanced capitalism banks also dominated the commodities and stock exchanges. At the international level Hilferding envisaged the world divided into a number of relatively hermetic imperial blocs. Although empires have long since crumbled, the current division of the world economy into three major trading blocs – the Pacific rim countries, Europe and the other Mediterranean economies, and the Americas – finds an echo in Hilferding's writings. In the case of each trading bloc one currency more or less dominates: the yen, the deutschmark, and the US dollar respectively.

In broad terms West Germany is the closest, albeit imperfect, contemporary example of finance capital. Its large universal banks dominate its financial markets. Historically both the UK and the US have exemplified the Anglo-Saxon tradition with other European economies and Japan falling somewhere in between. However, the UK and London in particular developed an expertise in international banking in recent decades, as will be clear from the next section. One should emphasise fundamental differences between the UK and the US in terms of the relative degree of regulation of the financial sector in both countries. Traditionally the UK has relied on a system of minimal statutory regulation in contrast to the US where both the banking and securities sectors are heavily regulated.[5]

In this chapter I define a financial centre as a network of related financial markets. Virtually all such centres have some international links today as a result of tendencies toward increased financial integration. The question is the extent of the development of such links in different centres. Thus in the literature one finds several competing concepts of international financial centres (IFCs).

For example, Reed (1984) uses a rather general criterion based on a centre's degree of influence on global asset and liability management. On this basis he proceeds to distinguish between three types of international financial centres:

- Host international financial centres. These centres attract foreign financial intermediaries but they exert no influence on global asset or liability management.
- International financial centres. As well as attracting foreign financial intermediaries these centres have a limited impact on global asset and liability management.
- Supranational financial centres. These centres act as the headquarters for a large number of internationally active financial intermediaries. Therefore they exert considerable influence on global asset and liability management.

Reed's typology contains a number of ambiguities. The basis for defining the third category is acting as the headquarters for a large number of internationally active financial intermediaries. However, this criterion fails to capture an important difference between centres like London in which large numbers of foreign financial intermediaries dominate activities and those like Tokyo where domestically headquartered financial multinationals rule the roost. This underlines the problem that the continuing basis of Tokyo as a financial centre may be more securely founded than London, for example.

Another problem in classifying IFCs is that dominance in one type of financial market is not a sufficient condition for dominance in others. To take one obvious example, Tokyo is now the premier international banking centre but London remains the leading foreign exchange centre. Chicago is something of an outlier since it is the leading international centre in futures and options markets but not in any other financial market.

In my view, financial centres' international links are best classified along the following three dimensions. The first is the extent to which a centre's client base or sphere of influence on the demand side extends beyond national boundaries. This could be related to Hilferding's concept of financial or trading blocs. The second relates to the degree of influence exerted by financial multinationals (especially those headquartered overseas) on the demand for and supply of financial services within a centre. Both sides of the market are considered because of the importance of the interbank market, for example (see next section). The third dimension is the proportion of turnover which is transacted in foreign currency as opposed to host country currency. In reality these three dimensions may not yield similar rankings or be of equal import in all centres.

In what follows I propose a two-tier ranking of financial centres which exercise international influence in one or more financial markets. I employ the term 'international financial centres' to depict the status of centres such as London, New York and Tokyo. This usage subsumes aspects of Reed's international and supranational centres. In my view the term 'regional financial centre' more graphically captures the position of less developed financial centres such as Paris and Frankfurt within Europe or Singapore in South East Asia.

In this chapter international financial markets in the UK are taken to be synonymous with financial markets in the City. This is because activity in international financial markets within the UK is concentrated in the Square Mile and the vast majority of the branches and subsidiaries of overseas financial intermediaries are located there also. Before discussing London's role as an international financial centre it will prove helpful to set out a fairly typical orthodox view of London's international role.

Davis and Latter (1989) discuss London's international role at the end of the 1980s and the thrust of their argument illustrates the largely uncritical mainstream complacency about London's leading international role. This is captured by the following quotation:

> Besides its domestic banking and securities business, London is a major centre for eurocurrency business, eurobond transactions, insurance, foreign exchange, fund management and corporate financial advice. It is also the location of a significant volume of international equity business, and the volume of activity on London's futures and options exchanges, though modest in comparison to that in the United States, has grown rapidly of late.
>
> (Davis and Latter 1989: 518)

In what follows I qualify some of the above views and generally present a more sceptical picture of London's future. Since London's comparative advantage in international financial markets lies in the banking field I focus attention on its role in banking markets, broadly defined. The discussion of London's lesser role in other international financial markets is correspondingly abbreviated.

LONDON AS AN INTERNATIONAL BANKING CENTRE

Historically London's reputation as an international financial centre rested on the performance of its capital markets rather than its banking markets. Witness London in the late Victorian and Edwardian periods as the leading centre for international issues of bonds and, to a lesser extent, shares and the accompanying export of capital. This accorded with the Anglo-Saxon tradition and the leading role of the Stock Exchange. The rise of the eurocurrency markets since the 1960s transformed that; London became the international banking centre *par excellence* although it was surpassed by Tokyo by the end of 1988 (see Table 2.2).

In this chapter I define international banking activities broadly to include both international (eurocurrency) bank lending and deposit business and foreign exchange activities. The size and importance of international banking centres can be quantified on the basis of three indices. Two are commonly employed in the banking literature. One is the number of overseas banking establishments located in particular centres and the other is the total amount of international bank lending advanced. A third index is the total amount of foreign exchange business transacted.

Overseas banking establishments

Although London was not renowned as an international banking centre in the nineteenth century foreign banks have been represented there for over a century. Among them one can distinguish three main groups: European, American and Japanese. Although European banks are the most numerous and long-established their share of lending is overshadowed by the other main groups. American banks initially benefited most from London's role as the leading euromarket centre, due partly to the central role of the dollar in the early phase of the euromarkets. They succeeded in capturing and holding the dominant market share of international bank lending from London until the early 1980s when Japanese banks assumed supremacy.

The history of foreign banks by year of establishment in London up to 1985 is summarised in Table 2.1. The table lists only banks which are directly represented by means of a branch or representative office. It thus excludes indirect representation by virtue of holdings in consortium banks, the significance of which had diminished by the 1980s.

Table 2.1 Foreign banks by year of establishment in London

	Pre-1914	1914–39	1940–59	1960–69	1970–74	1975–79	1980–85
Europe	9	5	10	15	35	46	52
US	3	5	1	20	24	8	4
Japan	–	2	7	4	10	3	14
Other	18	7	12	18	15	42	45
Total	30	19	30	57	84	99	115
Cumulated total	30	49	76	136	220	319	434

Source: Derived from the *Banker*, November 1986

Between 1914 and the end of 1985 the number of foreign banks in the City grew more than fourteen-fold. In absolute terms the bulk of the growth can be dated from 1960 which is an approximate starting date for the euromarkets. Expansion continued throughout the 1960s and gained momentum in the latter half of the 1970s and the early 1980s. Numbers virtually doubled between 1975 and 1985 but in recent years they have more or less stabilised with exits matching new entries.

Banks from European countries constitute the most numerous group represented in London. Their presence before the First World War reflected the hegemony of European banks during the last century. After that their rate of establishment tailed off until the 1970s. Well over half the European banks have opened London offices only since 1975, which is one of the spin-offs of Britain's entry to the EC and the 1992 proposals. Whilst one cannot deny the numerical importance of European banks in London they represent quite a heterogeneous group and as yet their influence on banking practices is relatively small by comparison with the American and Japanese banks, the two major national banking groups in London.

The history of Japanese banks in London may surprise some, for by 1960 their numerical presence of nine equalled that of American banks. Thereafter their numbers grew rather slowly until the 1980s when they experienced a renewed wave of growth. Nonetheless, by the end of 1985 their total of 40 was only about 60 per cent of the American total of 65. However, there is not a one-to-one correspondence between numbers of overseas banks represented and the amount of international bank lending.

American banks were attracted to London in the post-war period to service the banking requirements of the 800 subsidiaries of American multinational corporations which, by 1961, had located in the United Kingdom.[6] In other words the initial impetus was production led. Since then the burgeoning growth of the euromarkets provided the main attraction for both American and other foreign banks as international loans were increasingly booked from London.

Borrowing and lending eurodollars in London enabled US banks to transact banking business with a freedom and at interest rates that at the time were denied them within the United States, where regulatory restrictions such as those on interstate banking and on interest rates operated. This encouraged US banks to internationalise their operations earlier than they might otherwise have done. Finally, the existing expertise of US money-centre banks in wholesale banking techniques was readily applicable to the euromarkets.

International bank lending

International bank lending has expanded extremely rapidly in recent years. By the end of June 1990 outstanding cross-border lending by banks in the UK had attained a total of $952 billion.[7] This dwarfs the total of $184 billion for 1975. The fivefold growth since 1975 serves to underline the continuing spectacular growth of international bank lending via the euromarkets, despite the high inflation of the late 1970s and the new lending slowdown in the 1980s associated with the debt crisis.

Within the overall pattern of expansion of international bank lending the interbank market has emerged as a novel and prominent feature. Essentially it forms the immediate source of liquidity of the international banking system. Lewis and Davis (1987) report that about 2000 large international banks participate in this market either as suppliers of surplus funds or as buyers of short-term liquid assets. In 1987 Japanese banks alone accounted for two thirds of international interbank business and the bulk of this was transacted in London.

The concentration within the international interbank market is mirrored at the level of the distribution of market share as between competing financial centres. However, it should be borne in mind that London's hegemony over international banking markets in recent decades is based on what Coakley and Harris (1983) have dubbed its entrepôt role. That is, London acts as a clearing house for funds largely originating from and destined for overseas locations. Its entrepôt role in international banking markets means that the City is offshore to or divorced from the British economy in a double sense. First, it is divorced from most of the real sector of the UK economy with the exception of the multinationals and companies engaged in a significant amount of international trade. Second, it departs from the Anglo-Saxon stock market tradition although it has to be added that a number of commercial banks in London – British and overseas – have become involved in securities business.

Table 2.2 shows the market share of total international bank lending of the principal international banking centres from 1975

Table 2.2 Banking centre shares of international lending (%)

	1975	1980	1985	1987	1988	1989H1
UK (London)	27.1	27.0	25.4	22.1	20.9	20.5
Japan (Tokyo)	4.6	5.0	10.8	18.7	21.0	20.6
of which offshore	(– –)	(– –)	(– –)	(3.9)	(6.8)	(7.1)
US (New York)	13.5	13.4	13.3	9.9	10.1	10.0
of which IBF[a]	(– –)	(– –)	(6.5)	(5.4)	(5.6)	(5.8)
Offshore centres	11.6	10.7	18.5	18.0	18.5	18.4

Source: Bank of England
Note: [a] International banking facilities

through to the end of the 1980s. London's position contrasts with that of its nearest international rivals, New York and Tokyo, which is still largely that of the traditional international banking centre lending local funds to overseas clients. This is especially true for Tokyo where the Japanese banks could piggy-back on the huge current account surpluses being generated by Japanese exports in the 1980s.

From the rise of the euromarkets until the late 1970s London's market share of total international bank lending had varied between one third and one quarter. However, during the course of the 1980s, London's market share, despite being the largest, dropped to just in excess of one fifth while that of Tokyo and New York grew correspondingly. One reason for this is that London's entrepôt role declined in an era of slow overall growth associated with the debt crisis. Another is the establishment of offshore facilities in the US and Japan which enhanced the role of both New York and Tokyo at the expense of other offshore centres.

However, the leading role of London is by no means synonymous with a leading role for British banks, as emphasised by Coakley (1984) and borne out in Table 2.3. This table shows that, even in the case of London, Japanese and American banks accounted for more than half of all international bank lending in September 1990. The corollary of this was that UK banks were responsible for a mere 14 per cent of total international lending on their home territory. London's position contrasts sharply with that of Tokyo and New York where domestically headquartered multinational banks dominate international lending.

Table 2.3 Market share in international lending from London (%)

	Japanese	US	Other overseas	UK retail	Other UK[a]	Total
1)[b]	169.8	51.9	128.3	30.2	25.1	405.3
2)[b]	11.9	15.5	16.4	7.6	3.5	54.9
3)[b]	0.8	1.5	3.9	5.3	2.0	13.5
Total	182.5 (38%)	68.9 (15%)	148.6 (31%)	43.1 (9%)	30.6 (7%)	473.7

Source: Bank of England
Notes: a Includes merchant and other British overseas banks
     b 1): Currency lending to overseas sector
       2): Currency lending to UK private sector
       3): Sterling lending to overseas sector

The figures in Table 2.3 may exaggerate the role of Japanese banks as market leaders in London. From the 1960s to 1981 US banks in London held the dominant market share and it is only since then that the Japanese banks have become market leaders. In the 1970s and 1980s US banks played a leading role in the euromarkets until the onset of the Latin American debt crisis when debt provisions and new capital requirements forced them to curb balance sheet expansion. Moreover, their involvement with the UK corporate sector remains the largest of any overseas banking group and this is underlined by the level of their foreign currency lending to the UK private sector, which comfortably exceeds that of the Japanese banks. However, the activities of the Japanese banks are focused on international rather than UK lending. By September 1990 their total market share in London was more than twice that of US banks.

Foreign exchange transactions

The foreign exchange market is the one international financial market where London still enjoyed a clear lead over its principal rivals, New York and Tokyo, at the end of the 1980s. London's daily turnover in April 1989 totalled $187 billion, which easily surpassed that of its nearest rival, New York, at $129 billion. Table 2.4 shows total turnover in foreign exchange in March 1986 and April 1989 for the three major international centres.

Foreign banks accounted for no less than 80 per cent of principals' aggregrate turnover in London in 1989 with North

Table 2.4 Foreign exchange turnover

	London	New York	Tokyo
1986 ($ billion)	90	58	48
1989 ($ billion)	187	129	115
Change 1986–9	108%	120%	140%

Source: Bank of England

American banks being the market leaders. Even UK banks' dominance of cross-currency business involving sterling appears to be in decline. And despite London's current undisputed lead in foreign exchange turnover the challenge from both New York and Tokyo is intensifying, as evidenced by their relatively faster rates of growth since 1986. Foreign exchange business is closely related to euro-currency business which is shifting from London to Tokyo as Japanese banks and securities houses assume the dominant role of recycling Japanese trade surpluses and domestic savings. One can thus expect Japanese banks and Tokyo to pose a stiff challenge to London in the 1990s for leadership of the foreign exchange markets.

Conclusion

London's pre-eminence as an international banking centre has coincided with the rise of the euromarkets. By the early 1990s it still remains a leading banking centre as measured by total number of overseas banking establishments and foreign exchange turnover. However, the former is also one of London's weaknesses since so much of its banking business is dominated by overseas banking groups including American and Japanese banks. This renders it vulnerable to shifts of business to competing financial centres, especially with the advent of 1992, as will become clear in a later section. A shift has already occurred in international bank lending where Tokyo looks destined to consolidate its lead in the 1990s.

OTHER INTERNATIONAL FINANCIAL MARKETS

London's leading role in international banking markets is commonly assumed to carry over to other financial markets but this is not always the case. In this section I summarise London's international role in non-banking financial markets.

International bonds

London's supremacy in the euromarkets is not confined to the eurocurrency markets; from the beginning London established itself as the leading eurobond centre. Eurobonds are international bonds issued outside the country of their currency of denomination. At the end of the 1980s London still remained the leading eurobond centre. In recent years the eurobond market has received a fillip from the growing links between it and derivative markets. The latter include the swaps market[8] centred principally on London and New York and the equity warrants market. The growth of eurobonds with Japanese equity warrants was a notable feature of the market in the late 1980s.[9]

London's supremacy extends to the primary, new issues and secondary markets. About 65 per cent of new issues and three quarters of secondary market trading takes place in London.[10] Most of these activities are dominated by foreign banking houses. For example, in 1990 only one British house as opposed to three French houses figured among the top twenty eurobond lead managers. Further, London's role depends partly on restrictions in other markets, such as the witholding of taxes on income in Germany or the fact that newly issued eurobonds cannot be sold into the US during the 90 days after the issue. Finally, London's role is partly dependent on the attitude of overseas regulators. In the case of eurobonds with equity warrants the Japanese authorities have considered proposals that include greater price transparency and having warrants listed on the Tokyo stock exchange. In the early 1990s the bear market in the Tokyo stock market may prove the decisive factor in the demise of equity warrants.[11]

International equities

The Big Bang reforms instituted in London in 1986 made it unique among competing international financial centres in granting an entrée to securities business to banks and especially to commercial banks. London's reforms and the earlier Big Bang in New York can be viewed as an attempt at modernising the Anglo-Saxon financing tradition. Unfortunately, in the early and mid-1980s many financial intermediaries overestimated the future role of international equity markets in general, and that of London in particular, and invested heavily in trading floors and related information and communications technology systems. The October 1987 crash served to underline the excess capacity in London's equity markets and since then a quarter of total members, including several multinational firms, has withdrawn from these markets.

Table 2.5 shows that the market value of both domestic equity and total domestic and overseas equities turnover in London lags well behind that of Tokyo and New York.

London was the leading European centre but Frankfurt is beginning to challenge its European supremacy. Despite its smaller market value and its virtual complete lack of reform (as compared with London, Paris and Amsterdam), by the late 1980s Frankfurt's total equity turnover was catching up with that of

Table 2.5 Major stock exchanges, 1989

Exchange	Market value (September 1989)	Equity turnover (1989Q3)
	($ billions)	
Tokyo	2,460	300
New York	1,855	204
London	509	75
NASDAQ	233	50
Frankfurt[a]	179	65
Paris	188	17

Source: ISE *Quality of Markets Quarterly*, Autumn 1990
Note: a Frankfurt is employed as a shorthand for the Federation of Exchange in Germany

London. In fact its domestic equity turnover now exceeds London's. The reunification of the two Germanies has boosted their share of global stock market turnover although probably at the cost of some short run instability; turnover in Frankfurt in the first quarter was some $69 billion. Despite the long stock market tradition in the UK, London's domestic equity turnover represents just 5 per cent of world turnover, reflecting the decreasing importance of the UK industrial base *vis-à-vis* other capitalist economies.

One of the benefits of Big Bang for London was the establishment of Europe's first screen-based trading system in international equities. The system is known as SEAQ International and it displayed prices in 557 international companies in June, although only about 200 were actively traded.[12] This was the largest number of foreign stocks listed on any stock exchange. On the same date some 350 foreign companies were listed in Frankfurt which put it in second place. As a result London's turnover in foreign equities exceeds that in other major centres, but one wonders for how long, as trade in European equities (which account for two thirds of London's turnover in international equities) may migrate back to the country of domicile in the wake of reforms. This issue is complicated by a debate over the future of European stock exchanges which we return to in the next section.

Futures and options

These derivative markets are one of the peculiarities of international financial markets in that they are dominated by a centre which in other respects is distinctly second division. Chicago, with its two exchanges – Chicago Mercantile Exchange and Chicago Board of Trade – is responsible for almost four fifths of global business in these markets. Its dominance is due mainly to an early lead over its rivals and an agreement within the US not to list the same products on rival exchanges. New York is pressing for reform of the latter, which might erode part of Chicago's dominance.

Futures and options markets in London are fragmented into six separate exchanges which account for only 7.5 per cent of world turnover. Within Europe the Paris MATIF (Marché à Terme International de France) exchange has expanded rapidly since its opening in 1986 and is already offering stiff competition to London in both futures and options. In fact, turnover in traded options in both Paris and Amsterdam exceeded that in the

London financial options market by a wide margin in October 1989. Moreover, in 1990 MATIF agreed to link up with Globex, the electronic trading system devised by Reuters for the Chicago exchanges. More competition is expected from the Deutsche TerminBoerse (DTB) in Frankfurt which opened for business in January 1990.

Partly as a response to the growing competition from other European centres two mergers have been proposed in London. Early in 1990 a merger between London's futures (LIFFE) and traded options (LTOM) exchanges was agreed and is due to be implemented in 1991. In addition a merger has been proposed between two of London's commodities exchanges: the Baltic Futures Exchange and London FOX (Futures and Options Exchange). The latter trades in soft commodities contracts.

LONDON'S FUTURE ROLE

To evaluate London's future role one needs to consider a number of factors. These include the particularities of its success to date, the effects of the 1992 proposals, and the question of European monetary union (EMU). I first examine the major reasons for London's historical success in some markets.

London's advantages

Among London's many cited advantages (such as its convenient time zone location or use of English language and commercial law) it seems to me that only two stand up to close scrutiny. One is what Grilli (1989a) has called thick market externalities and the other is the nature of regulation. Without doubt a relative lack of regulation was, and remained, one of London's major comparative advantages over New York and Tokyo until the late 1980s. As deregulation proceeds in both these centres in the 1990s, as inexorably it did during the 1980s, so will the balance of financial hegemony be tipped in their favour. Deregulation within Europe is more complex since it is tied up with the 1992 proposals which I deal with separately below.

The intuitive idea behind thick market externalities is that a firm's productivity benefits directly from the presence of competing firms engaged in the same or related activities. It follows that productivity in financial products and services depends on the size of the market. The latter is another major factor in explaining the growth and concentration of financial markets in centres like London.

Grilli (1989a) argues that large markets lead to improved matching of products and customers on the output side and on the labour input side as well. Large industrialised economies in principle enjoy a comparative advantage in attracting financial intermediaries. Established financial centres benefit from the inertia produced by thick market externalities and thus are difficult to displace. Finally, Grilli considers that liberalisation and deregulation are likely to favour countries and centres with developed markets. The latter forms the basis for his conclusion that London's position in Europe is unlikely to be challenged in the near future.

Grilli's (1989a) optimism about London's future in a European context ignores or underestimates several factors. The first is that even now its supremacy in financial derivative markets is being challenged by Paris and, to a lesser extent, Amsterdam. In the 1990s Frankfurt can be expected to step up its challenge. In this context the proposed merger of London's futures and traded options exchanges must be viewed as a defensive move. It is interesting to note that the Bank of England has acted as a prime mover in this merger. The second and more imponderable factor is the effects of the single European market in 1992.

The 1992 European Financial Area proposals

Within the overall framework for a single European market by 1992 the area of financial services has been singled out for special attention. Fifty of the Community's 300 or so directives for 1992 are designed to create an integrated market for financial services to be known as the European Financial Area or EFA. By early 1991 about half the financial directives had been passed. These financial directives have two purposes. One is deregulatory in that it involves the removal of impediments. These impediments could relate to flows of money or capital such as cross-border capital controls or they may pertain to restrictions on markets as in the case of barriers to entry. The other purpose of directives is to set out minimum rules and standards in the operation and regulation of banking and other financial markets across the Community.

The end objective is freedom of establishment and services in all financial markets. This is to be achieved on the basis of a single licence or passport granted by any one EC member state or authority. The regulators will issue the passport to their home companies and will regulate these companies' operations throughout the Community. This is known as the home country control principle. The mutual recognition principle implies that other member states will recognise such authorisations on the basis of the harmonisation of minimum regulatory procedures.

To date most progress has been achieved in harmonising EC banking markets. The basic rules for banking markets are embodied in the Second Banking Directive (SBD) which was agreed in December 1989. The SBD envisages a single EC banking licence granting the holder freedom to establish branches and provide services throughout the Community. The banking model favoured is the more liberal universal banking model which, after 1992, will permit banks to supply a wide range of financial services, from securities business and advisory work to traditional banking business.

What are the likely effects of the SBD on financial centres? The underlying universal banking model is likely to favour those already operating within the universal banking tradition. This may give a boost to German banks generally and Frankfurt in particular. However, London may also gain since Big Bang has encouraged a move in favour of universal banking principles on the part of the larger UK commercial banks. The other more subtle effect of the SBD may well work to London's disadvantage. The single banking licence means that all those non-EC banks already established in London can now more readily set up branches in Frankfurt, Paris and other EC centres. In this respect, the current presence of large numbers of overseas banks in London may turn out to be something of a mixed blessing.

The future of securities markets in Europe is less clear-cut. Some progress has been made on less controversial issues such as a ban on insider trading and common listing requirements on stock exchanges. However, progress lags well behind that in banking markets. Britain, which has most to gain in these markets, is pushing for the equivalent of a single licence in the securities markets but there is disagreement over capital ratios. Meanwhile, Big Bangs are occurring in stock exchanges across Europe which, with the benefit of hindsight, are avoiding London's mistakes. The major question is which trading system will predominate within Europe after 1992: a network of centralised national stock exchanges or a decentralised screen-based market.

At the beginning of the 1990s European stock exchanges were split between support for two competing proposals. The Paris Bourse was supporting a move toward a network of linked national exchanges making markets in an European list of 200–300 stocks. The London exchange was pushing for a screen-based secondary market based on SEAQ International operating on an European scale. In a sense London could be seen as attempting to extend the reformed Anglo-Saxon tradition to Europe as a whole.

Prospects

One big question mark about the future in the early 1990s concerns the effects of progress toward EMU. Currently the UK government appears reluctant to agree to progress as rapidly as other EC members, such as France and Germany, toward full monetary union including a common currency, the so-called Stage 3 of the Delors Plan. The main issue affecting EC financial centres is the possible location of a future European central bank (ECB) in one of the EC's three major financial centres: London, Paris and Frankfurt. The current British government's attitude *vis-à-vis* full monetary union would appear to preclude London as the preferred location. Equally, the desire of many EC member states to use monetary union as a means of replacing the existing *de facto* deutschmark standard would seem to rule out Frankfurt. This leaves Paris as the only possible major centre for a future ECB. This would give a fillip to its role as a financial centre and correspondingly detract from the status of its two main rivals.

In the medium term the underlying strength of the economies of the UK's EC competitors is likely to favour their financial centres. This applies particularly to West Germany and France. With the dismantling of the Berlin Wall and ongoing financial reform in the enlarged Germany the role of Frankfurt is likely to be enhanced despite some short-term difficulties. One imponderable in the case of a united Germany is whether Berlin may seek to wrest back from Frankfurt its former position as Germany's leading financial centre. In any event German financial markets are likely to benefit most from the anticipated wave of foreign investment into Eastern Europe in the 1990s. In the meantime Paris can only benefit from the French government's commitment to the development of information technology ideas, such as the 'smart' plastic card which contains a microchip for storing client information.

CONCLUSION

One of the main themes of this chapter is that London's position as an international financial centre is currently not as secure, and in future may not prove as enduring, as most commentators assume. True, it still remains the leading centre for eurobond, international equities and foreign exchange business, but in each of these markets it is under threat from and likely to be overtaken by international competitors like New York and Tokyo. In all this the imponderability of the future competitive position of the European financial bloc *vis-à-vis* the US and Japanese blocs make it difficult to paint a more glowing picture of London's continuing international pre-eminence.

London's future as a regional financial centre will be bound up closely with prospects for the UK economy and EC-wide events such as progress toward the 1992 EFA and toward monetary union. Banking within the EC in future will be based on the liberal universal model envisaged in Hilferding (1910) that may favour continental banks which have enjoyed a longer universal banking tradition. The future shape of securities markets is less clear-cut but London's supremacy in international equities may not be permanent as business trickles back to domestic centres. Finally, it appears unlikely that London can figure as a location for a future European central bank, given the Conservative government's attitude toward Europe. It is not inconceivable that by the middle of the 1990s London will be struggling to compete with Paris and Frankfurt for financial hegemony within Europe.

NOTES

1 This chapter is a reworking of Chapter 3 of my PhD thesis, *Aspects of the Integration of International Financial Markets* (Open University, 1991). I am grateful to Leslie Budd and Laurence Harris for helpful comments on earlier drafts.
2 On the abolition of exchange controls see Artis and Taylor (1989). On the Big Bang see Goodhart (1987). Both these topics are discussed further in Chapters 4 and 6 of my thesis.

3 Hegemony is often employed as an undifferentiated concept. In my view it is useful to distinguish between at least three aspects: economic, financial and political/military hegemony.

4 'Europe's Capital Markets' Survey, p. 13, *Economist*, 16 December 1989.

5 In the US the banking and securities businesses are segregated by the Glass–Steagall Act which has been subject to pressure for reforms in recent years.

6 For more details of the role of American banks in London see my Chapter 8 ('American Banks Credit to UK Corporations') of Harris *et al.* (eds) (1989).

7 International lending is defined to comprise all foreign currency lending (to both residents and non-residents) and sterling lending to non-residents. Cross-border lending comprises lending to non-residents only. It thus excludes currency lending to residents.

8 See Blake (1990) on the swaps market.

9 See 'Out of warranty', *Economist*, p. 127, 7 April 1990 on the warrants market.

10 Davis and Latter (1989), p. 519.

11 See *Financial Times* Survey on 'Japanese financial markets', 15 March 1990.

12 ISE, *Quality of Markets Quarterly*, July–September 1990, p. 36.

REFERENCES

Artis, M.J. and Taylor, M.P. (1989) 'Abolishing exchange control: the UK experience', *Greek Economic Review*, 11, 1.

Blake, D. (1990) *Financial Market Analysis*, London: McGraw-Hill.

Coakley, J. (1984) 'The internationalisation of bank capital', *Capital and Class* no. 23.

—— (1988) 'The international dimensions of the stock market crash', *Capital and Class* no. 34.

Coakley, J. and Harris, L. (1983) *The City of Capital: London's Role as a Financial Centre*, Oxford: Blackwell.

Davis, E.P. and Latter, A.R. (1989) 'London as an international financial centre', *Bank of England Quarterly Bulletin*, 24, 4.

Goodhart, C.A.E. (1987) 'The Economics of "Big Bang", *Midland Bank Review*, Summer.

Grilli, V. (1989a) 'Europe 1992: issues and prospects for the financial markets', *Economic Policy*, 4, 2.

—— (1989b) 'Financial markets and 1992', *Brookings Papers on Economic Activity* no. 2.

Harris, L., Coakley, J., Croasdale, M. and Evans, T. (eds) (1989) *New Perspectives on the Financial System*, London: Croom Helm.

Hilferding, R. (1910) *Das Finanzkapital (Finance Capital)*, English translation by T. Bottomore (1981), London: Routledge & Kegan Paul.

Lewis, M.K. and Davis, K.T. (1987) *Domestic and International Banking*, London: Philip Allan.

Reed, H.C. (1984) 'Appraising corporate investment policy: a financial center theory of foreign direct investment', in C.P. Kindleberger and D.B. Audretsch (eds) *The Multinational Corporation in the 1980s,* Boston: MIT Press.

3

FINANCIAL BUILDING BLOCKS IN THE CONTEXT OF A CHANGING NATIONAL AND INTERNATIONAL ENVIRONMENT

Nick Robinson

One of the main themes running through this book is the fast pace of change which has been seen in the whole world's financial system and, in particular, in the activities of the City of London. In this chapter, we look at some of the economic factors which underlie this rapid change.

This chapter is concerned with the international environment and is structured around the following key elements – financial innovation, financial instruments and financial building blocks. We begin by looking at the broad economic developments which have operated on a wide scale and which have lain outside the control of the banking system.

First among these is the shift in the balance of economic power between nations. Although many other factors also play a part, there is a clear link between the general economic power of a nation and the importance of its banks in the world financial system. Thus, in the days when Britain dominated the world economy, British banks dominated the financial system and this dominance extended well beyond activities linked to Britain or even to Britain and its Empire. British banks were also pre-eminent in the financing of world trade and in channelling savings between countries of the world, even when these financings involved countries with few or no other connections with Britain. The relative decline of Britain and rise of the United States was followed by a similar shift in the relative importance of these countries' banks. Now we see Japanese banks mirroring the rise of the Japanese economy while US banks decline. European banks also show some resurgence, which reflects the increased cohesion of the European

Community. This is not to say that British banks are now unimportant in an absolute sense. They continue to play a very important role in the world financial system and are still regarded as fierce competitors by banks in many other parts of the world.

A second major factor has been the trend towards increasing competition among banks in their domestic markets. Many countries have moved from relatively protectionist stances in which their domestic banks are given special privileges over actual and potential competitors and so have some degree of monopoly power. Many countries have allowed foreign banks to set up local offices which compete with indigenous banks, while many have also allowed other institutions to offer at least a limited range of banking services. These trends are illustrated in Britain by the large rise in the number of foreign banks in London, by the issue of credit cards by a wide range of institutions, by the provision of chequeing accounts by building societies and so on.

A third major fact has been the increased volatility in the world's financial markets which has been seen since (and has been partly caused by) the breakdown of the Bretton Woods system of fixed exchange rates. Thus exchange rates, interest rates and commodity prices all became much more volatile in the seventies and eighties than they were in the fifties and sixties. Thus the fifties and sixties are increasingly coming to be viewed as peculiar oases of calm in the longer sweep of history, although for many people who started their careers in the late forties or early fifties, the stable decade may still seem to be the 'norm' which was then followed by two strange and difficult decades.

THE BANKS' RESPONSE

Although banks could do little or nothing to influence these changes they could certainly respond to them. Increasing competition forced banks to become much more sensitive to customer demand while at the same time forcing them to look carefully at costs and revenues. Cross-subsidisation was gradually reduced and an increasing number of activities were viewed on a stand-alone basis, to be continued only if they made a satisfactory contribution to profits. Costs were reduced by improved delivery systems such as dispensing machines and computerisation. There was a tendency for business to be split into two types – the 'mass' market offering simple products and providing profits only through high sales volumes coupled with low unit costs, and the 'quality' market in which products have sufficiently high value added to command prices high enough to provide profits at relatively low sales volumes. This process may be likened to some airlines which, in the same aircraft, offer large numbers of 'no frills', low cost seats together with a few premium class seats sold at much higher prices.

Also, markets became more globalised as banks increasingly offered services in markets in many time zones. Arbitrage opportunities have been exploited and, as a result, markets have become increasingly interdependent and increasingly similar. To give a general example, if a country's financial market is relatively inaccessible to foreigners while domestic participants are restricted in their ability to participate in foreign markets, interest rates in that country can be maintained at levels quite out of line with those in the rest of the world (although we should not underestimate the spur of competition on financiers to find profitable ways around the regulations).

At the same time, there has been a trend towards securitisation. The old model of a company and its financiers involved several specific relationships such as loans which involve agreements between the two parties concerned. Increasingly, companies have turned towards securitisation, that is, the raising of finance by means of financial instruments which can be bought and sold on markets.

In addition, volatility has given rise to greater interest in risk management. Volatility in exchange rates or interest rates can seriously damage a company's competitiveness and hence its profit performance. Increasingly, corporations, individuals and national governments seek ways of identifying their exposures to these international prices and then managing their exposure so that they become more closely in line with their own preferences.

Finally, there has been more attention given to the theory and practice of corporate finance. Banks hope to earn large fees by presenting new and imaginative financing proposals which allow corporations to take advantage of tax laws, acquisition opportunities and so on. Some indication of the pace of developments in these areas is given in Table 3.1.

Table 3.1 Amount and value of financial instruments

	US Treasury bond futures[1]	Eurodollar futures[1]	$/DM futures[1]	Crude oil futures[1]	US$ Interest rate swaps[2]	Currency swaps[3]	Net international financing[4]
1977	32,101	–	134,368	–	–	–	24
1981	13,907,988	15,171	1,654,891	–	–	5	64
1985	40,448,357	8,900,528	6,449,384	3,980,867	140	75	183
1989	70,303,195	40,818,269	8,186,221	20,534,865	1,000	317	396

Source: Bank of International Setlements
Notes: 1 Number of outstanding contracts, end year.
2 Billions of US$ notional principal. 1989 figures refer to end 1988.
3 Converted to billions of US$ principal. 1989 figures refer to end 1988.
4 Converted billions of US$. 1989 figures refer to end June.

THE PROCESS OF FINANCIAL INNOVATION

So far, we have tended to look at the demand side of the market rather than the supply. However, to answer the question of *how* banks have been able to change the range of products and services we need to look more closely at the supply side.

One important explanation of the process of financial innovation is the discovery by the world's financial institutions that the financial instruments which they have at their disposal (such as forward contracts, swaps and options) can be thought of as financial building blocks. Close analogies can be drawn between the products which financial institutions can construct with their financial building blocks and the things that children can construct with their plastic or wooden toy blocks. Some of the things which children construct look very impressive and difficult at first sight but, once we see how they are made by carefully putting together a number of simple, basic building blocks, we begin to see the power of the blocks and to understand how they can be used. The same is true of the financial building blocks. Complicated financial structures can be broken down into their components and so can be made easy to understand. Similarly, once a problem or opportunity can be thought of in terms of the blocks, it becomes much easier for a financial institution to select and put together the blocks which are needed in order to construct something to solve the problems or to take advantage of the opportunity.

Thus the process of integrating the world's financial markets towards a single homogeneous entity owes a great deal to the simple financial instrument or building block, known as a 'swap'. Illustrative transactions which represent this process are:

- European bank issues fixed rate yen debt in the euromarkets and swaps it for floating rate deutschmark.
- A British company issues dollar-denominated commercial paper in New York and swaps it for fixed rate sterling debt.

Without the swap, which allows the borrower to arrange his liabilities as he wishes while still taking advantage of market opportunities, globalisation would have taken place far less quickly, if at all. The same instrument can be used to mitigate against the adverse impact of volatility and, as we discuss later, swaps can play an important part in the management of risk.

The process of securitisation, involving the replacement of borrowing and lending by means of contracts with banks by borrowing and lending using instruments which are traded on exchanges, has been made possible by the multiplication of the financial building blocks.

A brief comment on hedging

The idea of hedging exposure provides a good vehicle with which to introduce the relationship between financial innovation, financial instruments and the building block approach to financial engineering. To give an example in the context of foreign exchange, Figure 3.1 shows the impact of the dollar on a hypothetical company which has a dollar exposure such that it suffers from a strong dollar. The left-hand side of the figure shows that the stronger the exchange rate of the US dollar the worse the profits of the company will be. The right-hand side of the figure centres the risk profile on the forward rate and shows that deviations in the dollar from its forward rate will lead to corresponding deviations in profits. These diagrams illustrating the company's exposure are often known as 'risk profiles' or 'exposure profiles'.

Hedging involves reducing the company's exposure by adding something to its portfolio with the opposite 'exposure' or 'payoff' to the entity's own exposure. Exposure is then removed because any change in the environment which worsens one exposure will improve the other and vice versa. Hence Figure 3.2, which shows that a movement in the dollar which worsens the performance of the company (shown by the line labelled 'underlying exposure') at the same time improves the payoff to the hedge (shown by the line labelled 'payoff to the offsetting arrangement') by an exactly equal amount. Such offsetting arrangements can take many forms, ranging from the takeover of another company which gains from a rise in the dollar and so has the opposite exposure profile to the first, to the use of an off-balance sheet financial instrument such as a forward contract. We now explore this latter method in more detail.

FINANCIAL INSTRUMENTS

Three well-known financial instruments with profiles similar to those shown in Figure 3.2 are forwards, futures and swaps. Let us look at each of these in turn.

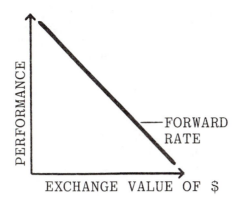

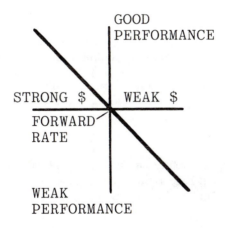

Figure 3.1 Risk profiles

Forwards

We examine two types of forward, currency forwards and interest rate forwards. A current forward contract involves an arrangement be- tween a bank and a named customer and is therefore non-traded. The contract imposes an obligation on each part to exchange currencies as specified. Finally, no action is required by either party until the contract reaches its expiration date, where-upon the exchange of currencies takes place.[1] At expiration, the value of the contract will depend upon the difference between the

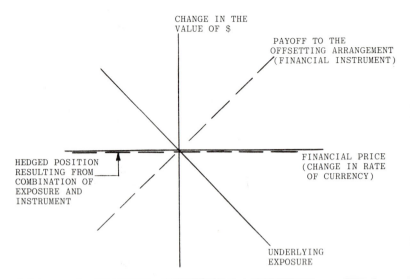

Figure 3.2 Hedging through offsetting arrangements

forward rate written into the contract[2] and the spot rate on the expiration date. Should the spot rate turn out to be equal to the forward rate, the contract will expire with a value of zero, because there is no price difference between taking delivery of the currency at the pre-agreed rate and buying it on the spot market. However, should the spot rate turn out to be different from the forward rate, the contract will have a value equal to the difference between the two rates multiplied by the amount of currency involved in the exchange.

Interest rate forwards are typically known as FRAs – forward rate agreements or future rate agreements. The FRA, being a forward interest contract, is similar to a currency forward. A major difference, however, is that there is no requirement on either party to make a deposit or loan. At its expiration, the value of the FRA contract, which is settled in cash, will depend upon the difference between the forward interest rate written into the contract and the spot rate, together with the notional amount of loan or deposit. Comparison between the way in which each type of forward is valued can be summarised by means of the general picture shown in Figure 3.3. The more the spot rate at expiration differs from the rate in the contract the greater the absolute size of the contract's payoff, a disadvantageous move to a negative one.

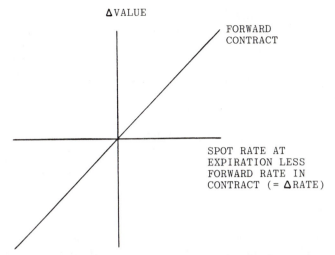

Figure 3.3 General picture showing a payoff to a forward contract

Futures

For our purposes here, we consider only the value of the futures contract at expiration. If we ignore the process of marking to market, we can see that a futures contract looks very similar to a forward contract. If the spot rate at expiration turns out to be equal to the forward rate in the futures contract, the futures contract will expire with a value of zero because there would be no difference in cost between taking delivery of the currency as per the contract and buying the currency on the spot market (or, in the case of an interest rate future, between a loan or deposit made at the interest rate in the contract and one made at the spot rate). However, should the spot rate turn out not to be equal to the forward rate, the forward contract will have a value determined by the extent of the difference between the two rates and the amount of currency (or notional amount of loan or deposit) to be exchanged.

A diagrammatic exposition of a futures contract would look the same as Figure 3.3, thus showing the similarity between a forward contract and the corresponding futures contract.[3] However, once the process of marking to market is taken into account, we cannot determine so simply the value of the futures contract at expiration.

This is because its value will depend upon the daily movements in the forward rate for its expiration date. Thus an early rise in the forward rate followed by a fall towards the eventual spot will place a different sum in the margin account[4] than an early fall followed by a rise towards the eventual spot, even though the eventual spot may be the same in each case.

Swaps

A currency swap is similar to a long-dated forward with the complication that the re-exchange of principal takes place at the spot rate prevailing at the start of the swap rather than at the forward rate. To compensate for this the counterparties exchange interest payments, which effectively convert the spot exchange into a forward exchange. The interest rate swap involves a string of interest payments paid by each of two counterparties.[5] A typical swap might involve one counterparty paying a fixed rate of interest throughout and the other paying a fixed rate determined by the movements in market interest rates.

Because swaps involve a series of payments, their payoffs cannot be shown as a simple function of just one spot rate. Nonetheless, the same principles apply. If each spot rate in the series turns out to be equal to the relevant forward rate the string of interest payments will have a value of zero.[6] Thus instead of deviation in spot rate, we use the concept of net deviations in the string of spot rates.

Options

Unlike the three instruments discussed so far, the owner of an option contract is not obliged to exercise it. In practice, the owner will exercise the option only when it will be to his advantage to do so. Consider a call option on the dollar which allows its owner to buy 10,000 dollars for 18,000 deutschmarks at a pre-arranged date in the future. If, on that date, the dollar is worth more than DM1.80 the owner of the option will exercise it. He provides DM18,000 and the writer of the option is obliged to hand over $10,000 – a sum worth more than DM18,000 at the spot exchange rate. Hence the payoff at expiration depends on the exercise price of the option and the spot price at expiration, as shown in Figure 3.4. In practice, the owner of the option will usually have paid a premium for it so that the net payoff or profit from the option will be its value at expiration less the net terminal value of the premium paid. The option removes most of the downside exposure while leaving the benefit (less the option premium) of the upside exposure.

It is worth noting that the profit to the writer of the call option is the reverse of the profit to the owner. If the owner pays DM18,000 for $10,000 which are worth more than DM18,000 he makes a profit on the deal; the provider of those $10,000 makes a corresponding loss. Now consider a put option on the dollar. Because the put option gives its owner the right to sell at a pre-arranged price, it thus has payoffs at expiration.

THE BUILDING BLOCK APPROACH

The similarity of their payoffs suggests that forwards, futures and swaps have more in common than meets the eye. In some ways they do, because each can be thought of as being assembled from financial building blocks, each of which is one day long. The future is perhaps the most obvious illustration. The future will initially be priced according to the forward rate expected on its maturity date. At the close of each day's trading that forward rate will be recorded and any change from the previous day's close will lead to a marking-to-market of the contract and a cashflow in or

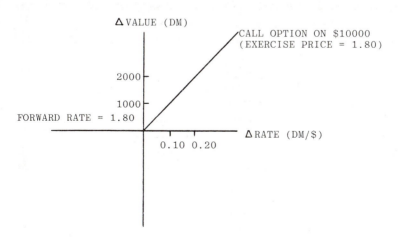

Figure 3.4 Payoff to a call option on $10,000

83

out of the margin account. This process explicitly recognises that the future has one day fewer to run before maturity.

The least obvious illustration is perhaps the forward contract because neither party is obliged to do anything until the contract matures and, apart from accounting considerations, it is not valued during its life. However, it can still be constructed from one-day blocks. A forward can be thought of as being made up of one-day blocks joined together so tightly that the 'cracks' between them cannot be seen and the forward looks and behaves like a solid block spanning the period between its birth and its expir- ation. A future covering the same period is made up of the same one-day blocks but they are loosely joined so that the cracks between them are visible. The marking-to-market process effectively pulls the daily blocks off one by one, leaving behind an ever-shortening string of blocks as time passes to maturity. The swap, with its six-monthly difference cheque, is less extreme than either, for its one-day blocks are joined together tightly over six-month periods, with a crack visible between each of these periods. Again, the difference cheque process effectively pulls the six-monthly blocks off one by one leaving behind the ever-shortening remainder of the swap.

These ideas are illustrated in Figure 3.5. The option shape contains a 'kink' and so looks unlike a forward, a future or a swap. However, we can show its similarity by considering the combi- nation of buying a call option, and writing (selling) a put option, each of which has an exercise price equal to the forward rate. As is known from the put–call parity theorem, these options will have equal prices (premia) and so – ignoring bid offer spread – the combination will involve no net cash flow. Hence the payoff (and profit) from the combination looks as shown in Figure 3.6.

Thus options, swaps, forwards and futures can be seen to belong to the same family. Perhaps the one-day option is the basic building block. Take a one-day call and subtract a one-day put and the combination becomes a one-day forward as shown in Figure 3.6. Clip together one-day forwards with appropriate 'cracks' and the combination becomes a forward or a future swap. In fact, it can be shown that an option can in turn be constructed from cash and a loan. Perhaps, then, cash plus a one-day loan are the basic building blocks. The search for the basic building block may be interesting in its own right but for our purposes it is sufficient to remember that forwards, futures, swaps and options can be thought of as variations on a theme.

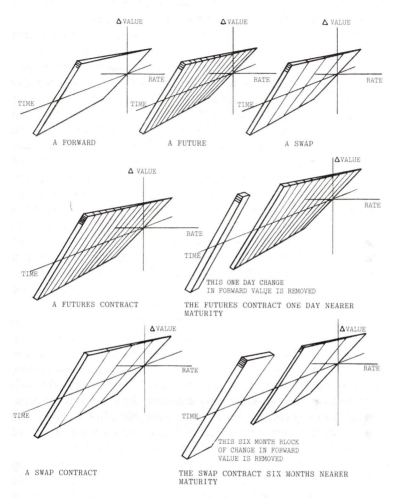

Figure 3.5 Marking-to-market building blocks

Exposure management with the building blocks

The market seems to be full of new-fangled financial hedging instruments these days and banks sometimes add to the confusion by giving them their own brand names with the result that the same instrument may be known by four or five quite different names and so appear to be four or five different instruments. A

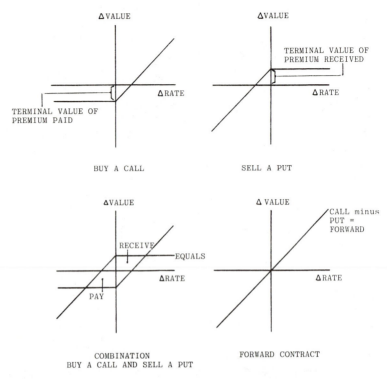

Figure 3.6 Buying a call option and selling a put option to produce a forward contract

good way to beat the confusion is to think of the instruments as being made from simple financial building blocks so that we can see that bankers are using the blocks to assemble many different products, just as a child uses its own toy building blocks to build castles, cars or aircraft. Almost every hedging instrument product contains the same blocks put together in different ways.

To illustrate this, consider the case of a deutschmark-based importer with a dollar obligation whose exposure profile can be shown as in Figure 3.1. The stronger the dollar, the greater the sterling cost of that obligation and the worse the importer's results. Now let's think of the use of a call option on the dollar. This gives its owner the right but not the obligation to buy a specified quantity of a currency at a specific price and time. Hedging the importer's currency exposure with a call option on the dollar produces a result as shown in Figure 3.8. So far so good, but the price is relatively high. To many potential users the price is so high that options don't feature on their shopping list.

However, increased familiarity with options and other building blocks of financial engineering shows how 'value-for-money' solutions can be found. The exercise price of a call option is an important determinant of its price. The higher its exercise price the cheaper the call option will be. The option user seeks to protect himself from even the small adverse movement of the exchange rate from the forward rate prevailing when the option was bought. However, not every potential user will want so powerful, and therefore so expensive, protection. Many are well able to live with small movements in rates and want to guard against only the large adverse movements. To do this, they use an option with a higher exercise price than the forward.

To reduce the up-front cash cost of protection even further, consider buying a call option and selling a put option with exercise prices chosen so that the two options have equal value. We now have an instrument with several proprietary names – the range forward, the tunnel, the zero-cost option, the collar, the floor–ceiling swap, the cylinder, etc. This instrument, which often involves no cash outlay, removes all the downside exposure beyond a predetermined point (determined by the exercise price of the call option) and pays for this removal all the upside exposure beyond a different point (determined by the exercise price of the put option). In the middle range the exposure remains.

But that may not suit the corporation perfectly. An alternative is to take the same call option once again and consider selling a put with the same exercise price and on the same amount (say $1 million) as the call. The call is out of the money and the put is in the money. Thus, mark for mark or dollar for dollar the put is more valuable than the call. To produce equal value, the put must be written on a smaller amount than the call and so it will have a smaller adverse impact on the corporation should it be exercised against it. This put–call combination, known as a participation or a profit-share option, involves no cash outlay yet gives protection against the downside while leaving a share (with no upper limits) in the upside.

The list is endless. If needs and opportunities can be properly specific, then it is usually possible to put together a combination of financial building blocks which will satisfy those needs and take advantage of those opportunities.

The 'shapes' and 'colours' of financial building blocks

We have so far looked at the use of the building blocks in the context of exchange rates. To continue with our analogy, we have looked at the one colour of blocks which are appropriate to the currency markets. However, just as we can find currency forwards, futures, swaps and options, so we can also find interest rate forwards (FRAs), futures, swaps and options. If we use interest rates on the horizontal axis in place of exchange rates, the payoffs of these interest rate instruments look similar to those of the corresponding currency instruments. Thus we can think of the building blocks as having different colours (indicating the market to which they are appropriate) but similar shapes (indicating their similar payoffs). Nowadays the range of interest rate shapes is as wide as the range of currency shapes. Volatility in other markets has led to the production of blocks in other colours, such as the commodity-indexed swap or a future linked to an index of stock prices such as the Standard & Poors 500 Index, an index showing the movement of the shares of 500 US-quoted companies.

So far we have considered using the building blocks for simple exposure management but, as financial institutions have gained experience in handling them, so an increasing range of uses has emerged. We now turn to some of these uses, illustrating each with examples.

These uses come under the rubric of matching borrowing costs to ability to pay. Many institutions – for example, sellers of consumer durables or real estate developers – find that, because of their customers' sensitivity to interest rates, their sales revenues are reduced when interest rates rise. Hence, if they finance their operations by means of an ordinary floating rate loan they are doubly exposed, with their debt-servicing cost rising just as the income available for debt servicing falls. At first this may seem an unfortunate, but insoluble, problem. However, many banks now offer reverse floating loans whose charges are inversely related to market interest rates. A loan agreement under which, for example, a borrower pays 18 per cent minus LIBOR rather than LIBOR provides the required matching of costs and ability to pay and so removes interest rate exposure. This is illustrated in Figure 3.7.

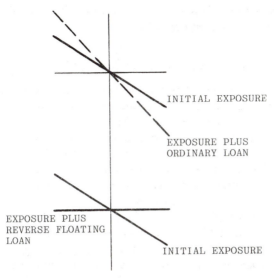

Figure 3.7 Matching of borrowing costs to ability to pay

Innovative as a reverse floating loan may seem, it is no more than an ordinary floating loan coupled with a fixed-floating inter- est rate swap whose notional principal is twice that of the loan amount.

To give another example, some time ago the price of oil fell below ten dollars per barrel, thus forcing a well-known oil company to increase its borrowings. However, because the reduced oil price lowered the company's credit rating it found itself being asked higher interest charges just at the time it needed the money! This problem was solved by issuing a bond which paid the larger of either 11 per cent per annum (where 11 per cent was considerably below the rate which the company would normally pay) *or* the value of one half of one barrel of oil per $100 borrowed. Under this arrangement, by which the company sold the bond buyer's call options on oil and took their value in the form of a 'subsidised' interest rate, the company matched its costs to its ability to pay. While the oil price remains below $22 per barrel and the company is relatively badly off, it continues to pay an exceptionally low rate of interest. Should the oil price rise above $22, the company will pay higher interest rates, but the company will also be cash rich and well able to pay these rates.

Wouldn't it be helpful to a gold mining firm, which is exposed to fluctuations both in gold prices and also in interest rates, to be able to finance its operation in gold; that is, to make interest payments in the form of gold and thus protect itself from fluctuations both in interest rates and in gold? What a novel approach, yet banks have already made loans with both principal and interest payments fully dominated in gold.

In the exchange rate context a further example of this kind of management is a Currency Conversion Facility (CCF), sometimes called – a little misleadingly – a Dual Currency Loan. Under this facility a borrower takes out a loan and simultaneously gives the arranger the right, at a predetermined future date, to convert the loan into a specified alternative currency at a predetermined exchange rate. The value of this currency option is passed on to the borrower in the form of a 'below-market' interest rate. Thus the *possibility* of higher payments in the future, should the option be exercised, is accepted in order to gain the *certainty* of lower interest charges today. This arrangement is attractive to borrowers who have liabilities in one currency (the dollar, say) and assets in another (the DM, say). By borrowing dollars, convertible to DM, the borrower can raise funds at a lower cost today. If the dollar falls against the DM, the option will be exercised and some of the benefit from the weaker dollar will be lost because the cost of the loan will then be higher than it would have been otherwise. However, the loss would only apply to the loan with the inbuilt option and the costs of its other outstanding dollar loans would be lower, so the borrower would still be better off. To show the situation another way, think of a borrower's circumstances measured on a scale of 0 to 10. Today's environment has pushed some heavily indebted borrowers down to 3. As the dollar falls they will move up again, say to 8. By entering into a CCF today's circumstances can be raised to 4, at the cost of rising to 7 rather than 8 should the dollar fall. Many borrowers would find a certain 4 today and a possible 7 in the future preferable to a certain 3 and a possible 8. Of course, each of these uses can be reversed to make similar changes to rates earned by depositors, rather than to rates paid by borrowers.

An environment in which executive freedom is maintained suggests that interest rates may fall and tempt firms to switch from medium-term to short-term funding so that they can enjoy lower interest costs once rates fall. The trouble is, should rates rise unexpectedly, the firm's costs will turn out to be unnecessarily high. Banks can put together a short-term funding programme with an interest rate cap (i.e. a series of call options on interest payments) which will allow the firm to benefit from reduced funding costs should interest rates fall, while retaining an upper limit should the environment change and rates rise. If rates fall the company pays lower interest charges and the options expire worthless, while if rates rise the options expire in the money and so compensate the firm for movements above the level set in the cap.

Commodity indexation can provide a useful form of hedging. As we pointed out at the start of this chapter, commodity prices have fluctuated as widely as currencies and interest rates. Wouldn't it be ideal for an oil user such as an airline to be able to protect itself from fluctuations in oil prices without having to change its long-standing arrangements with its suppliers? This can be done by buying oil forward, by buying a call option indexed on oil, or by entering into an oil-indexed swap. The Chase Manhattan Bank has already arranged several deals of this kind and has become the market leader in this rapidly growing area. To give an example, consider an oil producer wanting to lock in the price of a volume of its crude oil for a period of say two to three years.

A bank such as Chase can arrange a purely financial transaction – or swap – which will offset the effect of a decline in the price of crude oil. The swap will in no way affect normal sales and delivery procedures. The net impact of the hedge will be that the company will receive crude oil revenues which are effectively fixed, whether market prices rise or fall. Similarly, an oil consumer such as an airline, chemical or utilities company can arrange a swap for a portion of its consumption that will generate a payment to compensate for a rise in oil prices. Again, the hedge will offset the effect of any oil price change. Thus, the oil-indexed swap can be seen as having the familiar swap 'shape', but a new 'colour' differentiates it from a currency swap or an interest rate swap.

Financial engineering is a rapidly growing area of activity. This reflects the demand for protection in today's volatile world and the ability of the financial system to provide instruments which give such protection. As we suggested at the start of this chapter, increased familiarity with the instruments reveals a growing range of possible uses for them. It is a rare problem which cannot be solved, or at least greatly reduced, by applying the building block approach of financial engineering. The same little blocks, used in different ways, explain a great deal of the changes which we have discussed so far in this chapter.

We turn now to one of the most important influences which followed from successive Thatcher administrations' drive towards freer markets and less regulation. This was the breaking down of barriers preventing institutions from entering into various activities, known as 'Big Bang'. Big Bang and its effects are discussed at greater length in subsequent chapters so here we will make only a few comments. Many banks decided to enter into securities trading and, during the preparations for Big Bang, set up (often through acquisition) their trading capacity. Most were ready to admit that in many areas, particularly gilt trading, there was significant over-capacity but each expected the process of reduction to be spread over a long period and each hoped to be among the survivors. In the event, the swing in the government's finances into budget surplus and the stock market crash of 1987 led to a sharp fall in trading volumes and the over-capacity problem became acute. Many market participants decided to reduce or eliminate some of their trading activities and there were substantial redundancies. Further cutbacks in staffing levels in the future are still expected.

A POSTSCRIPT ON THE ROLE OF THE CITY OF LONDON IN THE UK ECONOMY

We look now at the impact of the City on the rest of the economy. Clearly, the City's financial institutions are a major source of employment for people living in and around London. The 'City' is also an important source of foreign exchange earnings. However, several criticisms have been made of the City. One is that salaries paid are disproportionately high and that knock-on effects raise costs for other domestic employers. A counterargument is that the City is exposed to international competition, that it deals successfully with such competition and that it must pay salaries which are comparable to those which could be earned in other financial centres.

Another criticism is that the City is excessively outward-looking in the sense that it tends to divert funds from the domestic economy towards overseas economies. A counterargument is that the return on capital has until recently been relatively low in the UK. If domestic investors had found funds difficult to obtain, the return on capital would have tended to be high. Also, if the return on capital is lower in the UK than elsewhere it makes good sense to place savings abroad and earn a higher return than could be earned at home. Put in more technical language, the growth of gross national product would be faster than the growth of domestic product.

A further criticism is that the City is over-cautious and that it does not make a proper contribution to domestic economic growth. In this context, the City is said to have a short time horizon and to want overly quick returns from its investments. It is said to be reluctant to lend to new entrepreneurs with good but untested new ideas. Banks are accused of taking little long-term interest in the companies, compared, for example, with German banks which tend to be major shareholders in German companies. These types of criticisms are difficult to assess but are often countered by a 'proof of the pudding is in the eating' type of argument. Since 1979 there have been no exchange controls in the UK and British individuals and companies have been free to deal with financial institutions elsewhere if they wished. Foreign banks are free to set up in the City and to compete with British institutions. If they felt that the criticisms of these institutions were justified and if they felt that by offering a different approach to customers they could make profits, they would presumably do just that. Furthermore, British City institutions earn large incomes from overseas customers des- pite competition from other institutions for the same business.

CONCLUSION

In recent years, towards the end of the decade of the eighties, the world's financial institutions have changed enormously, partly on their own initiative and partly in response to major changes in their operating environment. The institutions of the City of London have proved to be no exception. At the time of writing the financial world faces a high challenge in the form of the opening up of Eastern Europe and its consequent need for investment. Within the European Community, the plans for 1992 are leading to increasing cross-border competition as witnessed by the rivalry between the London International Financial Futures Exchange (LIFFE) and its French equivalent, the MATIF, and now the German Futures Market, Deutsche TerminBorese (DTB). In response to such other European competitive pressures, LIFFE and the London Traded Options Market have merged during 1990. As might be expected these changes have led to complaints of unfair practices and protectionism which are sometimes lumped under the general complaint of a lack of 'a level playing field'. Despite many justified fears, there seems to be a widespread feeling that these developments offer more in the way of opportunity than in the way of difficulty. In particular, there remains a strong feeling that, by continuing its tradition of fair dealing combined with innovation and imagination, the City of London will long remain a key player in the world financial arena in the 1990s, albeit a rather different political and economic environment than that prevailing in the eighties.

NOTES

1 We are dealing here with issues of cash flow. Some countries may require parties to show the contracts on their balance sheets while accounting laws may require them to estimate their eventual value and to show any changes in their profit and loss accounts.
2 We shall assume that this rate is the market rate as quoted in newspapers and on Reuters screens, etc. Different rates will be quoted to different customers in order to take account of differing credit risks, but we shall not bother with this issue here. In other words we shall consider deals made between institutions with the best possible credit ratings.
3 Those familiar with futures will know that the currency future, unlike the currency forward, does not require the exchange of the underlying currency amounts, its value being settled in cash.
4 We are here taking into account interest payments, both when they accrue to the margin account and also when they are foregone on alternative instruments as the margin account requires 'topping up'.
5 In practice, the two flows are netted out and a single difference cheque is exchanged.
6 That is, their net terminal value will be equal to zero. Because the cash flows occur at different times, their absolute sum will be zero only in the most unusual circumstances.

REFERENCES

Cooper, I. (1986) 'Innovations: New market instruments', *Oxford Review of Economic Policy*, vol. 2, no. 4.
Cooper, I., Bain, A., Donaldson, J. and Price, L. (1987) *New Financial Instruments*, London: Chartered Institute of Bankers.

Robinson, J.N. (1987) 'The growth of financial engineering', *The Business Economist*, vol. 19, no. 1.

Smithson, C.W. (1987) 'A Lego approach to financial engineering', *Midland Corporate Finance Journal*, no. 4.

4

THE PRIVATE CLIENT STOCKBROKER

Helpful agent or relic of the past?

Michael Lenhoff

This chapter is concerned with the stockbroker who acts on behalf of the private investor. It reviews the institutional aspects relevant to the private client stockbroker, including in this the legal framework to which the stockbroker must adhere. The scope and nature of the agency function which the private client stockbroker undertakes and executes on behalf of his client is then examined. This area will occupy the bulk of our attention because it provides the *raison d'être* for investment management. It also happens that what we shall say applies with equal force to private client business around the world. In contrast, our discussion of the institutional aspects is rather specific to the financial services industry in the United Kingdom.

In dealing with the institutional aspects, we shall first clarify the role of the stockbroker and then distinguish between agency business and principals business. In discussing the new financial regulations, the concern is less with the legal framework and more with the costs imposed in 'complying' with the Financial Services Act. The focus then shifts to the role of investment management, and to an assessment of what continues to be the still hotly debated controversy over active versus passive portfolio management styles. The case for and against the efficient markets hypothesis is examined and we take a fresh view of the role of active portfolio management. We then extend the case for active management by looking at a relatively new aspect, namely international asset allocation.

STOCKBROKERS: ARE THEY ALL ALIKE?

The term 'stockbroker' applies only to those individuals or corporate entities who are members of the London Stock Exchange, which is a recognised investment exchange under the Financial Services Act 1986. Generally, however, the term 'stockbroking' is something of an anachronism and has come to be rather loosely applied to a number of functions which fall within two broad categories of business. These categories are agency related businesses and market making or principals type businesses. The distinction between the two does not lie mainly in the nature of the risk inherent in their respective businesses, since the operating environment and the customer base is usually common to both. The relevant distinction relates rather more to their position taking. The agent transacts business on behalf of others and collects fees for doing so. The role is purely that of an intermediary between buyer and seller acting on behalf of one or the other or both, a broker in the strictest sense of the word. The agent takes no position in the market and performs his function without incurring any conflict of interest. The stockbroker with a market capacity invariably does the same sort of 'job' as the agent, with the exception that he goes a stage further by risking capital as a principal, as well as an intermediary, and becomes a position taker in the market, going either 'long' of a security or 'short' of it.

An agency function subdivides into two main areas: a distribution arm which combines equity research and sales, and an investment management arm. The latter can include anything from discretionary portfolio management to the 'passive' style most typified by the advent of index funds.

Another relevant distinction relates to the client base. Broadly, this base divides neatly into two groups: institutional and private clients. The former group comprises pension funds, insurance funds and so on; the latter comprises individuals. Agency business as it relates to the client base usually consists of an equity distribution service aimed more or less exclusively at institutions. An investment management service is usually directed at both types of clients, although the tendency has been to specialise either in the private client area or in the institutional area. Larger integrated investment houses tend to provide investment management services in both areas.

The private client stockbroker, with whom we shall be concerned, provides a number of investment management services. We shall concentrate on the discretionary side of these activities because it is this aspect which tends to dominate private client business. It also represents the main area on which the great debate between active and passive management has focused. Figure 4.1 displays the variety of ways in which a stockbroking function can be provided.

THE REGULATORY FRAMEWORK

This section describes the background to investor protection and the new regulatory framework for UK financial markets. It focuses on the cost of 'complying' with the new rules and regulations. Any transgression constitutes a criminal offence and is punishable by a prison sentence of anything up to seven years. So, the price of fraudulent behaviour is high. On the other hand, the benefit which investor protection confers has yet to be fully borne by the consumer. In time it shall be!

The Financial Services Act 1986 and the new regulatory environment which it spawned all stem from work commissioned by the Conservative government in 1981. Professor L. Gower, an authority on company and commercial law, was asked to review the relevant legal framework of the time and propose recommendations for investor protection. The first part of the Gower Report, which was submitted in 1983 and published in 1984 (Cmnd 9125),

Activity \\ Client	Agency		Market Making
	Investment Management	Distribution	
Private	Discretionary Advisory Dealing	Advisory Dealing	
Institutional	Discretionary	Advisory Dealing	Research Specialist

Figure 4.1 Types of stockbroking activity

98

set out the original proposals for a regulatory framework. These proposals were based on the view that, whatever structure evolved, it was important to ensure that it would not be rigid, since such a structure could easily discourage existing business from operating in the United Kingdom and/or drive prospective business away.

The Financial Services Act (FSA) requires the Secretary of State to be the ultimate authority responsible for the provision and supervision of the regulatory framework. In practice, this overall function is delegated to the Securities and Investment Board (SIB) which in turn devolves supervisory responsibilities to a number of 'self-regulatory organisations' (SROs). It is through these bodies, acting as agents for the SIB, that investment business receives its authorisation. SROs lay down the rules which are relevant to the sector of the industry and these provide the basis for judging who is fit and proper to do business.

Figure 4.2 sets out the present structure of the regulatory framework for UK financial markets. At present, there are five separate SROs, each of which has its own set of rules on the conduct of business, including the business of unsolicited calls, advertising and investment recommendations and the segregation of clients' money. It is the responsibility of each SRO to ensure 'compliance' by its membership with the rules and also to ensure that this is done to the satisfaction of the SIB. Any breach of any rule by any member of any SRO which leads to financial losses being sustained by investors is a criminal offence and private investors are entitled to sue for damage. The process of regulation of UK financial markets is evolving. The general framework may move towards a more conventional banking regulation approach with the appointment of David Walker, formerly a director of the Bank of England, as head of the SIB.

Compliance costs and investors' benefits

Professor Gower was of the opinion that investor protection was in the national interest; that it was to the benefit of both consumers and suppliers of financial services to have a properly regulated market which did not hamper or impede in any way, shape or form the efficient delivery or use of a service. His view was thus that, while the market should pay for the day-to-day regulation, the ultimate regulatory authority should be paid for from the public purse.

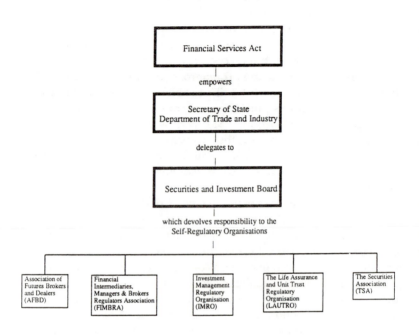

Figure 4.2 Statutory framework for investor protection

Note: The Financial Services Act also specifies various exemptions for institutions which may conduct investment businesses outside this basis framework. These fall within the general categories of Recognised Investment Exchanges, Recognised Professional Bodies and Recognised Clearing Houses. Again, each of these is bound by separate rules and is ultimately responsible to the SIB.

The first point which ought to be made is that the cost of putting into place a structure for compliance has not been exorbitant. Second, in various instances it has led to enhancements and gains in 'production' efficiency, allowing more business to be undertaken without incurring more cost; but the collective regulatory bodies have yet to be fully self-financing. Eventually, the membership body of the SROs will fully finance the cost of the UK regulatory framework and investors in turn will fully finance this. But, of course, this cost is not widely known about and member firms which have undertaken to comply with the Financial Services Act have only a vague notion at best of the extent of the costs which they themselves have incurred to date.

The usual distinction between fixed and variable cost is not an easy one to apply to the compliance costs imposed on the individual firm. Much of the initial cost tends to be associated with the design and implementation of systems to ensure compliance in the widest possible sense and, ultimately, much of this cost is in the labour allocated to the function itself.

Table 4.1 sets out in a very rough and ready way the expenditure associated with the overall cost of compliance with the FSA. The figures are illustrative and relate to the burden imposed among the larger private client businesses. The cost of compliance as a proportion of the overall expenditure is relatively small but probably representative. While the data tend to be unavailable, we reckon that for small (but similar kinds of) businesses the maintenance costs are proportionately higher.

As Table 4.1 shows, there are two basic components to the cost of compliance: the initial and the maintenance items of expenditure. The initial cost falls largely on labour and on the software required to satisfy compliance with the Securities and Futures

Table 4.1 Costs of complying with Financial Services Act

Initial expenditure (£000s)		Maintenance expenditure (£000s)	
		(1989 prices)	
Labour	300	Compliance unit	208
Software	100	Accounts & settlements	210
Hardware	15	Capital requirements	60
	415	Subs/Memberships	32
			510
		As % of total cost	3.2

101

Authority (SFA), the main SRO to which members of the Stock Exchange and/or agency or principal businesses belong.

The second general category of expenditure involves the cost of maintaining the surveillance and compliance structure. Maintenance costs also reflect the varying degree to which a business engages in a wide spread of agency-related activities (for example, commission business, acting as private client stockbroker, unit trust manager, financial services and so on). To that extent, they are variable costs dependent on the type of function performed as well as size and exhibit the economies (and diseconomies) associated with different levels of output.

As Table 4.1 shows, the cost of maintaining the compliance structure represents a relatively small proportion of the overall operating benefits to consumers, who should bear some, if not all, of this cost. To the extent that producers share some of these benefits, insofar as the gains in efficiency fall through to the bottom line sooner or later, there is a case for making producers bear some portion of the cost. However, the agent is now more vulnerable than ever to prosecution if the rules and regulations are transgressed. Not only is the agent more easily and severely punishable than before, clients are more able to gain compensation. It is the investor who is the ultimate beneficiary of protection and, as such, it is he who should bear the greater part of the cost of compliance.

In fact, investors have been bearing this cost in various ways. Some firms have simply instituted a levy in the form of a bargain charge to help cover cost. Others have incorporated the additional costs as part of their fee structure, either in terms of commissions or management charges. Some have employed a combination of all three. Unit revenues can be determined once costs, bargain levels or volumes have been projected. The fee structure is then revised in the light of the desired unit revenue, the intention being to recover the entire cost of compliance from the investor.

ACTIVE VERSUS PASSIVE MANAGEMENT: HOW RELEVANT IS THE EFFICIENT MARKETS HYPOTHESIS?

The question of whether investors should bear any cost at all hinges ultimately on how well the professional investor serves his client. In the end, the issue is likely to be judged by the performance of an investor's portfolio relative to how well he might have

102

done on his own or relative to a particular benchmark, such as a market index. A large and well-established body of literature relating to the 'efficiency' of the stock market indicates that the professional adds relatively little in the management of portfolios to justify his charges. This is much to the consternation of the professional investor who generally believes he can outperform the market.

Advocates of efficient markets theory insist that outperformance (in the sense of more return for less risk) is purely a random phenomenon. Those who achieve it are lucky. Skill is irrelevant because stock prices move on 'news'; the arrival of news is random and cannot be accurately and consistently predicted with respect to 'timing' or 'fundamental content'. Such provocative statements win few friends among practitioners, yet the evidence suggests that, on balance, professionally managed portfolios cannot outperform randomly selected portfolios of equities with equivalent risk characteristics. The conclusion may be hard to swallow; but it appears to hold particularly well. The performance figures (total returns with income reinvested) in Table 4.2 relate to the class of professional market. This class of investor attempts to differentiate his product either through segmentation of the market or through a thematic approach to stock selection. This investor purports to add value for the fees charged for the possession of superior skills at detecting fundamental value or specialist skills at timing purchases and sales. In the UK, the managers of unit trusts offer their expertise and promote their vehicles with as high a profile as their performance figures permit. If there is any 'test bed' for the efficient markets theory, it is among these professionals who claim they can and do outperform the market.

Table 4.2 The relative performance of UK equity unit trusts: proportion (%) which underperform in any given year

Basis	1979	1980	1981	1982	1983	1984	1985	1986	1987	1988	1989
1. Offer to bid	91	89	79	85	69	92	76	71	43	96	99
2. Offer to offer	72	72	38	66	36	68	41	33	16	72	93

Source: Micropal (total returns with income re-investment)

Table 4.2 sets out the recent record for the 'on shore' unit trust industry in the UK. It shows the proportion of the industry in each of the ten years to 1989 which has underperformed the FT-A All Share Index. While there is a case for arguing that a stringent test of how well these funds perform should make no allowance for the unfavourable impact of the 'offer to bid' spread on portfolio returns (if the managers really do add value), this cost should be relatively unimportant in a comparison. To be generous, we have presented the results on both an offer to bid and offer to offer basis, but the table shows the record is surprisingly poor either way.

The record provides an unpalatable conclusion for the one class of investor who stakes a reputation on the claim that he can 'outperform'. It would seem that he cannot. Indeed, what better evidence is there in support of efficient markets theory? The case is spawned for the passive practice of investment management and for the growth of index funds. A damning indictment if ever there was one. We shall return to this point later. First, we look at the formidable hypothesis itself.

The essential feature of the efficient markets hypothesis (EMH) is the 'fair game' interpretation provided in an early formalisation of the theory (Fama 1970). In this, the expected return is commensurate with the degree of risk taking implicit in the stock market. Or, to put it the other way round, to achieve higher returns it is necessary to increase exposure to market risk. The EMH assumes implicitly a model which generates the underlying structure of risk and return inherent in the market; that this model is known to all investors; that each understands what constitutes the relevant information set appropriate to the model; and that, as a result of fully processing this 'relevant information set', equity prices (and hence implied or expected returns) reflect 'fair value for risk'. To put it otherwise, there are no bargains or overvalued situations on which investors can profitably and consistently, over time, take long or short positions.

Two implications follow from the 'fair game' proposition. First, if prices really reflect the information relevant to the underlying model of asset prices, then 'news' is the only 'cause' for a change in prices. Since there is no reason to expect the arrival of new and relevant information to be anything other than 'random' in nature, the period to period change in a stock price should follow a 'random walk'. It thus follows, from this so called 'weak form' of the efficient markets hypothesis, that trading strategies based on past behaviour of stock prices, such as technical analysis, will not yield consistent excess returns for risk. If the market is efficient and investors outperform, it is because they are taking excessive risks. So much for the first implication.

The second implication follows from the assumption that the underlying model of risk and return is known and that relevant information is fully utilised in generating the expected returns implied by the model. The implication is that there are no market anomalies, no 'unfair' values which can be exploited, and that there is no viable trading system based on fundamentals which exists and which generates excess portfolio returns for risk. As we shall soon see, this theoretically appealing proposition is at variance with some well-known empirical regularities.

First, proponents of the EMH believe it carries a clear lesson: be suspicious of stockbrokers who say they can make money by exploiting charts, fundamentals or market anomalies. Second, while the case for indexing portfolios to a benchmark index (for example, FT-A All Share Index in the UK) does not stand or fall by the EMH, market efficiency does provide compelling grounds in favour of indexing. Third, and perhaps most important of all, if anomalies exist, it is one thing to recognise them and quite another to profit by them. Failure to do so may just as well be construed as further evidence in favour of the EMH.

Cracks in the EMH

The difficulty with all this theory is that, if markets are really efficient or, alternatively, if the random walk is an appropriate description for the behaviour of stock prices, why have so many of the largest price movements in recent years occurred on days when major items of news (remember, news moves markets) were absent? The lack of association on numerous occasions between quite volatile and often erratic movements in stock prices on the one hand, and relatively insignificant fundamental news or 'flash points' on the other, is the basis of the more recent wave of academic research now challenging the tradition of market efficiency. The challenge has focused on the informational premise of the EMH as this is the bedrock of the theory. It begs the question: how do investors know what constitutes relevant information in the first place unless they know the underlying model of stock market behaviour? Asset prices fluctuate far too widely to be justified on the basis of fundamentals alone. Some authors, for example Levy (1983), argue that the Capital Asset Pricing Model (CAPM) is not even a testable model, but a tautology which is incapable of empirical rejection.

A recent and thorough investigation to test for the impact of fundamental and non-fundamental type news on the US stock market had limited success in explaining the variation in stock prices (Cutler *et al.* 1989). The authors began their investigation by seeking to determine how much of the variation in stock prices could be explained by unexpected macro-economic news. They used monthly data for the period 1926 to 1985 and yearly data going back as far as 1871. Their conclusion was that not much more than 50 per cent of the movement in stock prices could be explained by macro-economic news as they had defined it.

Concerned that the remaining and unexplained 50 per cent of the variation in returns may be due to factors other than economic variables, the investigators turned their attention to the potential impact political or non-fundamental developments might have on asset values. Here, they took two approaches. The first was to consider the reaction of the stock market to major non-economic events, by considering only those events which were carried as the lead story in the press and reported in the business section as having affected the market. This was done for the post-1940 period and included many momentous political and economic events.

While these events produced some market reaction, the surprising finding was how small or how limited the reaction was to such significant political and/or non-economic news. An alternative route looked at the fifty largest single-day changes in US stock market history since the Second World War to see what link there was, if any, to the 'news' of the day, but this approach produced little as well. For most (but obviously not all) of the largest returns, the authors concluded that the information cited by the news media as the 'cause' of the market move appeared not to be significant or fundamentally shocking.

This illuminating study is only one of a growing number of investigations into the informational premise of stock market efficiency. The conclusion seems to be that stock prices fluctuate too widely to be justified by fundamentals alone. Oddly, this crack in the efficiency of the stock market offers as much of a case in support of indexing portfolios as does the EMH itself. Both the weak and semi-strong forms of market efficiency imply that no one investor has an edge over any other investor in the use of public information. Thus, when an investor occasionally outperforms, it must be no more due to skill than to the 'laws of chance'. On the other hand, if investors cannot specify the appropriate model of asset prices, how can they judge what constitutes the relevant information set?

The shoe now seems to be on the other foot. Whereas the widespread acceptance of the EMH placed the burden on the active fund manager to make his case, the onus would now seem to fall on the efficient marketeer to produce the underlying model and the relevant information set. No more can the efficient marketeer pour scorn on the prospect that there are genuine market anomalies which offer more return for risk. The possibility that anomalies exist has to be admitted and, moreover, the scope that they provide for genuine outperformance is best taken more seriously than before. This is not to say that the EMH is no longer relevant. It is relevant. But it remains at best a very rough and ready approximation for the behaviour of a market which has yet to be fully understood.

MARKET ANOMALIES

Until the middle of the 1970s there were relatively few studies which did not conform with the overall thrust of the efficient market hypothesis. The bulk of the empirical research did tend to support it even though a few genuine puzzles had been discovered. Those puzzles, such as low price to earnings ratio stocks outper-forming high ratio stocks, and the 'p/e effect' (Basu 1977), were followed by a host of other apparent market anomalies as the EMH came under attack in the latter half of the 1970s.

These major anomalies centred on studies concerning the 'January effect', the 'size effect' and the 'growth effect'. The first was an almost accidental discovery whereby Rozeff and Kinney (1976) found that there was a seven times higher monthly return for January compared to other months on New York Stock Exchange prices, dating back to the early 1900s. Subsequent studies, such as Dimson and Marsh (1988), pointed out that lower January returns would have been experienced if a different kind of stock price index been used. Such a critique led to consideration of other contributing factors such as size. Banz (1981) and Reinganum (1981) discovered that small firms earned higher than

107

expected returns after adjusting for risk. Furthermore, Keim (1985) later found these excess returns were 'temporarily concentrated', half of them being concentrated in the first five days of trading. Moreover, there was a correlation of high January excess returns in stock that had exhibited negative returns over the previous year. Subsequent work by Reinganum (1983) and Roll (1983) failed to throw light on the issues. Gultekin and Gultekin (1983) provided a form of sensitivity analysis by assessing whether the 'January effect' was uniquely institutional to the UK market. Their study found a 'January effect' of sorts in fifteen of the sixteen other markets they studied. Subsequent work shifted emphasis to other effects such as 'weekends', 'holidays' and 'turn of month'.

The final anomalous effect, 'growth', came to light through the work of Solt and Statmen (1989) which pointed out that stocks of growth companies provide lower returns than stocks of companies lacking growth opportunities. Growth companies were defined in the terms of the Tobin 'q' ratio.[1] In the course of their investigation several things came to light. Firstly, the 'q' ratio was positively correlated with market capitalisation and p/e ratios. This result appears to be at odds with the evidence that many small companies on low multiples (p/e ratios) turn out to be the growth companies which become big companies on high multiples, and with the size effect itself. Secondly, portfolios that contained stocks of companies with the highest 'q' ratios yielded negative excess returns, whereas portfolios with the lowest 'q' ratios had positive excess returns. In other words, stocks of companies with no growth prospects, but which also happened to be small companies and on low multiples, outperformed the stocks of companies that were reckoned to have growth prospects but were large and stood on high price to earnings multiples ('q' ratios).

What is the significance of this extensive list of stock market anomalies? Clearly, if profitably exploited, the anomalies weaken significantly the ground on which the EMH has rested as a formidable proposition for so long. Research of this kind is as vulnerable to criticism as the EMH and most of the anomalies have something in common. Value seems to be their common denominator and possibly the anomalous returns are the reward for the very special but relatively rare set of skills possessed by those few professionals who are adept at using them. Indeed, this seems to be the very ground which staunch advocates are prepared to concede (Samuelson 1989).

Thus there is scope for the discretionary account manager to add value in portfolio management. Anomalies seem to exist, but the attempt to differentiate the product through specialisation has not always helped the active fund manager to make his case.

ASSET ALLOCATION: A FURTHER STEP IN PORTFOLIO MANAGEMENT

Investment is not a science. No matter how much rigour is brought to bear on the subject, no matter how much quantitative analysis is done, in the end one has to judge the future largely on the basis of anecdotal and very inconclusive evidence relating to the present. The past is helpful in setting out the historical record. But the lessons it provides are only one of several essential ingredients for profitable decision making; experience and judgement, for which there is no substitute, are others. Typically, among private client stockbrokers, these essentials are brought to bear at investment policy meetings which are often the forum for the firm's investment policy. It is through this committee that a firm's investment philosophy derives substance. The members are practitioners and investment specialists. In this section we look at the issues that are likely to be formed on behalf of the private client.

An investment policy committee (IPC) usually serves a variety of needs. The more formal product of an IPC's deliberations is often a benchmark asset allocation which can then be tailored to suit individual clients with different income needs, tax positions and so on. The decisions taken by an investment policy committee might therefore reflect its perception of the general background relevant to asset markets. The resulting 'model portfolio' or 'model asset allocation' would then be incorporated, one way or another, across the range of discretionary monies under management.

The Model Portfolio

Should an IPC be proposing a model portfolio in the first place? Or should it simply be suggestive of direction? A model portfolio is a natural extension of strategic thinking. Without it, there is no yardstick for gauging the degree to which the IPC is being aggressive, taking too much risk for the return it is getting, or getting too little return for the risk it is taking.

However, the model portfolio should not prevent an account

109

manager from 'swimming with the tide'. At any moment in time, an account manager's position is very unlikely to resemble a model portfolio. But when the account manager chooses to unwind his tactical position, here is a benchmark or reference asset allocation to which he can refer. A more aggressive stance implies a higher risk level with correspondingly higher expected returns.

Table 4.3 sets out a model portfolio with norms and ranges for a sterling-based private client. It is intended to be a balanced portfolio with the emphasis on long-term growth and has, therefore, a large normal weighting for equities. The model portfolio is constructed in a way that incorporates the various points raised throughout this paper. The norm for the balanced positions is 15:85: 15 per cent for fixed interest, 85 per cent for equities. This is based on our own experimentation with a mean–variance optimisation model. The point to emphasise is that the 15:85 split represents a norm which may be viewed as the degree of balance appropriate to private clients who are moderately risk-averse and choose long-term capital growth from equities with an element of capital preservation.

As it stands, roughly half the 'normal' allocation to equities is to the overseas markets. On the face of it, this seems aggressive but the chronic weakness of sterling has justified this; we do not think sterling's position as a weak currency has changed or will change,

Table 4.3 Recommended model portfolio for private clients (%)

Cash & bonds	Norm	Range	Equities	Norm	Range	Commodities	Norm	Range
Dollars	0	0–10	US	10	5–20	Gold	0	0–10
Yen	0	0–10	Japan & other Pacific Basin	15	5–20	Other	0	0–10
Sterling	15	10–40				All	0	0–10
European	0	0–10						
All	15	10–40	UK	40	35–65			
			W. Europe	15	5–20			
			Emerging markets	5	0–10			
			All	85	60–90			

so the ranges and the allocation to the fixed interest markets enable an even more aggressive position to be taken.

It is important to set one thing straight at the outset. Managing the account of a private client and managing a high profile unit trust are two very different things. With the former, the emphasis is on long-term growth but not to the exclusion of capital preservation. The pressures are different with a high profile vehicle, such as a unit trust, where the accent is on relative outperformance not absolute performance. The distinction is important and has a bearing on the choice between balanced and all-equity portfolios for private clients and the underlying costs and benefits of international diversification.

Balanced or all-equity portfolios

There is a compelling case based on historic returns for an all-equity portfolio, provided the client is a long-term investor. Suffice it to say at this point that if one compares major indices of stock and bond markets, no matter where you look, the record seems to show that, over the very long run, the return on equity investment exceeds by a wide margin the return on bond investment. This has been well-documented and we shall not comment further on the record. The BZW annual Equity–Gilt Study is an excellent UK example, but we know of similar studies showing similar results for other markets (see for example Hamao 1989 and Wydler 1989).

The record also shows that risk or the standard deviation of the returns (a convention adopted for measuring risk) is greater for equity markets than for bond markets. This poses something of a paradox. If investors seek long-term growth and never anticipate a call for cash from their portfolios, what difference should it make if equities are riskier than bonds? The return is still unlikely to be higher and therefore the risk of holding an 'all-equity portfolio' would seem to vanish in the long run. On the face of it, an all-equity portfolio appears justified.

Many practitioners have found that long-term bonds are not just an unsatisfactory asset in anything other than a deflationary environment; they are, to quote the results of a recent study by Peter Bernstein (1989), which expresses a widely shared sentiment: '. . . an unsatisfactory asset with expected return below stocks and with risk-reducing features below cash. The investor who includes bonds in a portfolio should therefore have clear and

111

positive reasons for doing so; bonds have no place in a portfolio by default'.

While there are few practitioners who would not have sympathy with this position, bonds still have a role to play, even if this is small. Some of the early applied work in the area of Modern Portfolio Theory showed that, when it came to international diversification, 'optimal' asset allocations, comprising both the fixed interest and equity markets, generally tended to outperform 'optimal' asset allocations over equity markets alone. This work extends the Markowitz type mean–variance model which assumed that investors are risk-averse (that is, require higher expected returns as compensation for what are perceived to be higher risks) and concerned with two things: the return on investments and the associated risks. In these models, the sample mean of the distribution of returns is assumed to be a useful proxy for expected return and the variance (or standard deviation of the distribution of the returns) an adequate proxy for risk. Risk-averse investors then seek to minimise risk taking for any given expected return. An optimal asset allocation is one which fulfils the desired objective.

More recent studies have also shown that passively managed index funds which seek to replicate the major market indices, such as those produced by Morgan Stanley Capital International or others, can underperform optimal asset allocations over a combination of world stock and bond markets. One pioneering study in this area showed that an optimal asset allocation which included the bond markets made '. . . it feasible to double or even triple the returns of a passive index approach for the same level of risk' (Solnik and Noetzlin 1982).

How are these findings to be reconciled with the fact that over the long run equities outperform bonds? The point to remember is that the results refer to optimal allocations, that is, to allocations which minimise the risk per unit of expected return. An all-equity indexed fund based on market capitalisation incorporates a weighting scheme which only by accident and not design is optimal. Secondly, if bonds have an advantage over equities only some of the time, then, no matter how infrequently these occasions arise, a portfolio which can combine both bonds and equities, skilfully choosing between the two, should be able to outperform an all-bond portfolio and an all-equity portfolio over the long run. Although bonds contain a lower risk profit than equities, historically cash has tended to provide comparable returns to bonds but for lower risk. What this adds up to seems to be the following: IPC recommendations ought to be directed towards a balanced portfolio, but this should be geared towards growth.

The value of international diversification

Recent evidence collected from UK consulting actuaries shows that the benefit of investing in overseas equity markets is partially lost because of the generally poor performance record in foreign markets. Not only does the foreigner underperform the local market, he underperforms the local investor. This reinforces the view of many account managers that, because they know their market better than any other market, their expertise alone justifies overweighting the local market and retaining the lion's share of the portfolio in the reference or base currency.

Another consideration is a finding of the most recent studies designed to establish the gains from international diversification (see, for example, Jorion 1985; Eun and Resnick 1988). These studies have demonstrated that when sample mean returns are used as estimates of expected returns (as they usually are in such studies) the simulations lead to a sharp deterioration of performance measures outside the sample periods used to calculate mean returns. There is also a large element of instability in the 'optimum' weights assigned to specific markets.

These are significant results because they suggest that past studies may have overstated the realisable portion of the potential gains from international diversification. Moreover, the more recent studies have shown that fluctuating exchange rates mitigate these potential gains, not just by making investment in foreign securities more risky by virtue of the unpredictable or random nature of exchange rate gains or losses, but because of significant correlation between exchange rates and cross-correlations between exchange rates and asset markets. Recently, it has become fashionable to distinguish the exchange rate effect from the view one takes on a specific market. The exchange risk outlined above, however, suggests that separating the currency decisions from the asset allocation decision may not be as profitable an exercise as some practitioners believe.

Given the preceding discussion it is tempting to ask: why bother

113

to diversify at all? As noted so often in the past, diversification is a mixed blessing in that it prevents assets from moving down in value together and, equally, it prevents them from moving up together.

Diversification reduces the specific risk of being in any one market and can help to smooth portfolio returns so long as market returns are imperfectly correlated. By correlation we simply mean the extent to which the returns in any two markets are contemporaneously (but not causally) related to each other. If the returns in any two markets move together with precision, the returns are highly and positively correlated. As it happens, the correlation of returns across markets varies enormously. This is a statistical fact and it means that some markets offer superior diversification qualities. Ideally, one wants to favour markets which have high returns for risk as well.

To illustrate these points *as simply as possible,* consider Tables 4.4 and 4.5. The correlation coefficients in Table 4.4 have been calculated for the major equity markets using quarterly return data for the post-1982 period. The first set is based on local currency returns; the second set incorporates exchange rate changes. Note that there is very little difference between the two sets of correlation coefficients. The key point, as far as the sterling-based investor is concerned, is that the correlation of returns is greatest between the US and UK equity markets and lowest between the German and UK markets. Without taking the analysis any further, the table suggests that, for a sterling investor wishing to diversify abroad, the German equity market would seem to offer superior diversification benefits to the US market.

Table 4.4 Correlation matrix of returns in equity markets

	In local currency				In sterling			
	UK	US	Japan	Germany	UK	US	Japan	Germany
UK	1	0.75	0.54	0.45	1	0.77	0.68	0.51
US	0.75	1	0.51	0.60	0.77	1	0.58	0.56
Japan	0.54	0.51	1	0.44	0.68	0.58	1	0.36
Germany	0.45	0.60	0.44	1	0.51	0.56	0.36	1

Table 4.5 Average return and risk in equity markets (%)

	In local currency			In sterling		
	Average return	Risk	Return for risk ratio	Average return	Risk	Return for risk ratio
UK	4.3	11.0	0.39	4.3	11.0	0.39
US	3.6	9.5	0.38	3.6	12.7	0.28
Japan	6.4	9.3	0.69	9.3	11.4	0.82
Germany	3.4	11.7	0.29	4.5	13.2	0.34

The return–risk properties of the markets themselves are also relevant. These properties are set out in Table 4.5 for the post-1982 period. The table shows that the Japanese equity market was un-equivocally a superior market from the point of view of both risk and return. As the table shows, it had a higher average quarterly return than the other markets and a lower level of risk (as measured by the standard deviation of returns), whether denominated in terms of sterling or local currency. When denominated in terms of local currency, the German equity market had inferior return–risk properties to the US equity market which, when denominated in terms of sterling, had inferior return–risk properties to other equity markets.

The crucial point to emerge from Table 4.5 is that the UK and US equity markets have broadly similar return–risk features. Given that the correlation of returns between these two markets is high and that the risk–return characteristics are roughly identical, there is little to gain over the long run by diversifying in a large way in the US market.

Size is not a prima-facie case for deriving norms or benchmark weightings for an asset allocation scheme. If this was so, Japan and not the US would deserve the largest benchmark weighting for an internationally diversified portfolio. The UK weighting would deserve a relatively small magnitude, even if sterling is the reference currency.

ALLOCATION OF ASSETS: A STRATEGIC DECISION

Asset allocation is intended to answer the broad question: where should investors put their money? Equity markets? Bond markets? Overseas markets? It denotes that the emphasis is strategic and not tactical, a distinction made relevant by the time horizon over which the investment decision is being made.

A strategic decision focuses on longer-term issues which are concerned with broad matters about the relevant investment back-drop. A tactical decision involves precision and timing; neither of these should be critical to the success or relative merits of the strategic decision.

The strategic decision sets its sights on macro-economic developments. The objective is to assess the implications of an economic forecast (on which there is some broad agreement) for expected returns in asset markets. The relevant strategy should appear robust against the backdrop of 'adverse news' as and when it arrives, month-in and month-out, in quite random fashion.

Performance comes, but is by no means guaranteed, by taking risks. Thus, the choice is between choosing the level of risk and settling for performance or expected return which is judged to be commensurate with the chosen risk level. The usual demonstration of this is the efficient frontier which shows the 'optimal' portfolios corresponding to known or assumed values for risk and return. The frontier is a theoretical construct obtained by varying the risk level an investor is prepared to tolerate for any given combination of returns in asset markets. All portfolios along the frontier provide a superior return for risk, for any given level of risk, over all portfolios inside the frontier. Thus, all allocations inside the frontier are inferior or 'sub-optimal' to those along the frontier.

CONCLUSION

The fact that an IPC meets monthly is not sufficient justification for recommending changes to a model portfolio. Changes should be soundly based on fundamentals and market timing should be relatively important. An IPC is under no obligation to propose changes for the sake of changes. Indeed, the frequency, or relative infrequency, of changes is a good measure of the extent to which an IPC's policies are robust enough to withstand 'adverse news' or to benefit from 'good news'. Frequent switching is also bound to be costly and unrewarding.

A certain cynicism surrounds the business of private client stockbrokers. In part, this is due to their track record which leaves much to be desired and, in part, it is due to the persuasiveness of the case for efficient markets. However, this case is being challenged in an equally persuasive manner. Numerous anomalies have been shown to exist and these provide opportunities for outperformance. The merit of the portfolio manager lies in the ability to recognise the value (or lack of it) that such anomalies present and to seize these opportunities as a means of enhancing portfolio returns.

For the proponents of efficient markets, the relevant question seems to be not whether outperformance can be achieved occasionally, but whether it can be achieved consistently over time. The majority of professionals who aspire to do so fail miserably. However, some do achieve quite impressive results and the fees they charge are but a small reward to a scarce resource. Even if the majority of investment managers were to be made redundant by passive investment techniques, one would still expect a nucleus of 'activist' practitioners to survive. Their limited and valuable resource would enhance the portfolio returns which over the long run tend to be consistent with the structure of return and risk in financial markets.

Is the private client stockbroker a helpful agent or a relic of the past? We think he is a helpful agent. Questions relating to the mix of assets in a long-term portfolio are rightly his domain. In backing his judgement, perhaps the more relevant issue in the active versus passive debate is not consistent outperformance as such and whether it can even be achieved, but whether or not the practitioner can be successful on enough occasions over the long run to make all the difference between mediocrity and truly superior performance. When looked at from this point of view, there can be little doubt that the private client stockbroker is potentially a helpful agent.

NOTE

1 The Tobin 'q' ratio is the ratio of the marginal efficiency of real investment to the market yield on equity. This ratio was generated when he developed a general framework for monetary analysis (Tobin 1969).

REFERENCES

Banz, R. (1981) 'The relationship between return and market value of common stocks', *Journal of Financial Economics*, 9, March: pp. 3–18.

Basu, S. (1977) 'Investment performance of common stocks in relation to their price–earnings ratios: a test of efficient market hypothesis', *Journal of Finance*, June: pp. 663–82.

Bernstein, P.L. (1989) 'How true are tried principles?', *Investment Management Review*, III, 8.

BZW (1989) *Equity Gilt Study*, January.

Capel-Cure Myers Capital Management Limited (1989) *High Yields: Are Institutional Investors Missing Out?* March.

Cutler, D., Poterba, C., and Summers, L. (1989) 'What moves stock prices?' *Journal of Portfolio Management*, Spring.

Dimson, E. and Marsh, P. (1988) 'Yielding up the secrets of smaller companies' dividends: twice the real growth rate of larger companies!', *Hoare Govett Ltd, Review of the First Quarter.*

Eun, C.S. and Resnick, B.G. (1988) 'Exchange rate uncertainty, forward contracts and international portfolio selection', *Journal of Finance*, March: pp. 197–246.

Fama, E. (1970) 'Efficient capital markets: a review of theory and empirical work', *Journal of Finance*, May: pp. 383–417.

Gultekin, M. and Gultekin, B. (1983) 'Stock market seasonality; international evidence', *Journal of Financial Economics*, December.

Hamao, Y. (1989) 'Japanese stocks, bonds, bills and inflation 1973–1987', *The Journal of Portfolio Management*, 15, Winter: pp. 20–6.

Jensen, M. (1989) 'Eclipse of the public corporation', *Harvard Business Review*, September–October.

Jorion, P. (1985) 'International portfolio diversification with estimation risk', *Journal of Business*, 15. 3.

Keim, D. (1985) 'Size related anomalies and stock seasonality', *Journal of Financial Economics*, June.

Levis, M. (1986) 'An exploratory investigation into the small size effect' (unpublished report), *Capel-Cure Myers*, July.

——(1989) 'Stock market anomalies: a reassessment based on the UK evidence', *Journal of Banking and Finance*, Winter.

Levy, H. (1983) 'The capital asset management model: theory and empiricism', *Economic Journal*, March.

Malkiel, B. (1985) *A Random Walk down Wall Street*, New York: Norton & Co.

Reinganum, M. (1981) 'Mis-specification of capital asset pricing: empirical anomalies based on earnings yield and market value', *Journal of Financial Economics*, March.

—— (1983) 'The anomalous stock market behaviour of small firms in january: empirical test of tax-loss selling effects', *Journal of Financial Economics*, June.

Roll, R. (1983) 'Vas ist das? The turn-of-the-year effect and the return premia of small firms', *Journal of Portfolio Management*, 9, Winter: pp. 8–28.

Rozeff, M. and Kinney, W. (1976) 'Capital market seasonality: the case of stock returns', *Journal of Financial Economics*, October.

Samuelson, P. (1989) 'The judgement of economic science on rational portfolio management: indexing, timing and long-horizon effects', *Journal of Portfolio Management*, Fall.

Solnik, B. (1974) 'Why not diversify internationally rather than domestically?', *Financial Analysis Journal*, July/August.

Solnik, B. and Noetzlin, B. (1982) 'Optimal international asset allocation', *Journal of Portfolio Management*, 9, Fall: pp. 11–21.

Solt, M. and Statmen, M. (1989) 'Good companies, bad stocks', *Journal of Portfolio Management*, 15,3: pp. 30–44.

Thaler, R. (1987a) 'Anomalies: the January effect', *Economic Perspectives*, Summer.

—— (1987b) 'Anomalies: seasonal movements in security prices: weekend, holiday, turn-of-the-month and intra-day effects', *Economic Perspectives*, Fall.

Tinic, S. and West, R. (1984) 'Risk and return: January and the rest of the year', *Journal of Financial Economics*, 13, pp. 561–74.

Tobin, J. (1969) 'A general equilibrium approach to monetary theory', *Journal of Money, Credit and Banking*, February.

Wydler, D. (1989) 'Swiss stocks, bonds and inflation 1926–1987', *Journal of Portfolio Management*, 15, Winter: pp. 27–32.

Zarowin, P. 'Short-run market overreaction: size and seasonality effects', *Journal of Portfolio Management*, 15, Winter: pp. 26–9.

119

5

FRAUDBUSTING IN LONDON

Developments in the policing of white-collar crime

Michael Levi

The purpose of this article is to describe and analyse some of the changes and continuities in the regulation of financial fraud in London, whose cost in money terms – *excluding* both unrecorded and tax fraud – as recorded by the two London police forces, has risen by 150 per cent since 1970 and in 1989 amounted to some £4 billion at risk. However, as other contributors to this book have emphasised, financial services activity in London (and the UK generally) is just part of a global phenomenon. During the 1980s, major banking and securities frauds hit Argentina, Australia, Brazil, Brunei, Hong Kong, Israel, Italy, Malaysia, Portugal, Singapore, the United Kingdom and the United States. Corruption scandals have arisen in all countries: developed and under-developed; capitalist and communist (before Eastern Europe moved towards a market economy).

The precise levels of corruption in different economic and social systems are impossible to ascertain, since so much is hidden. However, what is certain is that the policing of the upperworld raises many critical difficulties: first, the competency of policing organisations to understand and investigate fraud; second, their motivation to do so; and third, the political autonomy of police, prosecutors and judges from the groups – if any – who may be under suspicion of involvement in fraud. It would be a mistake to view any of these factors as being intrinsically static; we have only to imagine that this article was written in late 1986 instead of late 1990 to understand how rapidly the composition of 'upperworld criminality' – at least as measured by *prosecutions*, if not convictions – can change, from marginalised individuals and professional criminals in 1986, to these plus a small number of the most prestigious business names in the UK and US in 1989 and 1990.

Libel laws as well as scientific rules being as they are, in mid-1986 I would have had to observe that, although there was some reason to believe that influential figures unconnected with the Mafia were involved in illicit securities dealing in Britain and America, law enforcement agencies were unwilling or uninterested in bringing them to justice. Then we would have had to speculate on the allocation of responsibility for this to, *inter alia*, a general ideological harmony between regulators and regulated, to bribery, to political favour trading, to unintended or intended inadequacies of legal frameworks, or to simple incompetence. Now, things have changed. Senior figures in the most prestigious securities firms in the United States have been placed in handcuffs in the full glare of television cameras on the instructions of former US Attorney (and later unsuccessful Republican candidate for Mayor of New York) Rudolph Giuliani; former 'junk bond king' Mike Milken was jailed in 1990 for ten years following a guilty plea; the former chairman of Guinness was arrested in London – although, compared with the US, somewhat more genteelly at his solicitors' offices – for allegedly attempting to pervert the course of justice and later, along with other major entrepreneurs and professionals, was jailed for five years for fraud; and – in some respects most dramatically of all – as discussed by Chris Stanley in this volume, in November 1989, quite senior merchant bankers, brokers and a partner in a leading firm of City solicitors were charged with conspiracy to defraud in relation to the flotation and market making of Blue Arrow by County NatWest and Phillips & Drew, causing public furore at this and the fact of their arrest at their homes at 7 a.m. (It is arguable whether these arrests were operationally necessary and legally justifiable, and it appears that they were intended as symbolic gesture and/or general deterrent. But unmentioned by the press was the fact that this was not a particularly early hour for City personnel, and may have been the latest hour at which they could have been expected to be at home.) Thus, except where the underlying conditions remain stable, as may happen in some underdeveloped countries such as Haiti before the fall of 'Baby Doc' Duvalier, it is simplistic and unilluminating to assert that élites are immune from criminal justice.

The increased criminalisation of élite persons for financial crime – though still modest compared with levels of prosecution of those lower down the social scale – raises the question of how frauds are carried out and what sort of people practise these *modus operandi*. An extensive discussion of this is beyond the space available for this article, but what little survey research there has been suggests that some two thirds of frauds against large companies are carried out entirely by insiders or with inside help, and that where the people at the top of organisations have a lax attitude towards controls, those lower down the hierarchy will act likewise (Levi and Sherwin 1989). London's place as an important corporate finance centre, combined with the immense personal and institutional competitiveness in the world of mergers, take-overs and all forms of financial instrument fluctuations creates a massive premium on superior information and on business alliances, and this can readily spill over into insider trading, market manipulation and commercial espionage. Sometimes, this is done 'for the firm' (and, secondarily, for one's own performance-related bonuses and reputation in the industry); at others, it is done *purely* for one's own financial benefit, as in insider dealing, embezzlement and corruption. These are extremes on a continuum, as one may see from those mortgage frauds which begin as a method of loaning building society funds at cut prices to landlords and commercial property speculators, and may end in the loaning by several societies of funds on the identical real or non-existent property to professionals who then abscond with the money. In addition to these frauds by 'criminal professionals' at varied levels of the organisation from senior director to temporary secretary in the typing pool, there are also frauds by 'professional criminals' such as 'long-firm' (bankruptcy) frauds, the sending of bills for bogus or valueless services (such as telex directory frauds), the charging of 'advance fees' for promised future loans that never materialise, and various types of fraud based on false documentation (fraud against the European Community agricultural fund, maritime insurance fraud, forged bills of exchange and forged letters authorising the transfer of funds, normally by electronic means).

In Britain, commercial fraud is policed by the police, Inland Revenue, HM Customs & Excise and the Department of Trade and Industry. Sometimes, these agencies overlap, for example when 'long-firm frauds' are set up to get goods on credit without intending to pay for them, and defraud not only creditors but also value-added tax and income tax (Levi 1981). But each agency has its own domain. For example, the Department of Trade and Industry has overall responsibility for insolvency and for financial services regulation, including insider dealing and major company investigations. This aspect is discussed elsewhere in this volume by Chris Stanley, but it is important to stress that the majority of financial services regulation is aimed at fraud prevention rather than fraud investigation and prosecution.

The UK police are formally independent of central (and, *de facto*, of local) government, and their priorities are set by the head of each force in loose consultation with the public, their police authorities and the Inspectorate of Constabulary (see, generally, Reiner 1985; Weatheritt 1986). Prior to 1985, no UK government – Conservative or Labour – ever expressed much interest in the work or staffing levels of police fraud squads, so Chief Constables – who in both London forces have the title of Commissioner – were left very much to their own devices. Governmental agencies, however, derive their cues about their priorities from government policy direct. Although it may be sloppy political science methodology to infer governmental aims from governmental presentation, it is clear that, initially, the way in which 'the securities fraud problem' was presented in the UK was very low-key: in 1984/5, the Conservative government was plainly concerned not to alienate its political and financial supporters by imposing heavy regulation or compliance costs. This concern not to be misunderstood by the City as being tough on regulation is exemplified by the government's White Paper on Financial Services (Department of Trade 1985: 1) which forms the basis for the Financial Services Act 1986:

> This does not mean excessive regulation. That would impose unnecessary monitoring and enforcement costs; and would stop or delay new services and products being developed in response to market opportunities. The Government therefore intend that the regulation of the financial services industry should be no more than the minimum necessary to protect the investor. This will be in the interests of the customers of the industry as much as of the industry itself.

All the evidence points towards fraud regulation not being historically anything more than a marginal plank of government policy. It is within this broad political context of governmental indifference (relative to street and household crime) that I wish to discuss the policing of commercial fraud in London.

FRAUD AS A POLICING PRIORITY

Some may seek to 'explain' the policing (or non-policing) of commerce in terms of Ruling Class interests but, as I have contended elsewhere (Levi 1987, ch.4), such an approach provides a simplistic picture of 'capitalist interests' and, even if one were to accept that the non-policing of fraud was helpful to capitalism, fails to do justice to the relative autonomy of state and – in the case of the British police – local state institutions. Let us consider the facts in more detail.

Although with some 588 Fraud Squad officers in England and Wales, the police have more staff than the Department of Trade and Industry corporate regulation sections, they occupy what in many respects is a subsidiary role in policing the upperworld. The two London police forces have approximately one third of all the police fraud investigators and approximately one fifth of all the police officers in England and Wales, so it appears superficially that fraud investigation is statistically *over*-represented in those forces. On the other hand, since my 1985 survey showed that, in terms of sums defrauded and at risk, the London forces dealt with more fraud than all other forces combined (Levi 1986), it is arguable that the police there were (and are) relatively *under*-staffed. The determination of the appropriate weighting of police manpower in relation to the number and complexity of cases under investigation is beyond the scope of this article (and, perhaps, of human competence), but it leads us to address the question of how seriously the police regard fraud.

There are a number of ways of addressing this question. One is to look at how many resources are devoted to combating it; another is to examine police attitudes towards fraud. 'The police' are not a homogeneous group, and we should beware of taking the views of any particular individuals as being representative of majority opinion. Moreover, what is written in annual reports is often the product of, first, staff officers second-guessing what Commissioners (I am writing here of London forces, which do not use the title Chief Constable) would want in print and, second, the rewriting of these drafts by senior personnel; so, although they contain the Commissioner's imprimatur, the extent to which they are the pure product of his thoughts varies. Why should we focus on the views of Commissioners? However independent in practice 'street cops' are of 'management cops' (Bradley *et al.* 1986; Punch

1983; Weatheritt 1986), Commissioners do control the resources available to specialist squads such as fraud squads. Thus it is important to see how they – as well as 'the ranks' – view fraud. One fruitful initial source of police perceptions of social problems are the annual reports to their police authorities. These are interesting both for what they state and for what they leave out. After all, whatever one's views regarding the extent of and need for 'police accountability' (Morgan 1989) – particularly in the Metropolitan Police where the Home Secretary, not local representatives, is the police authority – these annual reports (and the memoirs of police officers) give a good indication of what issues senior officers believe are of greatest interest and concern to their police authorities, the media and the public. We may look to the general introductions in annual reports for insight into what senior officers think are the high priority issues of the day as seen by their reference groups.

It would be unfair to characterise even past police attitudes to commercial fraud as almost total neglect, as some commentators imply (Box 1983). Prior to the Second World War, interest and expertise in the policing of fraud was largely a matter of happenstance, even where large businesses were the *victims* (for instance of bankruptcy fraud), as well as where members of the élite were offenders against relatively powerless victims. To some extent, such an unsystematic approach to the policing of fraud may have been the product of rivalries between City of London Police and Metropolitan Police Commissioners. But it should not be forgotten that – Special Branch excepted – nationwide policing strategies, however effectively or ineffectively implemented, are largely the creation of the Thatcher era. The City of London may have been an exception – because of the prevalence there of financial services interests – but elsewhere the vigorous and competent pursuit of fraud was dependent upon whether or not there happened to be officers in the division who had some experience of such investigations. It is a matter for speculation what sort of service fraud victims received and how they filtered cases before reporting them to the police (see Levi 1981). However, though Scotland Yard set up a small Sharepusher and Confidence Trickster Squad in the 1930s for frauds occurring within its jurisdiction, it was only in 1946, when the Home Office became increasingly concerned about the prospects of fraud against demobilised Britons and Americans, that a combined London Squad was established, entitled the Metropolitan and City of London Police Company Fraud Department. Its head has always been a Commander of the Metropolitan Police – the equivalent of an Assistant Commissioner in the City of London Police – and City of London officers, though part of the combined squad, are for disciplinary purposes answerable to the City of London Commissioner and thus effectively independent of the Metropolitan Police Commander who heads their squad. (A similar accountability arrangement applies to officers seconded to the Serious Fraud Office, discussed later.)

THE METROPOLITAN POLICE AND VIEWS ON FRAUD

Since space is limited and this book is primarily about the City of London, I shall deal more briefly with the Metropolitan Police District than its importance warrants. During the 1960s, the principal areas of concern for the Metropolitan Police were long-firm frauds – businesses set up to obtain large quantities of goods without intending to pay for them, which were then closely connected with the Kray and Richardson gang operations (Levi 1981) – and various stock and insurance swindles. Since then, by the criteria of column space and rhetoric, commercial fraud has increasingly – though variably – attained social problem status in the Metropolitan Police area. Sir Robert Mark's first report, for 1972, displayed concern about the way in which fraud was becoming a target for criminals in the following terms:

> There is an increasing awareness that fraud can be easily and profitably carried out provided it is not too protracted, and that investigation so strains police resources that detection, if it occurs at all, may be long delayed. This is perhaps one explanation for the marked increase in the whole field of fraud from simple cheque cases to large commercial transactions.
>
> (Mark, Home Office 1973: 14)

What bothered him was the switch by 'criminal types' into areas of activity such as 'long-firm fraud'. This interpretation is reinforced by his further commentary the following year on what one might term the 'downmarket' aspects of fraud (Home Office 1974: 13). The theme of international cooperation in combating organised fraud was continued in his introductions to the annual reports in

1974, 1975 and 1976, possibly influenced by Sir James Crane, Commander of the Fraud Squad and later Deputy Assistant Commissioner, who rose to become HM Chief Inspector of Constabulary. Mark's expressions of concern about fraud may not have been reflected in increased manpower for the Fraud Squad, but assuming anyone below Chief Superintendent ever read them – which is far from certain – his words may have given symbolic encouragement to the Squad that what they were doing was not only important in itself but was also appreciated by the Metropolitan Police hierarchy. Thereafter, only in 1977 and 1978 did Sir David McNee mention fraud as an issue in his introductions, and he too focused on international fraud. The internationalisation theme is thus a persistent one though, judging from my observations and Anderson's (1989) neglect of fraud in his account of the politics of international police cooperation, it does not appear to have generated much practical pressure overseas. Neither Mark (1981) nor McNee (1983) referred to fraud in their autobiographies, though they both discussed extensively their battle against police corruption.

Sir Kenneth Newman, who followed McNee as Commissioner, was (and remains) an intelligent and strategic thinker on police matters who may have been more directly involved than most of his predecessors in the drafting of policy statements. It is thus significant that he did not comment upon commercial fraud in his lengthy introductions to policing London. In 1984, in his report on his first full year as Commissioner, he devotes almost all his space to outlining a model of preventative policing which excludes not only fraud but also most specialist crime investigation units. Commercial fraud receives no mention whatever and, indeed, the only mention of business crime is in a brief reference to the setting up of 'business watch' (Home Office 1984: 8 and 106), again as part of a crime prevention strategy. Though his post-retirement view of fraud in business is that it is very serious, in office the only significant concern expressed about it was in the context of charity fraud (Home Office 1985: 99), reflecting his (and many other police officers') view that the task of the police is to respond to popular sentiments about fear of crime, while retaining the autonomy to override such sentiments where they are 'irrational' or not 'cost-effective'.

Sir Peter Imbert's first report as Commissioner contains no mention of fraud in his introduction or statement of force objectives. His second report likewise omits fraud as a central policing objective. There is nothing about it in the section on crime prevention and, in the discussions of specific crimes, it is relegated almost to back marker status even within specialist squad activities. This is not an accident, for his introductory remarks make clear the populist basis for prioritisation:

> Opinion polls indicate that 'personal crimes', such as street robbery and burglary which are normally dealt with by local officers, have a greater impact on the public than organised crime, terrorism, blackmail and fraud, the policing of which tends to be the responsibility of specialist branches and squads. Therefore, the order in which the crimes are discussed here follows, for the most part, that public perception.
>
> (Imbert, Home Office 1989: 20)

In the later section on fraud (25), the listing of major fraud squad activities is followed by what appears to be a plea for a separate fraud squad cost component to be incorporated into privatisation flotation costs. Again, the theme of understaffing is communicated by mentioning that the complex investigations into mortgage frauds 'are usually undertaken by the branch, but the increase in this type of crime has necessitated enquiries by local officers'. (Cheque fraud was dealt with separately, stressing organised crime counterfeiting of company cheques.) This general approach is reiterated in the report for 1989 where an almost apologetic prelude to the work of the department commences with 'The work of the Company Fraud Branch may seem remote from the public at large but its work discourages crime which could affect the financial well-being of citizens' (Home Office 1990: 18). Elsewhere (12), the Commissioner laments the fact that asset confiscation work 'has created a considerable demand on resources, with costs of staff and necessary overseas travel being met to the detriment of other enquiries': a comment that would apply also to the expensive travel associated with international fraud investigations. Given the high cost of international (particularly European) travel, financial constraints as well as police attitudes inhibit the development of globalised policing.

In short, insofar as anything at all can be read into them, annual reports consistently suggest that commercial fraud is not seen to be a central problem in policing the Metropolis. Otherwise, the relatively small amount of discussion on fraud would have been enhanced. Such reports should be seen in their political context, however, and it remains an open question to what extent this sense of the relative unimportance of fraud reflects the personal views of successive Commissioners or merely their political (with a small 'p') judgements about what interests Home Secretaries and/or the London public as a whole.

CITY OF LONDON POLICE VIEWS ON FRAUD

By contrast, the recent annual reports of the Commissioner of the City of London Police pay far more attention to fraud, both in terms of the space devoted to it and in the gravity with which the issue is discussed. No mention was made of it in the forewords to the 1980 and 1981 reports, but each subsequent year has contained some comment in the foreword as well as more detailed remarks in the substantive sections.

In his report for 1982 (City of London Police 1983), Sir Peter Marshall, the Commissioner, drew the attention of the Police Committee to:

the work of the Fraud Squad and the perennial difficulties they face in investigating complex and international frauds. There has been an unprecedented focus of public attention on some spectacular features of self regulation in the financial institutions of the City; there are signs, albeit early ones, that steps are being taken to improve the control of doubtful practices and to afford better protection for the public. There are signs of greater willingness to improve co-operation between those agencies with a responsibility for enforcement and prosecution. These are welcomed by my Fraud Squad, which will continue to bear the main burden of investigating and bringing to prosecution complex cases where regulation and prevention have been unsuccessful.

I am aware, from the many letters I receive from both home and abroad, that the reputation of the City of London Fraud Squad is acknowledged internationally. It is my intention to ensure that that reputation is retained and enhanced.

(Marshall, City of London Police 1983: 7)

This panegyric was followed by the briefer remarks on the events of 1983:

The difficulties of investigating and prosecuting complex city frauds are highlighted once again. 1983 saw a level of public and governmental interest in this crucial field which could mark a turning point. I look forward to seeing a new framework for the protection of investors and await the recommendations of Lord Roskill on trial procedures with interest.

(Marshall, City of London Police 1985: iii)

In the report on 1984 (City of London Police 1985: iii), the note of progress is maintained, though perhaps with less optimism than hitherto. The report on 1985 (City of London Police 1986) included improved detection rates for 'large scale organised fraud' among the force objectives. Commissioner Owen Kelly mentioned the high priority given to Fraud Investigation Group (FIG) cases – the task force set up in 1985 which coordinated the Director of Public Prosecutions and the police, and which still remains in place for cases requiring more than routine expertise but which are not handled by the Serious Fraud Office – and that as a consequence:

the investigation time of non-FIG cases is necessarily prolonged. Whilst care is taken to ensure that fraudsters do not benefit from the situation, and that all complaints are treated as expeditiously as possible, it is inevitable that the workload will take longer to process.

A feature of some of the more spectacular of the fraud cases has been the news media attention they have attracted . . .. Our determination not to be drawn into the political arena has meant that we have been unable to be as forthcoming in our comments to the news media as we would otherwise have wished.

(Kelly, City of London Police 1986: 13)

The foreword of the report for 1988 is almost exclusively devoted to non-fraud crime. Its comments on the effective clamp-down on 'lager louts' and on the fact that secluded walkways and high-rise blocks do not produce high crime rates in the City of London – though the role in this of the social class composition of the Barbican and Middlesex Street residents is somewhat understated – dwarf the short paragraph which observes on an upbeat note that:

In April the Serious Fraud Office opened and officers of the

Company Fraud Department are now working alongside lawyers and accountants on the most complex cases. Early indications are that this closer co-operation will indeed help to bring about the much-desired speedy and effective prosecution of major fraud.

(City of London Police 1989: 6)

The draft objectives for 1989/90 mention fraud prevention as an important item. The section on the work of the CID notes that:

In August the role of the Cheque Squad was revised and a greater emphasis was placed on intelligence gathering and 'pro-activity'. Computer support is of tremendous benefit to the investigations and enhancements are being developed . . .. Cheque related crime is an increasing trend of criminal activity and . . . a Cheque Fraud Liaison Committee was established to ensure that there is a frequent and readily accessible forum for the dissemination of information held by the various parties.

(City of London Police 1989: 27)

The detailed and interesting section on the work of the Company Fraud Department stresses the changes brought about by the introduction of the Serious Fraud Office under the Criminal Justice Act 1987, and strikes a note of positive response to change:

[I]n a current enquiry very much in its early and labour-intensive period, a *Commission Rogatoire* was required within five hours to enable overseas enquiries to be instituted and the results made available to the investigative team in this country. Because of the close liaison and proximity of all involved, the relevant discussions, preparation, checking and forwarding of the documents was done within the time available. Under previous arrangements this would have been virtually impossible.

(City of London Police 1989: 30)

Later, commenting in detail upon the Johnson Matthey Bankers fraud, the Commissioner notes (31) that the trial judge 'praised the entire team for its "enormous hard work"'. He goes on to stress the proactive role of the department in developing contacts with the banks and, also on the theme of positive responses to change, the training of officers in asset-tracing to meet the demands of asset confiscation legislation for fraud as well as drug trafficking.

The report on 1989 contains a great deal of lucid discussion of fraud issues, both in the introduction and elsewhere, reflecting the development of a much more proactive (and self-confident) line within the force regarding fraud (City of London Police 1990). The report is upbeat about the impact of the Serious Fraud Office and the Criminal Justice (International Co-operation) Bill – now enacted – though fraud is not included specifically in the Force objectives.

There are approximately twenty six times as many officers in the Metropolitan as in the City of London Police, but the Metropolitan Police Company Fraud Department is little over twice the size of that of the City of London: its establishment is 153 compared with 65 (plus twelve officers on the City of London Cheque Fraud Squad, which is controlled by the CID, not by the Company Fraud Department). This manpower differential, and the annual reports quoted earlier, support the view that the Commissioner of the City of London sees fraud as a much more important policing (and/or political) problem than does his Metropolitan counterpart. This is captured not only in the rhetorical style and prominence given to fraud, but also in more material ways such as the proportion of the total forces who are in the respective fraud squads and the maintenance of the Cheque Squad by the City of London and its controversial cutting back by the Metropolitan Police. (This is part of the gradual erosion of the élite status of central Special Operations squads in the Metropolitan Police since the Mark era began in 1972.) This difference in policing priorities may reflect the relative absence of public order, organised crime and street crime problems in the City of London, but it also reflects the central importance of financial capital to the prosperity of the Force area. Even prior to the political and media scandal-mongering over fraud that has occurred since 1985, the City of London Commissioner repeatedly referred to the 'wide recognition' of the importance of fraud regulation and to 'public and governmental interest' in this 'crucial' area. Although total losses from fraud are far higher in the Metropolitan Police area – much greater than from other crimes in London (see Levi 1987, ch.2) – both crime and political constituencies are much more varied in the Met than in the City, where fraud is far more salient. Inasmuch as promotions depend on doing well at what promoters value, it is interesting but perhaps operationally irrelevant whether junior officers share these different perceptions of the significance of fraud.

There are no surveys of police or public attitudes to fraud in London. The few police/public attitude surveys that exist reveal that in a northern and southern police area of England (Levi 1987, ch.3) and in the United States (Rossi *et al.* 1985), the police rate fraud offences considerably less seriously than do the general public. In my view, this is *not* explicable principally in terms of the police reflecting established power differentials in society, though, in spite of the increase in police powers to deal with fraud since 1984, dealing with high-status offenders is more personally risky and technically difficult than dealing with lower-class suspects. However, the 'seriousness gap' *is* related to the lack of support and interest that emanates from further up the organisational and political hierarchy in Britain. At least prior to the Criminal Justice Acts 1987 and 1988, experience led many fraud squad officers to be aware that active pursuit was likely to end in overseas juris- dictional obstacles which the Director of Public Prosecutions was unenthusiastic about pursuing. Senior officer interest in fraud *may* have increased since the mid-1980s, due to increased attention to it by television, radio and in the main crime and news sections of newspapers, as well as in the business sections that non-specialist officers are less likely to read. At least at a formal level, asset confiscation provisions in the Drug Trafficking Offences Act 1986, the Criminal Justice Act 1988 and the Prevention of Terrorism (Temporary Provisions) Act 1989 have shifted police interest in the direction of crippling 'villains' financially, even though this is a drain on scarce police resources for which they are not formally compensated. Given Mafia and other 'Organised Crime Group' involvement in international fraud – a risk that may increase with even readier Italian access to London markets after 1992 – the interest in policing fraud that occurred in the FBI may extend to Britain, but tackling crime – even drug trafficking – by following the money trail will remain only a minority police involvement (see further, Levi 1991).

Another reason for police concern not to amplify 'the fraud problem' relates to the resource burden it imposes: a point repeatedly emphasised not only in my interviews with police officers but also in Commissioners' annual reports. (Though Sir Peter Imbert has restored the size of the Fraud Squad to what it was before it was cut by Sir Kenneth Newman.) In his report on 1975, Sir Robert Mark noted (Home Office 1976: 16) that investigation of major cases of corruption in the public sector requires 'detailed and lengthy investigation and . . . one investigation can often lead to a large number of time-consuming parallel enquiries which greatly increase the pressure on the inevitably limited resources available for this work'.

In the report on 1982, Sir Kenneth Newman heralds the beginnings of the 'task force', inter-agency coordination approach to commercial fraud investigations as follows:

Major fraud cases require protracted and costly investigations by police and to obviate the need for separate investigations, certain cases are being dealt with using the fraud investigation group approach with investigating officers being advised from the outset by the Director of Public Prosecutions and the Department of Trade.

(Newman, Home Office 1983: 53)

Not only officer-hours but also the international complexities are stressed. Thus, Sir Kenneth, referring to two multi-million pound frauds which *did* lead to arrests, states that:

In January a request was made for Fraud Squad officers to investigate allegations of fraudulent trading concerning the Bank International Limited of Grand Cayman in the British West Indies. The investigation lasted four months and was conducted in co-operation with the Department of Trade and Industry . . .

(Newman, Home Office 1985: 99)

In the report for 1985, it is reiterated: 'Internationalism in fraud has grown rapidly. Cross-border investigations through Interpol highlight an increase in international fraud and much time is spent dealing with enquiries received from Interpol member countries' (Home Office 1986: 45–6).

Similarly, the obstacles to police enquiries – both national and international – are frequently mentioned in the City of London annual reports. The report for 1980 sounds a note of despair when it states:

The difficulties facing investigating officers when unravelling complex highly technical international frauds are increasing and though much joint thought and effort has been expended in attempts to simplify the process and enhance international co-operation, little has been achieved and my officers acknowledge that their efforts to investigate and prosecute successfully this class of fraud are becoming increasingly frustrated.

(City of London Police 1980: 14)

The resource position has not altered noticeably since those words were uttered.

Nor does the priority given to training and career development within fraud squads give much cause for optimism. The prestige of fraud as a policing issue is indicated by its almost total absence from any education for promotion-bound officers attending Command Courses at Bramshill Police College, where strategies are developed for policing problems of the future. Fraud Squad training does not exceed one month. Moreover, it is general policy in most forces not to keep officers who are to be promoted in Fraud Squads for long: they are unlikely to serve for longer than three years in the Metropolitan Police Fraud Squad on any one occasion, though they may stay longer in the provinces and are often transferred back to the Fraud Squad at a later stage. So what we end up with is a situation in which the most difficult offences and the most high-status offenders are dealt with by comparatively inexperienced officers who receive most of their training 'on the job', without much debriefing and collective lesson-sharing from other cases. What is miraculous is that, due to their enthusiasm for mastering problems and 'feeling collars', the police achieve the results that they do. Lest this should appear to be an over-whelmingly negative view of amateurism in the policing of fraud, we should note that, at least prior to the late 1980s, the performance of the permanent career civil servants in the Department of Trade and Industry who dealt with the licensing of investment businesses and with the investigation of insolvency and company frauds has been abysmal compared with that of the police. For a vigorous critique of the role of the DTI, see Bosworth-Davies (1988) and, in more restrained style, the report on the collapse of Barlow Clowes (Le Quesne 1988), along with the overview report of the Select Committee on Trade and Industry into DTI investigations (1990). So permanence is not a sufficient condition for competence!

DEVELOPMENTS IN THE POLICING OF FRAUD IN LONDON

Although the historical policing of fraud could be characterised most accurately as a policy of benign neglect, there are two sources of more serious policing in the future which may alter that portrait considerably. The first relates to the draconian powers of investigation granted to the Department of Trade and Industry inspectors under Sections 177 and 178 of the Financial Services Act 1986, which, in cases of suspected insider dealing, enable inspectors to require information from any persons on pain of imprisonment for contempt of court and/or of de-authorisation from conducting investment business. This is dealt with by Chris Stanley elsewhere in this volume (see also Levi 1987, 1991). The second relates to the establishment of the Serious Fraud Office under the Criminal Justice Act 1987 (Wood 1989).

Since the banking, insurance and investment scandals of the 1980s brought fraud in the City into sharper focus, governmental interest has certainly grown. Although the London police are formally independent of the Home Secretary, this has translated itself into the policing of fraud via particular concentration upon high-visibility alleged investment frauds, many of which (with the notable exception of Guinness) occur within the City of London Force area because – pending further geographical changes in the organisation of the financial services sector – that is where their headquarters are located. The developments in policing and prosecution are not solely a response to the scandals of late 1986, since they were adopted in principle before these scandals broke. Following the recommendations of Lord Roskill's Fraud Trials Committee (1986: 27), the Criminal Justice Act 1987 established the Serious Fraud Office. This is a statutory body responsible directly to the Attorney-General, headed by a director who is independent of the Director of Public Prosecutions, and with some 80 accountants, lawyers, investigators and clerical staff, including several partners seconded from leading firms of City accountants such as Ernst & Young and Price Waterhouse (whose salaries are 'topped up' by their firms from what, for accountants, are the relatively modest civil service pay scales).

The Serious Fraud Office supplements but does not replace the Fraud Investigation Group of the Crown Prosecution Service, and is intended to collaborate and work closely with designated officers of the Metropolitan and City Police Company Fraud Department: thus far, more closely with the City of London Police, who have more officers than do 'the Met' dedicated specifically to work with the SFO. Its brief is to deal with 'serious' and/or 'complex' fraud, which in practice means frauds over £2 million which are interpreted by the SFO case screening officer and Director as being of public concern. (This is influenced by the media but is not a simple reflection of publicity.) Section 1 (3) of the Criminal Justice Act 1987 makes this remit quite open when it states that 'The Director may carry out in conjunction with the police investigations into any suspected offence which appears to him to involve serious or complex fraud'.

The Director of the Serious Fraud Office is given major powers to require documents and answers to questions as a result of the Act, tougher in some respects than those available under the Police and Criminal Evidence Act 1984 and almost as great as those in the Financial Services Act 1986 (see Levi 1987, chs 5 and 8; 1991; and Wood 1989). These provisions attracted hostile reactions from bankers and from the Law Society, who succeeded in modifying some clauses in Parliamentary Committee, but what is left is still a significant extension in 'police power' to deal with fraud outside the financial services regulatory framework. For example, the personal fiat of the Director gives access to bank accounts without a court order: this was done 344 times in 1990–1.

Except for revenue intelligence, which will be disclosed to others only for the purpose of a criminal prosecution by either the Serious Fraud Office or, in relation to an inland revenue offence, to the Crown Prosecution Service – see Section 3 of the Act – information obtained may be passed on not only to the police but to Department of Trade Inspectors, the Official Receiver and, under Section 3 (6),

> (c) any body having supervisory, regulatory, or disciplinary functions in relation to any profession or area of commercial activity; and
> (d) any person or body having, under the law of any country or territory outside Great Britain, functions corresponding to any of the functions of any person or body mentioned . . . above.

So, although differences in legal procedures and in police powers and priorities, allied to reservations about the diminution of sovereignty over criminal matters, make it harder to achieve the harmonisation of international criminal justice than of civil justice or securities regulation, developments in mutual criminal assistance in the late 1980s do provide a legal framework for dealing more effectively with international fraud. These changes should be seen within the context of the fast-developing sharing of information among securities regulators and (sometimes) among police, normally bilaterally (as in most US treaties), but sometimes under the aegis of multilateral organisations such as the Commonwealth, the European Economic Community, or even the OECD (1989), which have agreed to fairly routine exchange of previously sacrosanct revenue information. (The Companies Act 1989 allows the DTI to undertake enquiries on behalf of other countries even if no offence against UK laws is suspected.)

Despite these changes, the policing of fraud in Britain is unlikely to be transformed immediately into a high-profile 'fraudbuster' operation: the tradition of discretion and caution is too deeply ingrained. Nor are police agencies easy to internationalise: indeed, it is difficult to get them to agree to share intelligence *nationally*. But for the first time, an organisation has been created with a bureaucratic interest in taking fraud seriously. Formerly, the Department of Trade and Industry was always ambivalent about the significance of business control in comparison with business promotion, and the Director of Public Prosecutions had other major crimes to deal with which were more attuned to the traditional priorities of the culture of the Bar. And despite (or because of) the likely flow of staff from Serious Fraud Office and Self-Regulatory Organisations to higher-paid jobs in the financial services sector, the changes will make competence in fraud investigation a worthwhile step in a legal and/or commercial career. Attention will then have to be paid to conflict-of-interest rules regarding regulators leaving for jobs with firms (or associated firms) which they have investigated, though the track record of Britain in controlling subsequent employment of civil servants gives little cause for optimism that such rules will be implemented or, if implemented, enforced.

Notwithstanding these cautionary words, it would be wrong to be too sceptical about the significance of the moves in the direction of serious fraud control since 1985. The political momentum has not been as great since the 1987 General Election, but the self-interest, first, of financial services firms in damaging the prospects of their competitors with scandal and, second, of Britain in maintaining or creating investor and public confidence in its (contradictory?) 'tough-minded but flexible' regulation is substantial enough to suggest that measures to deal with fraud will continue to receive greater governmental and commercial priority than they did prior to the Big Bang of October 1986.

The expectations built up of the Serious Fraud Office – more by government and by the grandiosity of its title than by the SFO officials themselves – have been considerable, and the danger is that too short-term an evaluation will stress the criticisms – the acquittal of Posgate and Grob by the jury in the only major Lloyd's of London case to be tried; the enormous delays in the Guinness and Barlow Clowes cases; and the support for the ban on publication of the DTI report on the Al Fayeds' purchase of House of Fraser – and will not allow sufficient time for the learning of what is a very different style in a public law context for English lawyers, accountants and police.

If there is a drop in the number of fraud scandals, there will remain ample scope to speculate as to whether this reflects greater success in fraud prevention by regulatory agencies or greater success in scandal suppression. Alternatively, if the rate of recorded serious frauds increases, law enforcement officials will be able to argue – as they did with the rise in recorded rapes in 1985 and 1986 – that this reflects greater public confidence in their ability to deal with frauds and is therefore a success rather than a failure. (On confidence levels, see the data in Levi and Sherwin 1989.)

The impact of the police and prosecution agencies on fraud remains as problematic as in any other sphere of criminal justice. Will more prosecutions and convictions, and heavier sentences upon prestigious (or less prestigious) figures in the City of London have any significant deterrent impact? To ask this question in any spirit other than retribution calls into question what the purpose of criminal law ultimately is. Even on a less fundamentalist note, it is disappointing, but not wholly surprising, that one proposal of the Fraud Trials Committee (1986) that was *not* incorporated into the Criminal Justice Act 1987 was the establishment of a Fraud Com- mission that would monitor the work of the new anti-fraud unit: the annual reports of the Director of the Serious Fraud Office (1991) have become less bland since Barbara Mills QC became Director, but one cannot reasonably expect agencies to evaluate rigorously their own effectiveness or even efficiency. It would be unfortunate if this omission were to be interpreted by sceptical observers as indicating that creating the appearance of change in fraud regulation is a more important political objective than 'success' at dealing with fraud itself.

REFERENCES

Anderson, M. (1989) *Policing the World: Interpol and the Politics of International Police Co-operation*, Oxford: Clarendon Press.

Bosworth-Davies, R. (1988) *Too Good to be True*, Harmondsworth: Penguin.

Box, S. (1983) *Power, Crime, and Mystification*, London: Tavistock.

Bradley, D., Walker, N. and Wilkie, R. (1986) *Managing the Police*, Brighton: Wheatsheaf.

City of London Police (1983) *Annual Report of Commissioner for the City of London, 1982*, London: City of London.

——(1985) *Annual Report of Commissioner for the City of London, 1984*, London: City of London.

——(1986) *Annual Report of Commissioner for the City of London, 1985*, London: City of London.

——(1989) *Annual Report of the Commissioner of Police for the City of London, 1988*, London: City of London.

——(1990) *Annual Report 1989*, London: City of London.

Department of Trade (1985) *Financial Services in the United Kingdom: A New Framework for Investor Protection*, London: HMSO.

Fraud Trials Committee (1986) *Report*, London: HMSO.

Home Office (1971) *Report of the Commissioner for the Metropolis for the year 1970*, London: HMSO.

——(1973) *Report of the Commissioner for the Metropolis for the year 1972*, London: HMSO.

——(1974) *Report of the Commissioner for the Metropolis for the year 1973*, London: HMSO.

——(1976) *Report of the Commissioner for the Metropolis for the year 1975*, London: HMSO.

——(1977) *Report of the Commissioner for the Metropolis for the year 1976*, London: HMSO.

——(1978) *Report of the Commissioner for the Metropolis for the year 1977*, London: HMSO.

——(1983) *Report of the Commissioner for the Metropolis for the year 1982*, London: HMSO.

——(1984) *Report of the Commissioner for the Metropolis for the year 1983*, London: HMSO.

——(1985) *Report of the Commissioner for the Metropolis for the year 1984*, London: HMSO.

——(1986) *A Police for the People: Report of the Commissioner of Police for the Metropolis for the year 1985*, London: HMSO.

——(1988) *We Can Improve the Quality of Life: Commissioner of Police of the Metropolis Annual Report 1987*, London: HMSO.

——(1989) *Commissioner of Police of the Metropolis Annual Report 1988*, vol.1, London: HMSO.

——(1990) *Commissioner of Police of the Metropolis Annual Report 1989*, London: HMSO.

Le Quesne (1988) *Barlow Clowes: Report of Sir Godfray Le Quesne QC to the Secretary of State for Trade and Industry*, London: HMSO.

Levi, M. (1981) *The Phantom Capitalists: The Organisation and Control of Long-Firm Fraud*, Aldershot: Gower.

——(1986) *The Costs of Fraud*, unpublished Home Office report.

——(1987) *Regulating Fraud: White-Collar Crime and the Criminal Process*, London: Tavistock.

——(1991) *Customer Confidentiality, Money-Laundering, and Police–Bank Relationships: English Law in a Global Environment*, London: Police Foundation.

Levi, M. and Sherwin, D. (1989) *Fraud '89: the Extent of Fraud against Large Companies and Executive Views on What Should be Done about It*, London: Ernst & Young (accountants).

McNee, D. (1983) *McNee's Law*, London: Collins.

Mark, R. (1981) *In the Office of Constable*, London: Collins.

Morgan, R. (1989) 'Police accountability: current developments and future prospects', in M. Weatheritt (ed.), *Police Research: Some Future Prospects*, Aldershot: Avebury.

OECD (1989) *Explanatory Report on the Convention on Mutual Administrative Assistance in Tax Matters*, Strasbourg: Council of Europe.

Punch, M. (ed.) (1983) *Control in the Police Organization*, Harvard: MIT Press.

Reiner, R. (1985) *The Politics of the Police*, Brighton: Wheatsheaf.

Rossi, P., Simpson, J. and Miller, J. (1985) 'Beyond crime seriousness: fitting punishment to the crime', *Journal of Quantitative Criminology*, 1(1), pp. 59–90.

Select Committee on Trade and Industry (1990) *Report on Company Investigations by the Department of Trade and Industry*, London: House of Commons.

Serious Fraud Office (1991) *Annual Report of the Director of the Serious Fraud Office, 1990*, London: HMSO.

Weatheritt, M. (1986) *Innovations in Policing*, London: Croom Helm.

Wood, J. (1989) 'The Serious Fraud Office', *Criminal Law Review*, March, pp. 175–84.

6

CULTURAL CONTRADICTIONS IN THE LEGITIMATION OF MARKET PRACTICE

Paradox in the regulation of the city

Christopher Stanley

> *The empire's gone but the City of London keeps*
> *On running like a cartoon cat off a cliff – bang.*
> (Churchill 1987: 25)

Serious Money by Caryl Churchill opened to critical and popular acclaim at the Royal Court Theatre, London, in March 1987. The play is a verse drama about City People and evokes brilliantly the spirit of a particular moment in which 'Never before had so many unskilled 24 year olds made so much money in so little time' (Lewis 1989: Preface). The moment in which Churchill places her characters was a relatively brief period in the development of the UK money markets which will be temporarily delineated as that between 1984 and 1989.

The purpose of this essay is to investigate this period of activity:

1 What factors and circumstances set this period as being different to the prior regime of the City?
2 What changes were wrought during this period which have perceptibly altered the dominant ethos of the City?
3 What 'ended' so that in the future the period will be adjudged to have been a transient era of change?

The essay is divided into two sections. The first section is concerned with two cultural norms: Enterprise Culture and City Culture. These are not mutually exclusive categories of cultural reference since they inhabit familiar value-orientated (ideological) space. However, in treating them as distinctive categories, it is possible to differentiate the points of divergence which exist between them beyond certain common areas of value-orientation:

Enterprise Culture will be portrayed as a *prescriptive* imposition of a set of standards for social action. These are premised upon distinct ideological precepts for the implementation of a set of values that serve to legitimate previously perceived deviant behaviour, thereby creating a new hostility between State and City.

City Culture will be portrayed as a *descriptive* mechanism that defines the scope and context of City activity where the economic rationale of profit as a base-point standard of conduct serves to generate a subcultural code of ethics. This is manifested as a sanctioning device to prohibit malpractice and deviancy from the accepted code.

The second section of the essay is concerned with deviancy classi- fied as crime: City Crime and State Crime.

City Crime: That activity which deviates from established norms of conduct and is classified as a transgression of the prevalent subcultural code. City Crime may be a deviation from a State-prohibited practice and/or a deviation from a self-generated set of principles evolved from within the City. In either case changes in the nature of City activity have facilitated transgressionary behaviour. This has been uneconomic save within the limited range of self-gratification.

State Crime: Such patterns of transgression would previously have been contained in the sense either of being controlled so as to prohibit temptation or sanctioned through some form of ritual penalisation resulting in exclusion. In the period of the 1980s it was the State that, through the ideological vehicle of the Enterprise Culture, served to legitimate, and in legitimating to encourage, forms of market malpractice which would previously have been registered as malpractice. This process of legitimation was conceived upon an ill-founded economic rationale which served to challenge the prior, internally evolved, economic system of regulation. An externally imposed value- position resulted in an uneconomic system of regulation being developed merely as a symbolic gesture to contain a collapse of validating authority.

What was forcefully evolved in a relatively short period was a confused cultural scenario in which there was only a nominal authority to control and a subtext of legitimation of malpractice. This resulted in the fragmentation of traditional and established self-control mechanisms, a process that had deleterious economic consequences due to the loss of confidence which had previously existed.

A brief overview of the situation prevailing on Wall Street between 1984 and 1989 will be advanced to contrast with the situation in the City of London during the same period. Whereas on one level of analysis the dominant ethos of the same period on Wall Street was of immediate self-gratification ('Greed is Good') on a grand scale, with consequent damage to the economic principles of confi- dence, the institutional framework of the State and the subcultural norms of the arena of play itself have been unified in action to a remarkable degree in the enforcement of prohibition. The reasons for this illustrate a dichotomy between Wall Street and the City of London with regard to the cultural ethos of the two markets, and also the extent to which change has been imposed upon the City of London but negotiated on Wall Street.

ENTERPRISE CULTURE AND CITY CULTURE

For the purpose of this essay culture will be understood as conflictual rather than consensual, and its elements will be theorised as codes, conventions and rules which claim a pre-eminence by being constructed in common-sense terms that are, in reality, attempts by particularistic social groups to give their specific interests universal meaning (Althusser 1969; Hebdige 1979). The mechanisms for the understanding of culture are the inscribed signs and maps of meaning, those codes which are 'ideology masquerading as truth' (Barthes 1977). The issue of a subculture will be treated as a struggle for hegemony between competing interest groups, whose competition over normative reference points – the dominant and the subversive – becomes a struggle for, and over, legitimation.

Athough City Culture and Enterprise Culture may inhabit shared ideological space, they are nevertheless in conflict because they are struggling for hegemonic power. The City will be typologised as a subculture even though it is a central element in the economic discourse of civil society. The Enterprise Culture has

144

claimed a dominant cultural position in civil society by inscribing a code of immediate gratification with the reference to self as the source of its validation.

Enterprise Culture

But the British public's financial education
Is going in leaps and bounds with privatisation.
(Churchill 1987: 41)

The Enterprise Culture as an externally generated cultural form emerged in the 1980s as the *leitmotif* in the political thought and practice of the Conservative government in Britain. In Britain the Enterprise Culture was the ideological mechanism for the legitimation of social change. History was reinvented as a legitimating device couched in the rediscovered language of economic liberalism with its appeal to the efficiency of markets, the liberty of the individual and the non-interventionist state. These devices were supplemented and later superseded by attitudes, values and forms of self-understanding embedded in both individual and institutional activities (Keat 1991).

It has been stated that City Culture and Enterprise Culture inhabit certain parameters of common ideological space to the extent that both are mechanisms involving the maintenance and extension of the domain of the 'free market'. The point of divergence in this seemingly homogeneous ideological construct is the primacy endorsed by the Enterprise Culture of the paradigmatic status of both 'the commercial enterprise' and the consumer: meeting the demands of the 'sovereign consumer' becomes the new institutional imperative. Both forms are an anathema to the City for different reasons as is the cultural self-ethic which the State seeks to implement in social life: the 'enterprising' qualities of the individual where

[O]ne finds a rather loosely related set of characteristics such as initiative, energy, independence, boldness, self-responsibility for one's own actions, and so on. Correspondingly, an enterprise 'culture' in this second sense is one in which the acquisition and exercise of these qualities is both highly valued and extensively practised.

(Keat 1991: 3)

145

These qualities are inherent in the cultural construction of the City community but to institute them as a universal norm of social action entails the removal of dependency in key areas, for example the provision of state-supplied goods such as pensions and health care and their replacement by financial services marketed for the general public. Individuals become non-dependent and 'responsible' for these matters, as consumers. The sphere of consumption becomes an important nursery for the enterprising self. The problem for the City in this regard is that previously it had been the State and the City which had undertaken the roles of the providers of these financial services to the dependent sectors, through either the sale of gilts for the public sector borrowing requirement, or private sector insurance provision that mimicked the caring image of the welfare state. The consumer was now being encouraged to participate in the attainment of these services and to question and challenge the standard of provision.

To compound the situation there was rapid growth in the financial markets due to State encouragement through initiatives in areas such as share privatisation issues and global financial developments facilitated by technology ('follow-the-sun' trading). The amount of work generated precipitated the need for new players in the City, bringing with them, or adapting to, the principles of conduct advocated by the State and abiding in their actions not by the internalised norms and codes of the City itself. As Keat notes:

> [E]nterprising individuals are self-reliant and non-dependent. They make their own decisions, rather than wanting or expecting others to make these for them; and they take responsibility for their own lives, so that when things go wrong they do not assume there is always someone else to blame, or whose job it is to put things right.
>
> (Keat 1991: 5)

These individuals are goal-orientated in terms of their own personal ends. Their activities are directed toward the advancement of these goals and they are motivated to acquire whatever skills and resources are necessary to fulfil their aims effectively. Such an attitude limits the effect of a 'community' created set of norms and values in that individual conduct is assessed upon self-generated criteria of success. A subcultural construction of codifed action will therefore only be obeyed to the extent that it contributes to the facilitation of individual goals and will be transgressed if it presents an obstacle to individual advancement.

Hodgson has noted that what has occurred in British society in recent years is the ascendency of the Disestablishment and the demise of the influence of the Establishment (Hodgson 1990). The Establishment were those possessors of power and influence (including the Rules of the City) who shared values and used informal personal links to promote or defend those values. The Establishment cannot be understood as a distinct class but as an interlocking power network (constellation of interest) operating between the State, the Church, the universities, the City and industry (Scott 1985). The Disestablishment are those who consider themselves as 'outsiders' in the sense of being 'efficient, populist, materialistic, (and) rule breaking' and enterprising to the extent that 'they' are pro-business in advocating a belief in money as a positive moral force. Applying Pareto's notion of the circulation of élites, the Disestablishment is as much an élite as the Establishment. This reinforces the idea of conflict between cultural forms struggling for hegemonic power. The rule-breaking, transgressionary Disestablishment is in the ascendency because its actions are legitimated by the State through the imposition of Enterprising values which are the values of transgression. The State itself has as its principal officers Disestablishment members and sympathisers.

In the City the period 1984–89 was an era of crazy financial expansion in which a spirit of rule-breaking transgressionary behaviour was set free, encouraged by the State as part of a policy of collapsing the authority of a competing cultural regime. The City was not to acquiesce without engaging in a conflict which threatened to diminish the effect of its own partially articulated ethical norms in the face of the imposition of an ethically moribund regime of significance. The rise of fraudulent market activity begs the question of the survival of any form of regulatory code of social action founded on a collective metaphor of norm-based behaviour whose economic rationale goes beyond mere self-gratification.

City Culture

The City's not mine any more so let it fall.

(Churchill 1987: 30)

Perhaps Churchill's *Serious Money* was so popular because it had as its subject the commodity of money which in the 1980s became a valid possession and tool of wealth in its own right. 'The creation of wealth is not some unpleasant habit to which we have set our hand when we have nothing morally superior to engage our interests. It is the foundation of our civilisation' (Brian Walden quoted by Rushbridger 1990). *Serious Money* was one of a number of representations which set up a mirror to reality in portraying an era and an arena which had caught popular imagination. And the popular imagination is often caught by the mysterious and the unknown or only vaguely perceived. Certainly, this could be said of any common understanding as to the City of London and its money markets, but the public had been encouraged to take notice of the game and many had a small stake through privatisation issues. In part the structural changes wrought upon the City were a response to the creation of a shareholder democracy which the State encouraged and had to appear to be protecting.

The attraction of *Serious Money* was that it was a drama about the enclosed world of the trading floor, which is itself only a part of a international network of transactions, concerning deals encompassing figures beyond mere mortal imagining and populated by a meritocratic selection of dynamic characters representing all the material desires and aspirations of an international community: 'These are the best years of our lives, with information from inside' (Churchill 1987: 111). Churchill's portrait was far removed from the staid picture of the City of London as the bastion of severe bowler-hatted suburban Lloyds brokers, jobbers and bankers. But suddenly the City of London, with its overtones of the righteous spirit of trust, confidence and commercial municipality where 'a gentleman's word was his bond', became simply the City where 'my word is my junk bond' (Churchill 1987: 105).

Something had happened. In this section a number of diverse elements will be presented, forming the basis of a construction to attempt to answer the question: What is the City? These diverse elements are part of a map of codes which constitute the Culture of the City. It is a subculture to the extent that it is alienated from dominant cultural norms, but it is also a significant instigator of power relations through economic control. However, as with other subcultures, it presents a challenge to dominant hegemonic forms because it possesses a contained *style* which is a refusal to conform.

Serious Money is a play in verse. The City is a game with players. The verse of *Serious Money* represents the language of the City as an internalised discourse serving through its own regime of signification to validate itself through its very alienation. Only those players who know the script will be able to play. The language of the City is much like poetry in that it is a discourse of metre and rhythm, imagery and metaphors, its own pulse and beat. It is a language spoken through machine, be it telephone or computer, a technological language which is metaphysical to the extent that its theme is money. It is a language of allusion and illusion, self-referential because it is almost always shouted. For example: the use of animal metaphors (bulls, bears, stags), of sexual metaphors (Big Bang, Big Swinging Dick), of suicide metaphors (poison pills, golden parachutes); the reliance on acronyms: LIFFE, SIB, DTI, MBO. It is a language which is a construct of another language but reconstituted so that it has to be learnt. And in it is a language which is ever evolving on a global scale, a language available only to those having access or the ability to hack into the maze.

And within this protected maze is the actuality of the purpose of the City: Money. As Rothman puts it, 'Financial capitalism is distinguished by the buying and selling not merely of goods, labour, and services but of money' (Rothman 1987: 87). Money has the capacity to act as a medium of exchange for itself, and is itself the basis for what it signifies. Through options, swaps and futures money is traded for money. Less than 5 per cent of the billions traded on the currency markets every day mirrors an equivalent transaction in goods and services: 'The significance of this is that the conventional vector of cause and necessity which points from trade to finance, from things to money, has been reversed' (Rothman 1987: 95). And the things which are themselves traded as commodities are transactions on a futures basis, so that what is being traded in fact does not exist (the metaphysics of commodities): the ownership of the image and the ultimate fetishisation of the object. It is an arena of hyper/panic money in which 'Money is caught in the grand cancellation of the sign of political economy. It finds itself homeless and constantly put to flight. It is abandoning the "worthless" world of contemporary capitalism' (Kroker and Cook 1988: iv). With the cancellation of the referent money circulates faster and more violently to maintain itself as the universal clinamen and its value appears only 'at the vanishing-point of its afterimage. It is no longer one's filthy lucre, only that of the sanitized electronic display of the computer monitor' (Kroker and Cook 1988: iv).

Production and its attendant international rentier circuits is replaced by a new, technologically driven system of economic reproduction. It is as if, as Baudrillard has articulated, money has become part of the universal system of simulacra in which money as a symbol reflecting value in the real world is transformed into an image that ultimately masks and perverts this reality and marks the eventual absence of this reality: its own pure simulacrum (Baudrillard 1983: 11). Or, as Marx puts it, 'everything solid melts into air, everything sacred is profaned'. This statement points to the unreality that possessed the financial markets in the period under review and also to the fact that this process was mirrored by a transgression of codes.

Such a representation of City activity came to fruition in the years 1984–89 in which the world's financial markets underwent massive expansion due to the implementation of policies of economic liberalism in the UK and the US. In the longer term these years will appear as a coke-blip in the markets – self-generated but externally legitimated. On a superficial level of analysis the credo of 'Greed is Good' achieved universal acceptance as the dominant market ethic. However, although style is the primary indicator of the subculture, the refusal to conform, it should not be overly emphasised. The style of the City has undergone a period of transformation and there has been an internalised conflict, for example with the introduction of many new players and new forms of transactions and financial products. Cultural critics might centralise their discussion of the City by emphasising a new rapprochement between City and State in which ideologies have been transposed upon one another so that there is no conflict. But there still exist other subculture codes which form the basis for norms of action and the maintenance of conflict. These subcultural codes of the City had been developed over a significant period and were suddenly put under threat through the external imposition of new codes legitimating previously perceived uneconomic transgressor activity.

The analogy of the Club has often been employed to describe the operation of the City. Previously it had relied upon light self-regulation with occasional intervention from the external legitimating bodies of the State to enhance the effect of prohibition. If external intervention did take place it was at the request of the City itself. The Club atmosphere of the City, reinforced by its traditions, institutions, self-interest and by the essentially homogeneous character of its members, proved a fertile ground for self-regulation to develop and attain a degree of respect. It was a Club whose code of conduct was a practitioner-based system of regulation which used non-legal methods to discipline and gain compliance with ethical trading practice. As Veljanovski has put it:

> The effectiveness of this club-type arrangement rested on the membership of the financial world being fairly exclusive. One cannot discipline people if they do not share the values of the club and are free to decide whether to join or not.
>
> (Veljanovski 1988: 3)

In the senior levels of the various institutions and professional firms there was a degree of homogeneity which ensured common values and reinforced the informal 'codes' within which this community operated. 'The class system, with its institutions of social control, invariably subtle and exclusionary in their orientation, functioned with a predictability and efficiency which probably surpassed any practical system of legal regulation' (Rider, Chaikin and Abrams 1987: 11).

A number of the new players have not shared the values of the Club and have wrought economic uncertainty upon the City. The prevalent forms of controlling conduct were moral suasion, raised eyebrows, the stern rebuff over drinks and the prospect of the cold shoulder. Market discipline was maintained through informal means. The City's protectionism is based upon the idea that a self-imposed control mechanism provides a justification for an organisation's continued autonomy, and this is recognised as an inherent element for the maintenance of economic stability. Therefore the maintenance of this self-generated code of conduct, no matter how questionable, is important for the validity of the independence and freedom of the City from external intervention. What occurred in the period under review was the symbolic imposition of a competitive regulatory regime which sought to disrupt the internalised practices of the City.

A US INTERLUDE: MEANWHILE ON WALL STREET

I'm not talking greed.
I'm talking how I mean to succeed.
(My father came to this country – forget it.)
(Churchill 1987: 25)

There can be no doubt that much of the dynamism for the growth in the world's financial markets in the 1980s was generated from Wall Street. Investment houses such as Drexel Burnham Lambert and Salomon Brothers seized the time and were instrumental in the development of new products such as junk and mortgage bonds and new devices for intercorporate activity such as the leverage/management buyout and greenmailing. As in the UK under Thatcher, Reagan encouraged market activity so as to re-state America's place in the world economy. Undoubtedly, then, Wall Street underwent a period of hyper/panic financial (money) activity. But there are perceptible cultural differences between Wall Street and the City. With the advent of a new administration in the US it has been possible to catalogue the disasters which resulted from the lax management of the Reagan era. This has been underlined by the ill-concealed delight with which the old-money, Ivy League administration of Bush has allowed the collapse of Drexel Burnham Lambert, the corporate symbol of 1980s success.

Whereas the City is primarily the representative of the institutional investors (pension funds, unit trusts, investment houses) despite the encouragement of a shareholder democracy, in the US there is still a useful class of assertive owners (shareholders) such as T. Boone Pickens and H. Ross Perot who own the majority of US equity. Their power as active market players/makers (noticeably in the takeover wars of the period) is balanced by the US institutional investors which are growing in importance. These financial institutions are the spawning ground of non-owning, performance-tested managers with different motives for corporate action from the individual assertive owner. The rise of the institutions in the US, despite the continued presence of important individuals, leads inevitably to corporatism, as the State and business bureaucracies work together. The irony is that the private pension schemes which the Conservative administration in the UK backed to encourage self-reliance are actually incubators for the corporate state (Harris 1990).

152

It is only now being realised that the boom years of the 1980s in the financial markets of the United States have resulted in deleterious effects, for example the collapse of Drexel Burnham Lambert and the takeover of Shearson Lehman. Individuals have fallen in their attempts to validate the ethic of 'Greed is Good', notably its instigator Ivan Boesky and the creator of the junk bond market, Michael Milken. That the flaws involved in certain market practices have been allowed to appear is illustrative of differences in the relational structure prevailing between Wall Street and the White House as opposed to those between the City and Downing Street.

It has been suggested that during the period under examination the subcultural ethos of the City was forced to enter into conflict with the imposition of an externally State-generated Enterprise Culture ethos which sought to undermine the dominant position of the City as a central part of the economic discourse. This scenario has not been replicated in the relationship between Wall Street and the State over the same period. Undoubtedly, there was a period on Wall Street of insane avarice and ruthless immorality but the instigators of these trends, be they the finance houses or individuals, have been penalised. A significant reason for the exposure of the problems inherent in the pursuit of corporate greed is the institutional relationship between Wall Street and the State. Even taking account of Reagan's blessing on the attack upon the frontiers of financial prudence through the challenge to the stagnant mega-corporations in the form of corporate raider activity resulting in mega-merger mayhem and takeover wars, the equilibrium existing between American political culture and financial culture remained intact.

The traditional regulatory policy of the US government was to enable regulating institutions to have significant interventionist powers. The official policy of a particular administration may not have encouraged intervention in the financial markets, but the machinery of regulation which had been created after the 1929 Crash was invested with enormous scope through the Securities Exchange Act 1934, and later the Organized Crime Control Act 1970, to control financial activity unencumbered by any allegiance to an individual administration.

The Securities Exchange Commission (SEC) is a well-funded institution and has established chains of communication with the FBI, the Federal Reserve, *and the business community*. Depending on the evidence it can bring either a civil case where it can ban a violator from the securities industry and freeze assets, or pass the case to the office of the Attorney-General for criminal prosecution (see Levi 1987). In addition, the presence of gun-toting marshalls making arrests on the trading floor and the recent introduction of legislation providing for bounty hunters in search of a reward, coupled with the prospect of 'triple damages', has established the regulatory forces on Wall Street as a *tangible presence* as opposed to the *ad hoc* fragmentary approach adopted in the UK.

The climate of the US regulatory regime can be illustrated by the case of Michael Milken. Milken was employed by Drexel Burnham Lambert in the 1970s, at that time a relatively insignificant investment house on Wall Street but with pretensions to join the élite ranks of Morgan Stanley, First Boston and Salomon Brothers. Milken was at the forefront of the Drexel corporate strategy to achieve this recognition and his primary initiative was to exploit the, as then, neglected bond market as opposed to the established equities. He struck at the right time as the equity market slumped and investors were searching for alternative sources for the placement of their capital. As part of his initiative he created the junk bond (a high-yield, high-risk bond secured against the undervalued assets of a target company in a leverage buyout scenario). Junk bonds became a popular source of finance for corporate raiders in the 1980s and secured Drexel virtual dominance in what culminated in a $180 billion dollar market. Subsequently, the problems involved in highly leveraged takeovers were revealed (for example the collapse of the Campeau empire). But where Milken went beyond accepted market practice was in his tactics to secure business. He is alleged to have manipulated, bullied and deceived companies in addition to basing many of his decisions upon inside information. It is spurious to draw lines between sound business sense and sharp practice, but what is significant is the assumption that can be drawn in that the WASP-dominated chief executives on Wall Street did not want Milken in their midst. He posed a threat because he challenged the existing norms of acceptable market practice (advanced by him on grounds of restructuring corporate America) and entered into activities which were classified as deviant behaviour. The point is not that he did anything wrong in a business sense (although the flaws in his creation have been detected through collapse in confidence) but the way in which he achieved his objectives: in the manner of an Enterprising Individual. He was prepared to challenge the status quo. It was the WASP fraternity on Wall Street that instigated the State machinery which saw to his downfall. Milken has alleged a conspiracy between the State and Wall Street to have him removed from the field of play.[1] Michael Milken was subsequently indicted, fined and imprisoned for five years with an additional three years of community service. America's financial and political élite has stopped the transgressor in an effective demonstration of damage limitation, so protecting the delicate status quo of domestic corporatist relations. Meanwhile, in London, the situation has proved to be very different – the status quo is being challenged by the State through the legitimation of transgressing behaviour of Enterprising Individuals.

CITY CRIME AND STATE CRIME

City Crime

Fuck the DTI, Zac. I refuse to be defeated.
I don't care if I go to jail, I'll win whatever the cost.
(Churchill 1987: 98)

Those actions which constitute City Crime can be identified as those involving fraudulent activity. The fraud lies in the false appropriation of property through fraudulent means, and in the City this implies an abuse of position, trust and *confidence*. The abuse could be the use of unpublished, price-sensitive information for personal gain or the disclosure of information which is known to be incorrect to a potential investor. The gain will be of substantial economic benefit and the 'victim' difficult to identify. There can be no doubt that fraudulent activity has always existed in the securities market and this is the reason for the development of regulatory mechanisms, be they self-generated or externally imposed. A capitalist system engenders some degree of fraudulent behaviour because the criterion for the operation of the system is premised upon economic principles concerning profit maximisation and therefore the moral–legal boundaries with regard to social action are determined by a central economic premise. But for the system to work effectively in the sense of the maintenance of confidence in its operation, a degree of apparent or ostensible control has to be exercised. During the period under examination competing regulatory mechanisms and economic principles facilitated in undermining any effective controlling strategy.

The period 1984-89 was one in which fraudulent market practices increased. A survey conducted by accountants Ernst & Young shows that fraud over the period risked sums totalling £4 billion, which is over 100 times the sums dealt with twenty years before (Ernst & Young 1989). This figure does not represent the full degree of fraudulent activity, since it is a recording of detected cases. As Levi has pointed out, there is the 'dark figure of unrecorded fraud' (Levi 1987: 25). In part, the increase in fraudulent activity was endemic of the atmosphere prevailing in the markets over this period which has been identified as one of panic and hyper-financial activity in which rapid change in customary practice gave rise to a sense where the only certainty was that of the instantaneous. The atmosphere was one of greed and an excess of primitive accumulation and overconsumption. The veneer of control was tarnished as a jungle mentality took hold of many players and became the natural inclination of new entrants. The homogeneity which had been the principal control mechanism in the City's regulatory position collapsed. The jungle mentality is reflected in the popularity over this period of a number of classic texts on strategy such as Machiavelli's *The Prince*, Clausewitz's *On War* and the Chinese Military Manual of Sun Tzu.

> A couple of hitherto quiet types with Prussian names were now keeping copies of Clausewitz's *On War* on their desks. Investment bankers usually read *On War* secretly, not because they are embarrassed to be caught with it, but because they don't want to let anyone in on their technique. I recommended Sun Tzu.
>
> (Lewis 1989: 173).

This is echoed in a scene from the film *Wall Street* in which the protagonist Gordon Gekko reflects upon his philosophy for success and recommends as a guide Sun Tzu. The game became not one merely of survival, because there was sufficient work to go around, but how much one could consume. The atmosphere can be classified as an anomie of affluence. This theory was developed by Simon and Gagnon (1976) after Merton (1957). Merton's conceptualisation was formulated in terms of the influence of the economic and social conditions surrounding circumstances of chronic depression. But the anomie potentially generated by

156

unanticipated affluence was the central concern of Durkheim. Simon and Gagnon suggest a typology of deviant adaptation ultilising questions of commitment to approved goals and the degree to which achievement of substantial progress toward such goals is realised.

The use of Durkheimian analysis lies in its concern with the culture for action. One of the determining factors in deviant or transgressory behaviour is the culture in which the individual operates. Anomie is a state of culture conceptualised as normlessness, a condition of moral deregulation where the hold of norms over individual conduct has broken down. In Durkheim's original formulation (1898) he focused on the top of the social stratum as the primary location of anomie, for it was 'power and not poverty that facilitated too easily the personal achievement of socially inculcated cultural ambitions' (Box 1983: 40). Economic success generates a position in which the individual no longer feels constrained by moral and social norms. In a condition of pure individuation, as Box notes, the successful experience the sensation that anything and everything is possible ('everything sacred is profaned'). 'The less limited one feels, the more intolerable all limitation appears' (Durkheim 1898).

A number of points can be made concerning the relevance of anomie analysis to City Crime. First, the institutions of the City are under crimogenic pressures since they necessarily operate within an uncertain and unpredictable environment such that its purely legitimate opportunities for goal achievement are sometimes limited and constrained; therefore they foster transgressive behaviour by individuals. Second, during the period under review, anomie was likely to be engendered because the Enterprise Culture promulgated a commitment to the achievement of individual economic goals as a criterion for success, but the individual still operated within a framework in which the means of legitimately achieving those goals were only differentially available. A commitment to goals was assumed; it was the means of achievement which were problematic. Since the only method within a capitalist system of demonstrating individuality is through economic means it was possible in the City to conform on an individual basis quite easily. What occurred within the period was the legitimation of goals beyond mere conformity and the demonstration of affluence as an extension of individuality. These goals were to be achieved through the articulation of personal as opposed to collective metaphors. The City had traditionally been successful in generating a collective metaphor of the maintenance of confidence as a control strategy, whereas the Enterprise Culture attributed primacy to the personal metaphor of success.

According to Simon and Gagnon environments which engender the ascendency of personal metaphors are those dominated by the existential and accidental presenting a challenge to the individual to test out the most abstract fantasies. Certainly, this was the atmosphere in the City at this time, an atmosphere of overconsumption and immediate gratification. The individual player in the City was encouraged to indulge desire ('persons consuming themselves in an orgy of escalating appetites': Simon and Gagnon 1976: 367). The individual becomes, in a post-Mertonian conception, a conforming deviant in which, having acquired the means of gratification, there is a necessity to explore the dimensions of pleasure in such modes of gratification that 'their quest for new experiences . . . brings them quickly to the margins of deviance' (Simon and Gagnon 1976: 372). And yet the individual will, first, receive gratification from the performance of deviant behaviour and, second, will not feel constrained by the social and legal norms which would punish the less successful. The Enterprise Culture ethos successfully ensured that sanctions could be transgressed.

In relation to the City individual players no longer felt constrained by the subcultural codes of conduct which the Club atmosphere of the prior regime had engendered. The validating collapse of the City's authority as a primarily self-regulating community can be illustrated through an examination of what has become known as the Blue Arrow Affair. The report on County NatWest Ltd and County NatWest Securities Ltd by inspectors appointed by the Department of Trade and Industry under the Companies Act 1986 s.432(2) tells the story of the extent to which individuals were prepared to transgress the rules in relation to share dealings (Blue Arrow 1989). Blue Arrow's £837 million rights issue to finance a bid for Manpower was intended to be the high point for County NatWest and Phillips and Drew, proof that they could play alongside the City's leading dealmakers. The Blue Arrow rights issue was announced in August 1987 as one of the greatest bull markets in the City reached its peak. The issue was a flop – only 38 per cent was taken up. The failure of the placing left the underwriters with a large slice of the issue which was not disclosed to the market, contrary to the requirements of the law. The Blue Arrow share price was rapidly falling as the market crashed.

The report of the DTI Inspectors concluded that:

1 County NatWest should have disclosed its interests in more than 13 per cent of Blue Arrow shares.
2 The market was 'deliberately misled' at several times over the progress of the company's rights issue.
3 The conduct of senior corporate financiers at County NatWest was 'well below that to be expected from responsible executives'.
4 Three NatWest main board directors were criticised for failing to ensure 'the lawful conduct of business' by the bank.

The report was sent to the Serious Fraud Office and charges were brought against eleven people under Section 11 of the Prevention of Frauds (Investment) Act 1958, contrary to Section 1(1) of the Criminal Law Act 1977. The indictment alleges conspiracy to induce investors through the use of fraudulent statements, conspiracy to deliberately withhold information from the Stock Exchange and creation of a false market.

A number of the statements given in evidence and the inspectors' own comments point to the general atmosphere of contempt for the rules of the market prevailing at County NatWest and Phillips and Drew.[2] The report by the DTI was a serious indictment of the management of the National Westminster Bank and its investment banking subsidiary. It served to undermine the view that commercial banks could successfully merge with securities firms to create great financial institutions competing on a global scale. It also served to suggest that market makers were primarily concerned with the spirit of the law rather than the letter. The report pointed to the misleading of the market *as a matter of routine* and if the market had not crashed then the story would never have been told. The inspectors were told that it was common practice to ignore Stock Exchange rules and that at all times the principals were concerned only with the form rather than the substance of the rules with regard to disclosure of share holdings. The people to whom they were ultimately accountable – the main board of National Westminster Bank – did not have sufficient grasp of the business to supervise adequately. At a vital moment 'none of the three executive directors had sufficient experience to examine critically what they were being told . . . having raised one or two obvious points and having received some comfort in relation thereto, they accepted the position'.

This final point illustrates the divide which had been created over the period between trading floor and board level. The spiralling activity within the markets created an atmosphere of 'anything goes' and a situation in which the traditional ultra blue-chip major players no longer dictated the pace of change. Those on the trading floor at County NatWest wanted to increase their market share of action, just as Drexel Burnham had done in the US, and were prepared blatantly to disregard the rules in the process *as if the rules no longer applied.* At boardroom level the chief executives of the National Westminster Bank simply did not comprehend the nature of the game that their subordinate subsidiaries were playing. There was a clash of organisational cultures within one unified organisation. As one financial journalist put it:

> To give clearing bank executives responsibility for an investment bank dealing in securities and corporate finance advice is like putting paycorps officers in charge of an SAS unit. Financial controls at head office are not much help when your hardened troops are out fighting in the streets for rewards that it would take half a lifetime for a bank manager to earn in a high street branch.
>
> (Rodgers 1990)

The Old Guard were out of touch with the game and the Young Turks who had entered the City on the tide of optimism considered themselves unbound by traditional practices: the flare and greed that characterised the modern investment bank was the opposite of the qualities of a traditional clearing house. The Club rules no longer applied. The worrying aspect in this scenario is what happened to the protagonists in the Blue Arrow Affair. The eleven individuals on the indictment were either appointed to similar positions at other institutions or retained their positions in the two institutions concerned (*Observer*, 23 July 1989).

The final aspect of the Blue Arrow Affair is the role of the regulatory organisations which had been empowered by the Financial Services Act 1986 (FSA) to detect fraud and monitor the behaviour of licensed financial institutions. In the Blue Arrow Affair it was the Securities Association, the Securities Investment Board, the Serious Fraud Office and the Bank of England who should have been aware of the situation. As had happened in the Barlow Clowes affair (see Barlow Clowes 1989), the frauds which were perpetrated by those market makers involved in the Blue Arrow rights issue were undetected. The regulatory procedures of the Financial Services Act 1986 were in place but were ineffective.

The successful prosecution of the defendants in the trial arising out of the Guinness takeover for Distillers would seem to point to a shift to more effective regulation. But it must be remembered that the defendants in the first Guinness prosecution included three executives of the companies involved in structuring the bid and not the trading floor troops (a second trial involving the market makers is to be held in 1991). Although individual gain was a motive, there was also the issue of direct corporate control: there is no evidence to suggest that any of the defendants would have become involved except in the context of seeking to fulfil their duties as directors towards the shareholders. The actual loss in the perpetration of the crime is hard to define. The principal losers were the Argyll shareholders who suffered an opportunity cost. Distillers' shareholders were better off being bought by Guinness rather than Argyll. Thus the issue is one of economic benefit and corporate responsibility versus morality. Although some commentators treated the case as confirming the effectiveness of regulation, I would suggest that the case demonstrates the continuing independence of the judiciary and the jury system (despite the nominal sentences) as opposed to the strengths of the regulatory system. A number of actions within the case could be justified as legitimate economic action, as actions applauded by the State. But the Guinness Four were publicly caught and so were sacrificed.

In the concluding section of this essay the role of the State in the activities of the City will be examined and issues of duplicity, symbolism and legitimation of economic anomie raised.

State Crime

In the quickprofit shortterm direction.
We wouldn't interfere in a free market.
But we are of course approaching an election.
(Churchill 1987: 102)

Returning to the conflict between circulating élites, in this case the Establishment and the Disestablishment, it is possible to suggest that the ascendancy of the Disestablished desired to assert the primacy of its social codes of action (values) over those of the until then entrenched Establishment. This meant eroding the supremacy of the City in a key area of public life, namely the control of the economy. The mechanisms for the erosion of the role of the City as a competing subculture can be classified as follows. The first two of these mechanisms will be dealt with below, and the final one by way of conclusion.

1 The ostensible imposition of authority upon the City for the benefit of investors through a redefined regulatory framework.
2 Symbolism and duplicity in the enforcement of sanctions against transgressors.
3 The validation (legitimation) of a state of an anomic affluence.

Ostensible authority

The imposition of a new regulatory structure to supersede the previous *ad hoc* approach of self-regulatory rapprochement between State and City was the cornerstone in the State's attempt to limit the influence of the City. The Financial Services Act 1986 (FSA) was a symbolic gesture both in its apparent effect of offering to protect the 'innocent investor' who was being encouraged to participate in the operations of the City through privatisation issues and in its introduction of an impressive array of regulatory machinery, which in fact has had little effect in achieving this aim.

The history of the introduction of the new regulatory policy is illuminating since it illustrates the divisions between State and City. The movement toward electronic trading allowed the government to remove restrictive practices in relation to share trading commissions. The rapidity of change and the expansion of financial services within the City inevitably led to the failure of several financial institutions, including Norton Warburg and Johnson Matthey. The State was obliged to consider a new regulatory framework and appointed Gower to undertake a review of investor protection (Gower 1982).

The Gower Report suggested a detailed set of investor protection laws. He stated that

[L]ogic and tidiness . . . are of importance only in so far as they contribute to a legal regime which can be understood, which will be regarded as fair by those it affects and which, as a result will be generally observed and can be effectively enforced.

(Gower 1982)

As a result of his initial findings, which were criticised for not being founded upon rational economic grounds (Veljanovski 1988: 7–12), Gower suggested a basic principle of a comprehensive system of regulation within a statutory framework based on self-regulation subject to government surveillance, adding a rider that:

If self-regulation is to survive, the surveillance to which it is subject must be sufficient to provide a genuine curb on undesirable restrictive practices and sufficient spur to ensure that rules are kept under review and their observance efficiently monitored.

(Gower 1982)

The government departed from Gower's prevailing philosophy in its introduction of the FSA regime. While accepting the need to improve laws relating to investor protection, the White Paper emphasised the dangers of excessive regulation: regulation should be no more than the minimum necessary to protect the investor. In the age of enterprise, where individuals are responsible for their own actions, the individual has to be aware of an element of risk inherent in participating in the games of the securities markets.

The Financial Services Act 1986 was a symbolic gesture toward investor protection. The rhetoric of the provision lay in its ostensible objectives:

1 The promotion of efficiency and competition.
2 The inspiration of confidence in issuers and investors in the honest operation of the financial markets.
3 To ensure that the regulatory framework is flexible so as to facilitate future structural changes.

(Rider, Chaikin, Abrams 1987: 18)

The mechanisms for the achievement of these objectives were the principles of supervision, compliance, disclosure and accountability. The primary arbiter for the imposition of these principles was to be the hybrid Securities and Investment Board (SIB) charged with the drafting of rules subject to the remit of the FSA and monitoring the activities of the self-regulatory organisations (SROs) which are subject to the FSA. As Page has noted: 'to provide for a statutory power of authorisation and regulation to be given to a private sector body is unprecedented' (Page 1987).The SIB resides at the top of a regulatory pyramid. It has regulatory and enforcement powers but, unlike its US counterpart, the SEC, it is financed entirely by the City but is accountable not to the City but to the DTI. Beneath the SIB come the self-regulatory organisations (SROs) such as FIMBRA and LAUTRO, whose recognition is achieved through the implementation of rule books giving investors 'equivalent protection' to the rules developed by the SIB (Veljanovski 1988: 5). But the position of the SIB and SROs is also buttressed through the other bodies such as the Office of Fair Trading, the Monopolies and Merger Commission, the Takeover Panel, the Bank of England and ultimately the DTI. It is an impressive array of regulatory machinery.

However, the economic principles underlying the introduction of the FSA regime require analysis so as to illustrate the deliberate paucity in response of the State toward investor protection beyond mere symbolism. Previously the self-regulatory system of the City had attained its objectives relatively successfully through informal codes and reliance upon occasional State intervention through such devices as the Prevention of Frauds (Investment) Act 1958. Although a significant need for change was precipitated by developments within the international financial system, the FSA was introduced as a gesture toward enhancing new investor confidence by the apparent imposition of an externally generated set of legal principles for market practice.

One interpretation based on the experience of the US suggests that, given the costs, efficient markets afford investors adequate protection. And an efficient market is simply one in which all available information is reflected in the share price; therefore the primary regulatory mechanism which is desired is an enforceable definition of 'fraud on the market' (Stigler 1964). This has been provided for by the discretion of the SEC and the judiciary in individual cases. Further rules do not improve the quality of the provision of information and place costs of regulation upon the industry (and therefore the investor); also there is no account for regulatory institutional failure.

Another interpretation, paradoxically also adopting the US approach, would be the development of a regulatory agency such as the SEC which is armed with a formidable array of regulatory powers, developed as part of a process of negotiation with Wall

Street, financed by the State and enjoying business support. But, most significantly, the SEC has as its simple purpose the imposition of sanctions relating to fraud on the market.

In the UK the State arranged for a complex combination of legal and quasi-legal regulations and agencies to be implemented. Since its inception in 1986 the very complexity of the prevailing regime has illustrated its fundamental weakness: the costs of the regime are borne by the City but the authority for the regime rests with the State. The regime has served to limit the autonomy of the City in making it ostensibly accountable to society and collapsing its prior authority as a self-regulating community. But the economic philosophy of the State has been one of non-intervention in the markets, which it has achieved through the creation of an amorphous regulatory structure with only symbolic power (inadequately funded and subject to the overriding authority of the DTI). The 'innocent investor', who is really the Enterprising Individual, has been left to take the consequences of Blue Arrow, Barlow Clowes, Johnson Matthey, Eagle Trust, BCCI. . .

Symbolism and duplicity

The ideological motives behind the imposition of the new regulatory framework have been intimated. A free market position as advocated by the State since 1979 required minimal intervention into the activities of that market. However, in the adoption of a strategy of popular capitalism and shareholder democracy through privatisation, the State had to appear to be reacting to the alleged possibility that the traditional networks of control within the financial markets were inadequate with regard to the protection of the new investors. At an even more devious level of realpolitik the State had also to dispossess the internalised authority of the City as a competing validating mechanism for legitimation of social action through subcultural codes of practice. The FSA was an externally imposed control mechanism which served as a gesture toward the maintenance of investor confidence, not in the City but in the State.

In the event the FSA has served the purpose of a cumbersome sop to enable the State to feign intervention. But it has been at an economic cost, indicating a dichotomy between political ideology and economic principles. Without assuming that the prior *ad hoc* regulatory regime of the City was a preferable alternative, it can be suggested that the State has served to disrupt all forms of financial regulation through a fragmentary structure which leaves a regulatory void of uncertainty and erosion of confidence. The subcultural codes of the City were a recognition that some degree of regulation of market practice was desirable on the economic grounds of the maintenance of investor confidence. The credo of 'Greed is Good' validated by the 'Enterprise Initiative' policies of the State may be adjudged to have had short-term economic benefits, for example in the liberation of undervalued assets by corporate raiders against the stagnant mega-corporations such as the Hoylake bid for BAT and the Guinness bid for Distillers. In the long term (as witnessed in the US) the financial markets cannot sustain such unprecedented/uncontrolled financial activity without incurring deleterious economic effects.

The *appearance* of action by the State illustrates the successful articulation of duplicity and symbolism in the achievement of aims in this area of social activity. There is the obvious example of duplicity in the introduction of a regulatory structure which ultimately is accountable to the State through the DTI. The policy of the DTI under Parkinson, Young and Ridley has been overtly non-interventionist (for example, in the House of Fraser affair and the Hoylake bid for BAT). Therefore, guidelines for the interpretation of the enforcement of rules under the FSA policy on securities regulation have not been determined. The procedures exist but transgressors are not pursued: it is for the regulatory bodies to do this but with the burden of a complex array of possibilities, inadequate financing, overlapping jurisdictions, the lack of any formally established lines of communication and resort to a final arbiter who is loath to take action on ideological grounds. Two further examples illustrate this duplicity:

- The statement by Cecil Parkinson (then Secretary of State at the DTI) in the House of Commons when introducing the Companies Securities (Insider Dealing) Act 1985, which sought to make illegal dealing based upon the use of unpublished price-sensitive information, that the legislation would protect those innocent investors who would otherwise be 'at the mercy of the unscrupulous'. It has been alleged that at the time of his speech, the first major investigation by his department into insider dealing probed the affairs of Parkinson's own broker, Walter Walker, who was involved in an asset stripping–share

166

dealing ring involving Parkison's own portfolio (Plender 1989; 'At the Mercy of the Unscrupulous', Channel 4 Television, November 1989).

- Also in relation to insider dealing was the evidence given by Nicholas Ridley (then Secretary of State at the DTI) to the House of Commons Select Committee on Trade and Industry, when he said that he did not consider insider dealing endemic in the City and that the 10 convictions out of 19 cases was a good record in the five years since the legislation was introduced. At the same time the SIB released figures that it was investigating 15 cases of insider dealing a day (Waters 1990).

These examples of duplicity serve to illustrate an underlining symbolic imposition of authority and ostensible action. The primary symbolic gesture is the appearance of a legitimating code but a denial of its actual operation (enforcement). Legal relations (norms) are created, but in their creation are automatically silenced. On one level of analysis this is representative of a conspiracy between interests groups with shared motives (Box 1983). But with regard to the State and the City, concerning the regulation of financial services, the symbolism serves to legitimate the redefinition of competing ideological and cultural norms. The emplacement of the Enterprise Culture could only be achieved if Enterprising Individuals were allowed to achieve their personally defined goals, and this meant the legitimation of previously transgressive behaviour. The State enabled individual goals to be established and executed through the removal of competing norms of action (such as the subcultural codes of practice of the City) and the creation of new referents of behaviour. But the limits of self-legitimated action, even within a state of anomie, had to *appear* to be determined through a compromise between Enterprising Individual and Enterprise State. Thus there was a requirement for a symbolic legitimating framework and the apparent enforcement of legal relations through the token sacrifice of arbitrarily selected, conforming deviants.

Returning to the Blue Arrow Affair, a number of the protagonists under indictment have secured employment elsewhere within the City. It would seem that testing the limits of deviant behaviour, even if 'caught', has its own rewards and it will be intriguing to witness the gradual structural changes in organisational culture as the Young Turks of the 1980s enter the boardrooms of the investment houses in the 1990s, taking with them the legitimated jungle warfare tactics of the Enterprise Culture.

CONCLUSION: LEGITIMATION OF ANOMIE OF AFFLUENCE

Naturally there's a whole lot of greed and
That's no problem because money buys freedom.

(Churchill, 1987: 109)

The City has undergone significant structural change in recent years. In part, this process of transition began in 1974 post-oil crash and then as a result of global growth after a series of recessions. But it was in the 1980s that the character of the City underwent transformation, partly due to international competitive pressures but also because of the disruption of the status quo in the relationship between State and City. This essay has attempted to unravel some of the complexities of these structural changes and their consequences for the future of the securities industry in the UK. The imposition of a new cultural series of norms (the Enterprise Culture) within society has perhaps removed some of the mystique from the operations of the City. Certainly, the City is now meritocratic to the extent that any Enterprising Individual can play. But the economic rationale of the State in relation to the displacement of the influential subcultural codes of the City is crudely formulated. A postmodern spirit of free action without constraints of prior normative behaviour will engender uncertainty, a decline in the confidence which is the linchpin for successful market operation, and the achievement of short-term individual gratification through transgressing behaviour which is validated by the ideological authority of the State. The hegemonic cultural conflict between State and City appears to have been won.

NOTES

I am grateful to Lynne Williams who has commented upon and supported my research throughout.

1 The *International Herald Tribune* concluded that the conviction marked the passing of an era. No longer was the Master of the Universe able to create companies, move markets, guide the republic and move the world into a brighter entrepreneurial future. The real

Masters of the Universe, the ones portrayed in Tom Wolfe's *Bonfire of the Vanities*, saw to it that Milken, who flew too close to the sun, got his wings badly burned, just as corporate America is now suffering the after-effects of being badly burned by Milken.

2 See paragraph 4.26:

> We regard Mr Wells' attitude toward compliance with Class II requirements of the Stock Exchange as irresponsible, Mr Stainforth took no steps to discourage Mr Wells. The willingness of Messrs Fraser and Alcock to be parties to a misleading of the Stock Exchange enabled Mr Wells to succeed in his objectives.

and paragraph 8.29:

> We can find no justification for the way the market was misled . . . Those involved in making those decisions must have appreciated that the market was going to be misled.

REFERENCES

Althusser, L. (1969) *For Marx*, London: Allen Lane.

Barlow Clowes (1989) *Parliamentary Commissioner for Administration: The Barlow Clowes Affair*. First Report – Session 1989–90, London: HMSO.

Barthes, R. (1977) *Image–Music–Text*, London: Fontana.

Baudrillard, J. (1983) *Simulations*, New York: Semiotext(e) Foreign Accent.

Blue Arrow (1989) *Inspectors Report On County NatWest Limited and County NatWest Securities Ltd*, London: HMSO.

Box, S. (1983) *Power, Crime and Mystification*, London: Tavistock.

Churchill, C. (1987) *Serious Money*, London: Methuen.

Cooke, P. (1988) 'Modernity, postmodernity and the city', *Theory, Culture & Society* 5 (2–3): 475–93.

Durkheim, E. (1898/1951) *Suicide*, New York: Free Press.

Ernst & Young (1989) *Fraud 89*, London: Ernst & Young.

Gamble, A. (1989) 'Privatization, Thatcherism and the British State', in A. Gamble and C. Wells (eds) *Thatcher's Law*, Cardiff: GPC Books.

Gower, L.C.B. (1982) *Review of Investor Protection – A Discussion Document*, London: HMSO.

Harris, A., (1990) 'An early warning from Dr Doom', *The Financial Times*, 6 March 1990.

Hebdige, D. (1979) *Subculture: The Meaning Of Style*, London: Methuen.

Hodgson, G. (1990) 'Hatred and the Establishment', *The Independent*, 28 February 1990.

Keat, R. (1991) 'Starship Britain or Universal Enterprise?', in R. Keat and N. Abercrombie (eds) *The Enterprise Culture*, London: Routledge.

Kroker, A. and Cook, D. (1988) *The Postmodern Scene: Excremental Culture and Hyper Aesthetics*, London: Macmillan

Levi, M. (1987) *Regulating Fraud: White-Collar Crime and the Criminal Process*, London: Tavistock.

Lewis, M. (1989) *Liar's Poker*, London: Hodder and Stoughton.

Merton, R.K. (1957) *Social Theory and Social Structure* (2nd ed.), New York: Free Press.

Page, A.C. (1987) 'Financial services: the self-regulatory alternative?', in R. Baldwin and C. McCrudden (eds), *Regulation and Public Law*, London: Weidenfeld and Nicholson.

Plender, J. (1989) 'The rules on ministers' investments', *The Financial Times*, 25 November 1989.

Rider, B., Chaikin, D. and Abrams, C. (1987) *Guide to the Financial Services Act 1986*, London: CCH.

Rodgers, P. (1989) 'NatWest: why send in the paycorps to run the SAS?', *The Guardian*, 26 July 1989.

Rothman, B. (1987) *Signifying Nothing: The Semiotics of Zero*, London: Macmillan.

Rushbridger, A. (1990) 'Gentlemen and players', *The Guardian*, 1 February 1990.

Scott, J. (1985) *Corporations, Classes and Capitalism*, London: Hutchinson.

Simon, W. and Gagnon, J. (1976) 'The anomie of affluence: a post-mertonian conception', *American Journal of Sociology* 82: 356–78.

Stigler, G.J. (1964) 'Public regulation of the securities market', *Journal of Business* (37): 117–42.

Veljanovski, C. (1988) 'Introduction', in A. Seldon (ed.) *Financial Regulation – Or Over Regulation?*, London, Institute of Economic Affairs.

Waters, R. (1990) 'Ridley defends DTI record on insider deals', *The Guardian*, 7 February 1990.

7

OLD CITY AND NEW TIMES

Economic and political aspects of deregulation

Bob Jessop and Rob Stones

This chapter examines the relatively distinct economic and political logics behind government attempts since 1979 to make the City more flexible.[1] We will describe the neo-liberal accumulation strategy intended to save Britain from economic decline and the 'two nations' popular capitalist political strategy which is meant to save us all from creeping socialism. Although we believe that there is a strong strategic element to Thatcherite politics and policies and that the best way to make sense of Thatcherism is to explore its strategic dimensions, we do not claim that there is one single, overriding strategy: the strategic line is emergent and tendential, subject to change or reversal in the light of new circumstances, and even includes important *ad hoc* elements as well as broader, long-term objectives (cf. Jessop *et al.* 1989; Stones 1990). Thus we will argue that, although they have both been clearly discernible as key elements in the emerging strategic line of Thatcherism from 1979 onwards, the purpose, weight and vehicles of neo-liberal and popular capitalist objectives have changed several times. We will also argue that, in certain crucial respects, these twin strategies are internally inconsistent, individually self-defeating and mutually contradictory. In particular we will suggest that the Thatcher government's neo-liberal strategy was ill-suited to the needs of the intense international race for modernisation and that it was further deformed through their concern to secure political support through popular capitalism and social division. Our essay proceeds in five steps. First we describe the emerging crisis in the City to which the neo-liberal strategy represented one possible response; then we describe the rise of Thatcherism and assess its general political significance; third, we describe the attempts to make the City more flexible; fourth, we show how the neo-liberal strategy has been deformed by political considerations; and, finally, we show how Thatcherite strategies have made things worse economically and, if continued, will go on doing so.

A TALE OF TWO CITIES

As an ensemble of commercial and financial intermediaries, the City has experienced many changes. Its history since 1945 is complex but one clear trend during 'les trentes glorieuses' has been a growing division between two 'Cities' (Plender and Wallace 1985: 15–16). One conducted international business and came to be dominated by international concerns, the other conducted domestic business and traditional City firms could still play a key role. But both poles have undergone further reorganisation in the 1980s and each has benefited from Thatcherism's 'neo-liberal' and 'popular capitalist' policies.

At one pole, then, we find an 'international City' which has not only specialised in ever more complex and novel forms of international business but has also become dominated by foreign finance houses. For the City acquired a new international role in the late 1950s and 1960s which extended well beyond the sterling area. This was most obvious in three areas: the rapid growth in eurodeposit banking business and the eurobond market, the increase in foreign exchange dealing which followed the collapse of fixed exchange rates in 1972–73, and the need to recycle petrodollars after the first oil crisis. It was precisely these markets, however, which were soon dominated by foreign concerns. Expansion could occur in these areas because London was less tightly regulated than its main competing financial centres so that overseas institutions could operate more freely here. In this way London rather than New York or Tokyo became the leading international financial centre for international business.

But it was the Square Mile as a virtual 'offshore' base of operations which expanded – not the traditional City institutions already based there. These were still subject to exchange controls and restrictive practices which limited their opportunities to participate fully in the new markets. British institutions which had previously dominated international capital markets (in government and business loans) and commercial markets (in sterling bills of exchange) suffered a declining market share in both areas (cf. Reid 1988). For, as sterling declined as an international currency and British industry lost global market share, City institutions had a shrinking capital base which limited their scope of operations. In addition, their business activities outside the sterling area were officially restricted in order to safeguard the reserves and protect the pound's value. Both constraints impacted mainly on the power to raise and allocate investment capital rather than on overseas commercial and trading activities (such as insurance or trade finance in sterling). Institutions which were more concerned with these latter activities managed to grow in absolute terms because of the rapid post-war expansion in international trade and commerce. But they still lost market share. Moreover, with global deregulation and continuing preparations for 1992, the advantage London once enjoyed as the least regulated of the major financial centres is disappearing and New York, Tokyo and Frankfurt have become real threats to London's position.

At the other pole, a new 'domestic City' developed, continuing trends already evident in the 1930s. This had two main concerns: serving the financial and commercial needs of domestic industry, trade and household consumption and serving an expanding market in central and local government finance. It was still dominated by home-grown financial intermediaries which became more involved with the British economy as mass production and mass consumption prospered. Indeed the web of restrictive practices and entry barriers surrounding old-established British institutions helped protect them from foreign competition in key areas such as domestic securities, the marketing of state debt, or Lloyd's insurance market. It could not protect them in new markets, however, from domestic and/or foreign institutions which were more innovative and flexible. Thus even in this second pole of City activity an increasing share of the action accrued to foreign-owned transnational intermediaries with a British base.

This set of circumstances produced three paradoxical outcomes. First, despite the central financial role of traditional City institutions and their broad freedom from state control, their concern with short-term gain and narrow-minded 'trade association' consciousness led them to neglect the need for an economic and political strategy to promote their long-term interests.[2] Nor was this provided by governments of the day. For the latter were so involved in managing the short-term problems arising from Britain's relative economic weakness that they could give little thought or political energy to developing and implementing a long-term strategy to escape the resulting constraints. Second, commitment to the reserve and transactions roles of sterling encouraged these same institutions to focus on markets (in the overseas sterling area) which grew less rapidly; at the same time, measures taken to protect the pound harmed the domestic manufacturing base on which City strength depended. Third, the very protection from the state which was afforded by self-policing, cartels and restrictive practices rendered the traditional City institutions vulnerable to more flexible and innovative secondary or 'fringe' institutions and/or to more aggressive foreign intermediaries.

These brief remarks should put the alleged dominance of the City into context. Many of the so-called successes of its traditional institutions, whether ascribed to its alleged political hegemony or its economic drive, have been misunderstood. For they have often proved counterproductive in the long term (such as defence of sterling) and/or were really due to the activities of outsider institutions (such as the expansion of the euromarkets). Indeed, the cosy corporatist order which characterised the traditional core institutions in the City introduced rigidities which made it difficult to adjust to growth and innovation in both global and domestic markets. This can be illustrated for some of the central traditional institutions: the London Stock Exchange, merchant banks, clearing banks and Lloyd's.

In the case of the Stock Exchange fixed minimum commissions were seen to be unresponsive to the needs of big institutional investors. Single capacity, whereby the functions of jobbers and brokers were formally separate, meant that neither of these could participate in the rapidly growing eurobond business. Conversely, the growth of the eurobond market encouraged many large UK firms to issue international bonds rather then raise new funds on the domestic market – depriving SE members of business.

The traditional dominance of capital mobilisation by the merchant banks had been destroyed after the Great War. They had been compensated for this loss by developing links with British industry in the inter-war period. This domestic orientation meant a loss of dynamism and a failure to take advantage of international opportunities when they arose. Their neglect of the emerging eurobond markets in the 1960s and 1970s was compounded by neglect of futures and options markets in the late 1970s and 1980s, and latterly they were slow to move into securitising capital issues.

The clearing banks lost out to competition from both home-grown and London-based overseas competitors. This is particularly clear in eurocurrency markets, which is a highly specialist business demanding the right mix of skills and capital (cf. Coakley and Harris 1983).

Finally, the London insurance market reveals somewhat different aspects of the crisis of the traditional City. The Square Mile has become the leading centre for primary business with companies as well as the leading centre for all types of reinsurance. But both markets have been subject to entry by overseas firms. London has the advantage over competing centres of a relative lack of regulation. This environment helps new kinds of activities to develop such as the plan for an international reinsurance bourse, for 1991, to complement the high-values catastrophe market (Bank of England 1989: 520). Despite being innovative in many areas (cf. Hodgson 1986: 30), Lloyd's has lost ground to foreign competitors. This has been compounded by a series of financial scandals as the old system of self-regulation began to break down (see Hodgson 1986). These crises do not amount to a terminal structural crisis for the City but there have certainly been important institutions which seem only too eager to be driven off into the setting sun by more vigorous competition.

THE RISE AND SIGNIFICANCE OF THATCHERISM

There is no single pattern of economy–state relations which has been uniquely favourable to economic expansion since the Second World War. Growth has occurred under liberal, corporatist and dirigiste regimes but quite specific conditions are required for any given pattern to prove effective (cf. Marquand 1987). That the post-war British state has proved so ineffective in promoting economic modernisation can be explained through the virtual absence of the preconditions for any of the three basic patterns. The post-war settlement ruled out a purely liberal role for the state and market forces were distorted by monopolistic practices and the split between the City and industry. Corporatism was undermined because neither business nor unions were well enough organised to commit their members to corporatist bargains and the institutional ties among business, unions, parties and officials were too unstable for an effective corporatist policy regime. And the liberal state tradition, for all its ineffectiveness, ensured that state intervention occurred without an interventionist state (cf. Jessop 1989). This triple failure led to continual oscillation among liberal, corporatist and dirigiste strategies as the limits of each became apparent. This policy cycle accelerated under Mr Heath's Conservative government 1970–74 (with its celebrated U-turn in 1972 away from its liberal experiment towards abortive corporatist consultation and then ineffective dirigisme) and the 1974–79 Wilson–Callaghan Labour government (with its shift from a quasi-corporatist Social Contract based on a relatively one-sided union–government accord towards statutory controls and a [*de facto*] experiment with neo-liberal monetarism and austerity). The obvious failure of these corporatist and dirigiste experiments enabled Mrs Thatcher to claim that there was no alternative to the neo-liberal road and encouraged her administration to roll back the frontiers of the corporatist and interventionist state.

During its first three years of power the Thatcher government found it hard to develop a strategy which could consolidate its political power as well as manage the economic crisis. This was a deeply unsatisfactory period for the government. Indeed one radical right commentator noted that: 'in the first two years of the Thatcher government, half of the policy prescription – the micro-economic side – has not been implemented at all, and the macro-economic has run into a political swamp' (Batchelor 1981). From mid-1982 onwards, however, a new economic strategy began to crystallise: it combined macro-economic policies to counter inflation with micro-economic policies to stimulate economic growth and job creation by sponsoring entrepreneurialism and flexibility. This approach evolved patchily, in a trial-and-error fashion, and with varying degrees of success. It has been accompanied by the gradual development of a political strategy based on 'popular capitalism'. Defended by Mrs Thatcher as a 'one nation' policy which will transform every man (sic) into a home-owner, share-owner, portable pension owner and stakeholder in local services, this is intended to provide the social basis and legitimation for the Thatcherite regime in its efforts to roll back the social democratic welfare state.

NEO-LIBERALISM AND POPULAR CAPITALISM

As the government's economic strategy has evolved, it has become more neo-liberal in character. In this context 'neo-liberal' is being

176

used in its European sense to emphasise the commitment to expanding the role of market forces in the economy and not in the US–American sense of left-wing reformism or interventionism à la Edward Kennedy or Mike Dukakis. For our purposes the six most crucial elements of Thatcherite neo-liberalism are: a) liberalisation, promoting free market (as opposed to monopolistic or state monopolistic) forms of competition as the most efficient basis for market forces; b) deregulation, giving economic agents greater freedom from state control; c) privatisation, reducing the public sector's share in the direct or indirect provision of goods and services to business and community alike; d) (re-)commodification of the residual public sector, to promote the role of market forces, either directly or through market proxies; e) tax reductions and reform to create incentives to earn, save, invest, create and accumulate individual and corporate wealth; and f) internationalisation, encouraging the mobility of capital and labour, stimulating global market forces, and importing more advanced processes and products into Britain. These elements form the micro-economic basis of the Thatcherite supply-side strategy and complement the earlier and continuing commitment to a counter-inflation strategy based on some form of monetary and financial policy.

Seen in these terms Thatcherism should not be reduced to a narrow or technical monetarism nor to a limited attack on trade unions or the welfare state. It also involves attacks on the entrenched privileges of specific fractions of capital and the restrictive practices of private sector members of the service and professional classes. As well as tackling trade union powers, for example, the government has also begun somewhat hesitatingly to disprivilege farmers, civil servants, stockbrokers, lawyers and doctors.

In pursuing its neo-liberal programme the Thatcherite regime has been obliged to adopt complex and even contradictory strategies. In promoting liberalisation and internationalisation in the City, for example, it further weakened the already crumbling patterns of informal self-regulation; in turn this prompted new forms of state-sponsored, formally organised, corporatist regulation. Likewise, in privatising natural or *de facto* monopolies, it has been obliged to establish regulatory bodies such as Oftel or Ofgas. Again, in abandoning incomes policies as part of its deregulation drive and leaving training to market forces, it frees unions to exploit skill shortages and drive wages above productivity growth

177

in the private sector. In this sense we must treat the different planks of the neo-liberal strategy as elements in tension which are open to trade-off and may also demand flanking or supporting policies.

'Popular capitalism' is the political complement to Thatcherite economic strategy. It aims to replace the social democratic welfare state with a 'two nations' social security state in which the majority of citizens make their own provision for housing, education, health, pensions and personal services and the state provides a safety net by paying wholly or in part for privatised or charitable services for those who cannot help themselves. This has proved harder to implement than the neo-liberal economic strategy and many radical proposals have been shredded, postponed or diluted. The whole process has been far more hesitant and uneven than has transpired in the neo-liberal case. Political resistance as well as sheer impracticability have been particularly marked in the attempts to introduce market forces into the health service and education and many other areas of collective provision still show only marginal changes. But this does not exclude further measures to promote home ownership, wider share ownership, private medical insurance, portable pensions, student loans and education vouchers, and so forth. Nor does it exclude continued efforts to reduce the ratio of public expenditure to national income and/or to induce private provision through public squalor. However, as we shall see below, the third Thatcher government found it harder to square the circle of tax cuts, maintain fiscal subsidies to private and occupational welfare schemes, and increase public spending in those areas where state intervention or support was still needed.

We cannot explore all the implications of neo-liberalism and popular capitalism here. Instead we will focus on their implications for the City and the overall performance of the British economy. This is particularly appropriate not only because this volume is concerned with the City but also because both policies have been especially favourable to the financial services sector. Thus, if they have proven a mixed blessing even here, then their general eco- nomic import must really be open to doubt. We will touch briefly on this issue in our conclusions.

Plate 1 Battery Park City, New York

Plate 2 Inside the Broadgate complex

Plate 3 Broadgate Central Square

Plate 4 Bishopsgate frontage of Broadgate, Spitalfields market foreground on right

Plate 5 Artist's impression of Canary Wharf from Greenwich

Plate 6 Beaufort House, Aldgate

Plate 7 St Botolph's Church, Aldgate, with Beaufort House in background

Plate 8 Embankment Place, Charing Cross Station beneath

DEREGULATING THE CITY

The City has benefited hugely both from neo-liberalism and its supporting political strategy. It has become the world's leading international financial centre for serving the needs of international capital. Admittedly, this achievement occurred in part at the expense of those traditional City institutions least able to adapt and through the aggressive incursion of foreign multinationals. We also have our doubts about the long-term stability of the City in this new role (especially with the approach of 1992) but its massive expansion during the 1980s cannot be denied. For it has generated a vast increase in employment, investment and foreign earnings and has helped to sustain economic expansion in London and the south-east. Indeed, due to the general expansion of financial services within the UK economy, even older, less flexible City institutions have seen their aggregate business expand even as they have been losing ground to new competitors. As we have seen, the groundwork for this achievement was probably laid in the 1960s with the rise of the eurodollar markets; but Thatcherite policies have reinforced the concentration of financial power in the City by abolishing exchange controls, deregulating financial institutions and services, generating business through privatisation, encouraging a free flow of inward and outward investment by multinationals, sponsoring small business expansion, providing favourable tax treatment for some financial instruments as well as reducing levels of personal and corporate taxation, and promoting popular capitalism. All these measures stress the market-driven character of economic reorganisation and, although state intervention continues, it is no longer guided by a concern to secure the coherence of Britain's industrial base. This is to be left to the benign but invisible hand of market forces.

In pursuing this neo-liberal strategy the Thatcher governments have received support from progressive reformers in the City. Some of the state's measures were meant to be facilitative, such as the 1979 abolition of exchange controls or the abolition of the 'corset' on bank lending in 1980. Others were intended to abolish the City's restrictive practices and inject greater competition. Among these were the deregulation and liberalisation of building societies' activities and the reorganisation of the securities industry. We explore the latter in some detail below because it sheds interesting light on the overall development of the neo-liberal strategy.

179

The City has also become more flexible in other respects. Among the dimensions of flexibility we can cite the introduction of new 'back-office' technology to enhance efficiency in existing services as well as new technology to extend the range of client services. There have also been attempts to introduce more flexible working practices and more flexible hours of work in individual firms as well as to offer new financial products and services with or without the aid of new technologies. Again, inspired – perhaps unwisely in some cases – by speculation about future trends in the financial services industry, there has been frenetic competition among firms to locate themselves in an alleged new division of labour: a combination of giant one-stop financial conglomerates plus 'niche' or 'boutique' financial houses which specialise in high-value-added financial services. These changes parallel those in industrial production and the labour force as the transition to more flexible, supposedly 'post-Fordist' practices continues. However, the medium-term outcome in finance and industry alike of such corporate strategies, as much inspired by media and corporate hype as by technological and market changes, is far from clear.

In addition to the continuing flow of innovations in existing markets in financial assets, new markets have been created both for equity capital (e.g. the unlisted securities market from 1980, the 'over-the-counter' market, the third market and London Securities Exchange for smaller firms) and other financial markets (traded options, financial futures, etc.). The government has also been active in promoting more flexible provision of finance through the tax system (e.g. Business Enterprise Schemes) and boosting investment through privatisation, personal equity plans, changes in stamp duty, capital gains taxation, and so on. Indeed the success of the City in recent years can be attributed in large part to continuation of favourable tax status for institutional investment (pensions, insurance) and certain forms of saving (building society funds, home ownership), new measures intended to encourage stock exchange turnover (such as reductions in stamp duty on transactions), and to the typically neo-liberal preference for fiscal expenditure (tax subsidies and tax shelters) over direct revenue spending in support of industrial investment. Deregulation and liberalisation have reinforced these measures.

Deregulation and liberalisation have also been accompanied by re-regulation. In part this has involved strengthening the hidden 'prudential controls' exercised by the Bank of England. But a formal regulatory framework has also been established through the Financial Services Act 1986. Quite how this framework will work in practice is unclear – initial teething problems and the role of 'learning by doing' make it hard to predict the real pattern of regulation in five years' time. Some of the difficulties involved in forecasting can be seen from arguments that the new Securities and Investment Board represented a new type of negotiated corporatist franchise along American lines. How far the SIB can be compared with the American SEC is debatable but the point remains that re-regulation in whatever form has been widely regarded as an essential concomitant of the neo-liberal strategy. This is reinforced by some of the unpredictable effects produced through new technologies and services. In an age of accelerating financial innovation, electronic money, global telecommunications and computer-driven trading and arbitrage, financial services sometimes seem to have become too flexible – encouraging exaggerated swings in markets as well as providing new opportunities for insider trading, corruption and white-collar crime. So complete deregulation would render the whole system unstable and flexibility must be controlled. This is evident from the experience of Black Monday as well as the growing scandals of insider trading, share support operations, Lloyd's insurance scams, unscrupulous takeover activities, and so forth. Whether the new regulatory framework will ever be truly effective remains to be seen.

NEO-LIBERAL ADHOCCERY

So far we have presented the neo-liberal strategy as if it were a fully formulated, coherent general strategy for regenerating the British economy which has been most adapted to circumstances from case to case. But this lends too much coherence to the pursuit of neo-liberal measures. In many cases they are developed casually or through trial-and-error, and only with hindsight was it possible for government apologists and outside observers to attribute so many measures to a neo-liberal strategy. Once this general line was identified, however, it has been used to shape new policies.

The origins and impact of Big Bang provide an interesting test case here. For it shows that the neo-liberal strategy was indeed an important factor determining government policies towards the City and that these do not simply result from City pressure. But Big Bang also shows that the strategy is adapted to changing circumstances and that divisions do occur within the economic state apparatus about how best to pursue the neo-liberal line.

The changes in the securities industry were prompted by the 1979 referral by the Office of Fair Trading (OFT) of the Stock Exchange rule book to the Restrictive Practices Court. Eventually this led to the 1983 'Goodison–Parkinson' agreement which gave birth to three 'little bangs' and one Big Bang. The former involved: ending the single capacity arrangement whereby member firms specialised either in jobbing or broking, a two-stage relaxation of the rules on outside ownership so that outsiders could eventually wholly own member firms and inject capital into them, and new rules on membership of the Stock Exchange to widen participation. Big Bang itself occurred in 1986 as members had to abandon fixed commissions.

That the neo-liberal strategy is flexible can be seen from the Parkinson–Goodison agreement. In 1980 Mrs Thatcher had replied to a letter from Harold Wilson which urged an informal solution to the OFT enquiry so that legal action could be avoided: she wrote that the Director General of Fair Trading was legally obliged to pursue the case and no grounds existed for exemption. During the winter of 1982–83, however, the Bank entered secret talks with the Treasury and the Department of Trade (bypassing the OFT): it had become worried about the City's long-term competitiveness in the face of international competition. These talks resulted in an out-of-court settlement in return for Stock Exchange concessions which were eventually recorded in the Parkinson–Goodison accord in July 1983. Because of the resulting legal complications, the agreement had to be sanctioned through special legislation.

This change of tactic shows two issues were at stake. These are clearly discernible in exchanges between Sir Anthony Beaumont-Dark and two fellow MPs during the debate on the Restrictive Trade Practices (Stock Exchange) Bill. Beaumont-Dark welcomed the removal of the Stock Exchange's future from the hands of the OFT and the Restrictive Practices Court but he also feared that the Parkinson–Goodison accord would permit a massive foreign take-over of British-owned institutions. He cited the bid by the German Allianz group for Eagle Star (already cleared by the government) and insisted that 'we are talking not just about Eagle Star but about £3bn of investment that Eagle Star controls. Therefore, gently over the years the control of the assets of this country may pass quietly into foreign hands' (6th Series, vol. 49, 1983–84, col. 919). Ian Wrigglesworth of the SDP protested that Beaumont-Dark was living in cloud cuckoo land in talking about the City as though it were an island unto itself: he suggested that there was an inter-national market-place trading 24 hours a day (cols 919–20). At this point Beaumont-Dark became more didactic:

> If the hon. Gentleman and his party do not understand the difference between switching between investments in one world centre and another and control of the City of London resting in overseas hands, the SDP has a great deal to learn about the City . . . Where one's funds are controlled is impor-tant. It is important for the Government and the City to have a say over who controls them and in whose interests they do so. It is not insular to say that we do not want the City to be controlled by American, Japanese or Saudi Arabian interests. It should be controlled for the good of this country.

Later, towards the close of debate, Beaumont-Dark pressed the Under-Secretary of State for Trade and Industry, Alexander Fletcher, to clarify the government's position on foreign owner-ship of British companies. He was worried that it would 'say that anyone can buy it if anyone will sell it' (col. 924). The minister's reply bore the full stamp of the neo-liberal strategy in rejecting any state-imposed barriers to global competition in a deregulated Stock Exchange:

> We take the view that the City and our financial institutions are capable of looking after their own interests . . . The future of the City is very much in the hands of those who work and are shareholders in our City institutions. They will be bought out only if they sell out. They are able to choose between foreign investors and British investors if they decide that they want to take part in or form a larger financial conglomerate.
>
> (col. 924)

The government would only intervene if the free market was threatened. He added that the Fair Trading Act (1973) gave them adequate powers where a monopoly position emerged or the public interest was adversely affected (col. 924). Indeed Mr Fletcher had already warned City institutions about this at a City luncheon on 13 November in response to worries voiced by some

Stock Exchange Council members about a flood of foreign take-over bids. He had told Sir Nicholas Goodison, Chairman of the Stock Exchange, that the government would not intervene and advised the City to look after its own interests. UK institutions had done nothing but sit on the sidelines when US banks took stakes in leading City brokers: 'it's not a question of the City being taken over, but of the City selling out to foreign interests' (*Sunday Times*, 13 November 1983).

During the passage of this legislation in 1983–84, the Bank of England played a key role in fostering 'suitable unions' between stockbrokers and more strongly capitalised banks. Its aim was to create giant British investment banks which could compete with foreign investment houses. Indeed, between September and November 1983, David Walker, the Bank's executive director for City organisation, swapped views with over forty senior partners of Stock Exchange firms about actual or planned mergers (Reid 1988: 52). Although the Bank had government approval in encouraging these mergers, its motives were rather different. For, whilst the government was indifferent to questions of ownership provided the City retained its international role, the Bank was concerned about the threats of foreign ownership. In an inaugural address, its Governor, Sir Robin Leigh-Pemberton, clearly hinted that 'it would not be welcome if foreign purchasers were to swamp the City scene with their buying power'. The Bank would be disturbed, he said, were British-owned member firms to play a clearly subordinate role. This message was not lost on his audience (Reid 1988: 61). But this message could well have come too late. For, whatever the OFT, the government and the Bank may have intended, Nicholas Goodison later claimed that the delay in reform occasioned by the OFT's legal action had given American firms the chance to dominate the securities and investment markets after exchange controls were ended – and they had seized their chance (*Financial Times*, 27 October 1987).

MAKING THE ECONOMY MORE FRAGILE

Even if the new regulatory framework does work, it does not follow that the 'real' economy benefits from recent changes in the City. Indeed, as applied to the old and new Cities, the government's neo-liberal strategy has been harmful. A recent report in the Bank of England's *Quarterly Bulletin* raised doubts about the benefits of

London's role as an international financial centre. The report notes that:

> There may of course be disadvantages in hosting a major financial centre. Salaries and wages may be forced up, thus driving up rents and house prices, with undesirable social consequences. Regional disparities may be exacerbated and the congestion of local transport systems may be aggravated. The economy may face risks due to over-dependence on a single sector. The operation of monetary policy may become complicated by the need to nurture the financial sector. Regulation may need to be more complex than otherwise. Finally, it has sometimes been argued that the financial sector merely preys on the rest of the economy, adding to costs and distorting other markets – by, for instance, attracting able individuals who might be more socially productive in other areas such as manufacturing.
>
> (Bank of England 1989: 516)

Having conjured up this spectre, however, the authors at once proceed to exorcise it with various counterarguments. They then conclude that, 'on balance, the financial sector may be judged to offer substantial net benefits to the economy' (ibid.). We return to some of these suggested difficulties below but we also want to present some further arguments which suggest how the Thatcherite strategies have helped skew, if not deform, the mode of growth in Britain. This argument takes us well beyond Thatcherite policies towards the City as such but this can be defended on two grounds: first, that neo-liberal strategies more generally, as many commentators have noted, tend to reflect City views about the role of markets rather than manufacturers' views about the organisation of production; and, second, regardless of the intellectual justification and/or political pressures behind these strategies, they have often been geared towards government perceptions of City interests (and the services sector more generally) as well as towards calculations of the electoral interests of Thatcherism without too much regard for the long-term needs of manufacturing industry – especially of those firms with a largely domestic base of operations. Let us briefly illustrate this from six different areas of economic growth.[3]

First, in pursuing both banking deregulation and a monetarist counter-inflation strategy, Thatcherism has created conditions discouraging investment in the 'real' economy. Banking profits come from making loans; and financial institutions compete with each other by inventing new financial instruments. Deregulating and liberalising banking capital promotes this competition and helps banks to circumvent monetary restraint. In turn this makes it progressively harder for governments to control the money supply each time that tight money is needed for economic management. For financial innovation means that more credit can be advanced at any given level of interest rates and any given level of bank reserves. Deregulation has hindered Thatcherism's counter-inflationary strategy and has led to higher interest rates than would be required in a more closely controlled banking system. Thus, other things being equal, each successive round of tight money would be coupled with higher levels of unemployment, more bankruptcies and a larger drop in output. This hinders the recovery of the real economy and stimulates the growth of imports to meet upturns in demand. Even so there has been an increasing tendency to overshoot monetary targets.[4]

Second, by encouraging expansion in the financial sector, the neo-liberal strategy has increased financial claims on the 'real' economy. In a period when financial investment in global equity markets is increasingly liquidity-driven,[5] the danger arises that manufacturing productivity and industrial profits fail to keep pace with the growth of financial claims. This is especially worrying when other government policies have undermined industrial investment and growth. In response three effects are likely to occur: recurrent mini-crashes as speculative bubbles burst, inflation as wages and industrial profits struggle to compensate for the increased claims from the financial sector, or outward portfolio investment in the search for higher returns. We have already seen the October 1987 crash and a smaller version in 1989; a collapse in the housing market and high interest rates to control wage-push inflation; and consistently higher rates of overseas than domestic investment – both direct and portfolio (cf. Toporowski 1989). None of these augur well for the UK economy.

Third, in pursuing its policy of disengagement, the government has systematically run down its role in training and has tried to bring education and R&D activities closer to the market. Yet the recession which it engineered in 1979–81, the proliferation of small businesses and self-employment which it has encouraged, and the high interest rates which play a key role in its economic strategy have each contributed to the collapse of private sector training initiatives. At a time when high-grade flexibility depends on polyvalent skills, the government sponsors flexibility through hire-and-fire industrial relations legislation and adopts a low-cost, low-skill training policy. This has reinforced the low-skill, low-wage, low-productivity character of British industry. Interestingly, one of the few areas where skills are allegedly in adequate supply is financial services (e.g. Bank of England 1989: 521). Moreover, in continuing the traditional bias of successive British governments towards military and nuclear rather than civil R&D and pushing the latter towards the market, the Thatcher regime has helped retard modernisation and hindered competition in high-tech areas. As the pace of technological innovation accelerates and ever-new demands are placed on the workforce, this problem will become more severe (cf. Ashton *et al.* 1989; Freeman 1989; Robinson 1988). Taken together these factors could well contribute further to restrictions on the capital base of British financial institutions. In contrast the rapid rise to worldwide dominance of Japanese financial institutions is based on Japan's trade surplus, high levels of domestic savings and the global expansion of Japanese industry.

Fourth, in its drive to promote popular capitalism, the Thatcher regime has acted irrationally not just economically but also politically. It has pursued short-term asset stripping of the public sector for the sake of a share-owning democracy, cosmetic reductions in the PSBR, and tax cuts – all to the detriment of securing long-term improvements in competition and industrial performance. It has sought to maximise revenue through the sale of monopolies rather than to promote competition through breaking them up. It has sought to promote popular capitalism by the deep discounting of shares rather than securing the best price for the assets it is selling.[6] And, if we look closely at performance figures, there is little evidence that off-loading firms into the private sector improves their subsequent performance once allowance is made for the more general growth in profits after the 1979/81 recession (cf. Bishop and Kay 1989).

Fifth, by privileging owner occupation in the hope of electoral benefit, it has certainly given a major boost to the financial services sector. But it has also promoted a consumer boom on the basis of housing equity, aggravated the crowding out effects of the HSBR (housing sector borrowing requirement) on productive investment, and discouraged regional labour mobility from areas of high unemployment to areas of labour shortage. Moreover, in promoting owner occupation, it has created a vested interest which is proving fickle with the current downturn in the housing market. As Joe Rogaly commented in a survey of Thatcherism's prospects at the outset of 1990: 'this is what happens to Governments that base their political strategy on the creation of a property-owning democracy and their economic strategy on interest rates' *(Financial Times,* 19 January 1990). This, more than the wider (but not yet very deep) share ownership promoted by the Thatcher regime, could prove to be the Achilles' heel of its strategy of popular capitalism. Indeed, given that London and the south-east have higher rates of home-ownership, more expensive properties, and associated debts, any downturn would particularly affect the principal geographic as well as social base of Thatcherism. It is also possible that rising house prices are a crucial link in the wage–price spiral which Thatcherism has not yet managed to defeat.

Sixth, much of the apparent success of the neo-liberal strategy depends on trends in the south-east. In the 'north' it triggered far more job losses in manufacturing (both in absolute and relative terms) than in the 'south' (cf. Martin 1989). This came to pass through the combined impact of general macro-economic policies (such as tight money and high exchange rates) and specific micro-economic measures to restructure nationalised industries (which are over-represented in the 'north'). In contrast such government policies as internationalisation, deregulation, liberalisation, privatisation and tax cuts were especially advantageous to the City, rentier and producer service interests located above all in London and the south-east. Moreover, turning again to consider manufacturing, the central role of various low-profile forms of government aid (e.g. airports, research establishments, defence industries and motorways) in the south hardly suggests that neo-liberalism alone could ever drive a real expansion in output. It is overheating in the south-east which has prompted the recent deflationary attempt to engineer a 'soft landing' for the economy as a whole. The costs to this in future investment in general and growth in more depressed regions in particular have not yet been calculated. Whether manufacturing can recover to the same extent in the north is uncertain – especially with the likely impact of 1992 and the Channel Tunnel in further polarising growth southwards (see Martin 1989; Smith 1989).

188

Pulling all these different strands together, we can say that the Thatcher years have been quite distinctive in macro-economic terms. Some sectors have certainly expanded – most notably, of course, financial services. But much of this financial expansion has occurred through the increasing internationalisation of the City and its ever closer integration into the global circuit of capital. What this implies for the British mode of growth is less clear. Taking a more general view, however, economic growth in Britain has taken the form of a consumption boom financed from borrowing, from dividend and interest incomes, from redundancy payments, and from an increased volume of state benefits (unemployment benefit, pensions). In turn this is linked to a pattern of investment which is skewed towards sectors which service the consumption boom (retailing, distribution, personal financial services and credit) rather than those involved in tradeable commodities. This has been partially disguised by productivity increases in industrial sectors which have been reorganised since 1981, but this reorganisation has not restored the economy's overall manufacturing strength. But, since manufacturing matters, this is not a sustainable basis for economic recovery. The 'soft landing' hoped for by Lawson and Major is unlikely to secure this (cf. Glyn 1989).

CONCLUDING REMARKS

We have argued that the City and current government policy have mutually conditioned each other and evolved together. The relative decline of Britain's manufacturing base relative to Britain's competitors is well-known and its impact on the decomposition of the post-war settlement has often been retold. Here we have stressed how the crisis of traditional City institutions also contributed to Britain's relative decline and helped to prepare the ground for the Thatcher era. Well before Mrs Thatcher became Prime Minister, a new City was emerging to become the leading international financial centre in the world. This exacerbated the problems facing a weak state in managing the process of economic decline and reinforced the appeal of the neo-liberal solution favoured by the incoming Conservative regime. The wide-ranging neo-liberal economic strategy pursued by the Thatcher governments certainly reinforced emerging trends in the City; and City institutions rewarded them with increased support. In addition the 'popular capitalist' political strategy pursued by the Conservatives gave a further boost to the City: this time in its other guise as an ensemble of financial institutions concerned with housing, personal financial services and mass consumption.

Yet the overall effect of the neo-liberal strategy and its popular capitalist complement has been to hasten the decline of the British economy. Neo-liberalism has further weakened the already weak manufacturing base of the national economy and integrated it more closely into different spheres of multinational influence. It sometimes seems that Britain is being relocated at the margins of the three emerging poles of global economic competition: the USA, Europe and Japan. One is tempted to claim that, under Thatcherism, the British economy is becoming the 51st American state, a subaltern member of an emerging European Economic Space, and an outlying colony within a new Asian Co-Prosperity Sphere. Perhaps this is too pointed a remark; but the resulting balkanisation of the British economy which it indicates has certainly reinforced the low-wage, low-tech, low-growth syndrome (cf. Nolan 1989) and now seems to be threatening the survival of the City itself as a privileged 'offshore' island. Likewise, the pursuit of political advantage through popular capitalism has intensified social and economic inequalities and deformed the implementation of crucial elements in the neo-liberal accumulation strategy. Together these strategies first created a 'false dawn' in Britain's alleged 'supply-side' miracle and then produced the overheating which has required such strong deflationary action. If we are now living in a post-Thatcher era, as so many commentators now proclaim, then the interaction between City institutions, neo-liberalism and popular capitalism will have contributed powerfully to this 'new dawn'. It will also have made it much harder to reverse the continuing decline of the British economy.

NOTES

1 This chapter draws on previous work by Bob Jessop and his colleagues, Kevin Bonnett, Noelle Burgi, Simon Bromley, Tom Ling; and on research by Rob Stones. See especially Jessop 1986, 1989; Jessop and Burgi 1988; Jessop *et al.* 1989; Stones 1988, 1990.
2 On the lack of City concern for hegemony, see Stones 1988.
3 The arguments presented here were first developed in Jessop 1989.
4 For the analysis underpinning this claim, see Miller 1978; Jessop 1985; and Toporowski 1989.
5 This feature derives from Japan's financial surpluses and the deregu-

lation of US and Japanese investment houses; the Thatcher regime reinforced it by several legislative acts which encouraged funded pension schemes and contractual savings.

6 Whereas the average discount on new share issues in the private sector is 3 per cent, the average discount on privatisation issues before British Steel was 14 per cent: cf. Labour Research Department 1989: 21.

REFERENCES

Ashton, D., Green, F. and Hoskins, M. (1989) 'The training system of British Capitalism and its prospects', in F. Green, (ed.) (1989), *The Restructuring of the UK Economy*, London: Harvester Wheatsheaf.

Bank of England (1989) 'London as an international financial centre', *Bank of England Quarterly Bulletin*, November.

Batchelor, R. (1981) 'Thatcherism could succeed', *Journal of Economic Affairs*, 1, 137–45.

Bishop, M.W. and Kay, J.A. (1989) 'Privatization in the United Kingdom: Lessons from experience', *World Development*, 17, 1989.

Coakley, J. and Harris, L. (1983) *The City of Capital: London's Role as a Financial Centre*, Oxford: Blackwell.

Freeman, C. (1989) 'R&D, technical change, and investment in Britain', in F. Green (ed.) (1989), *The Restructuring of the UK Economy*, London: Harvester Wheatsheaf.

Glyn, A. (1989) 'The macro-economy of the Thatcher years', in F. Green (ed.) (1989), *The Restructuring of the UK Economy*, London: Harvester Wheatsheaf.

Green, F. (ed.) (1989) *The Restructuring of the UK Economy*, London: Harvester Wheatsheaf.

Hilton, A. (1987) *City Within a State: A Portrait of Britain's Financial World*, London: Tauris.

Hodgson, G. (1986) *Lloyds of London*, Harmondsworth: Penguin.

Jessop, B. (1985) 'Prospects for a corporatist monetarism', in O. Jacobi *et al.*, (eds.) *Economic Crisis, Trade Unions, and the State*, London: Croom Helm.

——(1986) 'The mid-life crisis of Thatcherism', *New Socialist*, March.

——(1989) 'Thatcherism: the British Road to Post-Fordism?', *Essex Papers in Politics and Government*, Colchester.

Jessop, B. and Burgi, N. (1988) 'Coal and the City: Flexibility and the State', Paper for International Conference on Strategies of Flexibilization, Roskilde, April 1988.

Jessop, B., Bonnett, K., Bromley, S. and Ling, T. (1989) *Thatcherism: A Tale of Two Nations*, Cambridge: Polity.

Labour Research Department (1989) 'Privatization does nothing for Performance', *Labour Research*, May.

Lisle-Williams, M. (1987) 'City and State in Britain', in A. Cox (ed.) *Finance, Capital, and the State*, Brighton.

Marquand, D. (1987) *The Unprincipled Society*, London: Cape.

191

Martin, R. (1989) 'Regional imbalance as consequence and constraint in national economic renewal', in F. Green (ed.) (1989), *The Restructuring of the UK Economy*, London: Harvester Wheatsheaf.

Miller, E. (1978) *Micro-Economic Effects of Monetary Policy*, Oxford: Martin Robertson.

Nolan, P. (1989) 'Walking on water? Performance and industrial relations under Mrs Thatcher', *Industrial Relations Journal*, 20(2).

Plender, J. and Wallace, P.(1985) *The Square Mile*, London: Century.

Reid, M. (1988) *All-Change in the City: The Revolution in Britain's Financial Sector*, Basingstoke: Macmillan.

Robinson, P. (1988) *The Unbalanced Recovery*, Dedington: Philip Allan.

Smith, D. (1989) *North and South: Britain's Growing Divide*, Harmondsworth: Penguin.

Stones, R. (1988) 'The myth of betrayal: structure and agency in the Labour government's policy of non-devaluation 1964–67', University of Essex, 1988: Ph.D. thesis.

——(1990) 'Government–finance relations in Britain 1964–67: a tale of three cities', *Economy and Society* 19 (1), March.

Toporowski, J. (1989) 'The financial system and capital accumulation in the 1980s', in Green, F. (ed.) (1989) *The Restructuring of the UK Economy*, London: Harvester Wheatsheaf.

Wilson Report (1980) *Report* of the Committee to Review the Functioning of Financial Institutions (Chairman Sir Harold Wilson), HMSO Cmnd 7937.

Part II

PATTERNS OF CULTURE, SPACE AND WORK

8

THE CITY AS A LANDSCAPE OF POWER

London and New York as global financial capitals

Sharon Zukin

The 'global cities' that have captured attention in recent years owe much to intense competition in international financial services. Partly a matter of providing world-class commercial facilities, and partly a matter of image-creation, the effort to attract geographically mobile investment activity changes a city's perspective. The old, diversified urban centre is cleaned up for new offices and cultural consumption; in the process, it becomes more expensive. Not surprisingly, governmental priorities shift from public goods to private development.

Local officials in New York and London have pursued this sort of growth with ambivalence. Forced to shed traditional allies from labour unions and the left, they have been disciplined by fiscal crisis, co-opted by property developers, taken in hand by financial institutions and quasi-public authorities, and scolded by national political leaders. For their part, national governments have eagerly anticipated the smaller world and larger cities that follow global financial markets. In the United States, the tradition of local autonomy precludes central government's taking a key role in directing New York's growth. In the UK, however, the national government has intervened to spur the City's eastward expansion. From 1980, activist conservative governments in both Britain and the United States broadened official support for the expansion of financial markets – and for an inevitable struggle between New York and London over priority of place. Competitive efforts to capture global markets in a single place would lead cities to the same general strategies. On the one hand, the geographical concentration of 'world-class players' in a small number of financial centres erodes traditional economic ties with certain areas of the world in favour of a more functional specialisation by financial product and activity (Walter 1988: 51). On the other hand, pursuing the same clients – mainly multinational corporations and individuals with high net worth – encourages financial firms to establish 'linkages' with other locally based financial institutions (Walter 1988: 59–60). Both London and New York have grown by means of these activities. Yet clients' growing sensitivity to price in financial transactions tends to intensify the low-cost advantages of different places. A milder regulatory climate, for example, brought many financial operations from New York to London in the mid-1960s, and existing facilities for international currency trading helped London to become the centre of eurodollar markets in the 1970s. In the 1980s, however, the search for expertise and deep financial backing in more unusual operations enhanced New York's concentration of asset-rich Japanese banks and worldwide institutional investors. New York also kept its advantage in supplying specialists in mergers and acquisitions and filling investment 'niches' (Cohen 1989).

It's all very well to describe such changes in terms of a traditional agglomeration economy. Yet the degree of conscious competition between cities that is involved, in a political context of seeking private resources for public problems, creates a new version of 'cities in a race with time'. Municipal officials of London, New York and even Tokyo must worry not only about the competitive ability of firms that are based within their realms – and the employment opportunities and tax revenues that might slip from within their grasp; they must also build an infrastructure that attracts and retains world-class financial actors. This infrastructure includes advanced telecommunications facilities, a computer-literate workforce, and new skyscraper office buildings that lift urban identity from the modern to the spectacular. Such an agenda differs substantially from earlier eras of local governmental collusion with business élites. Business competition today is increasingly seen as a joint public–private endeavour (Squires 1989). In the United States, this reaches beyond tax breaks to pure subsidy, as many of the costs of building infrastructure – from channels for fibre-optic transmis- sions and new educational curricula to speculative office buildings – are met by local government.

From this viewpoint, the social housing projects and downtown commercial renewals that followed World War II were only the prelude to a vaster, more symbolic reconstruction. The landscape of the global city, including public monuments and private housing, theatres, museums and other arenas of cultural life, appears more as a massive governmental responsibility than as the incremental pursuit of individual investments and social honours.

The urban response to global financial markets is thus a highly structured yet an extraordinarily open-ended game. Three factors are constantly in play:

- business relations between a spatially concentrated financial community and expansion-minded institutions based all over the world;
- political decisions made by a city government (or, in London's case, a national government) that is mortally concerned with business viability and also with fiscal solvency, tax rolls and riot prevention and
- consumption patterns of rich investors and their investment managers, who seek the cultural authenticity of the old city and the comfortable security of the new suburb.

These are all complex factors that imply their own contradictions, most notably, simultaneous centralisation and decentralisation of economic activity. But they also imply two common directions for analysis. First, such concepts as economies of scope and scale that are so important to micro-economists are only part of much larger collective arrangements that underlie both the symbolic and material realities of a global financial capital. Second, the interrelated effects of economic structure, institutional intervention and cultural reorganisation are most directly perceived in change in the landscape: creating the city as a landscape of power.

LANDSCAPE AND VERNACULAR

Cities always struggle between images that express a landscape of power and those that form the local vernacular. While power in modern times is best abstracted in the skyscraper outline of a city's financial wealth, the vernacular is most intimately experienced in low-lying residential neighbourhoods or *quartiers* outside the commercial centre. Much of the social quality of urbanity on which a world city depends reflects both the polished landscape and the gritty vernacular as well as the tension between them. New Yorkers point with pride, for example, to their 'city of neighbourhoods', whose architectural and economic diversity suggests the cultural and social heterogeneity of its population (*New York Ascendant* 1987: 13). Londoners praise their city's informal domesticity that rests on relatively small houses and a mixture of social classes in each area (Hall 1989: 16). By contrast, each global city has at least one densely built, centrally located, high-rise district that drives both property values for the metropolitan region as a whole and office employment in financial and other business services.

The coherent vertical landscape of this centre – the Wall Street area in downtown Manhattan and the City of London – is circumscribed by a segmented horizontal vernacular of working-class districts and low-income, immigrant ghettos. (On the incremental construction of a coherent vertical landscape, cf. Bender and Taylor 1987.) Yet the opposition between landscape and vernacular refers to more than mere architectural or art-historical categories. Just as *landscape* shows the imprint of powerful business and political institutions on both the built environment and its symbolic representation, so does *vernacular* express the resistance, autonomy and originality of the powerless. Their opposition, moreover, suggests an important *asymmetry* of power. Since élites are capable of imposing multiple perspectives on the surrounding vernacular, landscape implies their special contribution as well as the entire material and symbolic construction (Zukin 1991b PM).

The juxtaposition between landscape and vernacular in New York is easily visualised by taking the Independent subway line between Manhattan and Brooklyn across the Manhattan Bridge. On the Manhattan side of the East River, at the southern tip of the island, several generations of twentieth-century skyscrapers raise a profusion of gothic, flat-top and mansard roofs against the sky. The Woolworth Building was the tallest skyscraper in the world when it was built in 1913. Now it is dwarfed by the elongated twin cigar-box towers of the World Trade Center, completed in the early 1970s, and the lower yet no less massive commercial and residential development of Battery Park City, produced on 92 acres of landfill in the Hudson River in the 1980s, when speculative builders and public authorities favoured a civilised postmodern style. From the train windows one also sees in miniature along the waterfront the few remaining early nineteenth-century merchants' warehouses and the wholesale fish market that make up South Street Seaport, a commercial redevelopment of trendy bars, retail stores and tourist shops in a municipally designated historic landmark zone. Directly beside the elevated tracks are the red-brick, late nineteenth century tenements and loft buildings of China-town. The train rushes past open windows where ceiling fans revolve and fluorescent lights shine on Chinese garment workers, who are engaged in the only expanding manufacturing sector left in Manhattan. Beneath the tracks, oranges, mustard greens and purple eggplant spill over grocers' sidewalk stands, part of a crowded street life that some find similar to Hong Kong's. North of the bridge, where the subway re-enters the earth, a dense array of public housing projects is aligned along the shore. Built years before the waterfront was seen to have high economic value, these low-income apartment houses replaced some of the most crowded, dilapidated housing on the Lower East Side.

In London's East End, a more horizontal landscape is also chronologically segmented by financial capital and social vernacular, juxtaposing rich and poor in close proximity. The Docklands Light Railway connects the City's stern office buildings with the brighter, more reflective steel-and-glass or restored commercial centres at Canary Wharf, Tobacco Dock and the Royal Albert Dock, two miles away. The railway rushes past council flats whose building walls are striped with graffiti. It also passes clusters of small single-family council houses that stand as solitary out-croppings on ground cleared for new construction. Docks that have not yet been demolished or redeveloped are stark monu-ments to Victorian industry: huge, empty, lacking a function in the eight-square-mile, purpose-built financial quarter around them, where Canary Wharf alone occupies 71 acres.

Yet none of this is permanent. Just as landscape has often been transformed into low-rent quarters for the poor or artisanal work-shops, so has vernacular been changed into a new landscape of power.

This spatial metaphor unifies some of the disparate changes we see around us in the city, and couches our unease with an unfamiliar material reality. But change has not been so sudden as developments like Docklands and Battery Park City imply. Much of the landscape has been re-made incrementally. After all, London and New York have always had high property values, especially downtown and in the City. Further, gentrification proceeds by individual houses and streets; although it changes the 'character' of an area, it rarely occurs on so dense a scale as greatly to raise aggregate income or educational levels (Marcuse 1986; Nelson and Lorence 1985). And despite the perennial tension between the developers' urge to tear down and reconstruct and the residents' desire that things remain as they are, most large redevelopment projects, although often compromised in size and style, have in fact been built. Inured by previous battles over urban space, therefore, a liberal urban planner takes a moderate position on Docklands, suggesting that while building it was inevitable, it could have been done better. 'Like it or not', this reluctant critic says (Hall 1989: 15), 'it is so dazzling that it casts the rest of inner London's 124 square miles into a kind of deep shade.'

Seeing the landscape of the City is believing in its mission, for visual consumption holds the key to the old geographical centre's creative destruction. The very syntax, the rules by which we perceive it, have been changed and, as the rules have changed, so has the way we use the city.

New demographics certainly play a major role in this process. At the high end of the social scale, single-person and dual-income households, and a complementary growth of high-level jobs in financial services exert pressure on the city centre to provide aesthetic variety and contextual consistency rather than dilapidated structures and visible segmentation. This demand interacts with the centre's growing supply of new cultural producers, including artists, actors, museum curators, gourmet food entrepreneurs and a standing army of waiters, designers and boutique clerks, many of whom were trained for higher-wage jobs. Among low-skilled workers, however, income is too low to meet the rising costs of housing, and many entry-level jobs, even in services, have either been revamped beyond their skill or moved outside the centre. Remaining concentrations of low-wage households in the centre thus reflect statutory tenure, on the one hand, as in rent control and council housing, both rapidly diminishing, and quasi-communal provision of social services, on the other (Zukin 1991a, ch. 7; cf. Rose 1984).

The predominance of visual consumption in the central areas of the city also reflects three long-term trends in advanced industrial economies. Since the beginning of the twentieth century, the notion of value has increasingly been abstracted from material production, so that cultural and especially financial value emphasise *form* rather than the manufacture of concrete goods. Further, many people now derive social meaning from consumption instead of production, defining their roles outside the job and inside the supermarket, restaurant and regional shopping centre. Visual consumption, moreover, provides a common syntax for the language of international investment, as the global economy expands through such previously 'local' realms as cultural production (e.g. record production and distribution, movie studios and even food) and property investment (Zukin 1991a).

By both institutional intervention and cultural reorganisation, the landscape of the centre swallows up the vernacular. Ghettos are either bulldozed out of existence or gentrified; small commercial services are swept away by high-volume chain stores and high-price bistros, boutiques and tourist amenities. Wholesale markets and old manufacturing districts are re-viewed as historical artifacts and appropriated as signs of both landscape and consumption (e.g. South Street Seaport, Faneuil Hall, Covent Garden, Tobacco Dock). Symbols of the old centre are appropriated too. While Docklands' logo incorporates Tower Bridge, the actual development expands the centre two miles beyond it; Battery Park City's logo is Gateway Tower, a symbolic entry to the old financial district that lies behind the new World Financial Center.

'We have turned this area around', an official of London Docklands Development Corporation (LDDC) says about the new visualisation. 'We have changed the perception of it from the backyard of London to a city of the future' (*New York Times*, 15 October 1988). Or, as the Heath government intended when the first Docklands Joint Committee was formed in 1973, redevelopment would soon be 'bringing the West End to the East End' (quoted in Klausner 1986). Similarly, including public art with expensive corporate and commercial architecture helped writers visualise Battery Park City as a grand, romantic, yet accessible urban landscape in the tradition of Venice, St Petersburg and Constantinople (Deutsche 1988: 31).

As perceptions of the entire urban centre shift to a landscape of power, the use of the centre merges work and leisure, job and home, public arena and private refuge. Some might argue that these arrangements reflect the preferences of a sizable segment of the newly rich, or at least it satisfies their desire for convenience (cf. Thrift *et al.* 1987). In some ways too it replaces the older mix of activities in the segmented vernacular, valuing 'indigenous' or 'ethnic' suppliers to the extent that they contribute to an urbane ambiance. Thus it is not only the economic factor of higher rents that displaces old tenants, but also the visual and social coherence of a landscape that caters to a more affluent population.

A structural precondition of these shifts has been the abandonment of most urban manufacturing. Since the 1960s, New York and London have lost half their blue-collar jobs to automation, regional decentralisation and the internationalisation of industrial production. Certainly jobs in processing industries (e.g. chemicals, foods) and product assembly had located years earlier on the periphery or in the suburbs. Yet low rents and easy access to markets kept the garment and printing industries in the centre, along with a decreasing number of traditional crafts and, of course, the docks. The displacement of these jobs, however, freed the areas in which they were located for other uses. Property values that had been restricted by manufacturing plants and working-class housing could now reflect the inherent utility of a central location. Higher land values exerted pressure, in turn, on remaining industrial uses. The social meaning of this space was, moreover, freed for reinterpretation and new appropriation. The previously 'closed' vernacular of working-class districts, immigrant ghettos and industrial areas that were always regarded as dangerous and suspicious, especially after dark, was now 'open' as landscape to those who could consume it. These factors fed a wave of private-market property investment from new office construction to gentrification.

Historic building and district classifications have greatly contributed to 'opening up' the vernacular to a broadly defined upper middle class (cf. Wright 1985). So have restaurants, gourmet groceries and stores that sell artisanal or artist-designed products. These amenities lure consumers with cultural capital, i.e. the experience, education and time to seek them out (cf. Bourdieu 1986). And artists' districts – notably, Manhattan's loft district of SoHo – have also opened up the dingy charms of the vernacular by incorporating them into a landscape of cultural consumption (Zukin 1988).

While individuals change their use of the centre, geography reflects the centre's new functions. Clerkenwell and parts of Hackney lose their somewhat heterogeneous social character, emerging as enclaves of history that can best be apprehended by means of a guide. Spitalfields sheds the uneasy shadow of artisans' workshops, the wholesale market and Jack the Ripper to be presented as a prime site for commercial redevelopment. Docklands is re-created as a direct expansion of the financial centre on the one hand, and an urban frontier, on the other (Smith 1986; Crilley 1990). And if the railroad yards and canals at King's Cross are unified by Norman Foster's new urban centre, they will lose their 'inaccessible', somewhat desolate and inchoate quality: King's Cross will take its place between Camden and Islington in a coherent North London landscape.

A TALE OF TWO CITIES

With big projects like King's Cross and Docklands, London seems to escape traditional institutional bounds, i.e. the instrumental roles that are constituted by various territorial levels of government, social communities and public–private distinctions. In New York, on the other hand, big projects like Battery Park City or the 42nd Street Redevelopment at Times Square seem only to extend institutional precedents by which developers get to build what they want. For over 150 years New York's high land values have driven low-rent, low-class uses out of the centre, including working-class neighbourhoods, manufacturers and small crafts shops (Tobier 1988). But isn't each city really more complex? London's growth has been restricted by the Green Belt since the 1930s, as well as by political pressure by central government and an extraordinarily high percentage of housing stock in council housing; yet one observer of recent urban changes says that London is geographically and politically more mutable than New York (Savitch 1988: 170–1). For its part, although New York has always been in thrall to business élites, a change of mayors (albeit usually within the Democratic Party) and extraordinary mobilisation by citizens' groups, often in the law courts, have sometimes shifted the purpose and reduced the size of new construction, and occasionally slowed the pace of change (cf. Fainstein and Fainstein 1988).

Despite these differences, the landscapes of power that are emerging in New York and London are strikingly similar. This is hardly surprising, for redevelopment of the centre in both cities is commissioned and designed by the same worldly superstars, including developers, architects and private-sector financial institutions. Just as skyscrapers have become the *sine qua non* of place in the global hierarchy of cities, so do US, Japanese and Canadian builders and bankers represent the basis of global market rank. A city that aims to be a world financial centre makes deals with

Olympia & York and Kumagai Gumi, welcomes Citibank and Dai-Ichi Kangyo, and transplants Cesar Pelli as well as Skidmore Owings and Merrill and Kohn Pederson Fox.

Developers tend to use the same strategic tools. They seek to diversify their portfolios by spreading investment projects around the world, and find these investment sites according to computerised projections made by the same accounting, property and management firms, which are also organised on a worldwide basis (Thrift 1987). From the late 1970s, moreover, and especially since 1984, large US developers, their contractors and even their subcontractors have compensated for saturated office markets in North America by building in Western Europe, where lower vacancy rates are reflected in higher rates of return (*New York Times*, 10 October 1989). Even following the stock market crash of October 1987, overseas investors increased their development activity in the City. Foreign buyers have spent nearly as much on this sort of property investment as UK buyers since 1988, with landmark buildings in the centre purchased by Japanese, Middle Eastern and Venezuelan investors (*Estates Gazette*, 26 November 1988: 118–20).

Wrongly or not, the progressive lowering of barriers to multinational trade in services, as in London's Big Bang of 1986 and the consolidation of Western European markets in 1992, has encouraged this foreign participation. Yet unified markets do not require a large number of first-tier financial capitals. And the close links between trading practices in global market centres probably lead to a coordinated overexpansion of office space, like the coordinated retrenchment of personnel in New York and London following the stock exchange crash of 1987 and the increased volatility in the market in 1989. In other words – despite the common wisdom – it may no longer be a good idea to use property development in London as countercyclical hedging against loss of investment value in New York. Estate agents in London already anticipate a lag between excessive office supply and sluggish demand, led by a 42 per cent office vacancy rate in Docklands (*The Independent*, 4 January 1990: 5).

New York's office market should at any rate provide a cautionary tale. While foreign banks cut investments and employment less in New York than in London following the 1987 crash, and domestic financial firms either delayed massive layoffs or limited them to specific low-yield activities, office vacancy rates rose as US firms trimmed their payrolls selectively and physically consolidated operations. By 1989, 12 per cent of the best-equipped offices in the Wall Street area were unoccupied, as well as 22 per cent of secondary office buildings; in midtown, vacancy rates varied from 13 to 15 per cent (*New York Times*, 2 July 1989; 22 October 1989). By contrast, both downtown and midtown office districts experienced only a 9 to 10 per cent vacancy rate before the 1987 crash (opposed to 3 per cent in Europe). This downward trend was also reflected in the large amount of office space that was made available for sublet: 25 per cent in the Wall Street area alone.

Even the large money centre banks have added slack to New York's office market. While generally profitable and still expanding overseas, these financial institutions decided to sell some of the remarkable corporate headquarters buildings with which they were identified and move back-office operations outside Manhattan (*Business Week*, 3 April 1989: 94–5). Chase Manhattan Bank, long the linchpin of and major property investor in the Wall Street area, moved back-office operations to a new building in downtown Brooklyn. Citibank sold most of its diagonal-roof headquarters to a Japanese insurance company, building a distinctive new skyscraper across the East River in Long Island City. Storing assets in face of Third World debt and Japanese competition may have been only one among many reasons for Citibank's action, for the bank is playing an important part in the projected commercial redevelopment of the waterfront in that area of Queens.

But the pattern of playing musical chairs with office relocations has long been typical of New York's commercial property markets. City government subsidies and zoning changes have recently lured major developers from the overbuilt East Side to the West Side of midtown Manhattan, and office building owners attract large corporate tenants by offering special facilities, rent reductions, buildout allowances for tenants' improvements, and even a share of equity. These conditions allowed developer William Zeckendorf Jr to sign up the Madison Avenue advertising firms Ogilvy & Mather and N.W. Ayer and the Wall Street law firm Cravath Swain & Moore as tenants in Worldwide Plaza, his new mixed-use complex on Eighth Avenue north of Times Square (*New York Times*, 29 January 1989).[1]

Governmental connections also aid developers' efforts to create a locational advantage. During the decades that David Rockefeller directed Chase Manhattan Bank, he formed a business group, the

Downtown-Lower Manhattan Association, in 1957. The association's desiderata for protecting Chase's property investment in the area began with relocating the wholesale food markets to the Outer Boroughs, and included an ambitious programme to rebuild the municipal administrative centre, develop middle-income housing, attract university facilities and establish new bellwether skyscrapers that could compete with the more modern offices in midtown. The city government implemented most of this wish-list during the 1960s. Moreover, when David's brother Nelson was elected governor of New York State – a post he held from the 1960s to the mid-1970s – powerful state institutions were created and utilised for large-scale urban redevelopment. A new public authority, the New York State Urban Development Corporation, superseded local powers to condemn property, design projects and finance their construction by issuing bonds. The Battery Park City Authority controlled new waterfront construction. Meanwhile, the older Port Authority of New York and New Jersey, which manages most of the mega-scale transportation systems in the metropolitan region, used its jurisdiction over the port to commission its redevelopment. Mainly due to these institutions, the World Trade Center was conceived and built on waterfront landfill. To aid the process of marketing this mammoth space, some say, a local law requiring new fire protection devices was passed, hastening tenant relocation from older office buildings throughout lower Manhattan into the World Trade Center. The Rockefellers plied a winning strategy in the downtown office market with their influence over government, ability to move both public and private investment capital into new construction, and fine-grained understanding of the value of architecture as symbolic capital. This was in any event a period of manufacturing decline and business service boom, accentuated in property markets by the levers of public and private power (see Zukin 1988: 16, 43–6; Fainstein and Fainstein 1988: 175–7).

Until recently, in fact, commercial property development in New York was seldom constrained by popular protest or political opposition. In contrast to housing and highway construction, where community groups made their pressure felt, the business district in the centre was both materially and symbolically regarded as the province of business élites. Industrial decentralisation toward the Outer Boroughs, New Jersey and Long Island had reduced manufacturers' and workers' influence over land use in

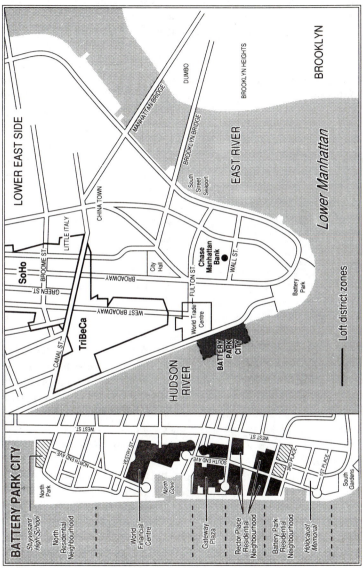

Figure 8.1 **Lower Manhattan and Battery Park City**

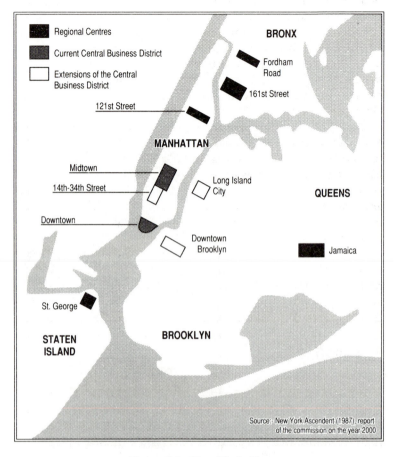

Figure 8.2 New York City

Manhattan since 1900. Zoning plans that were designed by bankers, lawyers and 'disinterested' reformers tended to restrict their use to ever narrower belts and pockets around the centre. Further, workers who depended on walking to factory jobs were first crammed into tenements on the Lower East Side, then encouraged to buy houses outside the centre by post-World War II home-ownership loans geared to suburban construction. The public-sector city builder Robert Moses, whose projects shaped so much of the city between the 1930s and 1960s, tended to favour housing over commercial development. By the sixties, large-scale removal of Manhattan residents occurred on only two, non-commercial project sites: the cultural complex at Lincoln Center and the primarily residential Upper West Side urban renewal area, both of which were intended to complement rather than expand the midtown business centre. Thus by 1970 no residential community remained to voice complaints about a 'change of character' in the centre.[2]

During the 1980s, however, the enormous expansion of New York's landscape of power was seen as having taken a toll on both 'quality of life' and 'affordable housing', two shibboleths of liberal opposition to business strategies. Yet without a tenacious working-class presence and pressure groups, as in Tower Hamlets and nearby boroughs of London, institutional bargaining focused mainly on trade-offs. On the one hand, the city government fully acknowledged the right to create private value by permitting taller buildings with more rentable space in congested parts of the centre. On the other hand, city officials tried to impose an obligation on developers to restore or renew public value, by adding plaza-like spaces open to public use, incorporating theatres or historic landmark structures instead of tearing them down, or refurbishing parks and subway stations near their building sites.

PUBLIC – PRIVATE LINKAGES

A hallmark of these exchanges is the concept of 'linkage', that establishes an explicit quid pro quo for specific development rights. Significantly, in New York, the relative absence of working-class and low-income housing in the centre indicates that any low-cost housing that a developer commits to build as part of a linkage arrangement will be located elsewhere, outside the centre. Rare exceptions – like Zeckendorf's renovation of apartments for Clinton residents in the neighbourhood of Worldwide Plaza – are devised by means of extended negotiations among community representatives, developers' attorneys, and staff members of city agencies and elected officials, especially the borough president. On-site housing renovations are always fewer than community groups demand, and cost the developers much more (so they say) than they can afford. But to the degree that developers want to reduce negotiation time, and improve the environment in which their project is marketed, the expense of linkage becomes a normal part of development costs.[5]

Linkage agreements, moreover, do not usually extend to employment. Construction jobs are understood to be determined wholly by the construction manager whom a developer selects. They are thus either given to the building trades unions, that are heavily white, highly paid and involved in complicated kick-back schemes, or earmarked for cheaper, non-union labour. Only construction that is directly subsidised by the federal government is subject to 'affirmative action' hiring rules and norms governing selection of minority subcontractors. These rules are often evaded. In any event, construction jobs seldom reach the hard-core unemployed on the Lower East Side or in Harlem, Brooklyn and the South Bronx.

By New York standards, therefore, the linkage-type arrangements that have been negotiated in London by the LDDC, the boroughs and various private developers are entirely acceptable. New housing for relocating Docklands residents at Beckton may be far from home, but not so far as it would be in New York City. Urban renewal projects have never returned displaced residents to their homes; when they have attempted to do so, the conditions of tenure have changed – especially rent structures but increasingly, as in Docklands, a conversion from 95 per cent rental to about 33 per cent owner-occupied housing (Committee of Public Accounts 1988–89: viii). Nor do displaced businesses generally return to their previous sites. Whether or not business owners eventually receive financial compensation, they often choose to move away or shut down when they are not forced out by higher rents, uncertainty and eviction (i.e. non-renewal of their lease). In the Urban Development Area in Tower Hamlets, for example, 580 firms employed almost 9,500 men and women in 1981; by 1984, only 385 firms employed about 8,000 people (Employment Committee, 29 June 1988: 292). Yet much of this job loss reflects the final disappearance of obsolete industrial sectors (e.g. sawmilling, manufacture of rubber products, non-ferrous metals and grain milling), as well as, we assume, the breakdown of local clusters of suppliers, distributors and manufacturers. In London as in New York, however, the restructuring of property markets at the centre *is not intended* to restore older economic uses. Thus the film producers, office equipment suppliers and manufacturers, and publishers who moved into Dockland's industrial facilities during the 1980s recruit from different labour markets than inner London's working class. In another version of musical chairs, they generally transfer their labour force from a prior location rather than hire on site. To the degree that these shops are unionised, moreover, institutional procedures restrict the hiring of new employees wherever they live or have previously worked.

For the most part, the new landscape of the centre is oriented toward business services, most of whose work-force commutes from outside the centre. In New York, white-collar employees who work downtown have commuted from uptown and the suburbs since the early 1900s (Tobier 1988: 85, 88, 101, 103). Similarly, in that part of Docklands on the Isle of Dogs, where most new jobs, even in industrial firms, are office jobs, 25 per cent of the work-force now commute to work from outside the immediate area (Isle of Dogs, Tower Hamlets, East London), and an additional 30 per cent commute from outside London. In 1981, by contrast, 35 per cent of all employees on the Isle of Dogs were residents of Tower Hamlets (Employment Committee, 29 June 1988: 293).

By 1987, when the Canadian developers Olympia & York signed on with LDDC to build a mixed-use complex at Canary Wharf, property markets ensured that primary employment in these facilities would be in office jobs rather than the high-tech industries and warehouses that had been foreseen in 1981. But East End residents, like their low-income counterparts in Harlem and the South Bronx, are not educated to fill these jobs. Learning English as a second language even when they stay in school, and hardly proficient with computers, young residents of 'vernacular' communities suffer a skills mismatch with new jobs in the centre as they become available. In New York, a recent hard-nosed review of the city's competitive ability to retain major employers in financial services placed the highest priority on improving labour force quality. Labour shortages that were beginning to be felt at the end of the eighties reflected not only nearly full absorption of potential workers from the suburbs, but also a lack of basic reading, writing and mathematics proficiency among the urban young, as well as a lack of understanding of 'job expectations with regard to punctuality, appropriate dress, and interpersonal skills' (*Meeting the Challenge* 1989: 11).

The business association that sponsored this study recommended increased collaboration between the financial services industry and the New York City Board of Education. One part of this public–private partnership would focus on curriculum reform; another would address job placement and job readiness problems. While personnel from financial services firms would create a constructive presence in the high schools as auxiliary advisers and teachers of a sort, following a pattern already set by IBM, the report also proposed that financial services firms work directly with educational administrators and professional teachers, 'recruiting, managing, and training educational staff to adequately prepare students for future employment' (Meeting the Challenge 1989: 15). In several ways this marks the US approach to reducing the local– global mismatch in world financial centres. Not only does the report call for a partnership between the public and private sectors, but the direction of this partnership would be guided by employers' requirements. Educational skills and acculturation to the corporate world represent an old set of employment criteria. More importantly, the current set of employers' expectations would replace expensive in-house training with city-financed programmes. Employers would also intervene in teacher selection and training.

Another direction is suggested by the Canary Wharf Social Contract and additional agreements that were negotiated in 1987–88 by Olympia & York, Tower Hamlets Council, the LDDC and labour and industry committees in construction. Everyone acknowledged the same structural problems that were described in New York: industrial decline and decentralisation from the city, geographical concentrations of hard-core unemployment, partial replacement of semi-skilled blue-collar by highly skilled white-collar jobs and a skills mismatch between requirements for these jobs and achievement levels of the local population.[4] But at Canary Wharf, the private developer agreed in principle to encourage the employment of local residents on the construction site, seek suppliers among local businesses and set up training facilities to qualify local workers for jobs within the development area. After setting those general conditions with LDDC, Olympia & York signed a more specific agreement with Tower Hamlets borough council to establish an educational trust of £2,500,000, to be paid in nine annual instalments during the course of construction at Canary Wharf, and 'use its best endeavours to ensure' the employment of 2,000 borough residents at the development site, either in construction or eventual (office) jobs (Employment Committee,

18 May 1988: 243–4). This expands the concept of the (US) Boston Compact.

But an immediate problem arose in the skills mismatch between local adults, who had been trained for semi-skilled industrial jobs, and the construction work that was required on the site. The developer mobilised representatives of local government authorities, LDDC, the national Manpower Services Commission, the Construction Industry Training Board, the construction trades union and the multinational construction manager, Lehrer McGovern Bovis, which had recently been created by a merger of two large US and UK firms. With costs paid by the private developer and the national government's MSC, a recruitment and training centre was set up on site for local residents to become construction workers in short-handed specialties like electrical work and steel erection. Training courses would be shared by the trades union and a newly cooperative industry board (Employment Committee, 18 May 1988: 244–6).

Although Olympia & York has gone further toward meeting local employment needs in London than in New York, several issues remain unresolved. First, the developer does not directly control either the construction manager or the financial and business services firms that will occupy the project's 15 million square feet. While Lehrer McGovern Bovis successfully completed Olympia & York's World Financial Center in New York's Battery Park City, the construction managers can clearly develop their own networks of suppliers and subcontractors from all over Europe and the United States. The extent of simultaneous new construction in Docklands and elsewhere in London has in fact required Lehrer McGovern Bovis to put out contracts from crane operation to woodworking in many countries. These subcontractors and suppliers are not bound by the Olympia & York employment agreement with Tower Hamlets. It is questionable, moreover, whether such future tenants as Crédit Suisse First Boston, Merrill Lynch and Morgan Stanley will agree to be obligated by O & Y's employment norms. This limitation becomes more acute as firms that serve global financial markets respond more drastically to market declines and fluctuating profit margins.

Another problem involves the gender mismatch between unemployed industrial workers, who are mainly male, and the largely female work-force that has expanded with growth in business services. Insofar as new Docklands employment will continue to be drawn from the relocation of back-office jobs from the City, these jobs will be primarily staffed by women. To some degree, the increase in female clerical employment has cushioned the impoverishment of low-income minority groups in New York. Yet it has widened the income disparity between native-born black men and women and also benefited public-sector more than private-sector employees. It also has less effect in certain immigrant communities where women do not speak English and are not encouraged to seek work outside the home. To the extent that East End residents, especially those in Bengali communities, share these conditions, they may not find work in Docklands. Macroeconomic conditions also affect employment. Interest rates, tax laws and restrictive public policies may in general delay financial firms' expansion.

A more specific factor reflects the potential overexpansion of redevelopment projects, especially in the office market, in inner London. Just as midtown Manhattan siphoned office jobs from the Wall Street area, Battery Park City attracted financial services from other buildings in lower Manhattan, and back offices have been relocated to northern Queens and downtown Brooklyn, so does London risk gaining jobs in one borough at the expense of another. While King's Cross may anchor upscale property markets across North London, for example, its office buildings may draw tenants that would otherwise move to Canary Wharf (*Chartered Surveyor Weekly*, 9 June 1988: 9). Moreover, new office construction within the Square Mile of the City is intended to attract headquarters and front-office locations, but in a more cautious economic climate it may retain back offices that would have moved to Docklands. Certainly the area around Liverpool Street Station needed more up-to-date office facilities; whether there are enough jobs to fill them, however, is an open question.

A final, perennial problem reflects the tensions in all public–private co-operation. The New York City government frequently feuds with developers over their failure to implement signed agreements while enjoying the benefit of additional development rights. Citizens' groups also call attention to the gap between developers' profits and their contributions to community facilities. Although the LDDC managed to get Olympia & York's agreement to contribute a major share of construction costs for the new light railway line to Canary Wharf, the two have disagreed about O & Y's obligation. Cost overruns have reduced the developer's share of expenses, prompting additional infusion of public funds. In light of the promises that were made, pressuring Olympia & York on this point is hardly conceivable. Sanctions against multinational developers who have many projects in other major cities are held hostage to competition in global financial markets.

Olympia & York is an especially difficult developer to target. Their financing has been innovative and relatively free from the usual pressures exerted by bank loans, for they sell commercial paper to cover costs. They often enter projects, moreover, at the bottom of a market. While this made them saviours of both the World Financial Center, to which they committed themselves before any tenant had expressed interest, and Canary Wharf, which they took over after the initial consortium of US and UK banks had failed either to finance or start to build, it also makes opposing them more difficult. Their ability to limit or diversify their investment, specialising in commercial development, on the one hand, and taking an equity position in competitive projects, such as King's Cross, on the other, gives Olympia & York added leverage. This is enhanced by their stated preference for long-term project commitment. Finally, the Reichmanns, who wholly own O & Y, negotiated the major part of their London role directly with central government. This gives them both a substantial financial guarantee (as for improvement of the Jubilee underground line) and impressive political backing.

Foreign firms' increasing role in global financial centres raises another thorny question. City governments that can no longer rely on the national state to finance construction are drawn to multi-national developers like Olympia & York who can assemble large pools of capital and work fairly quickly. In the absence of elected city government, a specialised public authority is usually even more impressionable. The expertise that large foreign firms require 'on the ground' they pick up from local (junior) partners. Financial markets are also attracted to foreign firms that can bring bigger capital assets, larger international networks and special expertise to bear on increasingly complicated transactions. Yet foreign firms can evade laws or guidelines, such as affirmative action norms, that have been established to benefit local populations (on Japanese banks, see Cohen 1983) even while they are swept by other local institutional norms, such as high salaries and high turnover for the most sought-after financial analysts (as

Japanese financial firms in New York have recently experienced). Under these conditions, foreign investors increase their equity in world cities. By 1988, foreigners owned 20 per cent of all office space in Manhattan (*New York Times*, 27 June 1988) and were becoming more active in London than UK office developers (*Estates Gazette*, 26 November 1988: 127–8).

It is interesting to consider, however, in what forms does 'foreignness' remain a distinct quality in global financial centres. US firms have had a strong presence in London advertising and corporate law since the 1960s and 1970s. As takeovers and other business transactions require special expertise, London and Tokyo call upon more US consultants and advisers (e.g. the support personnel assembled for and against Sir James Goldsmith's bid to take over BAT in 1989). Similarly, national governments have eased many barriers against entry into local markets by foreign suppliers of business services. Although licensing still remains a matter of 'local knowledge' (Noyelle and Dutka 1988), foreign firms have steadily won approval to act as lead agents in governmental bond sales and other financial markets.

A local source of competition may be more troubling to both New York and London. The decentralisation of business services throughout the metropolitan region may strengthen the area as a whole while impoverishing the initial core. Many corporate headquarters have relocated different activities to specialised centres in the effort to cut costs, ensure a skilled and docile supply of labour and enhance both external prestige and internal commitment to the firm. New York industrial corporations have moved both headquarters and research and development facilities to separate facilities in Westchester County (New York), Fairfield County (Connecticut) and Morris and Bergen counties (New Jersey) since the 1950s. In London, also, headquarters remain in the City or West End, perhaps decentralising to the Isle of Dogs. Ancillary paper-processing functions, a big part of the old central pool of employment, go to Reading or Harlow. R&D is in a country house in the Thames Valley near Henley or Marlow while various types of industrial production move farther afield (Hall 1989: 61; on 'jobs exodus' from London, see *The Times*, 2 January 1990). With continued computerisation and advanced telecommunications this trend can be expected to proceed, abetted by corporate consolidation following mergers and acquisitions.

The federal system of government in the United States empha-
sises decentralisation as a special problem. Jobs and tax revenues
gained in New Jersey or Connecticut may represent losses for New
York. In England, where a similar metropolitan region is forming
to the north-west of London, competition over the unequal
diffusion of economic growth may stir as much conflict as in New
York or London boroughs. But whether one views decentralization
as competition or merely expansion, for a number of years neither
New York nor London has grown as fast in business services as
national and provincial centres (Hall 1989: 54–5; Noyelle and
Stanback 1983; *Meeting the Challenge* 1989).

IN THE LONG RUN . . .

The material and symbolic reconstruction of the centre is a long-
term historical process. The sudden appearance of a Docklands or
Battery Park City masks the gradual effects of structural change,
notably, a shift from organising the city as an assortment of
concrete production spaces toward visualising it as a coherent
space of abstract financial processes and consumption. By the
same token, the seeming abruptness with which urban redevelopment schemes are adopted and abandoned reflects temporary
booms and busts in property markets and changing political alliances, as well as financial market advances and declines. Yet, in
addition to redeveloping 'capitalist' space, the landscape of power
reflects both the incremental institutional interventions of the
national and local state and the conscious cultural reorganisation
of business, political and artistic élites – those who wield *all* the
levers of social power.

Battery Park City and Docklands offer concise examples of the
morphological, geographical and aesthetic processes that are
involved. They are primarily sites that government has had to
market many times: first to private investors and developers, then
to banks and public and private bodies with the authority to
approve large-scale financing (e.g. bonds), also to a restive
citizenry that presses for both quality-of-life improvements (e.g.
low-rise building, low-density zoning) and affordable housing, and
finally to a broad segment of the public that has both financial and
cultural capital to consume the space the city has produced.

These processes lead, on the one hand, to an aestheticisation of
the project at the expense of a focus on critical social needs such

217

as housing and jobs (cf. Deutsche 1988). On the other hand, they lead to image-making that obscures the removal or incorporation of the segmented vernacular by the landscape of power of a world financial centre. Figures in this landscape are the co-operative artists, urban planners, and designers who find a useful function for their work in furnishing the new public spaces of commercial projects; they form a symbolic context for the material contributions of public officials, architects and developers.

Despite great differences between the political systems of New York and London, and different relations between their financial communities and the national economy (Coakley and Harris 1983; Ingham 1984), both major projects of contemporary new construction – Battery Park City and Docklands – show the same trajectory of a landscape of power (see Table 8.1).

Significant to globalisation, the redevelopment of the centre in New York and London has proceeded almost in tandem. While Docklands required, and still requires, the building of more transportation infrastructure, Battery Park City has merely spawned new streets and parks, essentially consumption amenities on the water (plazas, marinas, fountains).[5] Each project has been delayed by the continued belief among investors and developers that the project might be unmarketable, although the offices of the World Financial Center are over 90 per cent filled. Each crisis of investors' confidence was overcome by expanding the project's commercial facilities and reducing or removing the proportion of low-income housing. But the major obstacle to construction in both cases was eased by maximising the *private* role in development. Battery Park City Authority relinquished most of its instrumental role to private developers in 1979, and London Docklands Development Corporation proceeded the same way when it replaced the earlier, borough-dominated London Docklands Joint Commission in 1981. A belated interest in 'community development' on the part of LDDC in 1989–90 led the corporation to lobby central government for more social services without, however, denying the priority of private-sector demands.

Construction advanced on both sites to gradual completions and new arrivals through the 1990s. The more frenetic pace and much larger space at Docklands contrasted with monumental corporate architecture and an absence of old buildings at Battery Park City. But London suffered from the more massive resources required to build Docklands, the city's weaker attraction to foreign firms, and macro-economic conditions in the UK. In both cities, a recession in financial markets put all market-based development in doubt.

To this day we don't really know the economic conditions that maintain a world financial centre (Kindleberger 1974; Levich and Walter 1989). Nor do we know for sure what it should look like. But one urban planner thinks it inescapable that the multi-centred metropolitan regions that are now being built outside the centre will come to resemble the City: 'They will be specialized, high-intensity, high-rent centers, dedicated to performance of the region's higher-level functions' (Hall 1989: 78). Whether this will relieve the combined congestion and impoverishment of the City is an open question. It contradicts, however, the pleas for an *urbane* city frequently made by planners, civic élites and investors (cf. *New York Ascendant* 1987; Hall 1989).

A multi-centred city that would somehow dilute the arbitrary expansion of the centre negates the cheek-by-jowl juxtaposition of neighbourliness and imperial power that characterised New York and London at their commercial height in the not-too-distant past. The old contrast between a singular landscape of power at the centre and a segmented vernacular has deliberately been destroyed.

Table 8.1 Docklands and Battery Park City: a selective chronology

Docklands	
Covent Garden Market relocation planned	1961
Office construction banned in Central London	1964
First dock closure (East India)	1967
London Docklands Joint Commission formed	1973
Growth of eurodollar and eurobond markets	1973
Office construction ban lifted	1973
Docklands Strategic Plan published	1976
Inner Urban Areas Act passed	1978
London Docklands Joint Commission abolished – replaced by London Docklands Development Council	1979–81
Local Government Planning and Land Act	1980
Last dock closures (Royal docks)	1981
Billingsgate Market relocated	1982
Isle of Dogs Enterprise Zone established	1982

First apartments opened	1982
Rise of corporate borrowing by means of securities, development of futures trading	1982
Relocation of News International and Daily Telegraph and Guardian printing plants from Fleet Street	1986–87
Greater London Council abolished	1987
Olympia & York sign Master Building Agreement with LDDC and Tower Hamlets	1987–88
Docklands Light Railway and Airport opened	1987
Canary Wharf opened to tenants	1992
Canary Wharf to be completed	1997–98

Battery Park City

Downtown–Lower Manhattan Association formed, new headquarters of Chase Manhattan Bank built	1955–65
World Trade Center plan announced	1964
Dockers' jobs phased out, Battery Park City proposed by Governor Rockefeller	1966
Washington and Grosvenor wholesale food markets relocated to the Bronx	1967
New York State Urban Development Corporation established	1968
Pro-business development strategy adopted by Mayor Lindsay's second administration	1969
World Trade Center opened to tenants	1970
SoHo artists' district established by zoning	1971
Battery Park City Authority issues first bonds	1972
Decline of dollar, saturated New York office market, unemployment on Wall Street following stock market decline	1972–73
SoHo historic cast-iron district established; new construction in this area banned	1973
New York City fiscal crisis	1975
TriBeCa residential zone established by zoning adjacent to BPC site	1976
Battery Park City Authority leases land and cedes decision making to private developers; new master plan and financing adopted	1979–80
World Trade Center completed	1980
Olympia & York signed as developer of World Financial Center	1980
First BPC apartments opened to tenants	1982

220

| Linkage agreement signed to build low-income housing in Harlem and South Bronx | 1986 |
| World Financial Center completed | 1988 |

NOTES

1 It is interesting to note that Zeckendorf's investment partners on recent projects include Kumagai Gumi, who have also become active as contractors and developers in London (see *Estate Times Supplement*, Autumn 1987: 49, 52).

2 I omit discussion of the increasingly influential criticism of high-rise construction and 'cataclysmic' urban growth expressed by Jane Jacobs (1961), the destruction of urban working-class communities described by Herbert Gans (1962), and the cultural appreciation of old city buildings awakened by various architectural activists (e.g. Silver 1967) during the 1960s. This line of criticism eventually proved more effective than less organised citizens' protests against urban renewal and relocation from their neighbourhoods (cf. Caro 1975), leading, on the one hand, to historic preservation or landmark legislation by both municipal and federal governments and, on the other hand, to both the contextual and historical-reference schools of postmodern architecture, as well as more global critiques of modernism. The only residential community in US cities that has been able to establish and defend a niche in the centre during the past 20 years is that of artists, and they are successful to the extent that they do not conflict with the long-term development of commercial property markets (Zukin 1988).

3 Often these linkage arrangements are required for a project's approval by a community board or, in Zeckendorf's case, the city-wide Board of Estimate (abolished by a Supreme Court decision in 1989).

4 London differs from New York, however, on three key structural conditions. The growth of business services, as well as their concentration in New York, have been more rapid and more extensive than in London. Further, London has suffered more job loss in these services than New York. Finally, concentrations of the long-term unemployed tend to be in inner London (i.e. the East End) rather than in areas distant from the centre, as in New York (see Noyelle and Stanback 1983; Savitch 1988; Hall 1989).

5 The Wall Street area had been linked to both Pennsylvania Station in midtown and commuter suburbs in New Jersey by a special subway system established by the Port Authority under Governor Rockefeller in the late 1960s. From the mid-1970s, liberal spokespersons from the financial community stressed the need to improve the general subway system as soon as the pressing needs of the fiscal crisis were satisfied and, from 1982, when property markets improved, the subways did resume a programme of modest improvements. In 1989, a ferry service between Battery Park City and New Jersey was inaugurated – or

221

re-inaugurated, since these ferries had been phased out in 1967 and their waterfront terminals demolished. Despite a history of budget shortfalls and planning errors, the Port Authority paid much more attention to Manhattan's mass transit needs than the UK government did to central London's.

REFERENCES

Bender, T. and Taylor, W.R. (1987) 'Culture and architecture: some aesthetic tensions in the shaping of modern New York City', in W. Sharpe and L. Wallock (eds) *Visions of the Modern City*, Baltimore: Johns Hopkins University Press.

Bourdieu, P. (1986) *Distinction: A Social Critique of the Judgement of Taste*, tr. R. Nice, Cambridge MA: Harvard University Press.

Caro, R.A. (1975) *The Power Broker: Robert Moses and the Fall of New York*, New York: Vintage.

Coakley, J. and Harris, L. (1983) *The City of Capital*, Oxford: Basil Blackwell.

Cohen, B. (1983) 'The future of the investment banking industry', report prepared for the Office of Economic Development, City of New York.

—— (1989) 'The foreign challenge to US commercial banks', in T. Noyelle (ed.) *New York's Financial Markets*, Boulder and London: Westview.

Committee of Public Accounts, House of Commons (1988–89), 'London Docklands Development Corporation'.

Crilley, D. (1990) 'The advertiser and the architect: Remaking the image of London Docklands', paper presented at the annual meeting of the Association of American Geographers, Toronto.

Deutsche, R. (1988) 'Uneven development: public art in New York City', *October* 47: 3–52.

Employment Committee, House of Commons (18 May 1988) 'The employment effects of urban development corporations: memorandum submitted by Olympia and York Canary Wharf Limited'.

—— (29 June 1988) 'The employment effects of development corporations: memorandum submitted by the London Borough of Tower Hamlets'.

Fainstein, N.I. and Fainstein, S.S. (1988) 'Governing regimes and the political economy of development in New York City, 1964–1984', in J.H. Mollenkopf (ed.) *Power, Culture, and Place: Essays on New York City*, New York: Russell Sage Foundation.

Gans, H. (1962) *The Urban Villagers*, New York: Free Press.

Hall, P. (1989) *London 2001*, London: Unwin Hyman.

Ingham, G. (1984) *Capitalism Divided? The City and Industry in British Social Development*, New York: Schocken.

Jacobs, J. (1961) *The Death and Life of Great American Cities*, New York: Vintage.

Kindleberger, C.P. (1974) *The Formation of Financial Centres*, Princeton, NJ: Princeton Studies in International Finance, no. 36.

Klausner, D. (1986) 'Beyond separate spheres: linking production with social reproduction and consumption', *Society and Space* 4: 29–40.

Levich, R.M. and Walter, I. (1989) 'The regulation of global financial markets', in T. Noyelle (ed.) *New York's Financial Markets*, Boulder and London: Westview.

Marcuse, P. (1986) 'Abandonment, gentrification, and displacement: The linkages in New York City', in N. Williams and P. Williams (eds) *Gentrification of the City*, Boston: Allen & Unwin.

Meeting the Challenge: Maintaining and Enhancing New York City as the World Financial Capital (1989), report prepared by the Financial Services Task Force of the New York City Partnership.

Nelson, J.I. and Lorence, J. (1985) 'Employment in service activities and inequality in metropolitan areas', *Urban Affairs Quarterly* 21, 1: 106–25.

New York Ascendant (1987) Report of the Commission on the Year 2000.

Noyelle, T. (1989) 'New York's competitiveness', in T. Noyelle (ed.) *New York's Financial Markets*, Boulder and London: Westview.

Noyelle, T. and Dutka, A.B. (1988) *International Trade in Business Services*, Cambridge, MA: American Enterprise Institute/Ballinger.

Noyelle, T.J. and Stanback, T.M. Jr (1983) *The Economic Transformation of American Cities*, Totawa, NJ: Rowman & Allenheld.

Rose, D. (1984) 'Rethinking gentrification: beyond the uneven development of marxist urban theory', *Society and Space* 1: 47–74.

Savitch, H.V. (1988) *Post-Industrial Cities: Politics and Planning in New York, Paris, and London*, Princeton, NJ: Princeton University Press.

Silver, N. (1967) *Lost New York*, New York: Schocken.

Smith, N. (1986) 'Gentrification, the frontier, and the reconstruction of urban space', in N. Smith and P. Williams (eds) *Gentrification of the City*, Boston: Allen & Unwin.

Squires, G. D. (ed.) (1989) *Unequal Partnerships: The Political Economy of Urban Development in Postwar America*, New Brunswick, NJ: Rutgers University Press.

Thrift, N. (1987) 'The fixers: The urban geography of international commercial capital', in J. Henderson and M. Castells (eds) *Global Restructuring and Territorial Development*, London: Sage.

Thrift, N., Leyshon, A. and Daniels, P.W. (1987) '"Sexy greedy": the new international financial system, the City of London and the Southeast of England', Working Papers on Producer Services, no. 8, Universities of Bristol and Liverpool.

Tobier, E. (1988) 'Manhattan's business district in the industrial age', in J.H. Mollenkopf (ed.) *Power, Culture, and Place: Essays on New York City*, New York: Russell Sage Foundation.

Walter, I. (1988) *Global Competition in Financial Services*, Cambridge MA: American Enterprise Institute/Ballinger.

Wright, P. (1985) *On Living in an Old Country*, London: Verso.

Zukin, S. (1988) *Loft Living: Culture and Capital in Urban Change*, 2nd ed., London: Radius/Century Hutchinson.

—— (1991a) *Landscapes of Power: From Detroit to Disney World*, Berkeley and Los Angeles: University of California Press.

—— (1991b) 'Postmodern urban landscapes: mapping culture and power', in S. Lash and J. Friedmann (eds) *Modernity and Identity*, Oxford: Blackwell.

9

CITY FUTURES

Keith Cowlard

I believe the future is only the past again entered through another gate.

Sir A.W. Pinero, *The Second Mrs Tanqueray*, 1893: 4

Great cities grow from the synergy produced by the interactions of their component parts and by their ability to adjust to changes in their political, economic and technological environments. The City of London and the Port of London have been intimately bound throughout the history of the metropolis by the changing polity, economy and technology of international trading. The life story of this relationship describes a fascinating evolution from early mutual support and 'marriage' as each responded to the expansion of imperial trade during the nineteenth century; through the eventual dominance of one partner, when the City took controlling interests in the growing dock companies; then to 'divorce' as post-war investment in the Port declined and the docks began to close. Finally, to the tantalising possibility of some form of reconciliation: have the London Docklands now been developed to the point of possible remarriage with their former partners in the ever-changing markets of international trading?

CITY PAST: THE RISE AND FALL OF 'CITYPORT'

The establishment of London as a major trading centre in earlier centuries rested on two related developments in the capital: first, the provision of a physical infrastructure capable of handling the shipping and the cargoes; and, second, the creation of less visible support services necessary to facilitate the financing and insuring of a greater movement of goods. The first found expression in the development of the Port of London and the second in the growth of City institutions.

Custody of the Thames waterway had been vested in the Corporation of the City of London by Richard I in the twelfth century. By the sixteenth century 'Portus Civitatis Londiniensi' was thriving, Legal Quays had been built on the north bank of the Pool of London to handle all dutiable goods and, when these proved unable to cope with the increases in traffic, Sufferance Wharves were established on the south bank. The City Fathers jealously defended their jurisdiction over London trade, through what we will call 'Cityport', in recognition of the dominant position of the City. They licensed not only the Quays and Wharves but also their lightermen, watermen and porters. As the volume of trade continued to rise, the facilities again proved inadequate but: 'Any easement of the situation was viewed by the City as a derogation of the vested rights of the privileged holders of the upper berths' (Jarvis 1977: 57). The first Elizabethan age thus saw the expansion of imperial ambitions and the growth of trade on an, as yet, unmatched scale and the pressures exerted on London brought City and state together to provide mutual protection from its adverse consequences. By Royal Decree of 1580, the growth of the capital was to be contained within the effective purview of the City:

> The Queen's Majestie, perceiving the state of the City of London . . . doth charge and strictly command all manner of persons, of what quality soever they be, to desist and forbear from any new building of any house or tenement within three miles from any of the gates of the said City of London.

International trade continued its seemingly endless growth during the seventeenth century and, as a result, new support activities were created in the City which were to become the essential second feature of the platform from which the port could grow and lead to the eventual establishment of London as one of the major commercial and financial centres of Europe.

A kind of Stock Exchange was in existence by the 1670s for investment in shipping and trading companies; Lloyds coffee shop underwriters and other insurance facilities began in the 1680s; the Bank of England was established in 1694 and, together with the commodity exchanges, these provided the essential invisible services for the continued growth of Cityport.

Consequent to this impetus to trading links, the Quays and

Wharves found themselves overwhelmed and, amidst the growing losses of cargoes through delay and pilfering, merchants and shippers clamoured for expansion in the port. In 1796 the House of Commons received the report of its committee set up to investigate 'the best method of promoting sufficient accommodation for the increased trade and shipping of the Port of London'.

The plans debated nearly all involved dock or other facilities downstream, east of the City and beyond its immediate jurisdiction. Though dependent on the continuation of the prosperity of the port, the City, once more, strenuously opposed any developments to the east. But docks beyond the City walls were eventually built, starting with the West India Dock on the Isle of Dogs, which opened in 1802 despite the Corporation's final plea that it was 'pregnant with the evils before stated' (Figure 9.1). In 1733 Robert Walpole had unsuccessfully attempted to 'make London a free port and by consequence the market of the world'; the Warehousing Act of 1803 at last made that a possibility by creating licensed bonded warehouses and thus laying the foundations for London's subsequent lead as an entrepôt port (Pudney 1975: 32). Significantly for later history, the first such warehouses were built in the West India Dock.

Official opposition rarely clouds commercial sense and, from the start, the City interests became enmeshed in the dock companies. The first Board of Directors of the West India Dock Company included many prominent City men, four of whom later became Lord Mayor of London. The Chairman, George Hibbert, exhibited all the City, wharfage and merchanting interests that had previously been opposed to the development. City interests soon came to dominate the dock companies, and family connections and numerous cross-directorships compounded the intimacy of the association such as to cause one observer to remark on the Board of the London and St Katharine Dock Company that 'There was not a single director unconnected with commercial houses' (King 1868).

The symbiosis of City and Port was an effective one because it was founded on mutual interest in the growth of international trade through London. That the commercial interests of the one should so clearly dominate the other in the growth of Cityport can be illustrated by a list of directors' principal employments for two of the merged companies of 1868 (Table 9.1).

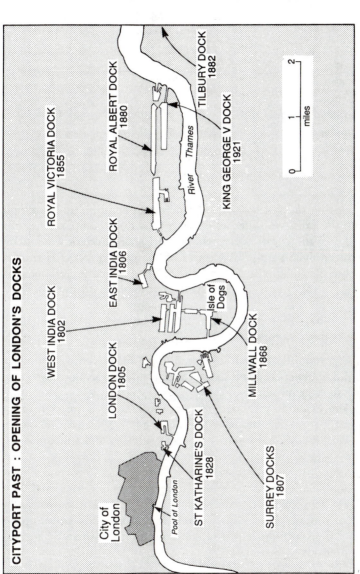

Figure 9.1 Cityport past: opening of London's docks

Table 9.1 Dock directors' principal employments, 1864

	East and West India	London & St Katharine
Banking	6	6
Insurance	26	19
Finance	1	1
Marine insurance	8	10
Shipping	4	0
Other	4	5

Source: Gardiner's Royal Blue Books 1868

During the last half of the nineteenth century, trade volumes into the port continued to grow, yet the dock companies' profits had begun to fall and dividends to shareholders were being reduced. The result was a series of company mergers created to secure the viability of the docks, which had to that period operated largely rival operations. But they were unable to offset the adverse effects of late-nineteenth century changes in the operation and technology of international trading which made them particularly vulnerable to a number of factors:

1 Commodities traded were changing. Ceylon Tea, for example, did not keep well and so the extensive dock warehousing was no longer required.
2 The expanding railway network was making it easier to move cargoes on quickly, again without requiring storage facilities.
3 The Suez Canal opened in 1869, altering the transport economics of much of the entrepôt trade of the port.
4 Sizes of ships were increasing and steamships in particular were unable effectively to use the earlier narrow-entrance docks.
5 The tropical luxury trade which had been the mainstay of the early docks gave way to more temperate mass-consumption cargoes which required new, more mechanised handling methods.
6 The docks had been built by rival companies and London had developed an uncoordinated port which found difficulty in competing with rival European ports.

228

But it was the special relationship of City and Port which added two crucial additional factors to the decline of the companies. First, it was the tradition that vessels anchored in mid-stream, beached on the banks of the Thames, or tied up at moorings. Much of the cargo was then transferred to small flat craft called 'lighters' for transport to a storage area. The early dock Acts contained a 'Free Water Clause' which gave the lightermen, licensed by the City, the right to enter the dock free of toll. In consequence many cargoes continued to be landed in the traditional ways, to the detriment of the company returns. Second, there is also some evidence that the symbiosis of Cityport added another perverse twist to the decline. Company directors' main interests were often outside of the docks themselves, relying heavily on the earnings from 'invisible' City activities which depended on the rapid throughput of cargoes out of the port, while the shareholders in the docks relied on the profits of the dock companies. The result was the subordination of shareholders' interests to those of the City 'customers'. This acted to the detriment of company profits at a time when the number of cargoes handled was increasing. Thus it was that the dock system may have been an early sacrifice to the growth of capitalist accumulation in the City (Halstead 1982: 39).

In 1908 the Port of London Authority was created to draw the ailing dock companies together under a single head. Briefly summarised, the subsequent history of the docks records the destruction of the Second World War, followed by new technologies of trade and cargo-handling, particularly mechanisation, containerisation and increased ship sizes, and the rise of major rival ports in mainland Europe. These changes ensured that Cityport never regained its earlier dominance and closures of the docks began in the 1960s.

During the 1960s physical decline and retreating investment in the docks to the east was matched by a building boom in the City. Financial markets were growing in a buoyant economy and there was unprecedented building of offices in the Square Mile. The media dubbed it 'the rape of the capital' and eventually the ever-starker contrasts between City and docklands prompted political action. In the City the speculative office building was to be dampened down and to the east measures were to be taken to revive the fortunes of the port.

In the City, the Location of Offices Bureau tried to encourage office activities to decentralise or move to the aided regions, while the Control of Office and Industrial Development Act of 1965 imposed office building permits in the south-east to reduce pressure. For a while it worked: in 1959 some 177,404 square metres of office space had been added to Central London; in 1965 only 9,615 square metres was built. The Hardman Report of 1973 recommended the decentralisation of some government offices and the Greater London Development Plan attempted to restrict major office building to the City and a limited number of strategic centres. Though slowed, the pressure for space in the Square Mile continued to rise into the 1970s.

In Docklands, the Greater London Development Plan proposed Action Areas in three specified localities for rapid renewal, and in 1971 Peter Walker, then Environment Secretary, enthused in Parliament about all the essentials being there for something big to happen and announced the urgent study of development possibilities in Docklands by the planning consultants Travers Morgan, who reported in 1973 on five possibilities ranging from major office development on the Isle of Dogs ('Europa') to majority public sector housing ('East End Consolidated'). The decision-making process was altered by a General Election, when the incoming Labour government rejected the report and set up the Docklands Joint Committee comprising the DOE, the GLC and the dockland boroughs. Their London Docklands Strategic Plan was published in 1976 and aimed to use public money in the social and economic regeneration of the area.

The plan adopted a needs-led approach, giving expression to the requirements of the local communities, and hankered for a 'flourishing and viable port in East London'. It intended to 're-dress the housing, social, environmental, employment/economic and communications deficiencies of the Docklands area' with a clearly zoned set of land-use proposals which aimed to renew the Isle of Dogs with local authority housing, open space and district shopping centres.

But formidable problems then stood in the way of that regeneration: public funding was limited and made worse by recession, much land was owned by public corporations who resisted efforts to get them to relinquish ownership, transport access was poor as a result of the uncoordinated development of the docks and, above all, the image of run-down areas and derelict docks all conspired to create an area in which major City insti- tutions would find it hard to recommend investment.

By the late 1970s the separation of City and Port, the demise of Cityport, had seemed complete. The Square Mile, though office completions were barely half those of the previous decade, continued in high demand and prime rents rose from about £2 per square foot in 1962 to £15 per square foot (£4.12 at 1962 prices) in 1978 (Manners and Morris 1986: 46). Yet in the port, the upper docks were nearly all closed. Once packed with the trade of the world, they now presented a sad, empty and derelict spectacle, apparently lacking the means of revival.

Yet, once again, it was the changing demands of international trade that were to give birth to new tensions in the City, to which it would have to respond. Bruce Kinloch wrote in *The Daily Telegraph* in 1976:

> If the City of London is to retain its hold on international trade and continue its high contributions to Britain's invisible exports, ways must be found, and found quickly, to provide offices which are suitable to overseas companies. Over half the remaining 3 million square feet of offices available in the City consists of property which was built prior to 1950, or built or modernised since 1950, without air conditioning. There is only just over 500,000 square feet of offices built or modernised since 1950 with air conditioning inside the central area.
>
> (*The Daily Telegraph*, August 1976).

CITY PRESENT

The New Right government returned in 1979 came in on a platform of free-market economic regeneration, private investment incentive and deregulation. Traditional planning, with its heavy dependence on local-authority controls, was seen more as a constriction on development than a quality assurance mechanism and it was to be opened up to more market forces. The new administration, imbued with an enterprise ethic, set about freeing the office development process from specific controls and creating a new private investment climate in London's docklands. That these aims coincided with the introduction of new technologies in global trading and the internationalisation of equities markets was a fortuitous circumstance that was to blow new wind into the sails of that special relationship between the City and its former port, and the catalysts of this were set to produce a surprising twist to the history of Cityport.

The Local Government, Planning and Land Act of 1980 introduced the Urban Development Corporation as a planning and development agency for inner city area regeneration. The London Docklands Development Corporation (LDDC) was established in July 1981 as such a centrally appointed agency, with wide powers to acquire land, including a 'vesting' facility to enable it to acquire publicly owned land, and powers to provide essential infrastructure and to direct the planning framework for the regeneration of the docklands.

It set about creating a new public and investment image for its 'Exceptional Place' through intensive advertising, buying and selling land and providing a relaxation of the planning regime to attract developers and institutional investors. It aimed to use public money to pump-prime the return of the private sector to the docklands. Eschewing a formal land-use zoning approach, the Corporation adopted a demand-led planning philosophy. This pursued a market-led strategy whose primary goal was to attract development first and to worry about essential infrastructure later.

The Enterprise Zone concept had been propounded by the geographer, Peter Hall, in a discussion of Freeports, and was taken up by Sir Geoffrey Howe in his Budget speech in 1980. The fundamental aim was to deregulate and provide financial incentives sufficient to prime market forces to reinvest in derelict inner city areas. The subsequent legislation provided for the designation of specific Enterprise Zones, in which a variety of financial and administrative inducements would be given to developers and businesses in order to speed up the regenerative process of problem areas. The inducements included ten-year exemption from rates and from land taxes on disposal, capital allowances and reduced planning controls. The Isle of Dogs became an Enterprise Zone in 1982 and this policy, together with the other LDDC inducements, proved potent attractants to this part of the former port, bringing in private entrepreneurial activity and capital to regenerate the area (Ambrose 1986: 223).

Though the LDDC's centrally organised political power with incentives to investment brought in the developers, it did not create an entirely free-for-all situation, for it issued its own development briefs to guide potential clients. In *The Isle of Dogs*

Enterprise Zone: The Guide the corporation stated that: 'The height of buildings and structures [should] be limited to no more than 120 feet.' Other measures to deregulate planning included the removal of the Office Development Permit, which had sought to restrict office development in the south-east, and the closure of the Location of Offices Bureau. These steps removed the remaining obstacles to office building in the capital. Thus deregulatory and market-oriented changes in planning coincided with other catalysts to provide the environment within which the fortunes of both City and Docklands were again to be drawn together.

Technologies new to docklands were transforming the rail, air and telecommunications accessibility of the area. The Docklands Light Railway created a link between the Isle of Dogs and Tower Hill, which will soon be extended to the symbolic heart of the City at Bank. This railway will provide an essential, though by itself insufficient, spine artery with a capacity of 24,000 passengers per hour and a 9.5 minute journey between Bank and the Isle of Dogs. 'Just 6 miles east of the City, London City Airport will give business travellers what they value most – time.' The advertising for the short-take-off-and-landing airport in the Royal Docks claims to provide rapid travel for City business people on short-haul flights to Europe. Also in keeping with the promulgated high-tech image, Docklands has two 'teleports' operated by British Telecom and Mercury to provide worldwide satellite telecommunications from the heart of the regenerating area.

The introduction of new information technology facilities to the financial world and, in particular, electronic dealing systems in securities led to a different set of demands in the architecture of the ideal office structure. The new facilities and dealing methods required larger floor spaces (dealing floors of at least two to four thousand square metres were suggested), higher ceiling heights and room to house the cabling and air-conditioning needed by the computer equipment, together with high quality lighting control and maximum flexibility of form to accommodate future change. Richard Rogers' Lloyds building was the extreme of the new form, with internal space cleared by removing service facilities to the exterior. In itself, this building became the object of argument over the future of office architecture, particularly in the City, but it did also serve to highlight the fact that in the Square Mile in 1975 only 6 per cent of office premises had been built after 1965 and 50 per cent were pre-war structures. If the future office was to be so different, could the City cope?

Big Bang signalled the deregulation of the Stock Exchange and the abolition of fixed commissions and coincided with the wider introduction of electronic facilities and the move to internationalise securities dealing. It was hoped thereby to secure for the City a pivotal position in global finance. With English the language of international dealing, a time-zone location which allows trading with both New York and Tokyo within a single working day, and long historical experience and reputation, the City looked set for an influx of foreign business and a renewed building demand. Demand for office space did grow in anticipation, foreign companies came in, often by way of merger, and the growing conglomerates increased the demand for larger purpose-built structures to mirror new corporate identities.

The catalysts loosened the spatial centrality of Threadneedle Street. The new technology of international trading no longer required face-to-face contact and, except perhaps for reasons of tradition or prestige, in theory the new financial institutions were free to locate anywhere. In all, they produced the right environment for the entry of a project which was to be the fulcrum of the refashioning of the balance between City and Port; a project so vast that it came to dominate the issues and hold the key to Dockland's ability to attract major private investors. In the demand-led planning approach, such projects are at once a wonderfully visible sign of enterprise achievement but also a liability, for so much can rest on a single development.

By adopting an approach which eschewed formal development plans, and relying upon the impetus of development incentives to attract business, the LDDC was opening up a potentially damaging mismatch between commercial development and infrastructure. Early developments in Docklands were small-scale and low rise so that deficiencies in infrastructure were not overly apparent, but a second wave of development was signalled when the more aggressive marketing of the LDDC landed this big catch. Once that had happened, demand-led planning provided its own spectacular growth multiplier, graphically illuminating the disparities between that development and the infrastructural underpinnings of transport, housing and community facilities.

Canary Wharf

The West India Dock had been the first of the main dock systems of London to be built to exploit the needs of international trading in the nineteenth century. Incredibly, 183 years later, it was also to be the site of a major financial and commercial project aiming to match the needs of international trading in the late-twentieth century and beyond.

A project covering 71 acres, providing 10 million square feet of space, which included 820,000 square metres of offices, and to be dominated by three 60-storey towers each 850 feet high, was planned for the former Rum Quay at Canary Wharf. 'Wall Street on Water' in the Enterprise Zone of the Isle of Dogs would be the largest development of its kind in Europe and looked set to capitalise upon the limitations of the City for the new global institutions.

> [Canary Wharf] responds to the need of the financial services sector for space in which to grow and thus secure London's future . . . these needs could not be met within London's Square Mile except through extensive destruction of the City's historic fabric.
>
> (Canary Wharf broadsheet, undated)

Controversy ensued. *The Economist* (26 October 1985) declared that 'the new jack-of-all-trades being created by the deregulation of Britain's financial markets do not sit comfortably behind the City of London's eighteenth century façades'. The Henley Centre predicted 57,000 new jobs on the Isle of Dogs, but remarked in February 1986 that office demand would probably be so great as to 'absorb Canary Wharf with no net fall in City employment'. Tower Hamlets Borough Council opposed the scheme, claiming that it contravened the provisions of the Greater London Development Plan and the LDDC's published guidelines for the area, and warned that it would 'weaken the vitality of the City office market'. *The Sunday Times* (24 November 1985), under the banner 'City Runs Out of Space', perceptively mused that: 'the City is now squirming in the face of what it sees as competition'.

Herein lay the essence of the refashioning of the relationship of City and Port. Was Canary Wharf to be simply an extension of the Square Mile eastwards? Was it an unlikely-to-happen and therefore irrelevant proposal? Or was it about to siphon off the cream of the expanding global markets from under the nose of the City and thus to reverse the roles of Cityport, perhaps by creating a 'Portcity' to reverse the dominant role?

The City had published a Draft Local Plan revision just before the announcement of the Canary Wharf proposal in which it proclaimed:

> The predominant role of the City today is that of a business and financial centre of pre-eminent international importance. This commercial role arose from its original function as a port, and the associated demand for banking, insurance and shipping services, brokers and commodity exchanges.
>
> (City of London 1984: 16)

The plan set out to consolidate that history by taking an overt conservationist approach, outlining 21 Conservation Areas and other measures of protection, which together covered 70 per cent of the Square Mile.

Property developers, architects and financiers reacted swiftly and vociferously. Peter Palumbo, after the City had again rejected his plans for Mansion House Square, complained: 'they are reducing the world's leading commercial centre to little more than a museum of moderately interesting buildings which a few tourists might occasionally glance at'. The Managing Director of Rothschilds warned: 'new organisations are not going to put up with refurbished buildings lurking behind Dickensian façades' and the Henley Centre summed up the problem: 'physical development is hindered by the proposed stringent planning regulations'.

Faced by widespread criticism and the implications of Canary Wharf, the City relented: conservation policy receded, plot ratios were increased to 5:1, and new development sites were found, in all sufficient to provide an additional 930,000 square metres of office space in the City over ten years. All this despite the fact that the City was experiencing unprecedented traffic congestion, much of its own making. When subsequent plans were announced to extend the Docklands Light Railway to Bank, thus directly connecting Canary Wharf to the heart of the Square Mile, the City, just as it had done in the nineteenth century, opposed development to the east. The Corporation cited problems of congestion at Bank, the safety of church foundations and security vaults. It was again unsuccessful in its pleas.

236

Yet by July 1987 the Canary Wharf project had begun to look less assured and the consortium faced administrative and funding problems. But in that month Canary Wharf was taken over by Olympia & York, a successful Canadian company with a high reputation in major project development. It had the resources to fund such a major project through, if necessary, several downturns in the economic cycle. The new company at once reduced the scale of the main towers, relocated them, and began to proclaim that Canary Wharf was assured and would provide 'The type of office accommodation for the 1990s and beyond . . . [to] reflect the architectural heritage of one of the world's great cities and at the same time offering a logical extension to it.'

CITY FUTURES

Financial markets, as Stafford shows in Chapter 1 above, are increasingly volatile and it is difficult to predict the eventual impact of the development rising above the West India Dock. Since the project was announced in 1985 controversy and argument have surrounded its relationships with office markets, the City and the former port. This can be clearly illustrated by the ways in which, in the span of just four years, views have changed. The prediction of metropolitan futures, resting as they do on the variable nature of international trading, is problematical in the extreme and the eventual nature of the City/port relationship far from clear. The LDDC was promoting the advantages of Docklands in 1986 amidst the euphoria which had been created by Big Bang: 'A City centre location with fast transport links to London, Britain, and Europe, advanced communications, attractive waterside environment with superb sites and unrivalled cost-effectiveness.' Prime office rents were then rising rapidly in the City as the availability of office space declined in the wake of renewed demand. 'Tenants requiring larger floorspaces are being forced to move outside the medieval street patterns of the City to peripheral areas and other parts of London' (Savills 1986: 19). The LDDC was seizing upon the growing disparity between City and Docklands prime office rentals (Table 9.2), exalting the advantages of the Enterprise Zone and other attractions to potential customers.

Demand in 1986 seemed insatiable and most observers felt that London would need development both in the City and at Canary Wharf in order to cope. Demand from foreign banks was

Table 9.2 Prime office site rentals, 1985–86

	1985	1986
City	33	37.5
Docklands	10.5	12.5
(at 1985 prices, pounds per square foot)		

Source LDDC leaflet, 1987

particularly strong and it still seemed that, 'there remains a strong commitment to the heart of the City . . . [it] continued to be the magnet for the majority' (Ellis 1986: 2) and that 'the City's claim to be the world's leading financial centre is being continually fortified . . . [now] the City's planners have adopted a more flexible attitude to office development in the area' (Baker, Harris and Saunders 1986: 3).

In 1986 Canary Wharf looked set to become simply a further appendage of the City, enabling the absorption of anticipated expansion of business and prosperity. This forecast was reinforced by market trends at the beginning of 1987. An acute shortage of office space in the City was forcing up rents, particularly in areas like Holborn and Aldgate, and demand looked set to outstrip supply for at least another four years. The assessment of Docklands was beginning to change when, first, Olympia & York rescued the Canary Wharf project and, second, Standard Commercial Property Securities completed 4,000 square metres at Harbour Quay, thus 'demonstrating the way in which projects in the Isle of Dogs enterprise zone, where there are no planning restrictions, has shifted from high-tech mixed use to office developments. That process can be expected to accelerate' (*The Independent*, July 1987).

But it was not to be that simple, for the increasing volatility of world equity markets during 1987 was shown on 19 October – Black Monday – when equities plummeted. Worst-case scenarios predicted 50,000 redundancies, and large projects like Canary Wharf, conceived in the boom of Big Bang, seemed less assured. Major securities firms were forced to rationalise as losses were sustained, and it seemed there would now be an oversupply of office space in the pipeline.

The prognostications proved somewhat over-pessimistic due to a number of factors. Rental growth steadied but continued to grow under the momentum of previous demand. Some major firms, including Morgan Grenfell, did withdraw from planned City developments, but contracts on most large developments were honoured. Professional services were growing in response to the financial sector expansion and these filled any gaps in demand created in the City and West End. Thus 1987 ended on a warning note with more cautious and retrenched office demands. Increased cost-consciousness in City finance houses had led to the shedding of staff rather than project abandonment.

By spring 1988 confidence had returned to office markets. Prime office rents in Docklands had reached £20 per square foot compared to the City Broadgate development that was commanding £40 to £50 per square foot. Continued shortage of office space was being emphasised by a massive increase in pre-lets on planned developments, and this was in spite of the year eventually being a record one for office completions in the City. Since Big Bang, demand in the City had been dominated by the need for large units and, by mid-1988, 780,000 square metres of offices were under construction in the Square Mile with a further stock of 24.25 million square feet in planning permissions. The City was set to increase its own office stock by over 25 per cent and to satisfy the demand even in the face of Canary Wharf (Jones, Lang and Wootton 1988).

But by the end of 1990 the doubts about the dependability and scale of future demand had been confirmed. A number of firms, in particular American banks, withdrew parts of their operations from London. By 1991, office completions in the City should be approaching 620,000 square metres and the City will see an expansion of its central and peripheral developments, with Broadgate, Ropemaker Place, Little Britain, Alban Gate and Royal Mint Court completed, and London Bridge City, Spitalfields, Bishopsgate Goods Yard, King's Cross and Waterloo still to come. These rival developments will severely test the claims of Olympia & York's Chairman, Paul Reichmann, that:

> London will be in the absolute forefront of Europe. International companies will want facilities they cannot find in the City, and that is another reason why the success of Canary Wharf is an inevitability . . . A model working environment for the next century, unparalleled in Europe.
>
> (*The Economist*, 9 August 1989)

As *The Economist* noted, it is '8½ square miles of twenty-first century London, perched on the edge of today's City . . . Yesterday it was it was being hailed as a white rabbit out of the hat. Now there is talk of it being tomorrow's white elephant' (*The Economist*, 9 September 1989). At the close of 1989 'up to 20% of proposed completions in the City and Docklands will not be built', and vacancy rates in Docklands were running at 42 per cent (Savills 1989: 16). By the end of 1990, as the recession bit hard on the financial sector, a sixth of all office space in the City and its fringes was empty (*The Independent on Sunday*, 16 December 1990).

Canary Wharf, then, conceived in the euphoria of 1986, started construction in the doldrums of 1988. The early years of the 1990s will witness a series of events that will add further uncertainty to the City/Docklands equation. The year 1991 should see the completion of Phase One of the Canary Wharf project with 460 thousand square metres of office space, and the near-completion of Phase Two. The year of the Single Market of the European Community, 1992, will give further impetus to the internationalisation of financial markets, and London will be a part of that process. The Second Banking Directive will, for example, enable any bank authorised in one member state to operate anywhere in the Community as a step towards a single market in financial services. In addition, 1992 marks the end of the ten-year span of the Enterprise Zone, removing special incentives on the Isle of Dogs, driving up rentals and increasing pressure for more intensive use of space. Current developments are already discounting to this eventuality.

Transport will remain the Achilles' heel of Docklands for some time to come. It is the product of a past geared to the carriage of goods rather than people, now exacerbated by the demand-led approach to regeneration of the area. Land and financial incentives to attract developers have been prioritised over infrastructural improvements and the reliance on private capital investment in Docklands, now being applied to transport facility developments, will further skew the network towards those who can pay, disregarding those who cannot, and pinning the future even more tightly to a few large schemes.

The 1990s will witness transport developments that will not only improve the access between the City and Docklands and increase commercial development pressures in both areas, but significantly exhibit a marked preference towards Canary Wharf and the Isle of Dogs. By 1992 London City Airport hopes to have improved European access by operating longer-haul 'whisper' jets from the

Royal Docks. The 1990s will see the completion of the Bank extension to the Docklands Light Railway and further extensions to Greenwich and the Royals, thus completing a network linking the heart of the City at Bank to the easterly extremity of Docklands, with Canary Wharf at its centre.

The year 1993 is the scheduled completion date of the Channel Tunnel, linking London to Europe and boosting Community trade, though the planning and specification of the rail link still remain to be determined. By 1992 improved road access from Canary Wharf to the City via the Ratcliff Highway should be operational, to be followed by other road improvements and the East London River Crossing which will link the M2 to the M11, just east of the Royal Docks, and relieve traffic in the Blackwall Tunnel/Isle of Dogs area. The planned extension of the Bakerloo Line to Stratford via the Isle of Dogs should be constructed in the early 1990s together with extension of the Jubilee Line from Charing Cross via Surrey Quays and Canary Wharf to the Royal Docks (see Figure 9.2).

Skewing of development is but one consequence of the demand-led strategies for regrowth in Docklands, yet it serves to highlight the dilemma of London as a whole as it faces the results of the abandonment of 60s style planning and the adoption of market-oriented approaches to urban development. If the 1960s can be characterised as a period of reconstruction predicated upon bureaucratic local authority, public sector financed, statutory planning, then the 1980s was a period of regeneration promulgated in the name of deregulated, decontrolled and private sector financed, demand-led non-planning. Among the legacies of the 60s are the residential tower blocks of the East End and the curtain-wall office blocks of the City, testimonies to an approach which left an impression of insensitive authoritarianism in the planning of people's lives. The 80s in Docklands is characterised by commercial development in the Isle of Dogs and an impression of regeneration insensitive to the needs of local people.

Both 60s (into early 70s) and 80s approaches were sincere in their beliefs, the one based upon public control, the other on market forces. Both were energetically pursued in the ethos of their period, the one in public reconstruction, the other in private regeneration. The Strategic Plan for Docklands understood the need for comprehensive co-ordination of land use and transport but lacked the financial underpinnings to move very far, while the

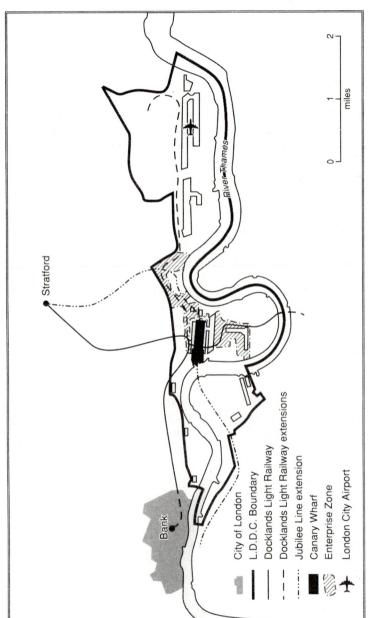

City of London
L.D.D.C. Boundary
Docklands Light Railway
Docklands Light Railway extensions
Jubilee Line extension
Canary Wharf
Enterprise Zone
London City Airport

Stratford

Bank

River Thames

0   1   2
     miles

Figure 9.2 Portcity future?

demand-led approach of the 80s had the finance in abundance but eschewed the need for planned infrastructural investment to precede major development.

Cities are extremely complex entities and major development brings with it a plethora of changed relationships which require anticipation. While the bureaucratic planning of the 60s left its legacy of problems, the failure to anticipate consequences and the inability of demand-led approaches to support essential infrastructure may be the legacy that will be left by the Docklands development. Already the LDDC is beginning to acknowledge the deficiencies, and is changing its approach to the Royal Docks plans, but this recognition of the problems of demand-led non-planning may have come too late for Docklands, especially since the essential spur of rising land values has been removed. In any case, the planning versus non-planning debate is a much wider issue, for the capital itself currently lacks any strategic authority capable of coordinated planning.

The removal of the Greater London Council left the capital without a direct strategic planning body and gave the boroughs the responsibility to produce 'Unitary Development Plans' which will incorporate strategic advice from the Secretary of State for the Environment. The London Planning Advisory Committee (LPAC), set up with representation from all the London boroughs to recommend to the Secretary of State what his advice should include, advised: 'that, outside these areas [including the City and West Docklands] no substantial new allocations should be made of land or buildings for major business development' (London Planning Advisory Committee 1988: 23). LPAC thus spoke for all political persuasions from the London boroughs and echoed the central area policies of the Greater London Development Plan – rational limitation of major commercial developments to a restricted central zone.

However, the subsequent official advice from the enterprise government of the second Elizabethan age offered no such majestic protection to the City as had its sixteenth century counter-part. 'Business development in Central London should not be restricted to a tightly-drawn core zone . . . boroughs surrounding the City of London should make every effort to accommodate such development' (Secretary of State for the Environment 1989: 5).

BACK TO THE FUTURE: THE EMERGENCE OF PORTCITY?

Cityport was created from a simple symbiotic relationship based on the growth of the physical trade of the world and this is acknowledged in the City:

> Ever since the Romans built the first quay along the Thames around 2000 years ago, the Port of London has contributed much to the wealth and growth of the City of London. The development of the City of London as one of the world's premier commodity and finance centres can be largely attributed to the cargoes and vessels that have passed through the port in great numbers over the years.
>
> (City of London Corporation 1989: 59)

Whether what might be termed 'Portcity' will yet herald a new symbiosis in which the eastern development in Docklands takes the lead in the relationship must remain uncertain.

As ever, divining the future is not an exact science. In the new economic and spatial order of the modernisation of the metropolis, Cityport, based on the visible trade of the world, may, or may not, be transformed into Portcity, positioned at the leading edge of the invisible electronic trade of the world (Hoyle, Pinder and Husain 1987). But it is undeniably fitting that Canary Wharf should be built, of all places, in the West India Dock. On 27 August 1802 *The Times* commented on the opening of the new West India Dock, which was to be the spearhead of the nineteenth century transformation of the City's eastern boundary: 'The Dock itself, appearing like a great lake, was an object of beauty and astonishment. The warehouses are the grandest,the most commodious and spacious we have ever seen, and are capable of containing a vast quantity of goods.'

Will the West India Dock again be the gate to London's future just as it was in its past? The commodious and spacious Canary Wharf, standing like a benediction above the new financial religion of Docklands, may aspire to be the symbol of the new age in international trading and it will certainly renew the links between City and Port. Such development may be required by the metropolis in the battle for global financial eminence but the continued growth of the financial services industry on the scale of the 80s must remain doubtful. Instead, Portcity may well remain an illusion as the events of the 90s unfold. City, Docklands and West

244

End may simply become parts of a greatly enlarged centre as a great city seeks its future global destiny.

REFERENCES

Ambrose, P. (1986) *Whatever Happened to Planning?*, London: Methuen.
Applied Property Research Limited (1988) *The Employment Potential of London Docklands*, London.
Baker, Harris and Saunders (1986) *City Development Review*, London.
Canary Wharf (undated) Broadsheet.
City of London (1984) *Draft Local Plan*, London.
City of London Corporation (1989) *Official Guide*, London.
Docklands Business World (1988) vol. 9, Oct.–Dec.
Docklands Digest (1989) vol. 3, No. 19.
Ellis, R. (1986) *The City Property Forecast*, London.
——(1988) *The Growing City: A Study of Future Office Demand*, London.
Estates Gazette (1988) 'City Ripples', 17 Dec.
Gardiner's (1868) Royal Blue Books, London.
Halstead, K.A. (1982) *The Economic Factors in the Development of Urban Fabric of London's Docklands, 1796–1901*, Unpub. Ph.D CNAA.
Hillier Parker (1989) *Rent Contour Map*, London.
Hoyle, B.S., Pinder, D.A. and Husain, M.S. (1987) *Revitalising the Waterfront*, London: Belhaven.
Jarvis, R.C. (1977) 'The Metamorphosis of the Port of London', *The London Journal*, vol. 3: 55–72.
Jones, Lang and Wootton (1988) *Central London Offices Research*, London.
——(1989) *Central London Offices Research*, London.
King, T. (1868) *The London and St Katharine Dock*, London.
London Planning Advisory Committee (1988) *Strategic Planning Advice for London*, London.
Manners, G. and Morris, D. (1986) *Office Policy in Britain: A Review*, Norwich: Geo.
Pudney, J. (1975) *London's Docks*, London: Thames and Hudson.
Savills (1986) *City of London Office Demand Survey*, London.
——(1988) *Isle of Dogs Survey*, London.
——(1989) *Docklands Office Survey*, London.
Secretary of State for the Environment (1989) *Draft Strategic Planning Guidance for London*, London.

10

THE COMING OF THE GROUNDSCRAPERS

Stephanie Williams

It was in Aldersgate late in 1987 that I first noted the phenomenon. Across the street from the Barbican, a vast multistorey car park built about 1965 was being demolished. It had been one of those buildings you took for granted, so nondescript that you had long since ceased to see it. Its demolition would have been unremarkable except that someone was also starting to bring down the building next door. Soon hoardings rose that stretched almost the whole of the long block that runs from the end of London Wall to the Barbican tube station. The gaping hole in the streetscape was enormous.

These sites in Aldersgate were literally next door to Little Britain by St Bartholomew's Hospital, just around the corner from London Wall and a stone's throw from St Paul's. They were less than five minutes' walk from even larger areas that investigation over the next six months also revealed were scheduled for redevelopment: Paternoster Square and Holborn Viaduct; great blocks in Fleet Street; Broadgate, Cannon Street and Spitalfields. The new buildings at Aldersgate were the commonplace examples, the examples of 'infilling', the ones that rarely get published even though they might contain, as did the first example that caught my eye, the deepest underground car park in the world. They were the first physical signs that the City of London was undergoing profound changes, change as dramatic as its nineteenth-century commercial expansion or the rebuilding after the blitz. In the process the whole of the centre of London itself was being affected. As I write, every major London station – Paddington, Victoria, Marylebone, Liverpool Street, Charing Cross, St Pancras, London Bridge, Waterloo and, the biggest of all, King's Cross – is associated with new developments. Meanwhile the developments in

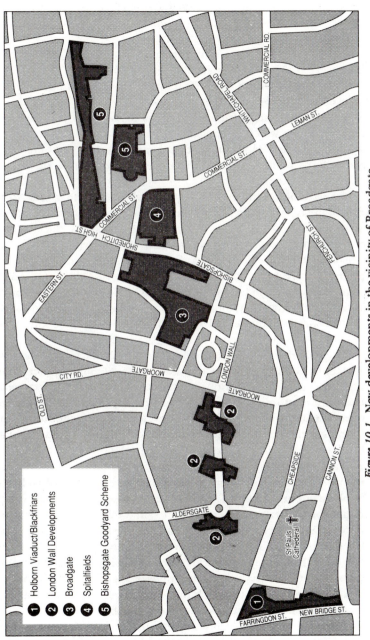

Figure 10.1 New developments in the vicinity of Broadgate

Legend:
1 Holborn Viaduct/Blackfriars
2 London Wall Developments
3 Broadgate
4 Spitalfields
5 Bishopsgate Goodyard Scheme

Docklands (see Chapter 9, Keith Cowlard) are themselves staggering. What is taking place represents the biggest remaking of London since the Second World War.

In 1986 when the new City of London Local Plan was published there were 6.55 million square metres of office space in the City (Murphy 1986). Within eighteen months consent had been given for twenty million square feet of office space to be completed by 1995 in the City and its fringes just over the river. Taking away the huge increases which Broadgate, Spitalfields and building over London Wall and Holborn Viaduct represent, the equivalent of over a third of the City's floorspace is in the process of being redeveloped (Rees 1988).

The shading on the map in Figure 10.1 gives some idea of the scale of the new buildings on the ground. Where two or three large buildings once stood, a single new one may take its place, swallowing up the open space between them. In areas where buildings date back beyond the turn of the century the changes to the streetscape are even more radical. Take the site of Leadenhall Court, a new block in polystyrene baronial style described as 'timeless' by its architects, Whinney Mackay-Lewis, for its owners, the City Corporation and Legal & General. Where once stood a cluster of as many as twenty small buildings, practically next door to Lloyd's, a single monolithic building of some 12,000 square metres of speculative office construction has appeared. Similar instances can be seen at the Danish Bacon site in Cowcross Street near Smithfield and, in the most celebrated case, in James Sterling's proposals for Mansion House Square.

The kinds of requirements seen as necessary for the modern financial institution – dealing rooms, flexible office space, ancillary services conceived as a key requirement in the days leading up to and immediately following Big Bang – do not allow for old-fashioned infilling. They need a whole city block. The basic equation for any new building – plot ratio, height restriction and size of the site – remains as inexorable as ever. But where in the past plot ratios of, say, 3:1 or 5:1 have been used to produce very high buildings, the climate of popular opinion is so fiercely opposed to towers that high-rise proposals are regarded as almost incapable of realisation. Hence the groundscraper: dense, deep-plan buildings that cover every inch of their site.

The massing of bigger and bigger sites is accompanied by the demolition of younger and younger buildings. Along London Wall and at Paternoster Square where most of the relics of the 1960s are concentrated it is a deliberate policy. These thin-clad, high-rise buildings so popularly detested, with their leaking façades, cheap details, low floor-to-ceiling heights, inadequate servicing and forests of internal columns, are, given the size and value of their sites, less expensive to demolish and rebuild than to adapt to the demands of new technology. Elsewhere, in Lutyens' Finsbury Circus and, even more explicitly, at the former Post Office in St Martin's le Grand (now the home of Nomura Securities), the guts of listed buildings have been scooped out wholesale and filled with new insides.

As in Tokyo, New York and Hong Kong, the daily advances in computer and communication technology are driving these changes. To do so, architects say they must be fatter, and the space between floor and ceiling greater than in those built since the war. They must have the potential capacity to carry huge trading floors and miles of service cabling for telephones and computers which can be called up anywhere in the interior. In temperate London sophisticated air-conditioning has become essential. Standby generators are *de rigueur* and rooftops carry a premium – a satellite dish is today a far more valuable facility than a banking hall.

These requirements are not only changing the configurations of buildings but also the construction budget. The main cost of a highrise building lies in its structure. But because the walls of a deep-plan building enclose a much larger area, the cost of ventilating and servicing increasingly sophisticated interiors has risen sharply in proportion to the costs of structure and cladding. The ratio of expenditure is further weighted to the cost of services due to their rapid obsolescence. Typically, structures today are designed for a life of fifty years, cladding for twenty five years and services (security power supplies, air-conditioning, fire-fighting systems, building monitoring and maintenance) for twelve. (This is carried further. Interior fittings are reckoned to have a life of 5–6 years, partitions are now designed to be moved every 5–6 months, and desk equipment is changed every two years.)

In contrast to the slim lines of the ideal skyscraper, where offices are built round the edges and designed to have a view, London's new groundscrapers require central courtyards and atria to bring daylight into their hearts. Because they also go deep underground one byproduct of the current wave of development has been a 50 per cent increase in archaeological finds each year since 1987.

Another, as yet uncharted, is the impact deep foundations will have on the City's water table.

As architect Richard MacCormac has pointed out, these new big office blocks have values more reminiscent of the Edwardians than Georgians. Buildings like these already exist on wide streets like Kingsway, the Euston Road and the Beaux Art boulevards of Europe (MacCormac 1987). The scale of today's site plans suggests that we are seeing a massing of building reminiscent of Paris at the turn of the century. There demand for retailing space led to the development of shops all around the perimeter of huge blocked sites, which themselves look inwards on courtyards. In entries for the 1987 Paternoster Square competition, the glazed public way through a densely covered environment was a consistent proposal. Because of the increase in floor-to-ceiling heights, there is a potential today for external expression on a grandiloquent scale. At street level the arcade is becoming more important. Similarity of street and site plan with the Edwardian model does not extend, unfortunately, to architectural merit. The challenge of building big and bulky has yet to be matched by substantial and inventive external design, or detailing that relates to richness and craft.

Sadly most of the new façades which are now being revealed are drearily banal and obviously machine-made. Huge thin sheets of preformed cladding of moulded concrete, aluminium and glass have simply been applied, as pieces of veneer from a manufactured kit, to the outside of a steel or concrete frame. Those with pre-tension mark the introduction of what for London is a new aesthetic: postmodernism. Exemplified most powerfully in Odeonesque style by Terry Farrell, it is being reinforced by others like Renton Howard Wood Levin, and several American firms, like Skidmore Owings & Merrill (SOM) and Kohn Pedersen Fox, who are now putting their stamps on London.

Fleet Street will see several examples of the style. Though a conservation area, bounded by the Embankment and stretching north to Holborn, the former newspaper district is being so radically overhauled that its character is no longer recognisable. Only two former newspaper buildings, the Daily Telegraph and Daily Express, are listed. Both have major redevelopments at the rear. The Telegraph building is now to be the London head-quarters of American bankers, Goldman Sachs, and has been designed by the American architects Kohn Pedersen Fox. Huge, monumental, in thirties-ish style with a vast convex curved glass-pane frontage, the new building with thirteen levels above ground will in fact scarcely be seen from Fleet Street but will look vast on the skyline. Here the existing elevations will be restored, but listed building consent has been required to redevelop the inside.

Likewise, the old City of London school on the Embankment is being replaced by the London headquarters of a second American bank, J. P. Morgan, in a building that would once have housed two of its neighbours. The designs, by the Building Design Partnership, were kept under wraps, but what has emerged is a classic groundscraper: with six storeys above ground and more below. An extremely deep-plan building, done in a neo-classical mode.

Fitzroy Robinson's plans for the Daily Express are similar. A mere seven storeys tall, but covering a huge site, the new building must be sited 27 metres back from Fleet Street. Another groundscraper has been designed by YRM for the former News of the World site. With a total of around 28,000 square metres of space (and room for approximately 2,500 people), the development is about two thirds the size of Goldman Sachs's. Reached from behind a Fleet Street façade, the new building is only eight storeys high, deeply planned around a central atrium. Below are three floors designed to accommodate financial trading. Renamed Whitefriars after a medieval Carmelite monastery that once stood on the spot, developed by the Japanese firm of Kumagi Gumi, and let to solicitors, Freshfields, it is a classic example of the current nature of the City's expansion.

PLANNING AND THE BOOM

Remarkably, this extraordinary building boom has been allowed to let rip with hardly a thought about where it is leading. 'It is an error to think that modern planning can be co-ordinated', Michael Cassidy, Chairman of the City Corporation planning committee, told me in an interview in 1988. 'What you are seeing here is a reaction against the comprehensive developments of the 60s developments like what you see at Paternoster Square, and that is a good thing. We don't want to find we make the same mistakes again.'

Cassidy did not hesitate: 'Part of the character of the City is its variety, its haphazard development. The way things happen accidentally adds to its charm.' His substitute for what he saw as the discredited planning approach of the past was the simple free-for-all. 'The market is deciding the pace of development – not the planners – and that is how it should be. Unless we have adequate grounds we cannot refuse permission: owners have the right to redevelop their properties.'

So what kind of City did he see in the future? 'One that is based on a core in the centre with a preponderance of historic buildings, surrounded by bang-up-to-date buildings around the edge which will support the services of the financial community.'

Few observers are so sanguine. If the current plans for the City result in a net gain of ten million square feet of new office space, it is likely that the working population of 330,000 could increase by more than 66,000. The impact of this increase, especially on transport, was regarded by Cassidy as outside the Corporation's purview.

Meanwhile great swathes of townscape are changed out of recognition. West of St Paul's at Ludgate Hill, nine acres of former railway land have been released for more groundscraper-style offices by a joint consortium of developers, Rosehaugh and Stanhope Properties. In the process Ludgate Viaduct has been demolished, restoring a mid-nineteenth century view of St Paul's from Fleet Street, and setting the psychological seal on the incorporation of the old newspaper district into the rest of the commercial City. At the same time, consents have been given which mean that virtually all of London Wall from Little Britain to Moorgate, including sight of the road, could eventually disappear under gigantic new construction. Never a street for pedestrians anyway, the new London Wall will be unrecognisable – and probably invisible from the ground. Drivers will flash in and out of patches of daylight as they travel under various monoliths above. London Wall is the centre of the high-rise breed of new buildings, plans for most of which are, like so much of Fleet Street, available if you seek them out in the Guildhall, but otherwise are shrouded in secrecy.

Here, for example, is architect Terry Farrell's replacement for Lee House, formerly nineteen storeys of steel frame and pre-stressed concrete built about 1965. Farrell's new building, Alban Gate, is on an epic scale. This is no groundscraper, something the Edwardians might have recognised. Nineteen storeys high, its scale relates to the building that was there before; this time it is reworked with a monumental curved roof-line, two vast central, open-air atria and façades treated in smooth, clean, broad-striped bands of glazing and grey, red and pink 'flame-textured' granite.

It is suspended over the road on an arch that itself is four to five storeys high. Nor does the building stand four square astride the street. One wing angles back over the podium towards the Barbican. Behind London Wall, Monkwell Square, which provided the original service access to Lee House, is being redeveloped as a garden square with new housing.

Alban Gate is a classic shell and core exercise on the US model; no electrics are distributed beyond the lift lobbies. The tenant must complete and furnish his space as he pleases according to the standards decreed by the developer. Each floor is independently air-conditioned; it will also be possible to remove sections of the floor to create new atria. Four floors have the big voids, high ceilings and clear spans to permit dealing rooms. Altogether the development represents a substantial 60,000 square metres, of which 37,000 is net office space. Whatever the lip-service being paid to the public (plans were exhibited on the site for ten days in 1986) and the welcome variety offered by its roofscape to the skyline, this is an uncompromising big business building that from the ground will be overwhelmingly monumental.

THE DEVELOPER AS PLANNER

Elsewhere in London demand for new kinds of office space has been fuelled by the results of Conservative policies of rationalisation and deregulation. The abolition of the Greater London Council (GLC) and the privatisation of nationalised industries have introduced to the market buildings and parcels of land that have been tied up in other uses or been derelict for decades. Today the headquarters of County Hall is redundant and awaiting conversion. For years British Rail had been taking steps to redevelop its land bank, but it was not until 1982 that it chose to perform the technically difficult feat of building over the tracks at Victoria Station. Now virtually every major London station is associated with a major private development, either completed or in the pipeline. This particular aspect of the remaking of London lies in the hands of a mere three developers: Greycoat, with Victoria and Charing Cross stations; Speyhawk, with Cannon Street and St Pancras; and Rosehaugh Stanhope, with Broadgate, Holborn Viaduct and King's Cross.

These schemes are huge, and profound in their implications. Not only do they require imagination to see what is possible over, under and around an operating station and strong nerves and financial stamina to deal with the intricacies of parliamentary approvals, planning permissions and construction, but with the demise of the GLC and an absence of strategic planning for London these developers have taken responsibility for whole pieces of cityscape. At the smaller end of the scale is Cannon Street. This site is about two acres in size and is built on the enormous brick vaults which support the railway track and platforms. Where the original glazed roof used to vault the station, a new block of offices, two storeys high and roofed with a garden, is being built within the massive original walls of the train-shed. A second building, equally deep-plan but four storeys taller, will span Upper Thames Street. The development will provide office space for over 3,000 people.

More awesome is Terry Farrell's Charing Cross. Here they have taken off the station roof and put up nine storeys of office building. Columns to support such a structure could only be sunk in two lines through the platforms: hence the high, double-arched structure from which the office floors are suspended. The resulting design is like something out of Hollywood in its heyday. On paper it looked just like an Odeon, but now completed it is robust and original, splendidly enriching the skyline.

Like Cannon Street, where the neighbouring streets are being repaved and tidied up, at Charing Cross it will now be possible to walk at high level from the South Bank across the river to Trafalgar Square. Villiers Street has been repaved; and the arches under Charing Cross are being supplied with new lighting, paving and deeper shops. Inside, the train station itself has been refurbished with, in Farrell's words, 'grandeur and style' and sports ceiling treatments inspired by the Moscow underground. But are these items not icing on the cake to appease the planners? How far has analysis of the implications bitten? Why, for example, has so much work been put into the area without improving the links between the underground stations? Have any plans been made to relieve the tremendous congestion of people now that Charing Cross station, already bursting to capacity in rush hours and lunchtimes, is suddenly to become the daily home for several thousand office workers?

Such considerations pale before the activities on even larger sites dominated by Rosehaugh Stanhope, the consortium formed by Stuart Lipton, the chief executive of Stanhope Properties, and financier Godfrey Bradman of Rosehaugh. Bradman, a close associate of the Prince of Wales in the latter's attempts to improve the urban environment, built a reputation under the Labour governments of the 1970s as a tax adviser to the very rich. More recently, as chairman of Friends of the Earth and the creator of a property company for self-building homes, he has developed a reputation for liberal thinking alongside financial infallibility. Lipton cut his teeth on the redevelopment of Tolmers Square which resulted in the big glass mirror building on the corner of Euston Road. After joining Greycoat Properties, he went on to do the well-conceived Cutlers Gardens, and then to put Victoria Plaza, with the largest dealing floor (Salomon Brothers) in London, above the tracks of Victoria Station. Lipton, with architects Arup Associates, pioneered 1 Finsbury Avenue, the first of the breed of groundscraping offices. Steel-framed with big efficient floorplates and a central atrium, the building was designed with considerable aplomb and constructed in less than a year. After failing to win the Coin Street site with Richard Rogers as architect, he left Greycoat: for Broadgate.

The development at Broadgate represents the largest planning permission in the history of London: fourteen buildings on 29 acres of former dereliction – disused railway land and a car park surrounding Liverpool Street station. To develop it Lipton had done his homework on architects, the best supporting professionals, and construction methods from abroad. He imported the US concept of shell and core construction: the developer builds the frame and cladding and runs the main services into cores in the building; the client completes the fit out of the internal spaces. With energy, and sheer force of personality, Lipton set a fantastic pace at Broadgate, achieving speeds of construction that were substantially faster than anywhere else in the world. In less than a year from the start of construction in July 1985 the first two buildings were completed. Together with the record achieved at 1 Finsbury Avenue, the process master-minded by Lipton has marked a revolution in the British building industry – while emasculating traditional suppliers. Everything that could be – from toilet pods to great sections of wall-cladding – was prefabricated off-site, the majority of it abroad, and craned into place as the steel structures were completed.

Broadgate reveals the new face of Lipton and Bradman's London on the ground. The big pluses are in the open spaces. The central squares of the early phases, designed by Arup Associates, on the west side of the site are coherent and attractively paved and a blessing in the congestion of the City. Their flavour is corporate-style North American rather than English or European: but then so are the buildings and their occupants. Even so the skating rink at its heart is crowded in winter and attracts children from nearby Hackney and Islington. While this imaginative centrepiece and its surrounding shops and restaurants are closely monitored and controlled, it is succeeding in making a certain impact on the 'dead at night' syndrome.

Architecturally, however, the quality of the buildings at Broadgate shows a debasement of the excellence seen in their precursor at 1 Finsbury Avenue. For Broadgate Arups have opted for honeycombs of granite and busy balconies on the façades. The glasshouse roofs of the building's atria are just fussy enough to start to look like gimmicks. The great danger, frankly acknowledged by Arups's Peter Foggo, who led the design team, was not having enough design and thinking time before pursuing an idea they had used before. With a team of four architects, the pressures on Arups were considerable.

Arups turned down the commission to design further phases of Broadgate, which were put into the hands of the Chicago-based architects, SOM. First commissioned in February 1986, planning permission was given in July 1987. Foundations were laid as soon as outline planning permission was received from the authorities; within three years this massive complex was nearly complete. 'Buildings should relate to the context of London, in their use of materials, texture and organisation', said James DeStefano of SOM, describing the scheme in 1988. He was referring to Phases 6–8 of Broadgate, a stretch of buildings forming a continuous façade seven storeys high, rising to twelve at the centre between the eastern edge of Liverpool Street Station and Bishopsgate. Some London. These phases of Broadgate display Beaux Art style massing to the buildings, Italianate stone arcades on the ground, granite cladding in the smooth-edge aesthetic of the Modernists, Victorian glass-coffered atria, Chicago 'cast-iron' corners, monumental New York 30s granite and wood treatments to the entrance halls and lift cars, and grand boulevard treatment for Bishopsgate itself, complete with Hawksmoor-style street furniture. All this was being manufactured and erected at breathtaking speed.

To the north of Bishopsgate, perched on massive foundations, a big glass block with an exposed steel structure spans the 80 metres above the throat of platforms 1–10 of Liverpool Street. In the same way that the air rights have been sold at London Wall, so maximum advantage has been extracted from a site that was previously occupied by a small metal bridge. Broadgate, however, is much more than the sum of its parts. It has revived a whole stretch of London that was derelict, to become an entirely new international office *quartier*. Not only has it made a significant contribution to the City's bid to remain the financial capital of Europe after 1992, it is also generating new life in the run-down borders of Shoreditch and Hackney.

A similar situation is under way on the other side of the City, where Lipton and Bradman are developing Holborn Viaduct. Here plans revolve around the realignment of the Holborn Viaduct to Blackfriars railway lines, and building above the tracks. Once again it will be the architects (Renton Howard Wood Levin) employed by the developer who will act as master-planners for this major piece of cityscape. The plans indicate a combination of clear pedestrian routes lined with shops, and as much office space as can be squeezed onto the site in the form of more of the not-too-tall, deep-plan 'quality' blocks we have seen; in total some 225,000 square metres are planned. A new station at Holborn Viaduct will transform an under-utilised suburban terminus serving the south, into a major new central London station with connections to Gatwick and Luton. While British Rail, the developer and the architects have put together the overall plan for the site, has any wider planning agency considered the implications of the 22,000 people who will eventually work at this new development?

Developments at Broadgate and Holborn Viaduct are dwarfed by the proposals for King's Cross. In the sense that these have been almost exclusively devoted to office use, they were easy. But north of King's Cross lie 50 hectares of quasi-derelict land owned by current and formerly nationalised industries (British Rail with 38 hectares, the National Freight Corporation with 18 acres, British Gas with 2 hectares and British Waterways with 1.5 hectares). King's Cross offers the greatest opportunity for urban regeneration in London since Docklands and is potentially far more fruitful. The chunk of land is large and comprehensible, and the surrounding infrastructure is in place. On the boundaries of

Camden and Islington, where a whole new prosperity is burgeoning, it is just off the Euston Road, where the British Library has now emerged. Next door, Sir George Gilbert Scott's St Pancras Chambers, the former Midland Grand, is to be re-worked into a luxury hotel and a club with service apartments on the upper floors. The station will be overhauled. In the undercroft, fronted by the railway arches beneath the hotel and station, will be shops, restaurants, a small museum, and two stages for live entertainment. The intention is to generate a kind of Covent Gardenish street life and 1,250 jobs.

But these are small generators of people, jobs and activity compared with the potential offered by the expansion of the present transport interchange to incorporate fast rail links to Stansted Airport and the Channel Tunnel. Three rival schemes were shown to the public in the summer of 1988 before British Rail decided which team of architects and developers to employ. Two of the schemes were workmanlike and predictable.

But a third voice struck the right note: in the centre of the site around the old Grand Union Canal, Foster Associates proposed an elliptical 16-acre park. It was utterly seductive. But the appeal of the scheme lay much deeper than the greenery: here were street lines which made sense and had purpose and which genuinely did descend from Nash. From a new arched 'gateway' (a great glass vault over a new railway terminal to be set between King's Cross and St Pancras) a grand arcade led to the park surrounded by a variety of business, industrial and residential buildings. Fosters had put forward four different strategies for developing the area. But in each the patterns of streets and open spaces were in the errant grain of London, and not in the hard-edged formality of a New York or Chicago. The beauty of this scheme was that it was not complicated; it did not try too hard.

Since those plans were first unveiled in 1988, the future of the King's Cross scheme has become shrouded in turmoil as the conflicting demands of Camden Council and local pressure groups come to bear on the amount of office space needed by the London Regeneration Consortium to finance the scheme. Fosters's outline plans have been re-worked countless times, and the equation of park, housing and amenities balanced against income-generating offices and shopping developments. Nowhere else in London has urban design become such a tool of the market. Problems have been compounded by the failure of the Department of Transport to confirm the location of the Channel Tunnel terminal and the downturn in the property market in 1990. How it will turn out is anyone's guess.

CONCLUSION

Broadgate is the completed example of urbanism by developer; King's Cross the next and far more ambitious challenge. Both reveal the extent to which the vacuum of power over the future development of London is being filled by the private sector developer. It is a situation that few regard with equanimity. With the demise of the GLC any pretence of strategic planning for London has vanished. As we witness the third remaking of the City of London in the space of 120 years, urban trends which became established under the Victorians – the squeezing out of small businesses, crafts and industry; the demolition of small lanes, interesting corners and elements of surprise; the building of bigger and bigger buildings devoted exclusively to office use – are today being extended over an ever-larger area into Islington, Hackney, Tower Hamlets, and Westminster and beyond.

If all the new groundscrapers are to be filled, the working population of the City and its enlarged neighbourhood must rise. Yet where are the businesses and people to fill them? When they eventually do come, how will they be transported, fed and entertained? Developers are not interested in controlling transportation, the increasing congestion of traffic, poverty, grime and pollution, or training school leavers for employment. Yet it is these problems which pose the greatest threat to the increase of the City's prosperity. It is time to realise that the development of London must be governed.

REFERENCES

MacCormac, R. (1987) 'Fitting in offices', *Architectural Review*, CLXXXI, no. 1083.

Murphy, S.J. (1986) City of London Local Plan, City of London Corporation.

Rees, P.W. (1988) 'City of London Local Plan. First monitoring report', April 1988, City of London Corporation.

11

AN URBAN NARRATIVE AND THE IMPERATIVES OF THE CITY

Leslie Budd

If H.G.Wells were to reappear in London today he might be tempted to feel that the imagination of *Things to Come* and *War of the Worlds* had become reality. London appears to be a continuous building site, with cranes and new structures competing for a hegemony of space and skyline as its urban shape is transformed.

Like any building site, London has abstract and concrete and internal and external characteristics. In offices, away from the building site, projects appear abstract as so many square metres, a number of storeys that require certain amounts of steel and concrete at a predetermined cost. Any project starts to become more real in the hands of architects, engineers and draughtsmen. They seek to represent graphically what the building will look like and by calculation confirm that its design is safe and long-lasting. The final form of the building is realised on the scurrying anarchy of the building site itself. The building site seems like a closed economy. The site workers are differentiated by skill and status and in their hands the designs of the professionals finally take concrete shape. The professionals have only intermittent contact with the workers, through site meetings with the workers' supervising engineers, and so on. The internal economy of the site interacts with the external one, within which it sits, in manifold ways. The general public's perception of their built environment then changes at a faster rate as technology speeds up building times. The public do not have access to the designs of professionals but do experience the changes that go on around the building site, albeit at a distance. What binds the internal and external characteristics of a building site economy are the larger forces of money and profit. They determine the purpose of the building developments and provide a flow of income to building professionals and workers and potential profit to firms that construct the buildings and those that manufacture and supply materials.

By the same analogy, the notion of a London urban economy displays both abstract and concrete and internal and external dynamics. In the way in which building sites completely or partly demolish old buildings and create new and refurbished ones, so the main impetus of an urban economy will be altered by the imperatives of new forms of economic and social activity. In London's case this has involved a shift from a decentralised manufacturing economy to a knowledge-based financial and business service economy. The demands of these newer, more dominant activities have led to demands for much more modern office accommodation and a more eastward development of London's geography. A way of accounting for these changes is to try to develop a narrative of this particular urban region.

This essay brings together a wide range of issues in order to explore London's narrative. It considers the relationship between money, time and space in order to show how changes in the world's financial markets affect people's lives in the way they use their time and space. Then the essay points out that the property sector has been very important in transforming the City of London in recent years. Because of a change in the financial environment, the property sector may be able to negotiate crises of the kind that afflicted this sector in the early 1970s a little better.

Marx's theory of rent is used to suggest that the mechanism which determines cycles in the property sector is different forms of ground rent, such as differential rent and absolute rent. Ground rent means the economic value of land, a counterpart to Marx's conception is the yield on property. These material circumstances then give the context in which a narrative can be developed. Despite the enormous changes that developments in the City of London have brought about, it is still too early to suggest that London's narrative has radically or permanently altered.

David Harvey has been an important contributor to the analysis of the relationship between money, space and time in an urban context. Harvey (1989) has also developed the notion of the spatial narrative, which in this chapter is given the general title of 'urban narrative'. He states that different material circumstances give rise to processes of constructing communities and their particular social and cultural practices, which in turn have a spatial dimension. Although the process of urbanisation involves a complex interaction between the forces of money, time and space, not all urban communities will develop in the same manner. Therefore, space can neither be treated as being homogeneous nor as if it gives rise to the same kind of spontaneous urban activities. A shorthand way of bringing this reasoning together is to say that each urban community has its own story to tell, its own narrative. Dr Johnson stated that the narrative was more universally accepted as a superior style of conversation. London's urban narrative has developed because its particular material circumstances have given rise to distinctive forms of urban development, social practice and behaviour. The question which arises is to ask whether there is an identifiable spatial or urban narrative for London. One knows that London is different from Paris, but if the imperatives of a knowledge-based economy become dominant, will that in itself bring about a change in the city's narrative?

One of the primary determinants of the spatial narrative of London appears to be the growing importance of the financial sector. This can be identified by comparing the size of the financial sector to national income. Table 11.1 summarises stock market capitalisation as a percentage of national income for various countries.

One could add several caveats to this table but the crucial point is that it shows the growth of the absolute size of the financial sector in the United Kingdom relative to its economy and competitors.

This chapter argues that changes in the underlying material conditions of London have challenged and to some extent changed the prevailing spatial narrative. The material imperatives of a decentralised manufacturing economy have been replaced by those of a knowledge-based business and financial services economy. The latter demands large-scale, high-quality and hi-tech office accommodation. The fulfilment of that demand radically

Table 11.1 Stock market capitalisation as % of gross domestic product

	UK	France	Germany	US	Japan
1978	36	12	15	38	33
1988	83	22	20	50	133

Source: Economist, 1989

changes the built environment and urban topography. It will be argued that the property sector is a key factor in the new imperatives that challenge the prevailing narrative of the city. It will also be argued that ground rent is the agency of booms and slumps in the property sector. That is, the appropriation and distribution of ground rent determines the cycles of destruction and recomposition of the property sector. A consideration of the theory of ground rent inevitably involves an analysis of land under capitalism. Land is both an object and instrument of production in a modern urban economy. As such it has the appearance of being a form of both fixed *and* circulating capital. This view departs somewhat from that of Harvey, who sees land as a form of fictitious capital,[1] and other Marxists, such as Bryan (1988), who see land as fixed capital. Through a consideration of these more fundamental debates this essay seeks to analyse *the* agency that determines cycles in the property sector. In drawing up an account of the property sector, a distinction is made between the crisis of the early 1970s and the possibility of the sector overreaching itself today. That distinction rests on the premise that the development of financial innovation in more liberal capital markets allows a better negotiation of crises through securitisation.[2]

In the final section of this chapter an analysis of what constitutes the material conditions of London's urban narrative is undertaken to show how those conditions have altered. Consequently, the urban narrative should also alter. It is argued, however, that a lag exists between the demands made by changes in the dominant economic activities and the spatial practices that make up a city's narrative. One important discontinuity is the provision of transport infrastructure to provide accessibility to residents' work and leisure practices. Infrastructure is built up over a long period so that providing new transport links does not occur as quickly as changes in the pattern of economic and social activities. Innovations in the financial environment have led to the prospect of land becoming a financial asset, traded like any other. But the notion of territory challenges these logical assumptions. It imposes an obstacle to the narrative and the treatment of land as any other commodity.

This chapter begins, however, with a consideration of the relationship between money, space and time in the light of changes in the international financial environment.

MONEY, SPACE AND TIME AND THE FINANCIAL ENVIRONMENT

The internationalisation of financial markets clearly imposes benefits and costs upon the host regions in which those markets are situated. The term 'internationalisation' has been used interchangeably with 'globalisation'. Similarly, 'deregulation' of financial markets has been interchanged with 'liberalisation' of those markets. At the outset, one needs to be clear about what these terms mean, if the effects that the changing financial environment has on London are to be captured. There is a subtle distinction between internationalisation and globalisation. The former has occurred because the multinationalisation of production led to the multinationalisation of finance and banking, to serve activities across many countries. The outcome of the multinationalisation of finance is that shares and other securities of, say, major American or British companies are traded in a number of financial market centres. Globalisation implies that the shares of those companies can be traded in all the major financial centres, twenty four hours a day. Due to different capacities and regulatory requirements, globalisation remains an aim, but not a reality, at present. The internationalisation of finance has occurred mainly because of technological and technical innovation, following developments such as Third World debt crises and the demand for more flexible forms of debt financing. This is usually associated with developments in computing that have resulted in screen-based trading of financial assets. However, given the large capital costs of investing in screen-based trading systems, a larger amount of business is needed, spread across a number of countries. The differences in the regulatory regimes of the United States and the United Kingdom contributed to the development of the eurodollar markets in the 1960s. As a result of the expansion of many American companies into Europe during the 1950s, excess dollars began to circulate through the European economies. Because of the restrictions on the creation of dollar deposits in the United States, a demand arose for an offshore dollar deposit market in Europe. The more liberal regime in Britain led to those markets being sited in London. In the mid-1970s the markets in shares and other securities in the US were deregulated. That is, many formal regulations or restrictions on trading were removed. The Stock Exchange in London was formally deregulated in October 1986 with the advent of Big Bang. Many other European financial centres are following suit to conform to the requirements of the Single European Market, after 1992. The process that underlies deregulation is liberalisation. That is, the markets themselves, through competitive trading, will establish the efficient and optimal allocation of capital finance without reference to regulatory restrictions. At the centre of this activity is the concept of securitisation, which is at the heart of much financial innovation. As shown by Robinson (Chapter 3) in this volume, other forms of securities can be generated from assets that have already been securitised. The latter are conventionally known as derivatives. In this different kind of environment the inertia of moving money around, the friction of distance and the constraint of time can be overcome. Liberal movement of capital, technological change and screen trading have broken down many of these barriers.

The relationship of money, time and space under capitalism is complex but some simple analytics can be drawn from this complexity. As Marx (1976) pointed out, money separates the buying and selling of time and that money bestows the basic means to gain free time. The credit system as 'the central nervous system of capitalism' (Harvey 1989: 96) coordinates differences in speeds of production and differentiation in the use of space. Empirically, these contentions can be confirmed if one conceives of the way in which satellite technology and computer-based financial trading allows an almost twenty four hour global market in financial assets.

A money economy allows integration over the most diverse forms of experience that are articulated through some negotiation of time and space. If money is an abstraction from relations of exchange and distribution, then speeding up the turnover time of production and the circulation of capital and revenues gives competitive advantage to capitalist enterprises. If capital conquers time and space, then periodic crises in accumulation can be overcome by displacements in time such as debt financing, swaps, options and other forms of financial innovation based on appropriating time. By the same token, appropriation of new spaces and their production also mitigate periods of crisis. Using these arguments, one can envisage the property sector and its development activities as one where money commands time and space. Developers wait for the appropriate conjuncture of time and space to extract profit (in the form of some right over ground rent). This process, where the property rights over the space to be reshaped are exercised optimally, in terms of time, appears to support Harvey's view that property can be treated as a form of fictitious capital, like any other financial asset. Despite the possibility of time and space being used in a different way from formerly, land is territory and cannot easily be restructured or repackaged like a conventional financial asset. Such an indivisibility means that it retains some features of fixed capital.

Property companies, and their major shareholders like insurance companies, also share a sense of territory. This extends to long-term risk-free assets like land. Even if they attempted to treat land as fictitious capital, through securitisation, problems of accessibility and the provision of collective services mean that expected returns on securitised land will not be immediate. The pattern and provision of collective services, such as transport, education and leisure facilities, are determined by the prevailing material circumstances; recent property developments in London have been responding to newer material circumstances. Accessibility lags changes in the material circumstances because of the relative fixity and indivisibility of transport networks. Reshaping and re-forming a network involves long lead times of, say, ten to twenty years, as current debates[3] on transport policy show.

Topalev (1974) argues that developers are able to parcel up tracts of urban land in order to appropriate higher levels of ground rent and surplus profits. Developers will also seek to determine accessibility in order to enhance the portfolio of developments by enhancing the attractiveness of locations. This leads them into a conundrum in that they may wish to internalise the benefits of a publicly provided transport network, but not to provide the means of accessibility themselves for fear of distributing external benefits to competitors. However, in a period where some developers have taken on virtual planning roles in the United Kingdom, such concerns may constrain developers' interests. They may wish to invest directly in accessibility and securitise that investment stake. In other words, developers may fund the provision of transport links and pay for them by bond financing, which would give investors a stake in the returns on the transport system. Those returns would be influenced by the enhancement of locations that developers have a stake in. The benefits to the developer would be two-fold. The external benefits of the transport link would be returned in the form of profits from debt financing the link. Secondly, the enhancement of location, through improved accessibility, would increase the value of the developer's landholding (Damm *et al.* 1980). Such a scenario, however, is an unlikely one for London at present.

THE PROPERTY SECTOR AND GROUND RENT

The relationship of land ownership and rent to capitalist accumulation is complex. The change in the economic imperatives of a major financial centre like London has resulted in the property sector of the economy being pivotal to any analysis of those imperatives. Indeed, the abstraction of international financial liberalisation comes together with the concrete changes in the built environment through the workings of the property sector.

In the post-war period commercial development has occurred on a massive scale in most major cities and London is no exception (see Table 11.2, below). This scale has led some theorists to note that cities have become entities with command and control functions based on the office rather than the factory (Mollenkopf 1978). Theoretically, these developments are concerned with the relation of commercial capital and interest-bearing capital to property development (Boddy 1981).

The basis of this debate is whether land is a form of fixed or circulating capital. What is disputed, is an interpretation of Marx's theory of ground rent and the role of land in capitalist development. Marx's analysis of land concentrated on agriculture and assumed that landowners were a distinct class who were parasitic on accumulation and that rent represented an interception of surplus value. As Massey and Catalano (1978) have shown, the majority of British land is owned by financial institutions. As a branch of banking and commercial capital, financial institutions recycle money capital, generated from industrial capital, through their investments in land. The ground rent and surplus profits appropriated are then recycled back through the circulation process. Turnover time of land development is rapid and thus land makes a major contribution to the rate at which capital and revenues circulate in the process of capitalist accumulation. Empirically, then, Marx's view seems threatened; theoretically, the issue is more difficult, especially when confronting urban land.

Land is bound up with private property, and private property is central to the social relations of capitalism. In this respect land is part of the tension between labour and capital. To restrict land to being solely a form of fixed or circulating or fictitious capital is to rob it of that tension.[4] Furthermore, as Massey and Catalano point out, the evolution of property companies has led to land having the characteristics of both fixed and circulating capital. These companies depend on land as a source of income and as an asset to raise finance in order to expand. When development activities occur, the distinctions between what constitutes improvements to land and ways of financing them become so fine that land also takes on the appearance of circulating capital. The crucial point here is the theoretical difficulties that are posed for analysing land when the institutional form of capitalism has altered. For example, the economic power of the City was historically derived from the landowning classes. In the modern era, banking capital now invests directly in land and generates forms of fictitious capital from its use. What poses the greatest threat in these kinds of debates is territory. Territory is crucial to the way communities are constructed. Property companies' and financial institutions' rational considerations of land, as a form of capital to be invested in, may be intercepted by irrational considerations of territory. Such considerations apply to city residents' spatial practices and the way they frame an urban narrative.

The capital markets are replete with examples of fictitious capital, such as equities, bonds and other forms of securities, which bestow property rights simultaneous to production activities. Capital markets and the credit system thus serve crucial and central roles in co-ordinating production and accumulation. The role of money in a capitalist economy logically extends to securitisation of financial assets and, thus, forms of fictitious capital. As Marx pointed out, mortgages are titles to future ground rent and shares bestow future surplus value to shareholders. Money is an abstraction from relations of production, exchange and distribution. The promise to pay the bearer on demand the notional sum printed on a banknote is in principle no different from any other paper financial asset. In a money economy, multiple transactions of goods and services are generated from a smaller proportion of money stock; a stock guaranteed by the lender-of-last-resort role of central banks. The same logic applies to the securitisation of financial assets; there is a production counterpart. Ultimately, there must be some concrete asset against which a financial instrument can be secured.

Complex financial innovation seeks to hedge risks of securitisation, the regulation of which is so complicated that it is becoming impossible. The same point can be made about land and property development – what is essentially bought and sold is the right to charge a form of rent. In this sense only, land can be treated as a pure financial asset – title deeds or leases can be securitised against the use to which land is put. The realisation of rents occurs continuously through redevelopment of land, so that claims on land and development are circulated through capital markets. It should be noted that capital markets co-ordinate and distribute economic surplus, but do not generate such a surplus. In this co-ordinating role, capital markets speed up the rate at which surplus value is circulated back into production and thus the rate of growth of capital accumulation. By the same token, the securitisation of property development will speed up the rate at which ground rent will circulate.

Marx distinguishes two elements of rent under the rubric of ground rent: differential and absolute rent. Differential rent is differential because of the existence of unequal rates of profits that industrial capital can derive from land that possesses unequal capacities. Differential rent is divided into two types, I and II, and it is the latter that gives rise to absolute rent. Absolute rent stems from the historic power of the landed classes to charge rent on all units of land under production, irrespective of fertility or location. Type I rent (DR I) occurs because capitalist farmers invest on new or uncultivated land. They produce surplus profits from cultivating that land because of the fertility of the land. These surplus profits are appropriated by landowners as differential rent type I. Differential rent, in general, arises from the monopoly of landed property over fertile land or that of superior location.

Differential rent type II (DR II) occurs because it is assumed that landowners can appropriate surplus profits generated by the application of advanced production techniques, or capital to improve location. Again, it is the monopoly power of the landowning class that can appropriate surplus profits, that appear internal to industrial capital, as rent. Whether this form of rent is appropriated will depend upon the competition between the users of land in a position to make bids of rent. In an urban economy differential rent is realised through differences in location leading to differences in productive capacity. Thus the magnitude of surplus profits depends upon accessibility and is therefore related to transport costs. A developer may be able to appropriate differential rent through manipulating accessibility and thus locational advantage. Differential rent in this context is the agency that is related to capital accumulation. In the absence of such an agency, surplus profits derived would be sat upon until some fortuitous occasion and not circulated via ground rent.

Absolute rent occurs socially because landowners will charge some rent, even on land with the least fertility. That is, a landowner who cannot appropriate a differential rent, because of inferior fertility or location, will still charge rent. Therefore absolute rent cannot be circulated in the same manner as differential rent. It can still arise in a modern urban economy because there is competition for favourable locations and landowners will charge rent for the least favourable locations.

Differential rent as the major agency determines cycles in the property sector. Predominantly it is differential rent type II (DR II) that is appropriated during property development. In the case of a parcel of denationalised land such as in Docklands, where derelict land of near zero value is invested in, it is differential rent type I (DR I) that is appropriated in the first instance. Successive investment to enhance location will then generate DR II at each stage. Institutional investment in land cycles surplus value from industrial capital through development. That surplus value is circulated via ground rent, but changes in the institutional form of capitalism can pose theoretical difficulties. This is especially the case with land speculation and the relation of rent to interest. If rent and interest are not clearly separate then rent could collapse into interest, during speculative moments, which is related to the functioning of the circuit of commercial capital. These difficulties can be empirically unscrambled to some degree by an account of the property sector in Britain in the post-war years.

PROPERTY DEVELOPMENT AND THE LONDON ECONOMY, 1970–90

Property development has been central to the changing imperatives of the London economy. The property boom and collapse of 1972 and 1973 is a powerful reference point. The recent downturn in the commercial property sector has led to commentators making a comparison with the events of early 1970s. That downturn has led to the Bank of England warning commercial banks about their levels of lending to the property sector (£30 billion at end of 1989). These events suggest a re-run of the period of the early 1970s, but it should be remembered that history is often a function of context and conjuncture. The different conjuncture is the globalisation and liberalisation of financial markets, in part based on the spread of securitisation. There is also a different composition of the assets, including land, held by financial institutions today. Financial innovation in property development has tended to lag behind that of other assets, but there has been a growth in the securitisation of property assets. The processes of globalisation and liberalisation have led property companies and financial institutions to include purchases and finance of property overseas in their internationally diversified portfolios. The difference between London of the early 1970s and the early 1990s is a different financial environment and regime. There is a great deal of literature about the way in which financial institutions distribute their funds across a balanced portfolio of assets.[5] Traditionally, property has been included in that portfolio, but shifts between assets across the portfolio are constrained because property has been a rather indivisible asset. Despite the indivisibility of this kind of asset and the friction of distance, changes in the financing regime of property development have overcome some of these problems. In the United Kingdom, debt finance from banks for property companies' development activities has tended to increase at the expense of pension funds and insurance companies' equity stakes in property companies. Table 11.2 shows the distribution of assets in the portfolio of pension funds and insurance companies over a twenty five year period.

At the same time, the internationalisation of financial markets has allowed international institutions to diversify a portfolio across a number of centres. Foreign investment in property in the United Kingdom for 1988 and 1989 was £3.1 billion, with Japanese companies accounting for forty four per cent of that total. Net investment by foreigners was £1.4 billion for 1989, whilst the equivalent net amount for British investors was approximately £2 billion. The combination of financial innovation and diversification, across national boundaries, has stimulated the development of securitisation in the property market. It still lags behind securitisation of more liquid assets. However, the ability of large international financial institutions and property companies to take a longer term view, combined with innovative financing

Table 11.2 Insurance companies and pension funds portfolio of long-term assets, 1964–89

	UK ordinary shares	Goverment securities	Land & property ground rents	Total
1964	3897 (27.8)	3168 (22.7)	1027 (7.3)	13986 (100)
1974	8447 (25.1)	6090 (18.1)	5498 (16.4)	33626 (100)
1980	38394 (49.8)	7479 (9.7)	20570 (26.0)	77063 (100)
1984	98969 (45.5)	9110 (4.2)	31052 (14.3)	217094 (100)
1989	171941 (52.0)	20846 (6.4)	44772 (13.6)	327702 (100)

Source: *Financial Statistics*, 1965–1990
(£m, current prices, percentages in parentheses)

and refinancing, means that domestic patterns of boom slump may be of less significance than formerly. Large companies are around long enough to collect rents, irrespective of the cycles in the sector. In an interview with a leading spokesman for a major financial institution, the *Financial Times* noted that some exposure to property risk was sensible in the present recessionary climate (*Financial Times*, 11 January 1991).

The financing of property development has changed significantly in the United Kingdom since 1945. In the immediate post-war period, yields on property were greater than long-term interest rates. Mortgage funds borrowed from insurance companies presented few problems. The returns on this investment were generated by the developers issuing long-term leases. In the 1950s and 1960s long-term interest rates began to rise as inflationary expectations grew. Developers responded by trading in part of their expected profit in return for lower interest rate finance.

Between 1963 and 1973, the property sector moved from boom to recession with controls on office development being imposed in 1964. However, by 1967, property company shares began to rise again as a shortage of space and inflationary pressures resulted in a significant rise in office rents. Given rising rents, capitalised by rising interest rates, existing assets became very valuable and takeovers of property companies became common. The inflationary climate that had assisted the swelling of cash balances of property companies ironically led to investment in property as a hedge against inflation. Many developers borrowed short-term for their developments, on the assumption that rising asset values would cover the costs of deficit financing. These rising asset values rode on the back of the development boom that began in 1970. However, the combination of a rent freeze in 1972, the post-1973 oil shock, ensuing inflation, rising interest rates and off-balance sheet adjustments to disguise negative cash flows contributed to the subsequent crash.

The collapse of property companies led to the secondary banking crisis, with a combination of Bank of England intervention and banks, insurance companies and pension funds bailing out property companies. One of the ironies of the crash was that the increased participation of financial institutions, in property companies and direct investments, tended to push up capital values and depress yields, thus exposing some property companies to risk that the institutions themselves ultimately but reluctantly helped to cover. As Table 11.2 shows, institutions again became keen buyers and property values rose sharply between 1978 and 1981 as a hedge against inflation. The recession of 1981–82 hit tenant demand and the rate of rent increases. The recovery in the economy led that of the property sector so that by 1987 rents and values began booming. But financial institutions have scaled back their investments, being replaced by the banks as major financers of this sector. The present shaky situation is suggestive of a re-run of the early 1970s, despite banks reconciling themselves to extending loans and thus interest in the property market. Why should it be different this time?

Like many of the financial markets, the property market has experienced market segmentation following the internationalisation and deregulation of markets. For example, the property companies which have experienced recent problems in the UK have been limited in their ability to restructure financially and take advantage of financial innovation by the structure of their portfolios and risk profiles. This innovation includes off-balance sheet techniques,[6] involving swaps and options. These off-balance sheets techniques expose banks, that lend to innovative property companies, to default because the profit and loss accounts of these companies do not reflect the true relation of assets to liabilities.

Unlike the early 1970s, banks are in a stronger position today. They have a claim on property assets that have future expected returns but will have to wait for rents and values to rise again; it could be a long wait. The strong demand for new purpose-built accommodation, since Big Bang, and the relative lack of such accommodation in London in recent years has led to lumpiness in the investment cycle. New capacity has been coming on stream at a time when the UK economy is heading rapidly into recession and the financial markets are in the doldrums in respect of activity. In terms of the relationship between an index of the property market and outstanding bank lending, the present situation does not reflect 1973. In the early 1970s the Financial Times Actuaries Property Index dropped 400 per cent whereas the adjustment after the stock market crash of 1987 was roughly 100 per cent. The high point of the FT property index, in 1990, was 1245.3, whilst its low point was 837.2. This compares with 1226.8 and 962.1 for the FT-All Share Index; at the beginning of 1991 both indexes have risen somewhat to means of 1035.6 and 977.78 respectively. This suggests that property has recovered a little more than equities. The other difference is the involvement of international property companies and financial institutions, and the fact that bank lending is only slightly above trend in the late 1980s, unlike the previous crash. Table 11.3 shows the amount of direct overseas investment in the United Kingdom property market for the decade. This investment reduces the vulnerability of the property sector to domestic crises but exposes any one global centre to the fallout from market crises in other centres.

Over-exposure to property risk has been the engine of financial crises in Japan and the United States during 1990 – having an impact similar to the property crash in Britain of the early 1970s. This has not affected London so directly but could have indirect effects on the portfolio decisions of international developers like Olympia & York, who are heavily involved in Docklands.

Table 11.3 Direct property investment from overseas

1980	1981	1982	1983	1984	1985	1986	1987	1988	1989
100	80	120	50	80	95	155	295	1400	2000

Source: Estates Gazette
(£m, current prices)

Between 1984 and 1988, 575,000 square metres of offices were built, in the City and City fringes, with planning consents for a further 10.9 million square feet, a doubling of the previous figures. This is a corollary of the expansion in financial services and business services following financial liberalisation. As the recession bites, excess capacity in the financial markets has led to occupancy rates increasing by only 3 per cent during 1990/91 and forecasts of average rents dropping by 20 per cent. Other estimates suggest that London will not need any new accommodation for ten years. The knock-on effects on new developments such as Docklands will depend on a number of international contingencies and the degree to which off-balance sheet financing does not disguise a financial house of cards. These contigencies include investors diversifying their exposure to risk by calculating correlations of portfolio returns between centres, as well as the global financial environment.

Despite most property debt being in the form of bank loans that are often syndicated, there is a large potential for property-backed bonds in the United Kingdom. Debt does raise gearing and is then vulnerable to downturns in the market, but bonds, being more divisible and easily tradeable, are often less risky than freeholds, if the credit rating of the issuer reflects their true financial worth. International investors, especially the Japanese, are often keen buyers of bonds rather than equities. Innovations, like the property unit trusts coming on stream in London in 1991, can make bonds attractive during market downturns. The downside risk of property-related securities is liquidity and these proposed unit trusts are to carry a liquidity health warning under the draft regulations of the Securities and Investment Board. In the present political climate many investors are 'flying to safety'. Given that the decline in the property sector has not yet created the financial crises of the order of Japan and America, exposure to property in London may be a future hedge against inflation.

Large international developers can ride out declines in the business cycles by parcelling up developments and influencing accessibility. Consequently, opportunities exist to enhance portfolios and gain ground rent, especially at a time when developers have taken on planning roles.

In an era when the London economy has become regulated by the imperatives of financial and business services, regulation is experienced most concretely in the changed built environment.

The property sector, then, has been central to that change. Accessibility in the form of transport costs and provision of infrastructure has a crucial bearing on the way in which this sector of the economy can reproduce itself. Accessibility and changes in transport provision are also important determinants in articulating a narrative for London and a notion of habitus for Londoners. This is considered in the next section.

A CHANGING URBAN NARRATIVE?

The basis of modern London stems from the period 1919 to 1939. A combination of planning acts, major regional plans and what are now the bases of London Underground Ltd and British Rail Network Southeast structured the roots of the city as it is known today. The major plans were based on the Barlow Report of 1940, the Forshaw Plan of 1943, the Abercrombie Plan for Greater London of 1944 and the Holden and Holford Plan for the City of London of 1951. The Barlow Report set the context for the 'planning' of the metropolis, whilst the planning environment was heavily influenced by the dictums of Ebenezer Howard's Garden City movement. Barlow laid down certain key principles such as redevelopment of congested areas, decentralisation of industry and balanced and diversified industrial development. The Abercrombie Plan, as the basis of a balanced planning approach to London, has been important historically for discussions concerning the London economy. Central to Abercrombie is a transport network to fulfil the objectives of the plan. However, the growth of transport provision in London occurred on a bifurcated pattern, established north and south of the Thames. In the north, Albert Stanley and Frank Pick extended tube lines out beyond the boundaries of London after 1933. In the south, Southern Railway, under the leadership of Herbert Walker, electrified lines and extended the system in a way similar to Stanley and Pick. The structure of London's transport provision is therefore based upon a pre-war pattern of settlement and an immediate post-war planning scenario based upon a perception of a planned urban economy determined by decentralised industrial activities.

The Garden City movement and the Abercrombie Plan are still important reference points, bringing together the three principles of the Barlow Report. Industry was to be decentralised along suburban arteries with complementary business services located centrally. London then appeared as the kind of balanced and organic urban economy described by conventional location theory. London has traditionally been structured by a bifurcation of its central activities. Commercial activities are sited in the east and political, administrative and major retail activities in the west. The shift in the pattern of activities from manufacturing to services, that has been a feature of every major economy, has affected London to perhaps a greater degree than other large western European cities. Big Bang represents a culmination of that shift towards services and thus the central locus of London's economy shifted with it. Bank of England figures (1989) show the magnitude of the shift to services over the last fifteen years. In 1975 Banking, Finance, Insurance, Business Services and Leasing (BFIBSL) contributed 7.2 per cent to Gross Domestic Product at factor cost. In 1988 this figure had increased to 13.9 per cent. Real output of BFIBSL grew by 82 per cent between 1975 and 1985 and 34 per cent for the period 1985 to 1988. The respective figures for the rest of the economy were 17 per cent and 11 per cent. Table 11.4 displays sectoral employment change in the London region for periods between 1951 and 1989.

Table 11.4 displays the obvious shift between sectors, but it also shows that there has been an absolute decline in employment in the London Region. If one looks at the annual growth rates of employment for financial and business services for London and the United Kingdom, a similar pattern emerges. In Greater London the annual growth rate for this sector was 1.9 per cent for 1978–81, 3.6 per cent for 1981–84 and 4.4 per cent for 1984–87. For the United Kingdom the respective figures are 3.8 per cent, 4.8 per cent and 5.9 per cent. This appears to confirm the initial

Table 11.4 Annual sectoral change in employment in London region

	Manufacturing	Services	Total
1951–61	+ 400	+ 18700	+ 1700
1961–66	– 30700	– 11700	– 14300
1971–74	– 49200	+ 24600	– 30800
1981–84	– 32300	+ 5400	– 33900
1985–89	– 400	+ 51000	+ 36000

Source: Buck *et al.* 1986; Bank of England 1989

conclusion. However, when distribution of income growth by region and by sector is considered, a rather more striking pattern emerges. It is clear that London and the rest of the south-east are contributing to economic growth and value-added at a faster rate than the country as a whole and in comparison to other regions (Murray 1988). The pre-eminence of business and financial services based in the south-east region of the UK appears to confirm a thesis of de-industrialisation and a core–periphery regional structure. The question then arises: what is one to make of these patterns in framing an urban narrative for London?

A change in the dominant economic and social imperatives of an urban region will affect the spatial narrative of the region. Many of the spatial practices that comprise the narrative will depend on residents' access to them. The suburbanisation of residential London, with the centre remaining the dominant area of work, means that the transport network, in the main, is not unrelated to the spatial arrangement of the service-based economy. After all, most of the property development in London occurred in the City and West End, both of which have good accessibility. However, the dominance of a knowledge-based economy has brought new spatial practices and an expansion into previously undeveloped areas like Docklands. Gentrification or yuppification of inner urban areas and a closer proximity of work and home are examples of new practices. Transport accessibility is still poor in many areas, especially Docklands. In the new material circumstances where land can be securitised by financial institutions and property companies, there will be an incentive to determine accessibility to property investments to enhance financial agents' portfolios. Large companies can either finance transport links or influence public policy. Olympia & York is developing a project at Canary Wharf in Docklands. It has offered a contribution of £400 million (1989 prices) to extend the Jubilee Line to Canary Wharf, amounting to 15 per cent over the life of the project, and has been given the go-ahead by the present government. This decision is a recognition of the new material circumstances by both policy makers and developers. In respect of the whole London region, there will be a lag before the new material circumstances feed through into new spatial practices via enhanced access to those new practices.

A number of French writers have developed a whole literature on the kind of process outlined above (Pincon-Charlot, Preteceille and Rendu 1975, 1986; Pincon-Charlot and Rendu 1982;

Pincon-Charlot 1986). This literature shows the way in which access to collective services ('équipements collectifs' is the French term) and the pattern of them veils the true economic structure on which those services are built. Rendu (1979) and Budd (1986) show how transport provision in the Paris region has been a function of economic class and political colour of the sub-regions of the region. In the case of London this kind of view seems more appropriate for the former material circumstances. Some of the French theorists have been influenced by the notion of 'habitus' (Bourdieu 1979). That is, the way in which an individual's immediate habitat is structured by forms of association, relationship, behaviour and services provides influences and determines the individual in relation to that space. Habitus is a generic way of speaking of spatial practices. The habitus of most of London's residents is still framed by the provision of collective services associated with former material circumstances. At present the newer circumstances, associated with a knowledge-based service economy, have had only a partial effect on residents' habitus and only in certain parts of the city and amongst certain classes and professions.

London as an international financial centre is in the forefront of the restructuring of the abstract forces of time and space because of the demands of banking capital. The concrete effect on the whole London urban region appears profound, in the sense that demands for a rapid increase in office space have transformed the appearance of London, especially in the City. What this chapter has argued is that a liberalised financial regime and its effect on property development have contributed to a displacement of the urban narrative beyond people's ability to control their habitus by the more normal material and cultural practices. Given long lead times in infrastructure provision and the rapidity of financial change, it is not so certain that a change in the urban narrative of London can be so easily identified or accommodated at present.

An apparently new urban narrative for London seems to evolve from a pattern of change brought about by the imperatives of a dominant financial centre. That pattern of change masks the material process underlying the apparent new narrative. The question is whether this type of narrative is permanent or whether, despite the massive re-forming of the built environment, all that appears solid can melt into air. As with the future of the City of London as the international financial centre of the European time zone, the constitution of London's current narrative is still problematic.

NOTES

1 Fictitious capital is so named because it does not contribute directly to the formation of surplus value (economic surplus in conventional terms). Marx gives mortgages and shares as examples of fictitious capital, and states that they are claims on future surplus value. That surplus value will be created by the application of constant (fixed) capital and variable capital (labour) to production.
2 Securitisation refers to a process of financial innovation whereby a financial instrument, such as a bond, can be produced against the security of an asset. In the event of default on the financial instrument the actual asset stands as security.
3 These debates have concerned various transport proposals. They include new toll roads in and around the inner suburbs of London and proposals for new and extended tube and rail lines.
4 I am grateful to Mike Cowen for bringing this point to my attention.
5 The literature of portfolio adjustment theory has a long history. Major theorists have included Tobin, and Miller and Modigliani, the latter being best known for their work on the portfolio preferences of corporate companies in the United States.
6 Off-balance sheet techniques include the setting up of shell companies whose only asset is the building development. In the event of the development not being completed there is no effect on the parent company's balance sheet. Another technique is to capitalise the interest of the project. That is, to roll up the interest costs and add them to the final cost of the development. Inventive accounting techniques can make capitalised interest appear as an income stream to the parent company. The net effect of these techniques is to make it very difficult for banks to ascertain the financial health of many property companies. They, as principal lenders, have the asset of the property development as collateral but they may have to wait to realise that asset, especially during market downturns, thereby weakening their own balance sheets.

REFERENCES

Bank of England (1989) 'London as an international financial centre', *Bank of England Quarterly Review*, November: pp. 516–52.
Boddy, M. (1981) 'The property sector in late capitalism: the case of Britain', in M. Dear and A.J. Scott (eds) *Urbanization and Urban Planning in Capitalist Society*, London: Methuen.
Bourdieu, P. (1979) *La Distinction*, Paris: Les Editions de Minuit.
Broadbent, A. (1975) 'An attempt to apply Marx's theory of ground rent to the modern urban economy', *Centre for Environmental Studies Research Paper*, 17.
Bryan, R. (1988) 'Land as capital: an alternative to Marx's theory of absolute rent', unpublished paper, Department of Economics, University of Sydney.

Buck, N., Gordon, I. and Young, K. (1986) *The London Employment Problem*, Oxford: Clarendon Press.

Budd, L. (1986) 'Equipements collectifs and political colour in the Paris region', *Department of Economics, City of London Polytechnic Working Paper*, 10.

Damm, D., Lerman, S.R., Lerner-Lam, E. and Young, J. (1980) 'Urban real estate values in anticipation of the Washington Metro', *Journal of Transport Economics and Policy*, XIV, 3: pp. 315–36.

Davis, E.P. (1989) 'International financial centres – an industrial analysis', *Bank of England Discussion Paper*, 51, September: pp. 1–26.

Duffy, F. and Henney, A. (1989) *The Changing City*, London: Bulstrode Press.

Harvey, D. (1989) *The Urban Experience*, Oxford: Basil Blackwell.

Itoh, M. (1988) *The Basic Theory of Capitalism*, Basingstoke: Macmillan.

Marx, K. (1976) *Capital*, vols. *1–3*, Harmondsworth: Penguin.

Massey, D. and Catalano, A. (1978) *Capital and Land*, London: Edward Arnold.

Modigliani, F. and Miller, M.H. (1958) 'The cost of capital, corporate finance and the theory of investment', *American Economic Review*, June: pp. 261–97

Mollenkopf, J. (1978) 'The postwar politics of urban development', in W.K. Tabb and L. Sawyer, *Marxism and the Metropolis*, Oxford: Oxford University Press.

Murray, R. (1988) *Crowding Out: Booms and Crisis in the South-East*, Stevenage: South-east Economic Development Strategy.

Pincon-Charlot, M. (1986) 'Social space and the provision of public services: segregation in the Ile de France region', in K. Hoggart and E. Kofman (eds) *Politics, Geography and Social Stratification*, London: Croom Helm.

Pincon-Charlot, M., Preteceille, E. and Rendu, P. (1975) *Equipements collectifs, structures et consommation sociale*, Paris: Centre de Sociologie Urbaine.

—— (1986) *Ségrégation Urbaine*, Paris: Editions Anthropos.

Pincon-Charlot, M. and Rendu, P. (1982) 'Distance spatiale, distance sociale aux équipements collectifs en Ile de France; des conditions de la practique aux practiques', *Revue française de sociologie*, XIII.

Preteceille, E. and Terrail, J-P. (1985) *Capitalism, Consumption and Needs*, Oxford: Basil Blackwell.

Rendu, P. (1979) *Equipements collectifs, gestion financière et couleur politique*, Paris: Centre de Sociologie Urbaine.

Richard Ellis Research (1989) *Office Space Survey*, London: Richard Ellis.

Tobin, J. (1965) 'Theory of portfolio selections', in F.H. Hahn and F.P.R. Brechling (eds) *The Theory of Interest Rates*, London: Macmillan.

Topalev, C. (1974) *Le Foncier Urbain*, Paris: Editions Mouton.

12

IN THE WAKE OF MONEY

The City of London and the accumulation of value

Nigel Thrift and Andrew Leyshon

> What does it do, in detail, to people; this pride of class and wealth; this indifference of trade; this reduction of human connections to their convenience for business?
>
> (Williams, Introduction to Dickens,
> *Dombey and Son* 1970: 25)

> As individuals succeed in wealth creation there can be no doubt that the majority will strive to exhibit that success by moving to the country.
>
> (Lilwall and Allcock 1988: x)

Over the last 150 years the City of London has often been described as a separate world from that inhabited by the vast majority of the British population, as a complex of wealth, prestige, authority and power dependent upon the rest of the world for its survival as much as upon Britain, and 'all the more formidable because of its geographical concentration, and the mutual sympathies of the men who ultimately control it' (Sandelson 1959: 141). Of course, it is possible to argue about the degree to which, over the course of history, the wealth and power generated by the City has cohered, and the degree to which it has influenced the British economy, state, society and culture. But it is clear that in the 1980s the City became more visible to the public gaze as a result of the interaction between changes in British society and changes in the City. In the case of the economy, the visibility of the City was made more acute by a general worldwide boom in the financial services industry and by specific increases in financial services employment in many parts of Britain, drawing new workers into the financial services labour force (Leyshon, Thrift and Tommey 1989). In the case of the state, the City's visibility grew with the increasing scale and influence of large financial services conglomerates which periodically were able to outflank the various state controls based upon the Bank of England and assorted regulatory mechanisms. In the case of British society, the more dynamic sections of the City became part of a new 'disestablishment' (Lloyd 1988a, b, c, d; Perkin 1989), a highly visible coalition of private business interests that was 'meritocratic rather than egalitarian, efficient rather than generous, individualistic rather than corporate' (Lloyd 1988d: 155). Finally, the City became imprinted on the national culture as an exemplar of a new Britain which was more conscious of wealth and more careless of egalitarian concerns. The rapidly growing cultural industries were able to serve up the City to audiences as a set of stereotypes. For example, young men and women working in the City were interpreted as Thatcher's stormtroopers in large numbers of plays, television series and films, and books, all the way from *Serious Money*, through *Capital City*, to *Nice Work*. It is thus that *Dombey and Son* takes on a new life.

This chapter will take the measure of some of the economic, social and cultural aspects (the three are inseparable) of the City's influence on Britain in the 1980s. The argument is a straightforward one that starts with the payment of large salaries and bonuses to many of those working in the City in the 1980s. In turn, these salaries and bonuses were converted into personal wealth. One of the ways in which this conversion was accomplished was via the purchase of scarce assets and which therefore had a 'positional' value (Hirsch 1978). Such positional assets have appreciated particularly rapidly in the 1980s. But these assets are not just a store of economic value. They also have a social and cultural value (indeed, this is one of the ways in which their positionality is defined). The purchase of these assets, therefore, became one of the ways by which the City's newly wealthy defined themselves socially and culturally and, over time, this definition (or set of definitions) spread to other parts of the business community, becoming more general in the process, both socially and geographically.

Accordingly, this chapter is in three parts. The first part considers the growth of the City's labour market in the 1980s, paying particular attention to the escalation in incomes that accompanied this expansion. The second part considers the choices that were made by the newly wealthy of the City, concerning which goods and services were particularly appropriate to buy. Particular attention is paid to the market in country houses. Finally, some brief conclusions are drawn.

MAKING MONEY: THE GROWTH OF THE CITY OF LONDON THROUGH THE 1980S

It is not our concern in this chapter to provide a full account of the economic growth of the City of London in the 1980s. That has already been done elsewhere (Thrift and Leyshon 1990). Instead, our intention is to select aspects of that growth which are most closely related to the chief theme of this chapter: the way that money earned in the City has contributed to the social and cultural transformation of Britain by the business community. In particular, this means focusing on the expansion of the City's labour market and the parallel increase in incomes.

Through the 1980s the City of London's labour market grew rapidly. There are, of course, considerable problems in defining what is meant by the City's labour market. Thus, the pattern of demand for labour has changed as the City's institutions have spilled out of the traditional area of City activity, the Square Mile, into the rest of inner London and even further afield. The pattern of supply of labour has also changed. Although the bulk of the City's labour force still comes from London, through the 1980s the long-established tendency to draw labour from the south-east and farther out was strengthened by an increase in long-distance commuting by rail (Leyshon, Boddy and Thrift 1989). Given the constantly shifting boundaries of the City's labour market, in both demand and supply terms, it is clearly difficult to provide exact quantitative estimates of the numbers employed in the City or their places of residence. So far as the administrative area of the Square Mile is concerned, numbers in employment have increased from 390,215 in 1981, to 413,711 in 1984, to 415,435 in 1987. Of these employees, 341,567 were engaged in service activities in 1981 (a definition nearer to indicating City types of activities), 357,939 in 1984 and 380,370 in 1987. Within financial and producer services, 186,235 were employed within the City administrative area in 1981, 206,452 in 1984 and 250,150 in 1987 (Census of Employment). A better estimate of total City employment would be provided by including those working in City types of activities in

284

inner London. No official data series provides such information. However, a survey by Rajan and Fryatt (1988) found that in 1987 the City administrative area accounted for only 71 per cent of employment in six key City activities (banks and discount houses, other credit-granting institutions, securities, insurance, accountancy and management consultancy, software services) and, given more recent moves out of the City by financial institutions, the percentage can only decrease in the future.

So far as supply of labour is concerned, similar difficulties are presented. Figures 12.1 and 12.2 show the place of residence of those working in the City in 1981 (the last date for which census figures are available). Not surprisingly, there was a clear pattern of decay with distance from the City and from the major road and rail links. Since 1981, this pattern has been 'stretched' with the development of Docklands, at least parts of which are enclaves for City workers, and by the continuing tendency for the City to draw its workers from farther and farther out from London (Evans and Crampton 1989).

In summary, the City's labour market expanded rapidly throughout the 1980s. The rate of expansion is in some dispute, but Rajan and Fryatt (1988) calculate that in the particularly frantic 'Big Bang' to 'Big Crash' period from 1984 to 1987, the average annual growth rate of employment was as much as 7.5 per cent. In the period from 1987 to 1992, Rajan and Fryatt calculated that the growth rate would still be in the order of 3 per cent per annum with the most sustained growth, over both periods, being found in banking, accountancy and management consultancy, and software services. This expansion in the numbers employed in the City was accompanied by an expansion of the City's labour market over space, in both demand and supply terms.

Of course, the City's labour market is not an undifferentiated mass. Over time, its composition has been changing as a result of changes in employer demand. Most importantly, the 1980s saw a general upgrading of the City's skills base which meant hiring more school leavers with 'A' levels, more diploma holders, more graduates and more of those with postgraduate qualifications. Thus, in Great Britain as a whole, banking, finance and insurance raised its share of graduate employment from 13.8 per cent in 1983 to 17.7 per cent in 1987. This increase coincided with the deregulation of financial services associated with Big Bang. This rise was particularly marked for males whose share rose from 14.8

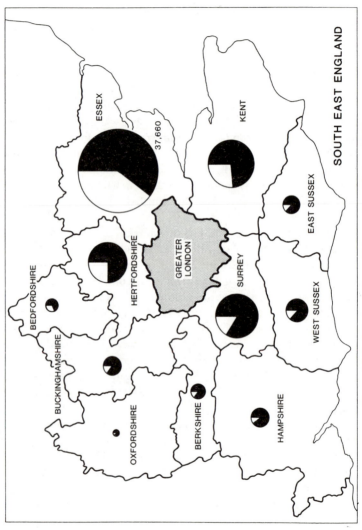

Figure 12.1 City work-force by area of residence, 1981

SOUTH EAST ENGLAND

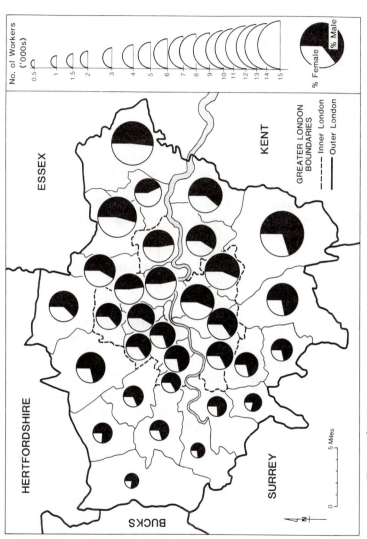

Figure 12.2 Number of City workers within Greater London boundaries, 1981

to 19.7 per cent, but also concerned females, up from 11.2 to 13.2 per cent (Creigh and Rees 1989: 21).

In turn, this upgrading of the City's skills base has meant that the proportion of employment in managerial and professional occupations increased, whilst the share of employment held by clerical staff decreased relatively (Rajan and Fryatt, 1988). The shortages of skilled labour induced by the City's need to upgrade its skills base also meant that through the 1980s more women and those from ethnic minorities have been hired. However, these groups remained under-represented and tended to be concentrated in the poorer paying clerical jobs which still account for nearly one half of the City's jobs.

The spatial extent of the labour markets of each of these different groups clearly varied. Thus, at one extreme, the City acted as a kind of 'vacuum cleaner', sucking up highly skilled labour. For example, graduates were pulled into the City from all parts of Britain to live in London and the south-east of England. At the other extreme, women and ethnic minorities (seen as undifferentiated groups) tended to be drawn from nearer to London, and to be more or less coincident with the pattern of supply of the City's clerical labour force (Figures 12.1 and 12.2).

PAY IN THE CITY IN THE 1980S

According to New Earnings Survey data, earnings in the City underwent a dramatic increase in the course of the 1980s. Average earnings were not just been above average earnings in Britain, but also above average earnings in the rest of London, and in the south-east of England. More spectacularly, the disparities have increased over time (Figure 12.3).

The reasons for such a rapid increase in earnings were many but amongst them the most important was a skills shortage induced by the general trend towards more skilled jobs in the City, coupled with the willingness of some firms to pay inflated salaries to buy in these skills. In the context of the City, 'skills' does not just mean proficiency in using particular management techniques or a particular technology, it also means the social proficiency associated with access to a web of contacts which provide new customers and other important information on markets and business more generally. One important manifestation of the skills shortage (which was obviously greater in certain kinds of jobs than

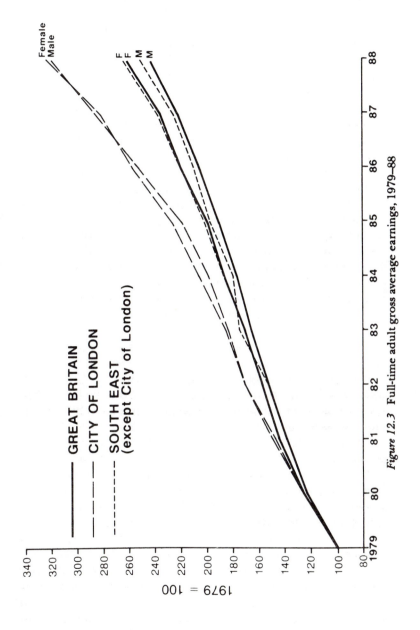

Figure 12.3 Full-time adult gross average earnings, 1979–88

others) was the constant poaching by firms of people or teams of people with particular skills/contacts from other firms, even in the less favourable market conditions of the late 1980s. This behaviour leads to particularly strong salary inflation because the value of such people or teams of people often comes to be associated with the salaries that they earn. Other factors also come into play in explaining the City's above-average earnings. First, through the 1980s the City increasingly became part of an international labour market for upper-echelon financial services workers based in the financial centres of the world. At the beginning of the 1980s salaries in the City were comparatively low by the standards of many of those centres. Through the 1980s the City was in the process of catching up, spurred on by an influx of foreign (especially US) firms used to paying higher salaries. In addition, more and more foreign nationals began to work in the City and in many cases they were used to higher salaries. Second, the institutional structure of the City's labour market became more complex: headhunting firms were commonly used to find particular kinds of workers (Byrne 1987; Jones 1989); labour market information (especially on salaries) became more freely available to both firms and workers; and so on. Third, and finally, career and salary expectations undoubtedly changed. Workers, in the upper echelons at least, became more likely to expect higher salaries and to expect to switch jobs in order to get them.

It is important to note here that earnings in the City do not consist only of salaries. In many City jobs, additions to basic salary are of crucial importance in boosting income (Reid 1988). Amongst these, the most important is the use of bonuses. These can be linked to the performance of the firm, or to individual performances (by, for example, traders) and can consist of straight cash bonuses or various share options schemes. In a number of cases these bonuses can form a very substantial proportion of final income. Another important addition to salary will consist of various perquisites, including mortgage subsidy, a company car or allowance for use of own car, help with costs of rail travel, life insurance, free medical assurance, low interest loans, subsidised meals and subsidised private telephone. These additions to basic salary are clearly unequally distributed according to seniority and type of job, but it would be surprising to find that in the 1980s those occupying managerial positions were not earning at least another 15 per cent of their salary through them.

In summary, it is clear that the number of well-off people in the City increased quite rapidly in the 1980s as a result of generally improved levels of income, combined with a gradual increase in the number of professional and managerial workers who were the chief beneficiaries of these increases in income, both relatively and absolutely.

But the story cannot stop with income. It is important to point out that the high incomes of the kinds which could be found in the City can be rapidly converted into a stock of assets, into personal wealth. The use of stock options as bonuses is just the most direct conversion of income into assets that is offered to those with substantial incomes. More usually, they make the conversion themselves by buying stocks, and shares, or opening deposit accounts, which provide them with another stream of income. Alternatively, they can buy appreciating assets like houses, or antiques and other collectables.

The process by which income was converted into personal wealth by the better off workers in the City was aided by four important processes. First, especially in the period leading up to Big Bang, many people gained instant wealth via golden 'handshakes', 'hellos' or 'handcuffs', large payments aimed at: buying partners or directors out of small firms which were to be integrated into larger ones; tempting people or teams of people with particular skills to join another firm; and persuading people or teams of people with particular skills to stay put. Second, many of those who work in the City do not have to accumulate wealth from scratch using only their salary and bonuses as a stake. In the City's upper echelons before Big Bang many of its leading firms had had a clear preference for recruiting into managerial or prospective managerial positions from a small pool of people (Thrift, Leyshon and Daniels 1987). These new entrants to the City labour market were more likely to have upper or upper middle class backgrounds associated with the major public schools and universities. They were therefore more likely to be wealthy, or to have wealth thrust upon them via inheritance (Table 12.1). With the increase in the number of foreign firms in the City, whose recruitment practices are more meritocratic, and the general increase in the size of the City labour force, the degree of selection from a narrow set of class backgrounds has clearly diminished but not, perhaps, as much as might be thought. Thus, many foreign institutions have shown the same bias towards products of Oxford, Cambridge and other top-rank universities like Bristol as their British counterparts. Again, it remains to be seen whether the leaders of City institutions in the late 1990s and 2000s will not prove to have the same narrow backgrounds as at present (Greenshields 1989) as the process of selection for higher office works through the system of promotion. In other words, in the case of the City the old adage 'to him who hath will be given more' may still have some force; the link between wealth and access to high incomes with which to generate more wealth has not necessarily been broken.

Third, the process of conversion of income into wealth has been helped by the active intervention of the British state. Various rules on capital transfer and capital gains have helped to make wealth

Table 12.1 Top executives in City institutions by school and university, 1986 (percentage)

A. By school

City institution	*School*		
	Public	*Grammar*	*Other*
Merchant banks	83	8	9
Stockbrokers	96	4	0
Clearing banks	56	21	23
Accountants	72	18	10
Insurance companies	58	15	27
Insurance brokers	77	13	10
Mean	74	13	13

B. By university

City institution	*University*					
	Top executives			*New entrants*		
	Cambridge	*Oxford*	*Others*	*Cambridge*	*Oxford*	*Others*
Merchant banks	37	35	28	37	27	36
Stockbrokers	37	43	20	26	15	59
Clearing banks	36	18	46	16	13	71
Accountants	23	29	48	1	1	98
Insurance companies	23	36	41	12	1	87
Foreign banks	Mostly foreign educated			28	23	49
Mean	31	32	27	20	13	67

Source Bowen 1986: 39

accumulation more feasible but undoubtedly the chief instruments of aggrandisement came in the successive budgets of the 1980s and most especially the 1988/89 budget which abolished all but one higher rate tax band. Many studies (Stark 1989) have documented the galvanising effect of these budgets on the potential for wealth accumulation amongst those with high incomes. For example, a 35-year-old City investment analyst with a modest income of £72,000 (made up of £70,000 salary and £2000 investment income) would have paid out £32,881 in income tax in 1987/88 but only £23,945 in 1989/90 (Knight, Frank and Rutley 1989). Fourth and finally, wealth accumulation has been made easier by soaring asset price inflation running far above the rate of product price inflation (Reading 1989a, b). Thus until 1987, at least, the market in stocks and shares boomed (and well-off people are more likely to keep their money in shares). Then, after 1987, a period of high real interest rates meant that those who had switched their assets into bank or building society deposits still gained. Even more strikingly, throughout the 1980s, markets in housing, antiques, fine art and other such assets all ran enthusiastically onwards and upwards (*The Economist* 1989).

It is, of course, exceedingly difficult to put exact figures on the total amount of income earned by City workers, but even the crudest calculations suggest that the gross annual earnings of City workers were £3.4 billion in 1981, £4.9 billion in 1984 and £6.9 billion in 1987. Taking into account the effect of tax, this left £2.2 billion to spend in 1981, £3.2 billion in 1984 and £4.5 billion in 1987. (This is a most conservative estimate since it does not include bonuses or the effects of various perquisites.) More mysterious is the amount of personal wealth that has been created out of the figures for income, but amongst the top 10 per cent of City workers (who earned £535 million in 1981, £763 million in 1984 and £1.4 billion in 1987) it can be safely assumed that personal wealth was being laid down at a very considerable rate.

SPENDING MONEY

The effects of the spending power provided by the boosted incomes and enhanced personal wealth formation of the City on the economy and society of London, the south-east of England and Britain as a whole remain a matter of fierce debate. Lee (1984, 1986) has argued that, in the mid and late nineteenth century, the high levels of consumer spending in London and the south-east (including those of workers in the City of London) were a powerful stimulant to the economy of the region, both qualitatively and quantitatively. Similarly, Rubinstein (1977, 1980, 1986, 1987) argues that the disproportionate concentration of high incomes and personal wealth in London and the south-east was an important determinant of the region's economic and social success relative to the north of England, and that this concentration flowed from finance and 'from London's other role as the centre of wealth, display, retailing, the professions, the press, and service industries' (Rubinstein 1987: 102). Clearly, such arguments are controversial, especially in the degree to which they underestimate incomes and wealth drawn from sources other than finance and commerce, and the degree to which they confuse pattern with process (Daunton 1989). However, even so, it seems clear that by the end of the nineteenth century, and probably before, definite and extensive impacts were being felt on the economy and society of London and the south-east of England as a whole, as a result of making money from finance and then spending it.

In the twentieth century, there seems little reason to suppose that these impacts have not continued, although on what scale they now affect the structure of demand is clearly extremely difficult to measure.

What seems certain is that spending generated by the incomes and personal wealth connected to the City of London has had identifiable effects on particular high-value markets. Of these markets, the most visible are those which have not only economic but also social and cultural resonance, that is, in which demand for goods and services is socially and culturally defined. These are markets in which money is deployed to buy goods and services which, when combined with other goods and services in particular practices, produce social and cultural advantage, what Bourdieu (1979, 1980, 1986, 1987) identifies as the accruing of 'social' and 'cultural' capital. Social capital refers to each person's insertion into, and accumulation of, a network of 'relationships of acquaintance and mutual recognition', that is a network of family, friends and business contacts. Cultural or symbolic capital refers to each person's accumulation of a stock of socially accepted competences all the way from a family name through ownership of 'appropriate' goods to formal educational qualifications. Roughly, the distinction Bourdieu draws is between knowing the right people and knowing the right things, although clearly the two are heavily interrelated, not least through their geography. Being in the right place is a crucial element of each type of capital. For example, 'to be seen at the right places, the right ski resorts in winter and the right watering places in summer, is important both for the symbolic capital involved and for the social and quasi-professional contacts that can be made or confirmed by simultaneous presence' (Marceau 1989: 146).

For those in the City who, in the 1980s, found themselves in possession of substantial incomes and, in some cases, considerable personal wealth, the challenge was to spend their money in tasteful ways, that is, in ways which would accrue social and cultural capital for themselves and their children. The new City wealthy were not alone in this objective. It was one shared by the rising 'disestablishment' which needed to stamp its authority on Britain, not just in the economic realm, but in the social and cultural realms too. In other words, Marx's abstract community of money had to be transformed into a concrete community of the moneyed. That required seeking out goods and services that could become a part of practices that would allow this to happen. Examples of markets for such goods and services were legion in Britain in the 1980s, extending all the way from the boom in simple status goods that demonstrate what Bourdieu calls 'honourability' (like expensive automobiles or antiques), through the expansion of arenas for aiding the for- mation of social capital (such as the interrelated rise of the Season and the corporate hospitality business, or the rise of certain field sports), to the rise of private day school education (which allows a child to accrue both social and cultural capital) (Thrift and Leyshon 1992). In the rest of this paper we will concentrate on just one of these markets in social and cultural transformation, the country house.

THE COUNTRY HOUSE MARKET

At the outset, it is important to define as precisely as possible what the commodity, 'a country house', consists of. Conventionally, the country house market is divided into three segments. The first and cheapest of these segments is the 'cottage'. Usually set in a rural village, it will have three bedrooms, two reception rooms, a bathroom and a kitchen and will also have about half an acre of garden (although this will vary quite dramatically). The second segment of the country house market is the five or six bedroom 'period house'. It will have three bathrooms, three reception rooms, a kitchen and a utility room, plus garaging for two cars and a considerable amount of land (up to five acres). It will often have been formerly a farmhouse. The third and final segment is the full-scale 'large country house' or 'manor'. This will have six to ten bedrooms, four bathrooms, three reception rooms, a study, a kitchen and most probably domestic accommodation (perhaps in a cottage set off from the main house). It will have extensive land (at least 15 acres) and garaging for three cars. It will almost certainly have outbuildings (especially stables) and most likely will include a tennis court and a swimming pool amongst its particulars.

The country house market has a number of common features which define it above and beyond the formal architectural parameters. Three of these stand out. First, the country house is 'historic'. Although there are examples of country houses built after the Second World War (Robinson 1984), they are rare and, significantly, they are likely to command a premium only if they are in a period style. In most places, more than 90 per cent of applicants to agents specialising in country house sales specifically want a period property, preferably Grade II listed (Paice 1989). Second, the country house should be vernacular in the broad sense; that is, it is built in materials and style typical of its local area and therefore blends harmoniously into the landscape. Third, and related, country houses should, as the term implies, be in rural locations. A quiet and attractive country setting is an integral part of the attraction of a country house. Thus 'Surrey has gone out of fashion . . . it is regarded as insufficiently rural and as one agent observed: "Today everybody thinks he's a squire"' (Country Life 1989: 20).

The pages of *Country Life* attest to the fact that a country house market existed before the 1980s but, except for some areas in and around London and the Home Counties, it was not a particularly active market. This was partly because the wealth and capital gains were not there to support it, partly because a national market did not exist, but rather a set of localised and often quite distinct submarkets, and partly because tastes ran counter to many of the values represented by the country house. In the 1980s all this changed: the market exploded into life. First of all, the wealth became available. In the first instance, this was undoubtedly the result of an injection of wealth from the City of London.

More than anything else, the Big Bang in the City of London has altered people's attitudes to country houses. For one thing, it has produced overnight a generation of young people who can afford to buy the houses that their elders were struggling to keep up for years.

(Country Life 1987: 10)

But if it was people from the City who set the market running, they were soon followed by other members of the newly wealthy private sector business class who had found a market which combined capital gains with social and cultural gains. An examination of typical country house owners carried out in 1986 confirms expectations (Savills 1987). In 1986, most new owners still came from the City. They were relatively young, with most men in their 40s and most women in their 30s. They were well off with 74 per cent earning more than £50,000 per annum and 41 per cent earning more than £100,000. Over half were purchasing their houses with cash. Those who had loans were willing to pay more than £2000 a month for a mortgage. As money from the newly wealthy started to pour into the country house market so substantial capital gains became possible, adding further to the market's attractions. Country houses are, after all, an important part of the British positional economy (Hirsch 1978), made up of goods which are inherently scarce. Seen in this sense, country house value comes from their absolute scarcity (since there can only ever be a limited stock) and their positioning in settings which are similarly in short supply. As one agent put it more succinctly, 'substantial demand plus fixed supply equals rising price. A period cottage away from neighbours and in pretty countryside will always perform well because it cannot be recreated' (Country Life 1989: 20).

Second, the 1980s saw a truly national market for country houses gradually come into existence. Before the 1980s, there were few chains of estate agents large enough to provide a national market in these houses. But in the 1980s, as the market grew, so those agents expanded apace, partly keeping up with it and partly creating it. Specialist agents like Savills, Knight, Frank and Rutley, Chestertons, Cluttons and Lane Fox all expanded and integrated their office networks; they began to do serious research on the market and to target potential buyers. By the year ending April 1988, one of the largest specialist agents, Savills, had a country house division turnover of £183 million. It sold 809 country house properties around Britain at an average price of £225,000 (Savills 1988). The expansion by specialist agents was paralleled by increasing interest being shown in the market by the large agency chains that were being set up by banks, insurance companies and building societies in the latter part of the 1980s. For example, Prudential Property Services set up a Prestige and Country Homes division in 1987.

Third, the 1980s saw tastes changing. The country house has been a potent symbol in Britain for a considerable period of time, whether at its most blatant as the patrician grand home, 'the abstraction of success, power and money . . . founded elsewhere' (Williams 1973: 299), or in its more domestic manifestations as the solid patrician period farmhouse, complete with squire, or as the Helen Allingham-like period cottage. In the 1970s these symbols were tarnished by a combination of recession and the prevailing structure of feeling, which was still based in the public sector and its associated modernist imagery (Wright 1988). In the 1980s these symbols were dusted off. The fog of the 1970s was blown away. Most particularly, country houses have become both a part of and a way of reflecting back a set of larger cultural discourses in a way that advantages the person who owns them. Their value as cultural capital has been inflated. These discourses are many but chief amongst them we can count the revival of historical feeling in the 1980s, helped along by the growth of conservation movements and the use of the past as a resource by the retailing and heritage industries (Wright 1985; Hewison 1987; Samuel 1989; Thrift 1989), and the increased interest in nature and the countryside, aided by the new devotion to pastoral versions of Englishness and the growth of the environmental movements (Samuel 1989; Howkins 1986; Thrift 1989). The country house has, in its different forms, amplified and extended these discourses, buoyed up by a wave of publications which have all helped to focus and fuel the fires of desire for ownership, ranging from stalwarts like *Country Life* through the agents' advertising and advertising-related magazines like *Savills Magazine* (first published in 1980) or Prudential's *Prestige and Country Homes* (first produced in 1988), to the vast flood of country house books which shows no signs of ebbing.

It is no surprise to find that, in these circumstances, those who buy country houses, as many surveys have shown, seem intent on buying a ticket to the past. Ideally, a house should be listed (in late

1987 there were 6000 Grade I listed buildings in England, a further 20,000 listed Grade II and 420,000 listed Grade III) and it should be recognisably 'historic'. In the 1980s, current cultural mores dictated that this meant chiefly houses in the Georgian or Queen Anne style. 'Working out what does constitute most prospective buyers' ideal of a classic country house is no problem at all for Jeremy Blanchard, of Humberts: ". . . Georgian," he declared' (Brennan 1989). This anecdote is borne out by a survey carried out by Savills (1987) which showed that 17 per cent of country house owners sought Georgian homes as their ideal, a further 15 per cent Queen Anne and 10 per cent Regency. Again, a country house needs to be in an unambiguously rural position to take maximum cultural advantage:

> [H]ouse-buyers are now seeking what one agent describes as 'a very comfortable form of the good life' where they can bring up their children in an attractive country environment within a rural community to which they can contribute. Through that they achieve a sense of belonging which enhances their quality of life.
>
> (Country Life 1989: 19)

The importance of a rural backdrop is not just about cultural mores. It also implies a quite specific set of social relations: cultural capital and social capital are interrelated. The 1980s have seen tastes change to the undoubted advantage of the country house. Buyers strive for monetary rewards, but the cultural and social rewards of ownership are not far behind. Certainly, the ultimate goal is clear.

Twenty estate agents were asked what their buyers would regard as an ideal country house. On this there was astonishing unanimity of view. It can be summed up in the description of one agent:

> [I]t is in a very underpopulated part of the country, which never sees tourists, but from which it is easy to get to London when wanted. There is a happy rural community where people know and like each other. The house itself is set in a park surrounded by a wall and entered by lodges. The drive sweeps up past beautiful trees. Then the house comes into view – slightly raised, overlooking a lake. It is not too big: seven or eight bedrooms and one good drawing room. The

scale is fine but not grand. The style is Queen Anne or
Georgian, and it must have 100 acres of land.

(Country Life 1989: 22)

The origins of the revival of the country house market and its
subsequent pattern of expansion can be traced through the
market's geography. Undoubtedly, in the early years of the revival,
proximity to London was a critical factor. Country houses had to
be within commuting distance of London: 'the stockbroker who
now has to be in front of his SEAQ computer at 7 am does not want
to live too far away from London' (Country Life 1987: 10). But the
country house buying habit soon began to spread outwards from
the immediate environs of London, for at least five reasons. First,
there was the sheer expense of country houses nearer the capital.
For example, by the year ending 30 April 1988, the average price
of houses sold by Savills' Henley office was £380,000 in contrast to
the average for the Norwich office of £134,000. This expense
pushed buyers without the requisite capital out of areas nearer to
London. The effect was cumulative over time – as the frontier of
high prices moved further and further out so those coming into
the market were less likely to have the requisite capital and had to
move further out again to find a house. Second, improved
communications helped to open up certain areas to interested
London buyers, especially the completion of the M25, and faster
train times on some inter-city rail lines. The most famous example
of this effect was the town of Grantham in Lincolnshire. With the
introduction of high-speed trains, journey times to London were
reduced to 75 minutes, and electrification subsequently reduced
them to an hour. The result was an influx of more than 200
London commuters and a country house price increase of 45 per
cent in 1987 (Van Cutsem 1988a).

Third, the stock of country houses near London is finite. Thus
the search had to be extended outwards. Certain counties, like
Oxfordshire, have a very limited stock of country houses relative to
demand so that prices in these counties spiralled rapidly upwards.
Other counties with a greater stock saw more moderate rises (it is
important to note that there are no extant stock figures for
counties, a situation which clearly makes it extremely difficult to
estimate exact supply/demand relations).

Fourth, there was the increasing spread of agents' offices out
from London and of information about houses in the rest of the

country back into London. Finally, there was the large rise in London house prices in the 1980s. This resulted in a considerable pool of people, who already had large salaries and were in a position to trade up, using their capital gains. For example, by mid-1987, an average four bedroom family house in Fulham cost between £300,000 and £350,000 with a journey time to the City, door to door, of about 45 minutes. At the same time, a six bedroom period house set in two acres of ground near Ipswich would have cost £275,000 to £300,000, with a journey time to the City, door to door, of 75 to 90 minutes (Van Cutsem 1988a).

Thus the London buyer spread outwards (Figure 12.4). In the period from 1984 to 1986, 15.3 per cent of country house buyers at Savills' Norwich office came from London. By 1987 the proportion had increased to 21 per cent. The Cambridge office saw an increase between the two periods from 14.1 to 17.5 per cent, Banbury from 11.7 to 22.2 per cent, Salisbury from 15.8 to 26.8 per cent, Hereford from 6.5 to 8.2 per cent and Wimborne from 3.8 to 7.6 per cent. (Meanwhile, offices nearer to London came to rely increasingly on buyers from London and the Home Counties as the only purchasers able to afford the prices.)

But, even in the mid-1980s, the country house market was clearly not restricted only to London (and especially City) buyers. The increasing wealth of the wealthier parts of the population in other parts of the country meant that the country house market was to some extent becoming independent of London. This was partly the result of the increasing economic propriety of a number of different parts of the country, which was producing large concentrations of higher incomes (Leyshon, Thrift and Tommey 1989), and partly because these wealthier parts of the country outside London experienced their own house price booms, which allowed people in these areas to trade up to country houses in areas further out again. Thus by 1987 a number of major cities were forcing up country house prices within their own spheres of influence.

Birmingham now affects Staffordshire almost as much as Warwickshire, while Hereford and Worcester are not far behind . . . Shropshire lags and continues to show plenty of scope for price improvement to match the other counties barely further in miles from Birmingham. Manchester's influence on Cheshire has produced in excess of a two-fold

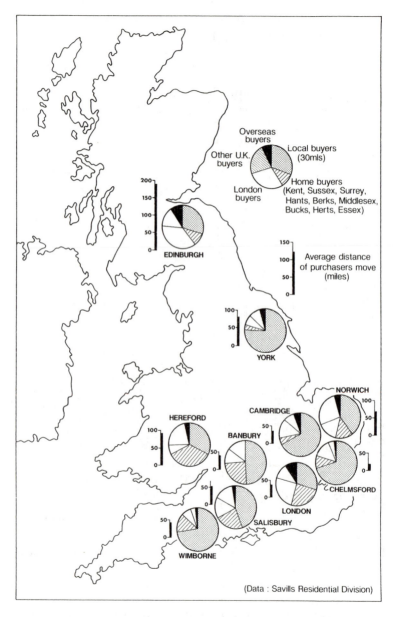

Figure 12.4 House purchase analysis, 1984–86

increase but Derbyshire and Lancashire have been less responsive. Bristol's interest in Gloucestershire, Avon and Somerset now collides cheerfully with that of London to bring about pronounced price increases.

(Lilwall and Allcock 1988: x)

Throughout the 1980s the highest country house prices were found in the Home Counties but over time the price differential between London, the Home Counties and the rest of Britain tended to decrease as country house prices in other parts of Britain rose: 'London is no longer in the position of rich relation to impoverished country cousins. Gone are the days when one could buy a Herefordshire manor house for the price of a terrace-house in Fulham' (Country Life 1989: 13). But undoubtedly a wedge of relatively high country house prices in the Home Counties persisted through the 1980s and was gradually joined in the course of the decade by the counties of Hampshire, Oxfordshire and Gloucestershire, all counties with a limited stock of country houses and a 'smart' image. Outside this privileged wedge, there was an intermediate zone of high country house prices created more recently that reaches west (to Wiltshire, Avon, Dorset, Somerset and Devon), north (to Essex, Cambridgeshire and Leicestershire) and east (into Norfolk and Suffolk).

By the end of the 1980s, the country house market had taken on all the characteristics of a mature market. It was liquid, it was national, it was split into identifiable market segments, based on different kinds of purchasers. Most important of all, it had the capacity to become self-generating as the wealth of the 1980s made in the City and elsewhere flowed through it in separate but related circuits of money, social and cultural capital. Thus one survey by Crowley Financial Services (Stewart 1988) identified three different kinds of purchaser based on the degree of their income or capital. The first of these consisted of younger purchasers looking for properties valued at under £250,000. They were taking the first step into the country house market via a mortgage financed by an income which would certainly be under £100,000. Usually these buyers required a 95 per cent mortgage but they might also have access to some capital in the form of gains on a house in London or an inheritance. The second type of purchaser consisted of older executives with substantial incomes, often already established in the country house market but wanting to trade up. The majority of purchasers in this group were in the 35–45 age bracket with young or grown up children and were seeking a better quality of life in the country – with riding, shooting, fishing, tennis, sailing and swimming nearby. They were also the highest paid group and were confident of borrowing £300,000 to £500,000, when perhaps they would have been reluctant to borrow even £50,000 half a decade earlier. These people required properties in the £250,000 to £1 million price range and already owned property which itself had increased in value so that their borrowings were usually no more than 70 per cent of the purchase price (Stewart 1988: 10).

Finally, there was a group of the very rich with sufficient capital to ensure that income was no longer a consideration. These purchasers made their money in company flotations and sell-outs. They rarely needed to borrow and were generally not concerned about the price of the house they bought. However, they were often prepared to pay a premium of anything up to 30 per cent for a property that was really outstanding. Importantly, within these gradations of purchaser, there emerged a clearly defined country-house-buying life cycle that made the country house market self-sustaining (Table 12.2). Knight, Frank and Rutley (1989) looked at three 'typical' households in this life cycle. The first consisted of a young couple (aged 35 and 32) with two children buying their first country house. The husband was an investment analyst in the City. They lived in London in Clapham or Battersea. They made considerable capital gains in the London housing market and may also have had access to a gift from parents or to an inheritance. They were in the market for a period farmhouse or perhaps a period cottage for weekend use. The household cycle is next picked up when the husband is a 45-year-old company director trading up from a period farmhouse to a manor house. Finally, the household life cycle is completed when both heads of household are in their sixties. They have decided to trade down to a period village house and to distribute the excess proceeds to their children. The whole process then starts again.

CONCLUSIONS

This paper has attempted to trace some of the effects of the proliferation of high incomes in the City of London and conse-quent changes in patterns of demand and consumption on the

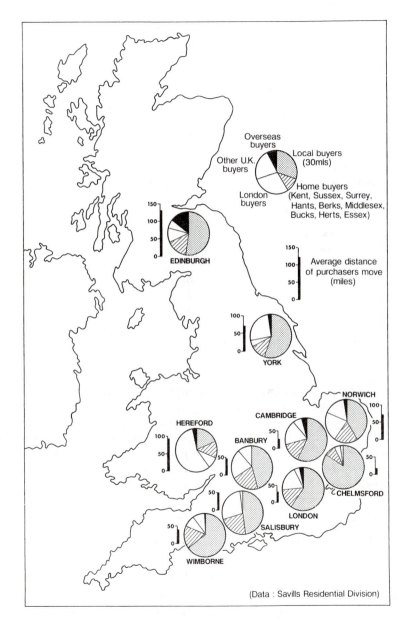

Figure 12.5 House purchase analysis, 1987

Table 12.2 The country-house-buying life cycle

	Household 1	*Household 2*	*Household 3*
Size of household	Husband 35 Wife 32 2 children	Husband 45 Wife 42 3 children	Husband 68 Wife 65 3 children
Current house	London, 5 bedrooms, 3 reception rooms, valued at £325,000	Period farmhouse, 6 bedrooms, 3 reception rooms, valued at £450,000	Period manor, 8 bedrooms, 3 reception rooms, valued at £1 million+
Aspirations	Period farmhouse	Period manor house	Period village house
Job of husband	City investment analyst	City company director	Retired City company director
Salary	£70,000 pa plus profit share	£130,000 pa plus profit share	£80,000 (pension)
Other income	£2,000 pa investments	£20,000 pa from investments	£26,000 pa from investments
Capital	£80,000 invested in stocks, shares, deposits	£350,000 invested in stocks, shares, deposits	£650,000 invested in stocks, shares, deposits
Total income after tax	£48,055	£75,655	£68,455
Existing borrowings	£40,000 mortgage	£50,000 mortgage (reduced from when present house bought)	£30,000 mortgage (reduced from when present house bought)
Borrowing power	£175,000	£400,000 (on income only)	–
Inheritance money from family	–	£220,000	–
Total funds	£450,000	£1,000,000	£1,000,000 (£600,000 for village house, £400,000 to be distributed to children)

Source: Knight, Frank and Rutley 1989

economy, society and culture of Britain. This has been done by reference to one commodity market only, the market for country houses. In the process it has demonstrated the importance of positional goods in asset appreciation. Positionality is the result of a complex interaction between not only economic but also social and cultural processes of the definition of scarcity. The country house market thrived in the 1980s because the commodities that it had on offer held out not only the possibility of economic gain, but also social and cultural gains. Indeed, it was precisely the ability of the country house to act simultaneously as a store of economic, social and cultural value which was its attraction. The scarcity of the commodity on offer was clearly an essential part of that ability. In particular, country houses were seized on by the new private sector 'disestablishment' as a way of accumulating assets, and as a way of providing themselves with social and cultural credibility.

The argument in the paper could be extended much further if space did not preclude it. However, two points need to be made in conclusion. First, the paper has only begun to explore the effects of the proliferation of higher incomes in the City, and more generally, on the pattern of expenditure in Britain. A laborious audit of a whole series of other commodity markets would be needed before the full measure of these effects could be understood. What is certain is that expenditure by those with higher incomes has hardly been restricted to the country house market. A whole constellation of goods and services is involved. Paradoxically, perhaps, this point can be well illustrated by turning back to the example of the country house. Expenditure on country houses hardly stops with the purchase of the house. It involves a whole series of other commodities, all of them with their effects on the structure of demand for particular goods and services. As Table 12.3 shows, buying a country house is likely to mean calls on the time of the chartered surveying and legal industries immediately, followed in short order by the removals and construction indus- tries and the furniture industry (no doubt including antiques and restorations) and the gardening industry. It may add to the growth of employment in domestic service. It will almost certainly help the fashion industry as the new owners 'tog up for the country' (Glancy 1988).

Second, it is important not to lose sight of the fact that commodities are part of the process of social relation. They are not something separate. The country house provides the example

Table 12.3 Expenditure on a country house

Initial Outlay (purchase price plus agents' fee, stamp duty, etc)	£537,500
Immediate expenses (Conservatory, etc.)	£54,000
Annual running costs (oil central heating, electricity, poll tax, etc.)	£5,150
Staff (gardener, domestic, nanny)	£16,840 per annum
Garden and land (Swimming pool, tennis court, etc.)	£62,350

Source: Stewart 1989: 57

again. Country houses are simply one of the most visible parts of a wider process of social interaction and class formation. The dinner parties, the weekend visits by friends or acquaintances, the reciprocal visits to kin, all these social activities centred around the country house will help to build up the 'invisible resources' (Marceau 1989) that will sustain the new disestablishment over future generations. The wake of money is long and sinuous.

REFERENCES

Bourdieu, P. (1979) 'Les trois états du capital culturel', *Actes de la Recherche en Sciences Sociales*, 24, 2–22.
——(1980) 'Le capital social', *Actes de la Recherche en Sciences Sociales*, 31: 2–3.
——(1986) *Distinction. A Social Critique of the Judgement of Taste*, London: Routledge.
——(1987) 'What makes a social class? On the theoretical and practical existence of groups', *Berkeley Journal of Sociology*, 3, 1–17.
Bowen, D. (1986) 'The class of 86', *Business*, November, 34–41.
Brennan, J. (1989) 'Agents caught short', *Financial Times*, 7 October, Property Supplement.
Byrne, J. A. (1987) *The Headhunters*, London: Kogan Page.
Country Life/Knight, Frank and Rutley (1987) *Buying a Country House*, London: Country Life.
——(1988) *Buying a Country House. A County Guide to Value*, London: Country Life.
——(1989) *Buying a Country House. A County Guide to Value*, London: Country Life.

Country Life (1989) 'Getting the edge', in Country Life/Knight, Frank and Rutley, *Buying a Country House. A County Guide to Value*, London: Country Life, 19–22.

Creigh, S. and Rees, A. (1989) 'Graduates and the labour market in the 1980s', *Employment Gazette*, January, 17–28.

Daunton, M.J. (1989) 'Gentlemanly capitalism and British industry 1820–1914', *Past and Present*, no. 122, 119–158.

The Economist (1989) 'Top and bottom of the art market', 29 October, 125.

Evans, A.W. and Crampton, G. (1989) 'Myth, reality and employment in London', *Journal of Transport Economics and Policy*, January.

Glancy, J. (1988) 'Togging up for the country', in Knight, Frank and Rutley/Country Life, *Buying a Country House. A County Guide to Value*, London: Country Life, xxiii–xxiv.

Greenshields, A. (ed.) (1989) *Who's Who in the City*, London: Stock Exchange Press.

Hewison, R. (1987) *The Heritage Industry*, London: Methuen.

Hirsch, F. (1978) *Social Limits to Growth*, London: Routledge & Kegan Paul.

Howkins, A. (1986) 'The discovery of rural England', in R. Colls and P. Dodd (eds) *Englishness. Politics and Culture 1880–1920*, London: Croom Helm, 62–88.

Jones, S. (1989) *The Headhunting Business: A Practical Users' Guide*, London: Van Nostrand Reinhold.

Knight, Frank and Rutley (1989) 'The family housing cycle', *Knight, Frank and Rutley Residential Reports* 2, London: Knight, Frank and Rutley.

Lee, C.H. (1984) 'The service sector, regional specialisation, and economic growth in the Victorian economy', *Journal of Historical Geography*, 10, 139–56.

——(1986) in J. Langton and R.L. Morris (eds) *Atlas of Industrialising Britain*, London.

Leyshon, A., Boddy, M. and Thrift, N.J. (1989) Socio-economic restructuring and changing patterns of long-distance commuting, Department of Geography/School for Advanced Urban Studies, University of Bristol (mimeo).

Leyshon, A., Thrift, N.J. and Tommey, C. (1989) 'The rise of the British provincial financial centre', *Progress in Planning*, 31, 151–229.

Lilwall, C. and Allcock, K. (1988) 'Value at a glance', in Country Life/Knight, Frank and Rutley, *Buying a Country House. A County Guide to Value*, London: Country Life.

Lloyd, J. (1988a) 'The crumbling of the establishment', *Financial Times*, 16 July, 6.

——(1988b) 'Preaching in the market place', Financial Times, 18 July, 15.

——(1988c) 'Serving Thatcher's children', *Financial Times*, 20 July, 20.

——(1988d) 'Death of the honourable Englishman', *GQ*, December, 152–5.

Marceau, J. (1989) *A Family Business? The Making of an International Business Elite*, Cambridge: Cambridge University Press.

Paice, C. (1989) 'Modern country houses. Winners or white elephants', *Savills Magazine*, no. 23, 55–7.

Perkin, H. (1989) *The Rise of Professional Society. Britain Since 1880*, London: Routledge.

Rajan, A. and Fryatt, J. (1988) *Create or Abdicate: The City's Human Resource Choice for the 90s*, London: Witherby.

Reading, B. (1989a) 'A return to stop-go', *Sunday Times*, 15 October, D9.

——(1989b) 'Letter to the editor', *Financial Times*, 19 October, 25.

Reid, M. (1988) *All-Change in the City. The Revolution in Britain's Financial Sector*, London: Macmillan.

Robinson, J.M. (1984) *The Latest Country Houses*, London: Bodley Head.

Rogers, B. (1988) *Men Only. An Investigation into Men's Organisations*, London: Pandora Press.

Rubinstein, W.D. (1977) 'The Victorian middle classes: wealth, occupation and geography', *Economic History Review*, 30.

——(1980) *Men of Property. The Very Wealthy in Britain and the Industrial Revolution*, London: Croom Helm.

——(1986) *Wealth and Inequality in Britain*, London: Faber and Faber.

——(1987) *Elites and the Wealthy in Modern British History*, Brighton: Harvester.

Samuel, R. (1989) 'Introduction: exciting to be English', in R. Samuel (ed) *Patriotism: The Making and Unmaking of British National Identity, Volume 1. History and Politics*, London: Routledge, xviii–lxvii.

Sandelson, V. (1959) 'The confidence trick', in H. Thomas (ed) *The Establishment*, London: Anthony Blond, 127–68.

Savills (1987) 'In search of perfection', *Savills Magazine*, 17, 5–8.

——(1988) *Placing Prospectus*, London: Savills/Kleinwort Benson.

Stark, T. (1989) 'The changing distribution of income under Mrs Thatcher', in F. Green (ed.) *The Restructuring of the UK Economy*, Hemel Hempstead: Wheatsheaf.

Stewart, I. (1988) '1988: the year of the country house', *Savills Magazine*, no. 21, 9–11.

——(1989) 'A layman's guide to country house costs', *Savills Magazine*, no. 25, 55–7.

Thrift, N.J. (1989) 'Images of social change', in C. Hamnett, L. McDowell and P. Sarre, *The Changing Social Structure*, London: Sage, 12–42.

Thrift, N.J. and Leyshon, A. (1992) *Making Money. The City of London and Social Power in Britain*, London: Routledge.

Thrift, N.J., Leyshon, A. and Daniels, P. (1987) 'Sexy greedy': The new international financial system, the City of London and the South East of England, Working Papers in Producers Services, 7, University of Bristol and University of Liverpool.

Van Cutsem, G. (1988a) 'On the move: update', *Savills Magazine*, no. 20, 9.

——(1988b) 'Communication is the name of the game and each generation they play it the same – or do they?', *Savills Magazine*, no. 19, 6–7.

Whitley, R. (1974) 'The City and Industry: the directors of large companies, their characteristics and connections', in P. Stanworth and A. Giddens (eds) *Elites and Power in British Society*, Cambridge: Cambridge University Press.

Williams, R. (1970) 'Introduction', in C. Dickens *Dombey and Son*, Harmondsworth: Penguin, 11–34.

——(1973) *The Country and the City*, London.

Wright, P. (1985) *On Living in an Old Country*, London: Verso.

——(1988) 'Brideshead and the tower blocks', *London Review of Books*, 10 (11), 3–7.

13

YUPPIES

A keyword of the 1980s[1]

Sam Whimster

This is a topic that excites. 'Yuppie' is not a value-neutral term. Yuppies provoke envy, hatred, derision, amusement, emulation, lust and, for the lucky few, indifference. Yuppie values encompass greed, ambition, conspicuous consumption, the pursuit of power and status, selfishness, an altruism raised to the level of personal taste, and a belief in private striving over the claims of public provision. The spectacle of the yuppie – the shirt-sleeved Stakhanovite of the office at his or her desk (for this is a unisex phenomenon) by 7 in the morning until 7 at night, the yuppie who relaxes by working out in the gym, perhaps taking in a wine bar for a little underindulgence of a glass or two of blush wine – is an image that exercises a strong fascination on the public consciousness at all levels of society.

If one surveys the output in papers, both tabloid and serious, magazines, in TV and films, literature and even poetry, it is quite clear that the British public appears to have a limitless appetite for all things yuppie. In a five-month period from August to December 1987 the British daily newspaper *Today* used the word a hundred times.[2] A simple content analysis reveals that the greatest frequency of use was for goods and services: cars, clothes, home furnishings, jewellery, filofaxes, gifts, gardens, travel and sportswear (22 items). The City of London merited 17 items and 10 of these were somewhat unfriendly references to the October crash. Thirteen items concerned politics (this was the period when the Labour Party was seen to be courting the yuppie voter). Health, food and sport received 12 references. The term cropped up 13 times in the TV, arts and entertainments pages. There were seven items on property ranging over Docklands, second homes, country houses, country cottages, long-distance commuting and, inevitably, house prices and mortgages. The yuppie way of life merited 16 references in this five-month period.

The same holds for more upmarket papers like *The Sunday Times* or *The Guardian*. Although the curiosity, fascination and hostility are differently inflected, analysis reveals the same bewildering range of topics that attract the term 'yuppie'. In addition the word has spawned a number of cognates: *buppies* (black urban professionals), *yummies* as in *The Sun* headline, 'We're Young Upwardly Mobile Muslims and we're in the Money', *swell* (single women earning lots in London), *dinkies* (dual income no children), *dockneys* (live in Docklands and work in the City) and *mockneys* (defined by Randolf Quirk as youth who have deliberately cultivated the language of the working class and made it work in an enterprise culture[3]). Finally there are the yuppie suffixes, as in *yuppiedom* and *yuppification*.

Faced with this barrage there is a temptation to dismiss the word as another case of media exaggeration of a transient social phenomenon. Sociology is quite well catered for by studies which designate the media as an unprincipled amplifier of images that bear little or no relation to society and as feeding the gullible public's threadbare prejudices on hooliganism, drugs and sex. I will resist this temptation and argue instead that the yuppie image is a response to often quite strong emotional feelings which have been occasioned by an unprecedented rate of societal change. This change has been both rapid and far reaching, and has led to an as yet unresolved turbulence in social values. The producers of the yuppie images, the deluge of social commentary, and its use in everyday language are all indices of a very real confusion in social values. Far from the yuppie being a media invention, the notion of yuppie has been one of the indispensable reference points, albeit not fixed, of British society experiencing the roller-coaster of change in the 80s.

My approach here will be to adopt something akin to Raymond Williams's notion of keywords. Williams says keywords present themselves. The keyword

> virtually forced itself on my attention because the problems of its meanings seemed to me inextricably bound up with the problem it was being used to discuss. I have often got up from writing a particular note and heard the same word again, with the same sense of significance and difficulty: often, of

course, in discussions and arguments which were rushing by to some other destination. I began to see this experience as a problem of *vocabulary*, in two senses: the available and developing meanings of known words. . .; and the explicit but as often implicit connections which people were making . . . -ways not only of discussing but of seeing many of our central experiences.

(Williams 1988: 15)

The 'discussions and arguments rushing by to some other destination' is very much an affliction with this particular keyword. Yuppies, popularly understood, stand for money, power, sophistication, sexiness (rather than mere sex) and style. The converse is equally understood: poverty, impotence and a crudeness in living conditions necessitated by the absence of those material and cultural goods. To sit down and write the note one has to cross this two-way expressway of popular sentiments, charged as they are by the strong emotions of greed and resentment. There is also the no less forbidding expressway of the social sciences where the heavy lorries of gentrification, privatisation, the service class, neoliberalism, the postindustrial society and its gaudy companion postmodern culture rumble past.

The approach I will adopt is to accept that 'yuppie' contains a number of 'available and developing meanings', and that these meanings are by no means consistent even when used by the same individual or social group. I will argue that the available and developing meanings of the word are insufficient to represent the experience of change over the last two decades. Although meanings cluster around a number of motifs such as hedonistic lifestyle, consumerism and upward mobility, these fail to do justice to the emergent social reality which is outstripping the available meanings.

It also has to be admitted that no overall social science paradigm has yet emerged which is sufficient to explain the complexities of the move towards post-industrial societies that has occurred over the last two decades. Using a popular acronym, like yuppie, is in no way a simplifying device, for the word brings together a range of sociological issues which number social structural change, social status, social class, consumerism, lifestyle, social mobility, personality, political and social values, and career. Hence a keyword approach involves a journey through the vagaries and incompatibilities of popular usage as well as the complexities of the social sciences. I am afraid that only too many of these difficulties will be exposed in what follows and I can only reiterate Williams's caveat that a keyword, while being out of the ordinary, cannot be regarded as a unifying word.

It is possible to be reasonably clear about the extent and nature of structural changes over the last two decades to British and American society, from which the majority of my illustrations will be drawn. For an account of structural change I turn to Daniel Bell's *The Coming of Post-industrial Society*. This now reads as a very creditable piece of social forecasting, even though some of the predictions have not happened in the way envisaged by the author at the beginning of the 1970s. The book has the advantage of having a clearly defined and, by now, well-known position, against which change can be assessed.

Bell forecast a number of trends in occupational structure, technology, the role of knowledge and the place of culture, against which the developments of the 70s and 80s can now be assessed. Bell spoke of his sense of being in a phase of interstitial time, of history in the making, and of passing from one age to another. The structural principles of the old system were those of property-bound social relations (social class), power structures centred on narrow ruling élites, and bourgeois culture based on notions of restraint and classification (Bell 1973: 37). Bell foresaw property differences becoming subordinated to the role of technology and science that in their turn would become central to the organisation of society. This change would have a 'revolutionising' effect on social structure: the economy's centre of gravity would shift from the production of goods to the provision of services, and the professional and technical occupations would predominate in postindustrial society.

There has been considerable debate over the nature of these structural changes and their interrelation. Notwithstanding that debate, in a very general sense it can be said that the 80s and the highly visible emergence of yuppies signalled the arrival of the trends forecast by Bell. He was not in any way complacent about the emergence of the postindustrial society. Above all he feared two developments. One was the ability of the system to operate according to an autonomous 'economizing' logic to the detriment of 'sociologizing' needs. This fear, it can now be seen, was well-placed. As is by now well-known, the result of neo-conservative politics in the USA and Britain led to the ditching of policy advisers, who had a concern with the common weal of society, and their replacement by the gurus of the market society philosophy. And as many of the other articles in this volume attest, the consequences of a market society philosophy have been profoundly destructive of those concerns that Bell refers to as public interest and that concern the sociologising mode (Bell 1973: 283).

His other fear was that the countercultural values adopted by middle class youth would cause a crisis of social integration. The virtue of Bell's position is that he took the interrelation between social structure and personality very seriously. For some this preoccupation with personality amounts to notoriety, for it was seen as part of a conservative backlash against the countercultural values of the 60s. The notoriety of this conservative position obscures the more interesting question as to how Bell was wrong in his prognosis on youth and personality. Yuppies are an unexpected revenge on the alternative society. Even though the outcome was quite the opposite of what Bell pessimistically foretold, tracing what did occur opens up a number of interesting insights on the interaction of personality and social structure.

FROM YIPPIE TO YUPPIE

In an article on how the term is used in America, Fred Shapiro disentangles a number of meanings, one of which can be labelled: from yippie to yuppie. This understanding of the term turns on the contrast between two very different lifestyles, a contrast unanticipated by Bell. This usage achieved national prominence in the States when a syndicated columnist, Bob Greene, ran a story (*Chicago Tribune*, 23 March 1983) about Jerry Rubin, the one-time leader of the yippies (Youth International Party). Rubin 'is now attempting to become leader of the Yuppies -- Young Urban Professionals' (Shapiro 1986: 139). This had all the ingredients of a good story. Political radicalism and countercultural values were rudely displaced by Rubin's wholehearted embrace of the values of Wall Street – getting on, knowing the right people, and money and income as the standard of social esteem. This was a radical repudiation of the world-rejecting values of the alternative society. It was through the rejection of consumerism, careerism and suburban America that the counterculture sought an escape to the inner world of personal experience, albeit spiced with the more surface delights of a sensual hedonism. This indulgence with matters of self and the inner self was accompanied by a fundamentalist conviction ethic (Weber 1971: 551–60) in the realm of politics that allowed neither a compromise with conservative politics – and there were good reasons to fear and hate its politics – nor with a more progressive liberal politics. As Rubin put it, 'liberal fuck offs who come on to the revolutionary really chummy-chum-chum' (Caute 1989: 269). The abandonment of the movement by Rubin was seen to mark the coming of age, somewhat late in the day, of the flower children.

By the mid-eighties commentators could afford to treat these changes in a jocular fashion. *The New Republic* did a clever parody of the transmutation from yippie to yuppie, publishing on the thirtieth anniversary of Allen Ginsberg's poem 'Howl' their own version, which they waggishly entitled 'Yowl'. 'I saw the best minds of my generation destroyed by stress/ frazzled overtired burnt-out/ jogging through the suburban streets at dawn/ as suggested by the late James Fixx/ career minded yupsters burning for an Amstel Light/ . . . who upwardly mobile and designer'd and bright-eyed and high sat up/ working in the track-lit glow of the Tribeca loft . . .' (*The New Republic*, 8 December 1986: 48). It is an amusing parody and from the vantage point of 1984 it is hard to see how commentators, like Daniel Bell, saw things in a very different light. In order to gauge the distance traversed from yippie to yuppie, the original of Ginsberg's great poem has to be recalled: 'the best minds of my generation destroyed by madness, starving hysterical naked/dragging themselves through the negro streets at dawn' . . . burning for the ancient heavenly/connection to the starry dynamo in the machinery of the night' (Ginsberg 1959: 11–12).

It was these modernistic, peyote-driven visions that so disturbed Daniel Bell. The rage against order, the annihilation of distance between inner being and the social state, the return to passions and lusts that did not rank very highly on a scale of sophistication of a complex and thoroughly differentiated society would, so argued Bell, undo the fabric of capitalism's superstructure. This would have been doubly ironic for, as Bell showed, capitalism had weathered the contradictions and crises at the economic and functional level, only to be undone in the realm of the immaterial, capitalism's superstructure. As it turned out he need not have worried. While much of *The Coming of Post-industrial Society* is now occurring, Bell's sequel, *The Cultural Contradictions of Capitalism*, has been proved to be redundant. The wags who penned 'Yowl' dedicated it to Jay McInerney, author of *Bright Lights, Big City* and *Story of My Life.* These yuppie novels are a celebration of the fast life – money, power, sex and cocaine. The yuppie had clearly learnt much from the previous generation. The choice was no longer between inner-directed behaviour and world rejection.[4] Yuppies both enjoyed themselves and worked. While dangers of excess still existed, they were no longer rooted in some psychic Ur-state. Jay McInerney's novels might occasion contempt in the mind of the cultural conservative – perhaps tempered with light amusement – but it is unlikely that they cause serious anxiety.

The phenomenon of the counterculture represents the first case in twentieth century industrial society of world rejection on a mass scale. The recreations of virtuosi like Allen Ginsberg signified for Bell a modernistic ex-stasis – a complete removal from the world as it is normally experienced. The counterculture represented a flight from the world and a rejection of the values of career, suburban life and conventional politics and power.

All of this makes the transition from yippie to yuppie so remarkable. But for those who did make, or were allowed to make, this psychic coming home, there is the question of how much emotional and cultural baggage was put into the pursuit of new patterns of yuppie career and patterns of consumption. There is also the matter of the second generation of babyboomers, born in the late 1950s and the 60s, and how much they partook of the counterculture which over the years – to cut a complex story brutally short – was being transmuted into popular culture. My simple answer is that it led to the formation of a more differentiated type of personality and a greater depth and variety of cultural responses open to personality, than had previously been available to the young middle classes.

The 1970s in America have received the attention of historians and social commentators, two of whom, Christopher Lasch and Tom Wolfe, continue in the same vein of *Kulturkritik* established by Daniel Bell. Tom Wolfe pejoratively labelled the 1970s as the 'Me decade' and Lasch castigated it as the 'culture of narcissism'. It cannot be disputed that there was a withdrawal from issues of community, radical politics and the creation of new ways of life – not least due to the political and economic climate of the 1970s. For my argument, however, it is the modulation of the sense of self

318

and consciousness and its receptiveness to new cultural objects that remains, even though the social concerns of communitarianism and radical politics became less central.

The 1980s mark a modulation away from self-absorption to egoistic striving and the conspicuous flaunting of cultural and consumer taste. While Wolfe described the 70s as the 'Me decade', *The Bonfire of the Vanities* – his step sideways into the novelistic genre of social realism[5] – describes the heroic bond dealer as a 'master of the universe'. To go from the introversions of 'me' to the aggressive ambitions of 'I' is, perhaps, to stretch the core personality thesis too far. But the fascination of *The Bonfire of the Vanities* is how the hero is humbled. Sherman McCoy Jr does not conform to the stereotypical yuppie where confidence and outward show always carry the day. In part, this is the novelist's revenge, the fictional arrival of *fortuna*, to a member of a group that appears to enjoy a hubris-free destiny. In part, though, Sherman's downfall is his failure to act egoistically enough. Only when he is successfully playing in the financial markets does he become a master of the universe. At other times his sense of confidence is undermined by his deferential comparison to his father. McCoy Sr is portrayed as an aristocratic lion, belonging to a school of financiers who did not experience self-doubt. Sherman belongs to a generation whose self-reflexive propensities are well developed. His doubts are given ample play in the area of cultural tastes. Unlike his father, who operates within an instinctive cultural framework, Sherman, while not being uninterested in culture, remains uncertain about his tastes in arts and the furnishing of his Manhattan flat, an ambivalence that is reflected in his relationship with his wife. In some matters, those of outward personal show – his car, shoes, suit – he is quite clear that these have to demonstrate his success. For a yuppie that should suffice, but Sherman's personality is a more complex amalgam that is unable to jettison conscience and an expressive dimension. The move from 'me' to 'I' is no more fundamental than the move from drop-out to returning to the fold. Rather they are modulations of a new consciousness of personality that originates in the 60s.

The British experience is different but similar points can be made. Peter York provides some acute observations on the British scene. The middle class, he asserts, was not big enough or rich enough to develop a consumerist culture centred on the self. Instead traditional middle class forms persisted and gentrification meant the continuation of traditional county and gentlemanly values:

> a significant number of people in this country who had the money and the education to make a run for Me now actually subscribed, and continue to subscribe, to a most mysterious and wonderful form of serial immortality, that of *One.*
>
> (York 1980: 98)

The One represents 'the aristocratic pleasure principle and the working of gentrification' where the gentleman, says York, 'is an obedient, polite, dutiful person. It is gents who *hold it in*' (ibid: 98). Gentrification here recalls an earlier ascetic ideal, developed in the public schools, which reached its zenith in the heyday of Empire and the Victorian age. The City of London, prior to the 70s, provided the main preserve of this type of ascetic gentleman, where the continuities of Empire to internationalism were at their strongest, and where the recruitment from officer caste into financial élite remained pronounced.

There was little in the British situation – the paucity of wealth and income, the inflexibility of its class structure and class attitudes and the absence of an indulgent 'Me' – to prepare public consciousness for the arrival of the British yuppie. Portrayed as ambitious, greedy, quick to make conspicuous displays of wealth and even quicker to seize on new wealth-making opportunities, and apparently unconcerned by matters of conscience or social good, the yuppie, televisually embodied by the young City dealer, marked the emergence of a triumphal 'I'. However, the continuity across age cohorts has not escaped notice. 'The post-war babies who metamorphosed from brats into beatniks and passed from hippiedom through yuppiedom are . . . now known collectively as the baby-boomers' (*Financial Times,* 14 December 1987). Peter York and Ann Barr, reviewing the progress of the yuppie from the vantage point of 1987, quote a stockbroker: 'Yuppies are youth culture hitting the business world'. As York and Barr comment, work has replaced leisure as self-actualisation (*Observer,* 8 November 1987: 21).

The thesis being advanced, then, is that one of the keys to an understanding of the yuppie phenomenon lies in a new type of personality which first surfaced in the late 1960s. At that time it came to fruition within an oppositional mode to that of orthodox society. But this should not obscure the consequent evolution of this personality. The changes in the 1970s and 80s did not simply leave the affects of the counterculture redundant. Rather they were absorbed within the youth and popular culture of the second generation of babyboomers whose job opportunities were being redrawn by the structural changes of the postindustrial society. This continuity and evolution can be traced despite the more obvious dissimilarities between opposition and conformity, communitarianism and individualism, public sector caring concerns and the favouring of the private sector.

LIBERTARIANISM AND EGALITARIANISM

Novels and social commentary do not amount to reliable empirical evidence. Yet they are extremely valuable in probing concepts like dimensions of personality where it is extremely difficult to establish empirical referents. There does exist, however, attitudinal data which can claim a much higher objectivity, even though tracking back from attitudes to underlying values and relating those to notions of personality is a somewhat fraught undertaking.

The most immediate finding of the attitudinal surveys is that young professionals (selected by age, residence and occupation) do not conform to a stereotype of self-interest on economic issues and a disregard of all other social and welfare issues. Yuppies, especially those in financial services, have more often than not been portrayed as the stormtroopers of the neo-conservative policies of Reagan and Thatcher. Greed is good, greed is healthy, and the rebirth of Mandeville's private vices/public virtues does not appear to be replicated among the young urban professional respondents in the social surveys.

In America political scientists took a close interest in yuppies during the 1984 presidential primaries, when it seemed for a time that Senator Hart was going to dislodge the favourite Walter Mondale. While Mondale represented the old democratic politics, the New Deal agenda of support for blue-collar workers, interventionist policies for farming and industry, moderation on defence and the traditional democratic support for equal rights and equal pay, Hart presented himself as a new image in politics: youthful, progressive, long on foreign policy issues, and strong on civil rights and equal pay. These latter issues are known as lifestyle political issues ('issues that engage voters' abstract values not their immediate self-interest' Hammond 1986: 490). In Britain they have been termed 'new agenda' issues (Heath and Evans 1988: 53–65).

It was thought that the young professionals' vote, while engaged with more abstract political issues, would also reflect a degree of inegalitarianism compatible with the ambitious consumerist image of the yuppie. In fact, the attitudes of young professionals are more egalitarian than those of the majority. But on personal and moral issues the yuppies were far more tolerant than the average on a range of topics: pornography, censorship, right to abortion, women's rights and racial equality (Carpini and Sigelman 1986: 502–18).

A similar pattern is repeated when the British Social Attitudes dataset for 1987 is interrogated.[6] On a scale of egalitarianism more professionals (selected as aged 18–44, holding managerial and professional jobs and living in the Greater London area) supported the Labour Party than the Conservative Party, and, again, more of them were in favour of governmental control of local councils and expressed a preference for more taxation and greater public expenditure rather than less. On so-called libertarian issues they showed a much larger support, compared with the average of the rest of respondents, for sexual equality, tolerance of homosexuality and pornography, and were against the death sentence and censorship.

The progressiveness of the political views of yuppies has been received with a degree of scepticism by supporters of the 'old agenda' politics. It is held that yuppies are egalitarian not out of self-interest but out of choice, whereas for the older constituency of the American Democratic Party or British Labour Party egalitarianism was an issue of social class interest. There is a suspicion that the yuppie support for egalitarianism is prompted by the need to feel 'good' about issues. In the United States Lekachman has voiced this concern. 'Yuppies are pro choice, in their careers, lifestyles and political representatives' (Lekachman 1987: 177). The same disquiet surfaced in Britain at the Labour Party Conference and the preceding TUC conference in the autumn of 1987, where a new-style political agenda was seen as displacing mainstream trade union and working class concerns. At the time Mr Bryan Gould, the main proponent of a new look to the Labour Party's programme, was accused of 'yuppiefying' the party. The neo-conservatives in both countries have also played on the supposed dissonance between affluence and egalitarianism of young professionals, and one has to note they have extracted a fair amount of political capital from this issue. (On the American situation see Paul Lyons 1989: 117–19.)

The attitudinal data by itself cannot discriminate between moral reasons internal to the individual and externally imposed or adopted desires. Progressive attitudes may be held as part of a lifestyle as opposed to choices made by moral agents. Recent consumption theories tend to stress the latter; though why this should be generalisable to a class so large and so varied as the new white-collar service sector occupations is not – at least without further research – immediately apparent. Further research is also required into the attitudinal data, in order to establish whether there exists a variability in attitudes according to public and private sector professions. One would expect significant variations within the large range of professions which, while sometimes generically termed the 'service class', displays a less than unitary composition (see Savage *et al.* 1988: 455–76).

The political issues of choice, welfare and the market remain, as ever, open to debate. Reconciling political choices with the needs of personality will certainly remain a feature of the 90s, especially with the arrival of environmental issues. Attitudinal data tend to make the focus specific to the actual respondents, whereas what is being argued here is that a more differentiated concept of personality became available as a resource for individuals to redefine their interrelation with the claims of the world. With the emergence of the postindustrial society in the 70s and 80s a series of new demands came to be made upon the individual. These comprise new patterns of life, consumption styles, the reordering of social class and status due to the changes in social mobility and, lastly, changes to career. 'Yuppie' as a keyword registers the confusion of people's perceptions of changes in social structure, whereas sociological investigation might be advised to examine how young professionals themselves cope with, adapt to and interpret the structural changes. The keyword registers its most marked confusion on the subject of upward mobility.

In Britain the obsession with matters of 'class' and status group distinctions has rendered the 'u' of yuppie more often than not as 'upwardly mobile' rather than 'urban', the latter being the main usage in the United States. There the acronym 'yumpie' was employed to specify upward mobility (Shapiro 1986: 141–2). It does not appear to have caught on, so testifying to the prevalent idea that the point in American life is to become middle class. The City's own layered social stability has been rudely upset by the rapid expansion of the 80s. Interview data (conducted by the author) show that 'yuppie' was never used as a self-description but as a pejorative term for other groups. Foreign exchange dealers, who are one of the more colourful and heterogeneous social groups in the City and who have attained their positions through their wits rather than educational qualifications, describe eurobond dealers as yuppies. Eurobond dealers are perceived as privileged in terms of parents and Oxbridge education. And the interviews of people working in merchant banks, with public school background, make it quite clear that the yuppie is the 'barrow boy' or the 'Essex oink' who previously would never have prospered so spectacularly with such educational and social credentials. This state of affairs has, to repeat, generated much confusion as well as social comment, neatly caught by Caryl Churchill in her play *Serious Money* where the old, Frosby, the ex-jobber, exchanges insults with the new, Grimes, the gilts dealer.

FROSBY.
  My lovely city sadly changes.
  Sic transit gloria! Glory passes!
  Any wonder I'm deranged,
  Surrounded by the criminal classes.
GRIMES.
  You've all been coining it for years.
  All you fuckwits in the City.
  It just don't look quite so pretty,
  All the cunning little jobs,
  When you see them done by yobs.

(Churchill 1987: 88)

The rate of expansion and the heterodox nature of its recruitment have produced not only a clash of cultures, but more importantly the need to create new social forms in consumer style, residence and social type in order to advance the claims of one group against those of others. In this situation subscribing to the self-effacing 'One' may well be non-adaptive. The 'barrow boy' commodities trader may well have no aspirations to old-style middle class tastes. As the term 'mockneys' suggests, indigenous East End ways may be more winning, and East End values translated to suburbanised

Essex may well be the contented expression of achievement. Do sons and daughters of the educated middle class, who now see the City as the élite career (*Economist*, 12 December 1987: 30), sub- scribe to the expressive and progressive ethos, values which a previous generation took into public sector professions? And is such an ethos likely to be engendered by the new intelligentsia of lawyers, accountants, risk analysts, economists, researchers and computer scientists? Lying behind these speculations is the thesis that expansion and qualitative changes require the creation of new social and cultural types, and the re-creation of pre-existing types. The confusions over consumption styles and upward mobility are indices of this need of social invention, and the absence, as yet, of any overarching cultural or sociological framework that will give people their social, cultural and status cues. In short, the availa- bility of meanings is deficient for the new yuppie stratum's own self-image.

The same confusions attend any definition by style of consumption. The authors of *The Yuppie Handbook* (Piesman and Hartley 1984) canonised the yuppie as a style of consumption.

> The male on the cover of *The Yuppie Handbook* is shown with a Cross pen, pin stripe suit, Rolex watch, squash raquet, Burberry trench coat, Gucci briefcase, coop offering pros- pectus, and L.L. Bean duck hunting boots, while the female yuppie is shown with a Sony walkman, Ralph Lauren suit, Cartier Tank Watch, coach bag, fresh pasta, gourmet shopping bag, and running shoes.
>
> (Belk 1986: 515)

When asked how they came upon the word 'yuppie', Piesman answered, 'We've heard variations of it – Y.P. is a West Coast phrase, also YO-Pro, Young Elite and Valley Crowd'. And Hartley, 'We picked Yuppie because it sounded like preppy and hippy and had the right ring' (Shapiro 1986: 139–46).

Apart from showing how careers may be made from confusion, these answers offer little in the way of sociological clarification. In a stabilised world of status, preppies should be distinguishable from upwardly mobile success. The preppie represents old money and exclusive private education and, despite a certain languid affectation of style, the preppie is meant to go on and achieve career success in the time-honoured WASP way. Yuppie, as upwardly mobile outsiders, emulate (to use Veblen's verb) the preppie. Outwardly, the two groups are identical but from the inside, presumably, the distinctions between the two can be made. This comes out in Louis Auchincloss's novel *Diary of a Yuppie* where the central character attends a private school for the last years of his secondary education in order to be in the right crowd (preppies) before moving on to one of the select colleges; not unakin to English parents taking their children out of comprehensive state schools and placing them in the sixth forms of public schools.

CAREER

In this last section I will bring forward some observations on changes to career patterns. Career provides the context within which the young professional has to operate, and offers an important link between the concept of personality and that of social structure. My argument here is that the outward-looking egoism of the young professional may well prove functional in regard to fundamental changes in the structure of career. These changes are analogous to the remarks made on upward mobility. Just as a fixed occupational structure through which a person rises through individual achievement no longer obtains, so career is no longer a pre-standing course through which the individual passes. Hence career will as likely be discontinuous as the assurance of upward progression.

According to Freidson, professional autonomy is the power of professions to define and control their own work. Through specialised knowledge professions obtain state-legitimated credentialism, self-government, a system of licensing and thereby a protected market situation (Freidson 1970: 71–84). This definition, it will be noted, does not take professions at their own self-evaluation. Also it suggests that professions have the ability to provide a framework for the careers of their members. There is considerable evidence that changes in economic and occupational structure are impacting upon the features of professional life itemised by Freidson. The City of London is a good example of these changes.

Amin Rajan provides evidence of how Bell's theses on the information/service sector economy have materialised in the City of London. The professions in the City prior to deregulation maintained job demarcations and fixed commissions, relatively low and stable amounts of business were transacted, and a service was provided to a customer on the basis of trust and personal relationships. The essence of professionalism here was the personal relationship. In the new City a service is provided on the basis of competitive price. Financial services now have to make a profit through the addition of a value-added component that derives from the professional's expertise. This may lead to a personal trust between professional and client but the primary factor is price competitiveness. Likewise, in a study of large firms in the services industry, Noyelle has argued that the factors of the increased use of technology, the deregulation and internationalisation of business, and the provision of higher education outside the firm have resulted in the weakening of upward progression for core workers and a minimisation of the corporation's responsibilities to those employees (Noyelle 1987).

For Rajan the role of information and technology has altered the nature of professional work. This has 'shifted the decision making nearer the seat of the action, namely the customer' (Rajan and Fryatt 1988: 5). The financial professional now has to make immediate decisions involving telephone-based client demands and screen-based information systems. City professions are no longer able to regulate the pace of information technology or to define the knowledge content of their members' expertise. The result of this process, argues Rajan, is 'more flexible organisational structures and a multiplicity of work skills in order to cope in an uncontrolled environment'. The work structure has changed in order to cope with flexibility of response. Large hierarchical organisations are ill-adapted, whereas firms with limited hierarchy, which maximise their breadth of expertises, are favoured. In addition the new professional seeks to maximise her knowledge through networks of contacts, both within and outside the firm (Hutton and Ley 1987: 136–7). These contacts run laterally not vertically. Large clearing banks appear to have the wrong organisational structure to thrive in areas like money exchange, fund management, foreign exchange, and bonds and shares broking. The successful, more specialised firms place the transactions process central to their organisation, and management, like secretarial and other service support, are adjuncts to the central activity of trading.

The cumulative effects of this information-driven knowledge economy and its increasing exposure to market forces are to redefine career in the City. In an environment which is regarded as subject to continuous change, professional control over the conditions of employment has been relinquished. Career as a course is no longer assured, rather it is the display of demonstrable ability that counts. Performance indicators define progress, and progress may be discontinuous. An expertise carefully built up of European equity markets (a peripheral knowledge in the 70s) can come into its own in the late 80s, just as an expertise in eurobonds may prove to be a less durable asset in the 90s. The shelf life of expertise has become shorter and less predictable. The implication of this is that the individual professional has to map out her new areas of specialism and the training skills she will require. The idea that individuals have to take control of their own career needs is emphasised by personnel experts in the City.[7] Accordingly, careers become the property of the individual, not that of firm or profession.

The quote from the stockbroker, referred to above, that 'Yuppies are youth culture hitting the business world' tallies nicely with the reversal of the Bell thesis that yuppies succeed because they deploy the resources of personality first generated in the 60s. But it misses the mark in suggesting that work, its intensity and duration, is itself a kind of game. Sport and leisure are of course notable parts of the yuppie lifestyle, and to treat work as sport appeals to the sense of yuppie *sprezzatura*. However, only the truly rich can afford this pretension. Yuppies *have* to work hard (see Pahl 1990), and this is a condition both of their success and of the loss of professional control. Glamour, excitement and high material rewards more than compensate in the financial services sector. But it is important to realise that deprofessionalisation and the loss of structured career are common to a wide range of professions, including public sector ones, even though they do not enjoy such lavish compensations.

Hence the assertiveness of yuppies is not solely some insufferable idiosyncracy but a necessary adaptive response to the changes in career. The egoism of the yuppie personality has come into its own as a response to increasing pressures. Moreover, it would follow from this thesis that the same assertiveness might also characterise the new public sector professional. There is no necessary reason to believe that public sector, 'caring' professionals, while disadvantaged for reasons of political ideology and underfunding, should conduct themselves with genteel altruism. To the extent that knowledge, skills, competition all operate to throw open the structure of careers, once again the assertive response may be the only way to succeed.

These points link to the argument presented in the Introduction to this volume. Financial capitalism has become a pervasive force in all aspects of life. Just as new financial instruments and aggressive takeover teams have led to a new insecurity in the environment of the firm, so people's life-world has undergone a similar destabilisation. A central feature of this process is the inflation in residential property prices which has rendered a crucial segment of the individual's life-world part of a financial market calculation. The home has become more than a material and cultural habitus; it has become a financial asset whose value and associated mortgage debt impinges on increasing aspects of everyday life. The rate of change of London house prices, as measured at mortgage completion stage, has outstripped the rate of increase in incomes.[8] This may not constitute such a problem for the successful young professional in law, advertising or finance. But as American commentators noted when yuppies first burst upon the scene, the new middle class service occupations do not offer a standard of living comparable to an earlier, smaller middle class generation (Belk 1986: 516). The older, more narrowly defined, middle class were able to afford larger houses and enjoy greater standards of collective and private services. The obsession with dinkies and their asset-rich elders, woofies, marks an edgy preoccupation with people's worth. Career now has to be thought of as an asset, as a flow of future income, to be offset against the debt burdens of housing, private schooling and consumerism. Children, parents, education, housing and residential location in relation to collective services all enter into this uneasy calculation.

That it remains an uneasy calculation – the offsetting of primary parts of one's life-world like housing, relatives, cultural habitus – distinguishes it from a qualitatively different level of calculation, commodification. Trading in the future contracts of homes, as occurred in Docklands in the mid-1980s, is to treat one's life-world as commodity. However, for most people (though this is gender specific), houses have to be lived in, children cared for, and careers worked out in terms of their balance of work commitment and leisure and culture. The point at which the impersonal yet pervasive world of finance and business intersects with the necessities of social integration represented by the life-world takes us to the limit of arguments that eddy around this keyword. Whether the young professional will work out an expressive and secular redemption (à la Habermas), or a salvation through consumption (Bourdieu), or whether he or she will be, at last, simply beyond redemption are questions and directions that should repay further investigation.

NOTES

1 Paul Lyons beat me to the draw with a similar title. Out of respect to Raymond Williams I have retained the above title (Lyons 1989: 111–22). An earlier version of this chapter was given at the Centre for Cultural Values at Lancaster University. The chapter benefited greatly from discussions I had with Ralph Schroeder, Richard Topf and Iwan Morgan, though they should not be held responsible for short-comings in my interpretation and presentation.

2 Results of a computer search using Profile. My thanks to Chris Smart and Neil Gosney at City of London Polytechnic Library, and to Jeremy Lawrence for his generous help.

3 Randolf Quirk on 'Start the Week', Radio 4, 8 January 1990.

4 Riesman *et al.*'s distinction between the inner-directed character of the traditional bourgeois and the outer-directed type of the large American bureaucracy mid-twentieth century (Riesman *et al.* 1950) is relevant here. See the recent article by Eugene Lunn who points out that Riesman's position should not be subsumed within Daniel Bell's *Kulturkritik.* Lunn points out this is a common but mistaken assumption: 'the possibilities of autonomous personal development – Riesman's actual regulative ideal – were greater within the age of "outer-direction" and consumer abundance, given the widespread freedom from economic want, the moral flexibility of the new personality type and the growing exposure to a variety of human experiences and values' (Lunn 1990: 64).

5 The novel is only different to journalism in that you don't include your subject's telephone number, says Wolfe. Social realism is not too distant from ethnography and can thereby claim the advantages of validity, though not reliability.

6 The British Social Attitudes dataset for 1987 was used. Yuppies were selected according to the following criteria: aged 18–44, living in the Greater London area, and belonging to the salariat as defined in the compressed Goldthorpe class schema (Jowell *et al.* 1988: 204). This yielded an average of 65 respondents on the main questionnaire, but this fell to 30 on the self-completed questionnaire.

7 Author's interview (15.11.89) with Rhiannon Chapman, Head of Personnel at the International Stock Exchange.

8 The overall percentage rise for the period 1978 to 1989 in average house prices, as measured at mortgage completion stage, in the Greater London area was 420 per cent (Council of Mortgage Lenders, *Housing Finance*, no. 6, p. 45). The corresponding rise in average

income for Greater London area over the same period was 245 per cent (*New Earnings Survey*, 1978, Section E, Table E9; *New Earnings Survey*, 1989, Section E, Table E117.2).

REFERENCES

Auchincloss, L. (1986) *Diary of a Yuppie*, London: Weidenfeld and Nicolson.

Belk, R.W. (1986) 'Yuppies as arbiters of the emerging consumption style', *Advances in Consumer Research*, 13: 514–19.

Bell, D. (1973) *The Coming of Post-industrial Society. A Venture in Social Forecasting*, New York: Basic Books.

——(1976) *The Cultural Contradictions of Capitalism*, London: Heinemann Educational Books.

Carpini, M. and Sigelman, L. (1986) 'Do yuppies matter? Competing explanations of their political distinctiveness', *Public Opinion Quarterly* 50 (1): 501–18.

Caute, D. (1989) *Sixty-Eight. The Year of the Barricades*, London: Hamish Hamilton.

Churchill, C. (1987) *Serious Money*, London: Methuen.

Freidson, E. (1975) *Profession of Medicine. A Study of the Sociology of Applied Knowledge*, New York: Dodd, Mead.

Ginsberg, A. (1959) *Howl and Other Poems*, San Francisco: City Lights Books.

Hammond, J.L. (1986) 'Yuppies', *Public Opinion Quarterly* 50 (1): 477–501.

Heath, A. and Evans, G. (1988) 'Working-class Conservatives and middle-class socialists', in R. Jowell, S. Witherspoon and L. Brook (eds) *British Social Attitudes. The 5th Report*, London: Gower.

Hutton, T. and Ley, D. (1987) 'The downtown complex of corporate activities in a medium size city, Vancouver, British Columbia', *Economic Geography*, 63 (2): 127–40.

Jowell, R., Witherspoon, S. and Brook, L. (eds) (1988) *British Social Attitudes. The 5th Report*, London: Gower.

Lekachman, R. (1987) *Visions and Nightmares: America After Reagan*, New York: Macmillan.

Lunn, E. (1990) 'Beyond "mass culture". The Lonely Crowd, the uses of literacy and the postwar era', *Theory and Society*, 19 (1): 63–86.

Lyons, P. (1989) 'Yuppie: a contemporary American keyword', *Socialist Review*, 19 (1): 111–22.

McInerney, J. (1986) *Bright Lights, Big City*, London: Fontana.

——(1989) *Story of My Life*, London: Penguin.

Noyelle, T.J. (1987) *Beyond Industrial Dualism: Market and Job Segmentation in the New Economy*, Boulder: Westview Press.

Pahl, R. (1990) 'St Matthew's and the Golden Handcuffs', *Kent Society Bulletin*, 14.1.90: 32–6.

Payne, G. (1989) 'Social mobility', *British Journal of Sociology*, 40 (3): 471–92.

Piesman, M. and Hartley, M. (1984) *The Yuppie Handbook: The State of the*

Art Manual for Young Urban Professionals, New York: Simon and Schuster.

Rajan, A. and Fryatt, J. (1988) *Create Or Abdicate. The City's Human Resource Choice for the 90s*, London: Witherby.

Riesman, D., Glazier, N. and Denney, G. (1950) *The Lonely Crowd. A Study of the Changing American Character*, New Haven: Yale University Press.

Savage, M., Dickens, P. and Fielding, T. (1988) 'Some social and political implications of the contemporary fragmentation of the "Service Class" in Britain', *International Journal of Urban and Regional Research*, 12 (3): 455–76.

Shapiro, F.R. (1986) 'Yuppies, yumpies, yaps, and computer-assisted lexicology', *American Speech*, 61 (2): 139–45.

Weber, M. (1971) *Gesammelte Politische Schriften*, Tübingen: J.C.B. Mohr.

Williams, R. (1988) *Keywords*, London: Fontana.

Wolfe, T. (1987) *The Bonfire of the Vanities*, London: Picador.

York, P. (1980) *Style Wars*, London: Sidgwick and Jackson.

14

BRICK LANE

A village economy in the shadow of the city?

Chris Rhodes and Nurun Nabi

I think those who sit in the top tier of the machine are immensely rash in their regardlessness, in their vague optimism that nothing really serious ever happens. Nine times out of ten nothing really serious does happen – merely a little distress to individuals or groups. But we run a risk of a tenth time . . .

(J.M. Keynes, *The Economic Consequences of Mr. Churchill*, 1925: 23)

The largest Bangladeshi community in Britain lives in the St Mary's, Weaver's and Spitalfields wards of the London Borough of Tower Hamlets. To the average Londoner and the tourist, the community and its area is represented by the proliferation of Asian restaurants and sari shops in Brick Lane. To the romantic eye Brick Lane offers some of the liveliness, colour and taste of an Asian city, while to the harder eye the poverty, squalour and struggle for a living are also evident.

No more than a few hundred yards to the west of Brick Lane, Middlesex Street forms the boundary between Tower Hamlets and the City of London. On the City side of the street a huge glass and concrete behemoth has just been completed and is waiting for the arrival of a firm offering financial or commercial services. It dwarfs the tiny shops on the other side of the street which are retailing clothing, watches and electrical household goods. In some streets off Brick Lane, the hulks of substantial Georgian houses are being restored to their original condition and offer the convenience of a trouble-free walk to work in the City. They sell for prices which exceed the annual turnover of many of their neighbouring Asian businesses.

So the City threatens to spill over into the three wards of Tower Hamlets through a process of commercial redevelopment and gentrification. What are the likely social consequences? Beyond saying that all those working and living in the affected areas are going to suffer from disruption, the answer is not straightforward and requires an examination of the community and economy of the three wards.

THE BANGLADESHI COMMUNITY IN TOWER HAMLETS

It is difficult to estimate the size of the Bangladeshi population in Spitalfields, Weaver's and St Mary's wards of Tower Hamlets. The last census figures available are from 1981, and they collected information only on country of birth, rather than ethnicity. Using these data as a base for projections on the current population nine years later involves many assumptions about fertility rates, mortality rates, patterns of local immigration and emigration. Any estimation can only be indicative. However, the Community Development Group recently commissioned a ward by ward study from the London Research Centre. This study suggested a 1989 Bangladeshi population comprising 80 per cent of the Spitalfields ward population (7081 out of 8822); 65 per cent of the St Mary's ward population (3993 out of 6105); and 30 per cent of the Weaver's ward population (2755 out of 9469). The Bangladeshi community is also much younger in all three wards, with about 48 per cent of the population aged fifteen and under, as opposed to 23–28 per cent in the population of the wards as a whole (Community Development Group 1990). As the young population makes its way through the system, increased provision will be required at all levels of education in Tower Hamlets. Bangladeshi parents have already experienced severe difficulties in finding school places for their children.

The overwhelming majority of the Bangladeshi population are Muslims following Islam. Islam places great stress on the performance of duties and obligations within the 'family', an institution which is much wider than in western tradition since it extends beyond one's relatives, and even friends, to one's neighbours and the wider community as a whole. To observe strict Islamic tradition, individuals must commit themselves to the material support of the wider 'family', to maintaining its dignity, and to compliance with the advice and opinions of elders. Free mixing of the sexes offends codes of decency, a fact which severely restricts women's lives outside the home.

The quality of housing is a major problem in the three wards. Many Bangladeshi families are housed in estates consisting of pre-war blocks of flats badly in need of replacement or refurbishment. A number of flats are run-down and damp, resulting in plaster and wallpaper falling off the walls. As Bangladeshi families tend to be large, the accommodation is frequently too small and overcrowding is common. In the worst cases seven or eight people share a room and have no cooking or washing facilities.

Several authorities have identified further problems. For example, the House of Commons Home Affairs Select Committee report, *Bangladeshis in Britain* (1987), noted that the Bangladeshi population suffers from a high incidence of physical illness. The report also identified a significant degree of underachievement in education by Bangladeshi students. Bangladeshis are also low users of social security, housing and welfare support and advice services. Language and cultural differences exacerbate these problems, making it hard for Bangladeshis to benefit from available education, housing, social security and social service provisions.

The immigrant generation of Bangladeshis in Tower Hamlets came to the area when young or middle-aged, when Britain recruited labour from Commonwealth countries in the post-war period. Originating in the state of Sylhet, which has an agrarian peasant economy, they received little education at home. In this country they had little chance to improve their education and knowledge of English. It is therefore to be expected that their educational level and knowledge of English is extremely poor.

This position handicaps the children of the immigrant generation. Parents find it difficult to provide support in the home for their children's education. It is likely that this problem is one of the factors underlying the high drop-out rate among Bangladeshi pupils, which results in many leaving school without qualifications, and in their poor representation in further and higher education. A particularly worrying trend identified by the Home Affairs Select Committee is that a majority of Bangladeshi teenagers are not fluent in English.

The Bangladeshi community in Tower Hamlets has given rise to about one hundred political, social and cultural organisations. Unfortunately, some of these organisations have a divisive effect and in recent years there has been polarisation both between organisations, and within the larger welfare organisations such as the Bangladeshi Welfare Centre, and the Nazrul Centre. (See the Bengali newspapers, *Notun Din*, 13–19 March 1989; and *Surma*, 22–28 September 1989.) Thus there is minimal coordination between these Bangladeshi organisations, in marked contrast to the smaller Pakistani and Indian Gujarati communities who show comparatively strong solidarity.

Despite all these difficulties, many Bangladeshis express a strong desire to remain in the area. This may in part be due to a commitment to the Islamic 'family', but undoubtedly problems with racial harassment are a factor. The surrounding wards of Tower Hamlets return a significant proportion of votes for ultra-right, racist political candidates, and Bangladeshis probably feel safer in a defensive enclave (Bethnal Green and Stepney Trades Council 1978). However, there is constant pressure on them to move out, due to a number of factors: the lack of family accommodation, and pressure from private sector commercial redevelopment and the increasing gentrification of the area, which is pricing many properties out of the reach of the low-paid Bangladeshi community.

THE ECONOMY OF THE THREE WARDS

A large majority of firms within the three wards are small businesses, and these provide the employment which underpins the minority community. Were it not for these firms, Bangladeshis would be thrown on to the open labour market where many would be severely handicapped by imperfect English, low educational achievement, an absence of marketable skills, and racism. Despite the outsider's view of Brick Lane, most of these small businesses are not restaurants; rather they are engaged in manufacturing, wholesaling and retailing, largely in the clothing, leather goods and footwear industry. Other activities, such as the provision of personal and business services, are minimally represented (Rhodes and Nabi 1989).

The business community in the St Mary's, Weaver's and Spitalfields wards is not ethnically homogeneous. The largest single ethnic group of owners is in fact indigenous (28 per cent). Bangladeshi owners form the next largest ethnic group (25 per cent), followed by Pakistanis (13 per cent), Gujaratis (12 per cent) and Sikhs (6 per cent). Other ethnic groups are also represented, though in much smaller numbers. The indigenous group is out-numbered by the other groups combined (Rhodes and Nabi Vol. 2 1989: 1).

When asked to rate the importance of the minority community to their businesses, it emerges that each of the groups says it relies to a different extent on the minority economy in the area. (Rhodes and Nabi Vol. 2 1989: 16) At one extreme, indigenous owners cite the community as important only for recruiting staff. At the other extreme, Bangladeshi owners say that the minority community is important in many ways. They rate the community as important for raising finance (and their businesses do show a comparative reliance on the ethnic banks and networks of family and friends for raising money). The community is also rated as an important source of business services.

However, the ratings suggest that it is Bangladeshi businesses' pattern of trading which lodges them most strongly in the minority economy. Bangladeshi manufacturers, restaurant owners, wholesalers and retailers all consider the community important for their supplies. Bangladeshi manufacturers, wholesalers and retailers all consider community customers important. In this way the Bangladeshi businesses as a whole present a picture (with the partial exception of restaurants) of a situation approaching economic self-sufficiency or autarky.

Because of this situation, the consequences of redevelopment of the area could be very serious for the Bangladeshis in particular, since the social and economic characteristics of the minority community could amplify the effects of even partial redevelopment. If their autarkic trading network is disrupted by redevelopment at any point, then other parts may be indirectly affected, even though those parts are not subjected to the effects of redevelopment themselves.

The amplification of the effects of redevelopment of the area may well be that much greater because of the economic geography of the community. A notable characteristic of the clothing industry is the way in which the sectors within it are distributed across the Weaver's, St Mary's and Spitalfields wards. Groups of streets, and in some cases single streets, concentrate on manufacturing, wholesaling or retailing. Thus the loss of Hanbury or Princelet Street (through redevelopment, gentrification or inflation of rents) could remove a substantial proportion of the clothing industry's manufacturing sector. If Commercial Street or Commercial Road were similarly affected, a substantial proportion of the wholesaling and retailing sector could go too.

To confirm this assessment, more research into the economy of the area is needed. But if it is correct, it is clear that, while some groups face 'a little distress' if the area is redeveloped, the Bangladeshis face a major crisis caused by severe disruption of the economic underpinnings of their community.

THE MANAGEMENT OF CIVIL ORDER

Britain experienced episodic breakdowns in civil order in the inner cities and industrial contexts in the early 1980s. The effects of the City's annexation of the western part of Tower Hamlets could have the same result. However, this is by no means inevitable: the displacement and disruption of white working class communities in Docklands areas such as Bermondsey has been accomplished with barely a ripple in the patterns of civil order – little more than sporadic harassment of incoming 'toffs'.

But will this be repeated in Tower Hamlets, or will the disturbances in Brixton, Toxteth and St Paul's offer the borough an image of its future? To answer this question requires some theorisation of how civil order is managed.

Whether or not the City of London spills over into Tower Hamlets and displaces the minority community working in its three eastern wards will be decided in a context dominated by national and international groups who can parlay their economic resources into the ability to get their way in the area: this much is clear. But stable popular compliance is an important asset for any state, and one which in the British context depends on a degree of responsiveness to popular interests (i.e. the interests of the populace) which is sufficient to maintain its image as a popular state (i.e. a state which in principle represents the populace). But this image is difficult to maintain in situations where sections of the populace have changes imposed on them, as will be the case of the minority community in Tower Hamlets. In such situations, the management of compliance becomes a problem.

Two groups in particular have to accept the image of a popular state. The first group is comprised of those who are at the receiving end of state action. If they do not accept that the state is responsive to popular interests then disaffection and, at the extreme, breakdowns in civil order result. The second group is comprised of those

338

liberal (in the sense of believing that the state should be responsive to popular interests), political and administrative actors who are necessary to carrying out the action. If they cannot convince themselves that the state is responsive to popular interests then they will become disaffected too, and they will frustrate and obstruct policy (in the absence of a conviction of some wider *raison d'état* – in circumstances which cannot be discussed here).

However, neither the risk of disaffection in the populace nor in state actors forms an inflexible constraint on policy, because the meaning of responsiveness to popular interests is subject to manipulation. Skilled political actors can stage-manage the appearance of responsiveness whilst still substantially imposing changes on the populace. It is in this context of stage management that conflicting assessments of the long-term prospects of the clothing industry acquire a particular political significance. The first assessment of the clothing industry is that it is undergoing a secular decline, as evidenced by a number of economic indicators in statistics covering national and regional trends, and is therefore incapable of regenerating the area and furthering the interests of the minority community. Whether or not national or regional statistics adequately represent the situation of the clothing industry in Tower Hamlets is debatable, but they do receive support from comments by some local businesses. Some businesses complain of increasing difficulty in meeting competition from Asian-made garments produced with cheap labour, and claim that the current strength of sterling exacerbates the position. This is a common complaint even though the local manufacturing workforce receives very poor wages, and though some workers and employees collaborate in various stratagems to minimise the payment of tax and national insurance contributions. One prospective entrepreneur's comments illustrate the difficulty. He had the idea of adapting traditional Asian clothing to western women's tastes. He found that choti (short jackets for women) could be made and hand-embroidered in Pakistan for less than the cost of printing the fabric and making it up in Britain. As a result of these pressures some firms resort to importing Asian-made garments, sewing on 'Made in England' labels, and selling them to the stalls in the Petticoat Lane market.

However, there is an optimistic, second assessment of the future of the clothing industry. The statistics and the complaints of some minority businesses offer only one side of the picture. The survey, which the authors conducted at the end of 1988, asked businesses to rate their prospects for 1989. Only a small minority (8 per cent) thought that they would be worse (Rhodes and Nabi Vol. 2 1989: 27). The survey also asked about employment prospects for 1989. Again, only a small minority (5 per cent) thought that they would be shedding staff (Rhodes and Nabi Vol. 2 1989: 5).

Of these two assessments of the future of the clothing industry, the pessimistic version may be made to play a useful role in the stage management of a physical and economic annexation by the City of London. It does so by draining the annexation of its provocative content by suggesting that annexation is destroying nothing that isn't facing terminal decline. When associated with promises of better business and employment prospects in the burgeoning business services sector, it further recommends itself as actually offering the community a brighter future.

This is certainly capable of persuading liberal politicians, administrators and technicians that collaboration in the re-development of the area can be carried out in good faith because the supervision of redevelopment appears to be a response to popular interests, even if they are interests which the community itself would not recognise. The conception of interests is proactive, based on superior specialist knowledge, rather than a reactive, populist response to the community's own inferior local know-ledge. Given this, the following comments can be made on the position of 'the state' and its actors as it bears on the redevelop-ment of the Spitalfields area.

The central British state is not a major player on the narrow issue of what happens in detail in Spitalfields. However, as should need little elaboration, under the direction of the Conservative Party the central state operates with a particular view, subject to debate, of how the regeneration of areas such as Spitalfields should be brought about. It will be achieved, if at all, through wealth created by economic growth in the private sector. This will best serve the interests of all those involved. Attempts at strategic planning by the state can only obstruct this benevolent process, especially strategic planning which tries to buck market trends.

As can readily be seen, this does not predispose the central British state to align itself against developments in Spitalfields caused by powerful economic forces: opposing such forces is wrong in principle and in any case those forces will ultimately operate to the benefit of those living and working in the area. This is the case even if those in the area do not realise it, a situation which arises because they have a lay (and hence mistaken) conception of their own interests which will have to give way in the face of superior specialist knowledge.

Nevertheless, under the present view of how regeneration may be brought about, the state may have an enabling role. This is particularly appropriate in the case of small businesses which (despite considerable evidence to the contrary) are held to have a particularly crucial role in innovation and growth in the economy. Accordingly, the government set up the Spitalfields Task Force as a catalyst for small business growth. Grants were given to a number of business development agencies, and several business and work skills training schemes, such as the City of London Polytechnic's Ethnic Minorities Business Development Unit, are also aided by state grants for their activities in the area. Whether or not such organisations are operating with a pessimistic, optimistic or agnostic conception of the future of the clothing industry, and are thus training and developing for redeveloped Spitalfields, the present Spitalfields, or are just training and developing without an overall strategy, is a question which would require too much detail in this context, as does the question of whether or not such organisations have sufficient autonomy from their central state sponsors to pursue an independent line. For the moment, all one can say is that organisations fall into all three categories.

At local state level, the London Borough of Tower Hamlets is certainly a major player in the issue of precisely what happens in Spitalfields. It is the planning authority for the area, though its decisions on planning permission are subject to appeal to central state level. Given this caveat, the borough has a key role in deciding on the development, for example, of the old Spitalfields Fruit Market, the redundant British Rail Bishopsgate goods yard, and the Grand Metropolitan brewery site at the north end of Brick Lane itself (see Figure 10.1, p. 247).

The borough is under the direction of the Liberal Democrats and operates with a particular conception, subject to debate, of the redevelopment issue. Broadly speaking, the conception involves regenerating the area, using private capital. Acquiescence to developers' plans is exchanged for concessions, so-called planning gains, to local community interests. It certainly does not imply optimism in the ability of the clothing industry to work for the development of the area, though provisions are made for small business units in the planning brief for the Bishopsgate goods yard site, for example. However, there is no detectable guarantee that premises will be available to displaced clothing firms, nor that there will be sufficient numbers. To offer a guarantee would at least require knowledge of the floor space currently occupied by Bangladeshi firms, and the floor space they would require after redevelopment: to date there is no research which has provided this information. In fact, there is no detectable strategic plan for the future of the Bangladeshi economy and community as a whole.

This conception informing Borough policy is not too far from that being operationalised by central government, though the details of the ideological understrappings might be different and involve the idea of partnership between the state and private capital. Again, the Borough is not predisposed by this conception to align itself against developments in Spitalfields caused by power-ful economic forces: those forces could ultimately be harnessed and operate to the benefit of those living and working in the area. This is the case even if those in the area do not realise it, a situation which arises because they have a mistaken view of their own interests. Again, the lay view will have to give way in the face of superior specialist knowledge.

Members of the community can also be convinced of the pessi-mistic assessment of the ability of the clothing industry to regener-ate the area, and of the suggestion that redevelopment offers better opportunities. The Community Development Group considers development as 'a unique opportunity for the local community to make a positive intervention and obtain substantial advantage for the people of the area' (Community Development Group 1990: 3). Funding from the Government's Task Force in Spitalfields and Business in the Community enabled the CDG to employ a professional team to produce a 'Community Plan' des-cribing a model of redevelopment adapted to the community's interests. The model contains a preferred allocation of land use between housing, business premises, open space, etc. and pro-poses the establishment of a community trust to manage land surplus to developers' requirements. The plan 'should ensure that much of the new development serves local needs and is accessible and affordable to people working, living and trading in the area' (Community Development Group 1990: 4).

WILL STAGE MANAGEMENT WORK?

These claims and manoeuvres are by no means guaranteed to stage-manage redevelopment effectively. Workers with some of the many business advice and support organisations in the area are not persuaded by the pessimistic assessment of the clothing industry's future and its ability to regenerate the area. They are also sceptical of the promise of improved business and employment opportunities. As one worker put it, the view that new opportunities will be offered suggests that a Bangladeshi sewing machinist in a back-room garment factory will be operating a computer terminal in five years' time. The implication is that this would demand an unrealistic degree of adaptability from the people involved, who simply do not have the skills and education to take up such opportunities quickly. Consequently, they oppose redevelopment, taking the view that a genuine response to the community's interests would be reactive, not proactive. The minority community, according to this view, already has skills and business knowledge of the clothing industry, and these should be built on with appropriate support, training and advice. But the keystone of the response they would support is a determined effort to provide and safeguard business premises in the face of the threat of redevelopment.

Neither is stage management of development guaranteed to work with the community. Sections of the community are suspicious of claims about the extent to which redevelopment can be made responsive to community interests. Consequently, there is some opposition to the CDG plan from organisations such as Save Spitalfields from Redevelopment, Spitalfields 2000 and the Spitalfields Small Business Association. The opposition centres less on the details of the community plan developed by the CDG (which in fact contains many attractive ideas) and more on the provenance of the CDG itself. The CDG advertises itself as 'an umbrella organisation with a wide range of individuals, groups and organisations from the three wards of Spitalfields, Weaver's and St Mary's' (Community Development Group 1990: 4). However, the names of those who attended public meetings, a list of organisations involved in the CDG, and the full aims and objectives of the CDG will not be available until a future volume of the CDG plan (Community Development Group 1990: 5). In fact it is evident that many community organisations were not

343

consulted. There is a further problem with the proposed community development trust, which will manage land surplus to developers' requirements:

> The CDG has not yet decided upon the final structure of the Trust, its range of activities, geographical remit, specific relation to section 52 agreement on the two sites, portfolio of land and other assets it will hold etc. Following the launch of the Community Plan and over the next few months we will enter into detailed discussions within the membership of the CDG, with the Council and with the developers in order to work out an agreed model for the CDT.
>
> (Community Development Trust 1990: 57)

Apparently, the community is to be told the terms and extent of its participation. This agenda, and general *modus operandi*, leaves the CDG open to the charge that it is a vehicle for controlling the concessions developers make in exchange for community acquiescence. In other words, as an attempt at stage-managing redevelopment, it fails to appear sufficiently responsive to the interests of the community, as articulated by the community itself. The failure is too transparent, and the attempt at stage management is not passing without challenge from community groups. But it has to be said that, between the poles of the Community Development Group and Save Spitalfields from Redevelopment, the majority of the Bangladeshi community do not know what is going to happen, and has not mobilised on the issue of redevelopment. We can do no more than talk about the conditions under which they would accept the pessimistic assessment of the future of the clothing industry, the promise of better opportunities, and hence redevelopment.

If redevelopment is to be accepted it will have to correspond in some measure to the way in which it has been stage-managed. This will not happen, first, if the community thoroughly persuades itself that viable firms are being decimated and, secondly, that promises of new business and employment opportunities were specious. Taking the first point, our survey revealed a well of optimism about business prospects, which certainly does not indicate that at present the minority business community is disposed to accept the view that their industry is finished. Rather it suggests that the community thinks the clothing industry continues to offer business and employment opportunities, and that if those opportunities are destroyed by redevelopment and anticipatory inflation in rents, the community will conclude that it is the redevelopment that will be to blame, not inherent faults in the industry itself.

Taking the second point, the community will have to be offered new business and employment opportunities. This raises the question of whether or not the community is primed to benefit from new opportunities, and the answer requires a further look at its characteristics. The central issue is the extent to which the community is open to innovation. The issue is complex, but a start may be made on the basis of information gathered in our survey. Again differences emerge between ethnic groups: Bangladeshi businesses show a comparative conservatism in business matters. There is a tendency for them not to see the relevance of new markets and new products to their businesses (Rhodes and Nabi Vol. 2 1989: 11). The corollary is their location in the clothing industry: in contrast to other groups they are almost exclusively located in the manufacturing sector where they are most likely to be experiencing the lowest profit margins and wages (Rhodes and Nabi Vol. 2 1989: 2). Alternatively, they compete with one another as restaurants in Brick Lane. The group which is most likely to suffer disruption as the result of redevelopment therefore seems, by virtue of its business conservatism, least well placed to take advantage of new opportunities which redevelopment might bring.

This being the case, it is appropriate to be sceptical about the degree to which redevelopment can be effectively stage-managed through the use of the pessimistic assessment of the future of the clothing industry and the associated argument that redevelopment will bring new opportunities to an economically moribund area. There is evidence that the community does not think that the clothing industry is moribund, and that the group likely to suffer most disruption is not primed to take up such opportunities as may be offered. On this basis it would seem unlikely that the community, the Bangladeshis in particular, will view the annexation of the area as being in any way responsive to their interests.

MAKING STAGE MANAGEMENT WORK

What would be required to make this programme of stage management work? First, the minority business community would have to develop the conviction that the clothing industry offered nothing but increasing difficulties and declining prospects. The state of the clothing industry at present is not sufficiently depressing for this conviction to develop. However, it could be the case that continuing competition from cheap Asian labour, the strength of sterling and high interest rates may change the situation. The impact of the European Market may also have the same effect, though in the absence of further research it could well be the case that the industry may be revitalised.

Secondly, redevelopment would have to offer the community new opportunities, and the community would have to be in a position to benefit from them. In the absence of further research, it is difficult to say what such redevelopment could offer. However, it is possible to comment on the ability of the community, particularly the Bangladeshis, to profit. As indicated above, a lack of openness to innovation could stand between the Bangladeshis and new opportunities which might present themselves. The nature of this impediment therefore bears some consideration.

In considering the impediment there is a strong temptation to invoke the notion of culture as an explanation. The ideal typical older Bangladeshi comes from Sylhet, a region of Bangladesh with a peasant economy steeped in Islam, and it is plausible to argue that the traditionalism of Bangladeshi businesses has its roots in what is essentially a premodern rationality. The decisive characteristic of this rationality is that it does not make the distinctions, typical of modern rationalities, between questions of religion and other areas of life. Business behaviour is therefore inseparable from the aesthetic and moral codes of Islam, as interpreted by the mullah.

This argument reflects certain characteristics of the Bangladeshi community. It is the case, for example, that some mullahs proscribe the use of British banks by Bangladeshi businesses as part of a general attempt to prevent the contamination of the community through contact with other groups. Pressures like these would act as a block to innovation, because innovation is made into a thorny religious and moral question.

However, this begs the question of why Pakistani Muslims, as indicated above, do seem open to innovation, whereas Bangladeshi Muslims do not. It may be that this question could be answered by investigating the social class and educational level of both the mullahs and laity, and the interests of the mullahs in the two cases. But a more fundamental objection to the argument is that it depicts the Bangladeshis as passive objects of a particular rationality, as beings with no capacity to initiate change – a point of view which in policy terms opens the way for the worst excesses of paternalism. However, like anyone else, Bangladeshis can make history even if they cannot do so just as it pleases them. A more fruitful approach would be to focus on what happens when a business plans to break into a new area. The central question would be whether or not it has resources which it can parlay into the power to realise its plan. The investigation of how a range of resources enable or disable an innovating business would form the substantive content of the argument. Without in the least pretending to do justice to the issue, the following serves as an illustration. As indicated above, Bangladeshi businesses in the clothing industry are, with very few exceptions, concentrated in manufacturing. What are the roots of this 'tradition'? The answer is not that this line of business satisfies the requirements of religion or is endorsed by the mullah, rather it lies in those aspects of the business's current situation which disable its ability to innovate.

First and foremost there is the issue of raising finance for the change. Whether or not a bank will loan money depends partly on the inherent plausibility of the proposed business plan, as defined by the bank. But it also depends on the current performance of the business, and a Bangladeshi clothing manufacturing firm working under the pressure of intense foreign competition cannot show the sort of track record that will inspire a bank manager. The problem is exacerbated by book keeping practices. Essentially, the firm keeps two sets of accounts. The official accounts understate the firm's turnover to minimise the firm's liability to tax. The number of employees are also understated: workers receive low wages and pressure the employer for payment in cash, without tax and national insurance deductions, and so the employees do not appear on the firm's books. The effect is that the official accounts, on which the bank manager will judge the firm's track record, make the record seem poorer than it is.

In other words, it is the firm's current situation that causes lack of innovation, rather than the entrepreneur's lack of innovation that causes the firm to remain in its current situation. There are other examples. For instance, the minute subdivision of the clothing industry means that the production process is highly fragmented. Bangladeshis working in individual firms therefore exercise a very narrow range of skills, and have minimal opportunity for acquiring new ones. The repertoire of the community as a whole is thereby impoverished, along with its ability to respond to change (Dufy 1979: 5). These factors do not seem to be related to any particular characteristic of Bangladeshis, differences in rationality included, though of course lack of fluency in English and any entrenched racism cause added problems. The fundamental problem is one of lack of power to change rather than motivation to change, and would be shared by any businesses in similar situations, regardless of ethnicity.

However, there are features unique to the Bangladeshis' situation which may act as disabling factors. A wholesaling business requires a different management approach than a manufacturing firm (or a restaurant). A manufacturing firm can be run on the basis of constant personal supervision by the owner, because the owner is on the premises. A wholesaling business requires the owner to be off the premises making contacts, thus needing a reliable person to mind the shop in the owner's absence. A frequent complaint from wholesalers is that it is difficult to recruit and keep reliable staff, with the added implication that goods and cash go missing. This problem is probably in part due to the fact that Bangladeshi firms cannot offer pay and working conditions of the sort calculated to generate staff loyalty – as would be the case with any firm operating under the same circumstances. Further, if the financial control of the business is informal and equivocal it invites suspicion and mistrust even if no pilfering and embezzlement result. So a lack of confidence in business control acts as a disincentive to innovation in areas where business administration will become more complicated. Again, this much would be true of any community in a situation where the widespread development of business skills is difficult.

But an obvious solution to the problem of trust would be for the Bangladeshi entrepreneur to involve his wife in the running of their firm. But, for the Bangladeshis, the female labour force is almost completely untapped (Rhodes and Nabi Vol. 2 1989: 26). Employment of women is minimal and, out of 940 small firms in our survey, only one was owned by a Bangladeshi woman. Keeping women at home safe from racial harassment is an issue, but a major cause lies in Bangladeshi codes of decency of conduct enforced by the mullah, which all but deprives Bangladeshi women of any economic role outside the home. Some of the young females currently attending the City Polytechnic's Bangladeshi Education Centre (an encouraging development) take their business courses with their chaperones sitting at the back of the classroom. Other minority groups, especially Sikhs and Gujaratis, are heavy users of female labour. Here is a situation in which Bangladeshi rationality does disable their firms' ability to innovate.

As a result of these and other factors, a Bangladeshi business thinking through the possibility of innovation would anticipate a web of problems, and great difficulty in solving them, and these act as a considerable disincentive to change. A feeling of inevitability about their current situation would result. This feeling explains the tendency, indicated above, for Bangladeshis not to see the relevance of business activities that lead to innovation, and so impairs their ability to take advantage of new opportunities that might be offered by redevelopment in the Spitalfields, St Mary's and Weaver's wards.

MAKING STAGE MANAGEMENT WORK: A SOLUTION?

For redevelopment to be sold to the Bangladeshis as responsive to their interests, they would have to be convinced that changing to new lines of business activity is a realistic possibility. They would have to see a number of conspicuous examples of firms like their own successfully taking up new opportunities, and conclude that they can do it too. That would require a full-blooded, coordinated programme of support and advice that addressed, in particular, problems of finance, premises and training. The Gujarati model of business development is an example of such a programme. The Gujarati business development model arose from a comprehensive Entrepreneurship Development Programme pioneered in India in 1970, which was designed to promote indigenous entrepreneurship, extending business training to the 'underprivileged, low-income poor . . . who have virtually no education or financial resources'. The programme has achieved its objectives fairly well, particularly in the state of Gujarat (Patel 1987: 109).

The programme has many conventional features. It has a procedure for selecting those who have the potential to be trained as entrepreneurs. It aims to develop trainees' entrepreneurial capabilities, teaches them basic managerial concepts, and ensures that each potential entrepreneur has a viable industrial project. However, it is more than a training programme. It also helps prospective entrepreneurs to secure financial, infrastructural and related facilities so that trainees' skills materialise in a viable industrial venture. The key to the programme's success is the integration, in a single coherent scheme, of training and systematic post-training support with the crucial provision of financial and material facilities, including premises.

In the different states of India this programme has provided a successful training model for entrepreneurship development and the programme is now run in 20 locations. 'Two programmes per year at each of the 20 locations develop 900 to 1,000 entrepreneurs and lead to the establishment of at least 500 industrial units, which in turn will employ at least 5,000 workers' (Patel 1987: 109).

THE FUTURE?

In the absence of a business development programme such as this, it seems very unlikely that the redevelopment of the Spitalfields, St Mary's and Weaver's wards can be sold to the minority community, Bangladeshis in particular, as being in any way responsive to their interests. Redevelopment and the destruction of existing businesses and jobs cannot be stage-managed by the promise of new business and employment opportunities unless those opportunities are made real for the groups whose lives will be disrupted. Making them real depends on the wholehearted implementation of a programme on the lines of the Gujarati model. Redevelopment without stage management would offer undisguised provocation to the minority community. A confident reply to the question of how the community would respond requires a good deal more research. The study of other forms of popular mobilisation (Rhodes 1983) allows some comments to be made on the parameters structuring developments.

The community's response will depend less on the level of misery that would be created by disruption due to redevelopment, and more on the community's experience of mobilising in its own interests and the way in which it organises itself. Two possibilities present themselves. In the first, a community facing provocation has generated stable organisations which have had some success in promoting its interests. Such a community would respond through those organisations for as long as they appeared to offer the best means of effective protest. This is reinforced if other forms of protest, direct action in particular, are met with resolute resistance on the part of the state (whether central or local) and especially if countered by outright repression.

To the extent that the Bangladeshi community in Tower Hamlets approximates this first situation, one expects its response to redevelopment to express itself through those organisations it has generated. But how close is the approximation? The sheer number of organisations, their lack of coordination and the controversy and polarisation that some seem to generate can only give rise to a sceptical view of their capacity to discipline the community's response.

There is then the question of the degree to which these organisations present themselves as being the best means of effective protest. A number of such organisations have been successful in gaining and administering good community facilities and services. However, the extent to which they can extract concessions over redevelopment is to a large extent in the hands of the state and developers. In particular, the state and developers will have to consider the capacity of community organisations to sell to the community the concession of half a loaf, when the community has sent them in to extract a whole loaf. This capacity would seem to be low, as a result of the organisations' apparently low ability to discipline explosive community mobilisation.

Finally, there is the propensity of the community to employ other means of protest, particularly direct action. The Bangladeshi population has no direct experience of a large-scale breakdown in civil order followed by firm repression. They have of course second-hand experience of the events in Brixton, Toxteth and St Paul's. Whether this has sufficient deterrent effect has to be taken into account.

The second possibility to be considered concerns a community in which organisations are short-lived and ineffective vehicles for promoting the community's interests. One would expect such a community's response to provocation to take volatile and individualised forms. One would expect episodic break-downs in civil order until repeated repression convinced those involved of the futility of this sort of mobilisation. Such a community would then face the prospect of reinforced alienation (in the sense of a reinforced conviction that the world is implacably unresponsive to the individual's interests and efforts), causing explicitly political protest and community-centred activity to degenerate into apathy and a rising incidence of crime.

351

To the extent that the Bangladeshi community approximates to this situation and is forced to acquiesce to redevelopment regardless of its effects, the outsiders' view of the village community centred on Brick Lane, whether they be tourists or the office workers of the redeveloped Spitalfields, will radically change: the taste of an Asian city will be of a thoroughly unwelcome, depressing and dangerous sort.

REFERENCES

Bethnal Green and Stepney Trades Council (1978) *Blood on the Streets*.

Community Development Group (1990) *Planning Our Future*.

Dufy, P. (1979) *The Employment and Training Needs of the Bengali Community in Tower Hamlets*, Commission for Racial Equality and Manpower Services Commission.

Patel, V.G. (1987) 'Developing indigenous entrepreneurship: the Gujurat Model', in Neck and Nelson (eds) *Small Enterprise Development: Policies and Programmes*, ILO.

Rhodes, C.J. (1983) 'Organised labour and the state', University of London, Ph.D. Thesis.

Rhodes, C.J. and Nabi, N. (1989) 'Small businesses in Spitalfields: a survey, Spitalfields Task Force'. This research was commissioned and funded by the Government's Task Force in Spitalfields.

NAME INDEX

SUBJECT INDEX

IUPUI
UNIVERSITY LIBRARIES
TODD WING LOWER LEVEL
INDIANAPOLIS, IN 46202-5195

IUPUI
UNIVERSITY LIBRARIES
755 W. MICHIGAN ST.
INDIANAPOLIS, IN 46202-5195